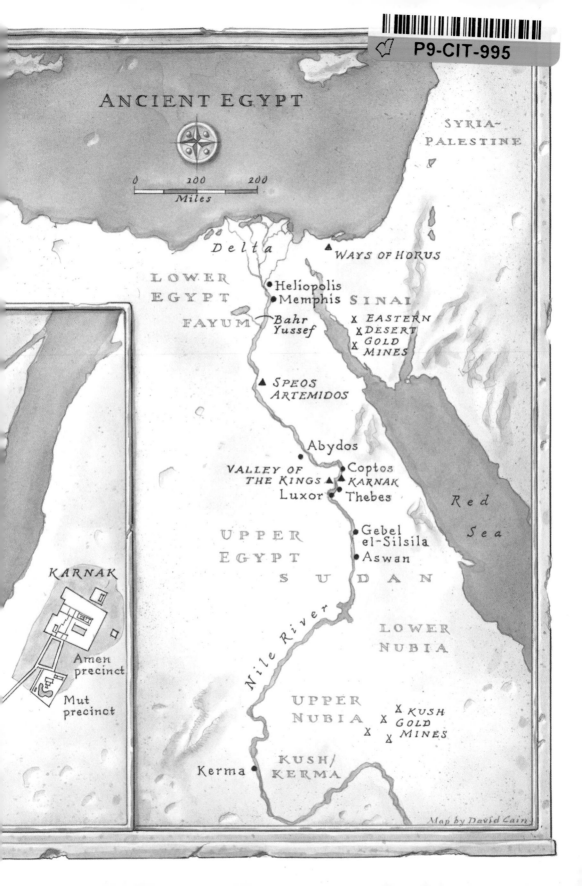

ANCIENT EGYPT

P9-CIT-995

SYRIA~
PALESTINE

0   100   200
Miles

Delta

WAYS OF HORUS

LOWER
EGYPT

Heliopolis
Memphis   SINAI

FAYUM   Bahr
Yussef   X EASTERN
             X DESERT
             X GOLD
               MINES

SPEOS
ARTEMIDOS

Abydos

VALLEY OF   Coptos
THE KINGS   KARNAK
Luxor   Thebes   Red

            Sea

UPPER   Gebel
            el-Silsila
EGYPT   Aswan

        S U D A N

KARNAK

                LOWER
                NUBIA

Nile River

Amen
precinct

Mut   UPPER   X KUSH
precinct   NUBIA   X GOLD
                X   X MINES

        KUSH/
Kerma   KERMA

Map by David Cain

Copyright © 2014 by Kara Cooney

All rights reserved.
Published in the United States by Crown Publishers, an imprint of the Crown Publishing Group, a division of Random House LLC, a Penguin Random House Company, New York.

www.crownpublishing.com

CROWN and the Crown colophon are registered trademarks of Random House LLC.

Library of Congress Cataloging-in-Publication Data
Cooney, Kara.
   The woman who would be king / Kara Cooney. — First edition.
      pages cm
1. Hatshepsut, Queen of Egypt. 2. Queens—Egypt—Biography. 3. Pharaohs—Biography. 4. Egypt—History—Eighteenth dynasty, ca. 1570–1320 B.C. 5. Egypt—Kings and rulers—Biography. I. Title.
   DT87.15.C66 2014
   932.014092—dc23

                                                                    2014000243

ISBN 978-0-307-95676-7
eBook ISBN 978-0-307-95678-1

Printed in the United States of America

Map copyright © 2014 by David Cain
Illustration on p. x and maps on pp. xiii–xv by Deborah Shieh
Jacket design by Chris Brand
Jacket photography by Sam Weber

10 9 8 7 6 5 4 3 2 1

First Edition

THE WOMAN WHO WOULD BE King

THE
WOMAN
WHO WOULD
BE KING

Kara Cooney

CROWN
New York

For Neil, with whom I have walked
through so many fires.

And for Julian, whose happiness
doesn't yet make him cry.

CONTENTS

CHRONOLOGY

New Kingdom 1539–1077 BCE

Eighteenth Dynasty	*1539–1292 BCE*
Ahmose I (Nebpehtyre)	1539–1515 BCE
Amenhotep I (Djeserkare)	1514–1494 BCE
Thutmose I (Aakheperkare)	1493–1483 BCE
Thutmose II (Aakheperenre)	1482–1480 BCE
Thutmose III (Menkheperre/Menkheperkare)	1479–1460 BCE
Hatshepsut (Maatkare)	1472–1458 BCE
Thutmose III (Menkheperre)	1460–1425 BCE
Amenhotep II (Aakheperure)	1425–1400 BCE
Thutmose IV (Menkheperure)	1400–1390 BCE
Amenhotep III (Nebmaatre)	1390–1353 BCE
Amenhotep IV/Akhenaten (Neferkheperure)	1353–1336 BCE
Smenkhkare/Neferneferuaten	1336–1334 BCE
Tutankhaten/Tutankhamen (Nebkheperure)	?–1324 BCE
Itnetjer Ay (Kheperkheperure)	1323–1320 BCE
Horemheb (Djeserkheperure)	1319–1292 BCE
Nineteenth Dynasty	*1292–1191 BCE*
Ramses I (Menpehtyre)	1292–1291 BCE
Seti I (Menmaatre)	1290–1279 BCE
Ramses II (Usermaatre setepenre)	1279–1213 BCE
Merneptah (Baenre)	1213–1203 BCE
Seti II (Userkheperure)	1202–1198 BCE
Amenmesses (Menmire)	1202–1200 BCE
Siptah (Akhenre)	1197–1193 BCE
Tawosret (Sitre merytamen)	1192–1191 BCE

Twentieth Dynasty	*1190–1077 BCE*
Setnakht (Userkhaure)	1190–1188 BCE
Ramses III (Usermaatre meryamen)	1187–1157 BCE
Ramses IV (Heqamaatre setepenamen)	1156–1150 BCE
Ramses V (Usermaatre sekheperenre)	1149–1146 BCE
Ramses VI (Nebmaatre meryamen)	1145–1139 BCE
Ramses VII (Usermaatre setepenre meryamen)	1138–1131 BCE
Ramses VIII (Usermaatre akhenamen)	1130 BCE
Ramses IX (Neferkare setepenre)	1129–1111 BCE
Ramses X (Khepermaatre setepenre)	1110–1107 BCE
Ramses XI (Menmaatre setepenptah)	1106–1077 BCE

(Based on Erik Hornung, Rolf Krauss, and David A. Warburton, eds., *Ancient Egyptian Chronology*, Handbook of Oriental Studies, sec. 1, The Near and Middle East [Leiden and Boston: Brill, 2006].)

Family Tree of Hatshepsut's Immediate Relations

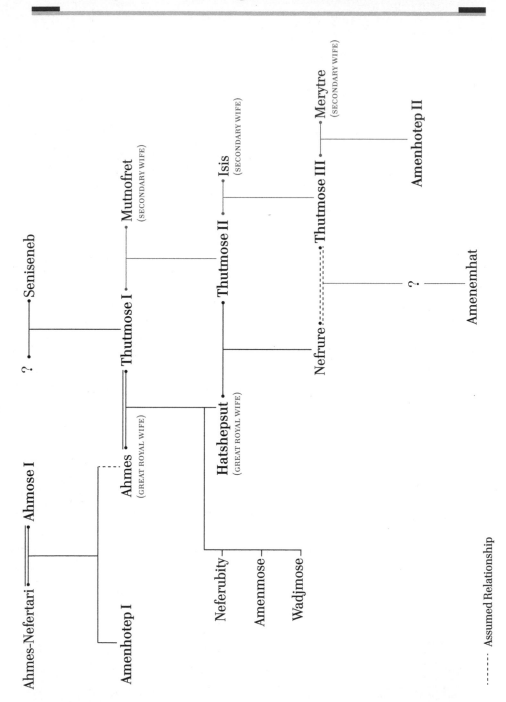

Certainty plays little role in this history of Hatshepsut. The nature of the information passed down to us is uneven, and because so many of her monuments were destroyed, the jumble of perceptions we are left with are from other people, many of whom lived millennia after her death. I have had to break many rules of my Egyptological training in order to resurrect and reanimate Hatshepsut's intentions, ambitions, and disappointments, by engaging in conjecture and speculation, and creating untestable hypotheses as I attempt to fill out her character and decision-making processes (even though I document my sources and accentuate my uncertainties). Any supposition on my part is warranted, I believe, because Hatshepsut remains an important example of humanity's ambivalent perception of female authority. Even in the absence of exact historical details and reasons behind Hatshepsut's actions, I can still track her rise to power by following the clues left behind by herself, other kings, courtiers, officials, and priests, thus filling out the circumstances of her life's journey as I go.

I have decided to forgo any long-winded analysis of architectural history, reliefs, statuary, text, and genealogy, instead focusing solely on Hatshepsut's narrative; you will find discussions of topics tangential to the main story in the notes. I have also eschewed reconstructions of Hatshepsut's ambitious building program, because the extensive evidence of it already fills many volumes. (Indeed, Hatshepsut's impressive architectural agenda has lured historians into creating a narrative of objects and buildings in lieu of a history of Hatshepsut herself.) This book is about a woman of antiquity and her interactions with Egyptian systems of government and power players, her decisions, her ambitions, her desperation, her triumphs, and her defeats. As I follow Hatshepsut's story from her ancestral beginnings to her bitter end, I will watch what she did and how she did it, within the context of her times, and present my hypotheses explaining her motivations and thought processes.

Many historians will no doubt accuse me of fantasy: inventing emotions and feelings for which I have no evidence. And they will be right. As I try to get at the human core of Hatshepsut, I will put many ideas and assumptions on the page; this is the best way for me to reconstruct her decision-making process. My conjectures, founded on twenty years of Egyptological research, are bounded and informed. What I say about Hatshepsut's emotions may not be right, but when I engage in conjecture, I do my best to qualify the statement, or to offer alternatives, or to clarify any uncertainty in my writing. The inexactitude remains, however, as is the case with any historical study of the ancient world.

This book is a kind of pause for me, something completely different from my previous Egyptological research dealing with funerary data sets and coffin studies. I have used all my skills as a researcher, but I have also allowed myself to think out loud, to infer and imagine, in a way I would not do in my other work. This book finds its origins in my intimate (and strange even to myself) connection to the ancient world, and I have to thank the countless scholars who share the same obsession with Egypt's past—generations of archaeologists who uncovered Hatshepsut's remnants in the dirt, philologists who translated and analyzed her texts, art historians who pieced together broken statues and found traces of her relief erased by chisels. They have paved the way for this biographical discussion of Hatshepsut's relevance.

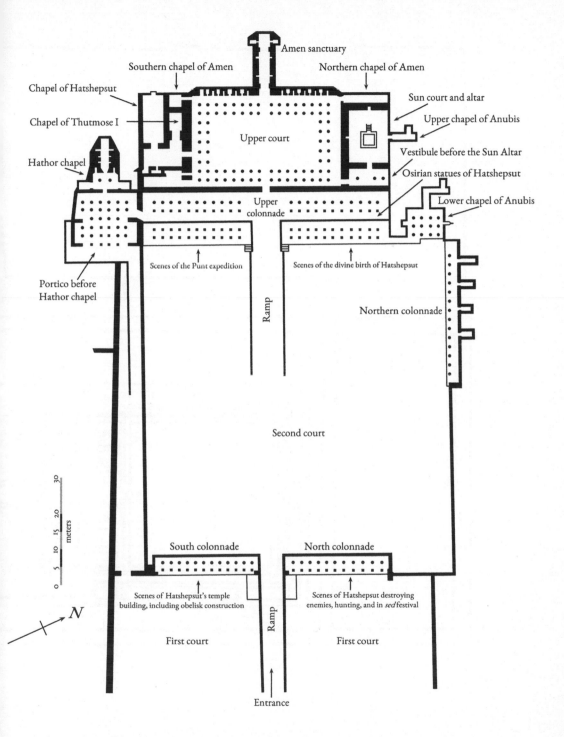

Amen sanctuary

Southern chapel of Amen

Northern chapel of Amen

Chapel of Hatshepsut

Sun court and altar

Chapel of Thutmose I

Upper chapel of Anubis

Upper court

Vestibule before the Sun Altar

Hathor chapel

Osirian statues of Hatshepsut

Upper colonnade

Lower chapel of Anubis

Portico before Hathor chapel

Scenes of the Punt expedition

Scenes of the divine birth of Hatshepsut

Northern colonnade

Ramp

Second court

30
25
20
15
10
5
0
meters

South colonnade

North colonnade

Scenes of Hatshepsut's temple building, including obelisk construction

Scenes of Hatshepsut destroying enemies, hunting, and in *sed* festival

First court

Ramp

First court

N

Entrance

Map of Hatshepsut's funerary temple, Deir el-Bahri, Thebes, Eighteenth Dynasty.
Map by Deborah Shieh.

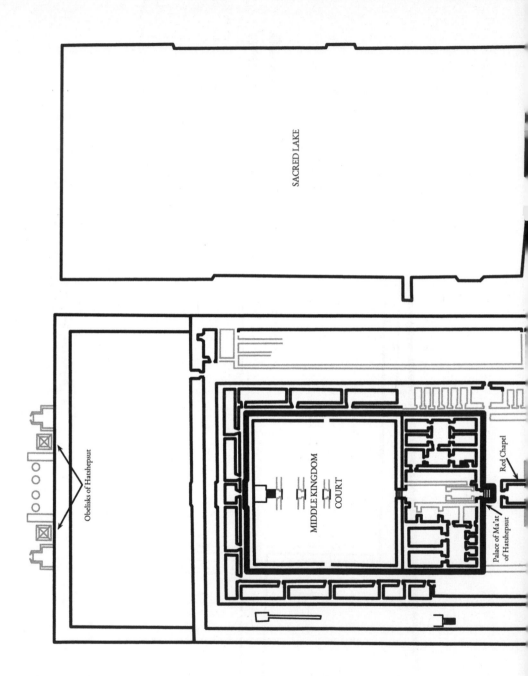

Map of Karnak Temple, Amen precinct, during the time of Hatshepsut.
Map by Deborah Shieh.

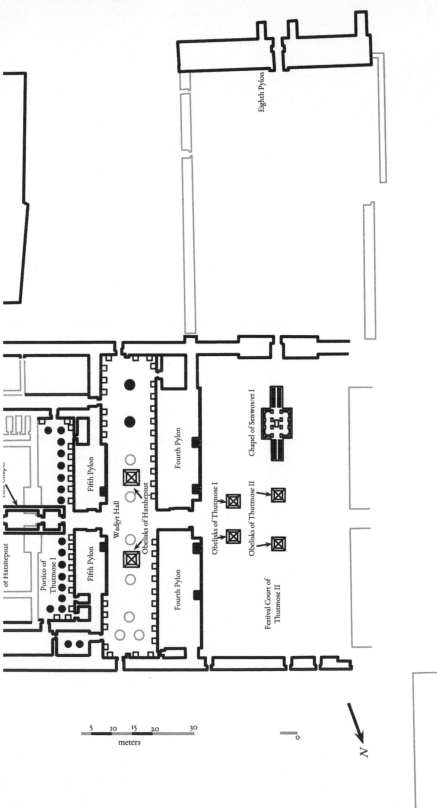

Eighth Pylon

Fifth Pylon

Fifth Pylon

Portico of
Thutmose I

of Hatshepsut

Wadjyt Hall

Obelisks of Hatshepsut

Fourth Pylon

Fourth Pylon

Obelisks of Thutmose I

Obelisks of Thutmose II

Chapel of Senwosret I

Festival Court of
Thutmose II

N

5   10   15   20   30

meters

0

Palace of
"I am not far from him"

Hatshepsut was the first woman to exercise long-term rule over Egypt as a king. Other Egyptian women had governed before her, but they merely served as regents or leaders for short periods of time. If we combine her regency and kingship, Hatshepsut reigned for almost twenty-two years. Even more remarkably, Hatshepsut achieved her power without bloodshed or social trauma. We have no evidence of any messy assassinations of her family members or attempted coups that nearly succeeded (led by her or anyone else). Though Hatshepsut's rise to power was clean and creative, it required every weapon in her arsenal—invoking her bloodline, education, political acumen, along with a deep (and sometimes radical) understanding of religious power.

So why do so few people today know the name of this extraordinary woman? We know about Cleopatra VII's murders, sexual exploits, economic excesses, and disastrous military campaigns. Hatshepsut was, as far as we can tell, not a seducer of great generals in charge of legions, for the practical reason that there existed no men greater than she. Rather than seduce mere mortals, she created a mechanism to publicly and inexorably prove the gods' love for her without having to submit sexually to men. She is not remembered for any disastrous battles because all her military exploits brought her people and her gods greater imperial wealth. There are no stories preserved about her conniving to procure cash because she had more money than anyone in the known world. She is not remembered for her nasty death because there is no evidence of her expulsion, murder, or suicide.

Hatshepsut has the misfortune to be antiquity's female leader who did everything right, a woman who could match her wit and energy to a task so seamlessly that she made no waves of discontent that have been recorded. For Hatshepsut, all that endured were the remnants of her success, props for later kings who never had to give her the credit she deserved.

Male leaders are celebrated for their successes, while their excesses are typically excused as the necessary and expected price of masculine ambition. A king's risk taking is more likely to be perceived as crucial and advantageous, something that can bring great reward if he wins. Even the sociopathic narcissism of a male leader can be suffered. Women in power who do everything wrong offer great narrative fodder: Cleopatra, Jezebel and her daughter Athaliah, Semiramis, Empress Lü. They are dangerous, untrustworthy, self-interested to a fault. Their sexuality and powers of attraction can bring all to ruin. History has shown that a woman who pushes the envelope of ambition is not just maligned in the history books as a conniving, scheming seductress whose foolhardy and emotional desires brought down the good men around her, but also celebrated in infamous detail as proof that females should never be in charge. In this regard, ancient Egypt was surprisingly contemporary, allowing Hatshepsut any opportunity to rule in the first place.[1]

But Hatshepsut saved the day and her dynasty by paving the way for a baby king who was probably gnawing on his crook and flail during his own coronation. And what may consign Hatshepsut to obscurity is our inability to appreciate and value honest, naked, female ambition, not to mention actual power properly wielded by a woman. Posterity cherishes the idea that there is something oppressive and distrustful about women who rule over men—that their mercurial moods have the power to destroy, that their impolitic natures ruin carefully tended alliances, that their agenda on behalf of their children will endanger any broader political interests. These critical perceptions make it difficult to properly rank Hatshepsut's achievements in history. We lose the opportunity to either laud her for her successes or dissect her methodologies and tactics. How does one categorize a female leader who does not follow the expected course of disaster and shame, one who instead puts everything to rights in the end, in a way so perfect that her masculine beneficiaries just sweep her victories under the rug and ignore her forever?

Why does Hatshepsut's leadership still trouble us today? Female rulers are often implicitly branded as emotional, self-interested, lacking in authority, untrustworthy, and impolitic. The ancient Egyptians likewise distrusted a woman with authority, and this context makes Hatshepsut's achievements all the more astonishing. For more than twenty years, she was the most powerful person in the ancient world. But when she finally died, all that she had built was instantly over; there would be no legacy.

Hatshepsut's achievements are relevant to us precisely because they were ultimately rejected and forgotten—both by her own people and by the subsequent authors of history. She was the most formidable and successful woman to ever rule in the ancient Western world, and yet today few people can even pronounce her name. We can never really *know* Hatshepsut, but the traces she left behind teach us what it means to be a woman at the highest echelons of power: she transcended patriarchal systems of authority, took on onerous responsibilities for her family, suffered great personal losses, and shaped an amazing journey out of circumstances over which she had little control.

We *do* have a great deal of information about Hatshepsut and the Egypt of almost thirty-five hundred years ago, and from that I have built this story of her life and what she created. All the details that will give us insight into her anxieties, grief, disappointments, and aspirations—from government offices, countless bureaucrats, palaces and temples, riverboats and horse-drawn chariots to the diseases and illnesses that threatened her and her family—are vital to understanding this woman.

As a social historian of ancient Egypt, I am drawn to the nitty-gritty of ancient life, particularly those circumstances that could not be conquered: disease, social place, patriarchal control, gender inequality, geographic location. I want to know how people coped in a world over which they had so little control and in which they had so little time to make their mark, a place where grief, sorrow, and apprehension were more commonplace than success and where most knew they could never create any kind of change in their life, beyond doing what their fathers or mothers had done before them. My Egyptological work on social life has enabled me to re-create Hatshepsut's world as best I can and thereby to know her better.

I have spent two decades studying the remnants that ancient Egyptians left behind—letters, receipts, funerary texts, coffins, funerary bandages, magical talismans—any attempt by people to work their social circumstances into something better. Most ancient Egyptians used the meager tools they had available to effect small changes in their lives—bribing an official to get a craftsman's job, demanding testimony from family members to divorce a husband who was physically abusive when he drank too much beer, disowning children in a last will and testament if they did not care enough for their parents—all the while knowing that most of life was already written by forces far beyond anyone's ability to change them. Hatshepsut was born into the highest echelons of society, to be sure, but even she had plenty of obstacles in her path, not least of which was her female identity. It took all her perseverance and creativity to strategize a change in her social circumstances beyond society's perceived expectations. Hatshepsut was a rare human being, a woman able to see beyond the machine and set forces in motion to shape her own destiny. She effected the ultimate change to make herself king. She did everything right, but none of it mattered. She was maligned not just by the ancient Egyptian rulers who followed her but also by nineteenth- and twentieth-century Egyptologists who were suspicious of her motivations and ready to judge her for taking what did not rightfully belong to her.

Hatshepsut's story should teach us that women cannot rule unless they veil their true intent and proclaim that their pretentions are not their own but only for others. They must claim to sacrifice themselves to service, declare that they have been chosen by providence or destiny for such a role, and assert that they never sought such authority for themselves. If a woman does not renounce ambition for ambition's sake, she will be viewed as two-faced or selfish, her actions fueled by ulterior motives. Maybe Hatshepsut was so intent on climbing the ladder to power, one rung at a time, that she never grasped these truths; perhaps she believed that she could change the system. And maybe we still believe the same thing.

ONE

Divine Origins

The Nile, lifeblood of the world's first great civilization, flowed calmly outside her palace window. The inundation had receded, and she could see the farmers readying themselves in the predawn hour, milking their cows, getting their sacks of emmer and barley seed ready to cast upon the rich black earth. In a few hours, the air would fill with the sounds of men shouting, children laughing, and animals bleating as they ran behind the plows, treading upon the scattered seeds and driving them into the soil. But for now, the sun was yet to crest the horizon. There was still time before she would be called to awaken the god in the temple. The girl dismissed her handmaiden to have a moment of privacy for herself.

Hatshepsut was around sixteen years old, and her life's purpose was over. Her husband Aakheperenre Thutmose, Lord of the Two Lands, King of Upper and Lower Egypt, may he live, was gravely ill, despite his youth. He and Hatshepsut had failed to produce an heir. She had only one daughter, Nefrure, who was strong and healthy but just two years old—not old enough to marry, reproduce, or forge the alliances that princesses so often do. Hatshepsut herself was the daughter of the previous king and was married to her father's successor—her own younger brother. She now sat as the king's highest-ranking wife. Her bloodline was impeccable: daughter of the king, sister of the king, wife of the king. Her biggest failing was not giving birth to a son: the heir to the throne would not come from her.

Why had Amen-Re, the king of the gods, not blessed Egypt with a son of pure royal blood? Why had he only given Hatshepsut a daughter? A man could spread his seed and produce offspring in profusion. A woman's womb could give but one child a year. And Hatshepsut's womb had been blessed only with a girl—or at least Nefrure was the only child that had lived.

Her husband did have some boys in the royal nursery—but from other mothers. The kingship should always pass from father to son; however, these boys were mere babies. The king had only been on the throne for three short years, not long enough to sire a stable of healthy potential heirs. And worse than that, the mothers of these children were nothing more than Ornaments of the King—pretty young things brought in to arouse the king's pleasure, with faces and bodies that would excite even the most sickly of monarchs. These girls had no family connections of any importance. How could one of these women be elevated to King's Mother? The idea was insupportable.

Hatshepsut understood that she wielded great power as queen. Her husband had never been in good health. His kingship had never been expected, but his two elder brothers died before they could take the throne. Thus Thutmose was not trained for kingship as he should have been. When they married, it was Hatshepsut who advised her brother on which officials to trust, which families to avoid, and how to make his mark as a monarch. It still seemed to her as if he had been plucked from the royal nursery one day, called to be king, to his own horror as much as anyone else's. The heartbreaking death of one brother after another had brought the crown to young Thutmose and the queenship to Hatshepsut. From as far back as she could remember, Hatshepsut understood that she was training for a life of great power and influence. But now it was all over. With no direct connection to the next king, she would be shut out of worldly affairs, her life's journey confined within luxurious palace walls.

But Hatshepsut still walked the halls of power as the God's Wife of Amen. And she sensed that it might be difficult for people to support the claim of an infant to the crowns of the Two Lands. Would their subjects watch passively as a young prince without connections, the son of one of the King's Beauties, was propped up as king? Such a vulnerable monarch could only be maintained if Hatshepsut stood behind him as his regent and made the decisions; otherwise, all would be lost; her father's

Thutmoside line would be broken after only two generations. Many great men of the court were emphasizing their connections back to the Ahmoside family—the kings who had ruled before her father—in an attempt to lay claim to the thrones of Upper and Lower Egypt; if the White and Red crowns passed to one of them instead of to a son of her brother, then all that her parents had entrusted to her would be lost. It would be a shameful end to her father's dynasty: dying out after only two Thutmoside kings— her father and her brother. Somehow she had to create the circumstances for a third Thutmoside king.

Hatshepsut was not only the King's Great Wife but also the God's Wife of Amen, and she understood how to use that position. She served as the most important priestess in all of Egypt and had been trained from childhood by Ahmes-Nefertari, the most revered and aged royal queen and priestess in the land. As Hatshepsut prepared for her duties at the temple, she decided to ask the god what to do. She would place the burden in his hands.

Somewhere beyond the palace, she heard the beating of drums and the shaking of sistra. It was time to awaken Amen.

Hatshepsut hurried into the temple of Ipet-Sut, the Chosen Place for the gods of Thebes, moving through a series of majestic plastered gateways, light-filled courtyards, cool columned halls, and dark, smoke-filled inner sanctuaries, to her own robing rooms. As was her daily custom, she bathed in the sacred lake within the temple walls; the dawn air chilled her flesh. Having been thus purified in preparation for the morning meal with the god, she was anointed with oils by her Divine Adoratrices and then dressed in a pure linen robe pleated with hundreds of folds pressed into the gauzy fabric. This particular morning was not a festival day, so the temple staff had to complete only the simplest of preparations, which included the slaughter of a bull for the god's meal of a few dozen courses of milk, cakes, breads, and meats. To Hatshepsut, this temple was a second home. She found comfort in the juxtaposition of its frenetic activity against a calm, divine presence. Frantic priests ran through their preparations in the outer rooms as she walked with her ladies deep into the very heart of the temple. The chanting and drumbeats now sounded more distant as she entered the small, dark, windowless sanctuary where Amen dwelled—a room filled with brightly painted relief whose low ceiling and close walls acted as a womb of rebirth for the god. Finally, she stood before the shrine of Amen himself; in the lamplight, gold and lapis gleamed through the incense smoke, a sight that never failed to set her heart pounding.

The First High Priest of Amen joined Hatshepsut in the sanctuary while the Second High Priest arranged the sacred texts and instruments. After all the offerings of food and drink were arrayed, the lower-ranked priest retreated from the sanctuary, wiping away his footprints as he backed out of the room. The next moments of the ritual involved waking the vulnerable god from his sleep of death. All but the most important priests waited outside in the offering hall, shaking their sistra and beating drums to calm the god and to keep danger at bay. Only Hatshepsut and the First High Priest were able to witness the god's visage and exposed body. The high priest was the first to approach the shrine of Amen. With cool and reverent hands, he removed veils covering the unknowable and hidden image. The fact that the Great God was an immobile statue of gold did not make him any less real.

Closing her eyes, Hatshepsut began the incantations to awaken the god, calling him to his meal. Shuffling behind her, the First High Priest burned wax figures of the enemies of Egypt, so that the sanctuary would be clear of any danger. All around them incense burned in profusion, narrowing her vision in the lamp-lit room to a tunnel with the god's image at the end. Hatshepsut then reached for her golden sistrum, ready to shake the sacred tambourine of Hathor to awaken the god.

As she chanted and shook the sistrum, she opened her linen robe, revealing her naked body to the Great God's eyes. Meanwhile, the high priest offered him food, starting with milk, because the newly awakened divinity was as weak as an infant, and then building up to great bloody cuts of freshly sacrificed beef as he gained strength. After the last course, Hatshepsut moved closer to the statue so that the god could complete his morning renewal. As the God's Wife of Amen, Hatshepsut was also known as the God's Hand, the instrument of his sexuality. Reverently, she took his phallus into her palm, allowing him to re-create himself through his own release. Outside the sanctuary, her Divine Adoratrices were chanting, their voices rising higher and faster with the urgency of the moment. She stood before his statue, opened her linen robe wide to reveal her young body, and chanted praise of Amen, King of All the Gods, Lord of the Thrones of the Two Lands, the Lord of All, until she felt his orgasm.

Her eyes were closed. Her head was dizzy from the incense, herbs,

and chanting. She felt herself fall to the floor before him—something neither she nor the high priest expected. With her eyes closed and her head
bowed down before his shrine, she began to talk to her sacred husband,
the god Amen-Re. She told him of the king's great sickness and impending death. She told him that a young Horus had not yet been chosen, and
that all the candidates were merely nestlings, puppies. She told him that
she had served him faithfully and would do as he asked. But all of Egypt
would soon be in mourning and silence. She needed to know what to do
to maintain the Black Land and Amen's rule in it. She was young, but she
could hold and keep power. She needed his guidance.

In return she received a revelation. He spoke to her. Amen-Re, Bull
of His Mother, Sacred of Arm, told her that she was elemental to the plans
in his mind: he had chosen her, Hatshepsut, to carry them out; he would
reveal his instructions over time, so she must be always ready, listening.
And he told her more, too, secrets of power and fearlessness that left her
breathless and weeping.

And then the revelation was over. In silence and in secret, her voice
shaking with emotion, she gave Amen a solemn promise. She would be
his instrument.

We have no historical record of Hatshep-
sut's worries and schemes upon the death of her husband, Thutmose II, but by examining her unprecedented choice to ultimately take on
the kingship we can imagine how an educated royal woman might have
understood and created a place for herself within Egypt's court. Because
the Egyptians enacted their politics through the rituals of religion, we
cannot know exactly where the affairs of government ended and the ideology started. Hatshepsut herself tells us in many monumental texts that
her assumption of power was decreed by Amen-Re, her father. Indeed, *she*
probably believed this to be true.

The nature of the evidence from her reign—her temples and monumental texts, the decorated tombs of her courtiers, her tomb in the Valley
of the Kings, all her statuary and painted reliefs, even the recent identification of a possible mummy—has encouraged us to understand Hatshepsut's story through the things she built and touched. She did not leave us
any letters or diaries. We have little access to the human emotions of her

story. The difficult part of a biography of any Egyptian king is that we fall into the gaps of the personal history left untold. If the king was meant to be a living god on earth, then naturally he had to be shrouded in ideology and not defined by his personality, schemes, plans, and ambitions. Unlike the Romans, who produced countless lascivious stories about their own emperors and senators, not to mention Cleopatra, that foreign seductress of good Roman generals, the ancient Egyptians played their politics close to the vest, and for good reason. The *system* of divine kingship and cosmic order mattered most to them, not the individual *person* who was king at a particular time. The institution of kingship was unassailable even when the dynasty was in jeopardy, when there was competition for the throne, or when a woman dared to take power. Among thousands of often meticulous Egyptian historical documents, hardly a single word betrays any human emotion of delight, heartbreak, jealousy, or disgust concerning political events.[1] The Egyptian ideological systems took precedence over the emotions, decisions, wants, and desires of any one individual or family. Gossip among the elite and powerful of ancient Egyptian society was almost unheard of, at least in any recorded form that we can decipher. Formality ruled the day. The drama of a public scandal was swept under the rug, never to be entered into official documents or even unofficial letters. The ancient Egyptians never underestimated the power of the written word; anything that smacked of personal politics or individual opinion was excluded from the formal record. It seems that such things could only be spoken of in hushed tones. Ancient Egyptians preserved the "what" of their history in copious texts and monuments for posterity; the "how" and the "why," the messy details of it all, are much harder to get at. And, for our modern minds, it is the recording of events that allows them to become real and valid.

Historians have the materials but lack the intangible substance behind them. We know from temple carvings that Hatshepsut gained power as God's Wife of Amen at least by the reign of Thutmose II, her husband-brother, in the early fifteenth century BCE (if not before), but we do not know whether she was the real power behind his throne. If she was, did she wield that power cruelly or wisely? We know that Thutmose II ruled for only a short time,[2] but history has not preserved the reason why: was he sickly or stupid or mad or lazy, or did he just die unexpectedly? We know from the tomb texts of officials who ruled under Hatshepsut that she acted as regent for the next young king, but we don't know how that reality came about or what anyone, including Hatshepsut, really thought about the situation of a young girl in charge of the most powerful land in the ancient world.

The Egyptians preserved Hatshepsut's body to last for eternity,[3] but they recorded little from her mind. Archaeologists have uncovered many temples, ritual texts, administrative documents about trade, quarrying, and mining, and countless statues of her, her daughter, and her favored courtier Senenmut, but we don't know the intricacies of her relationships. Egyptology has identified the trappings of the kingship, but it is very hard to locate the king among them. Do we even need to discuss Hatshepsut's thoughts and ambitions? Hatshepsut successfully scaled the mountain to kingship, after all, and perhaps that fact should be enough for us. But women in power are still suspect in the world of modern politics. Glass ceilings loom everywhere. If we can gain just a tiny glimmer into Hatshepsut's mind as she struggled with her own journey to transcend the strictures of masculine dominance in her society, we might better understand why women are systematically shut out of positions of authority. Given Hatshepsut's undisputed success as a king, why was the legacy of her rule stricken so quickly from Egyptian history?

Hatshepsut was born around 1500 BCE[4] into the Eighteenth Dynasty of the New Kingdom—although she herself would not have used the term—a time of nascent prosperity and dominance for Egypt. Control over the southern mines and quarries in Nubia had recently been reestablished, and gold was once again pouring into the country. The recent wars with the Hyksos of Syria-Palestine had made every landholder, official, and warrior rich.[5] Elite Egyptians who had followed their king on campaigns were rewarded with the wealth that a well-waged war was meant to bring—chariots, horses, live captives, and gold. Not only had the borders been secured by the hawkish early Eighteenth Dynasty kings, but the distasteful invasions of generations of Hyksos from Syria-Palestine had been made invisible—either by violently expelling the foreigners back to the northeast or by allowing their settlement and Egyptianization in the Nile delta. Hatshepsut would have heard dozens of tales about the exploits of elite Egyptian men who besieged great Hyksos cities or met the enemy in open battle, returning with bloody severed hands cut from lifeless corpses, proudly displayed as trophies at court.

But before Hatshepsut was even born, despite Egypt's resurgence on the imperial stage, there were storm clouds brewing. King Amenhotep I, who had helped to create all this prosperity, was facing a crisis. Despite twenty years of rule, there is no evidence that he produced any children at all.[6] We can imagine the King's Mother, Ahmes-Nefertari, hovering around him and procuring new queens and concubines for him after marriages to both of his sisters failed to produce the hoped-for boy—or any child for that matter. The Egyptians veiled any reference to disastrous outcomes related to the king in their formal historical texts and monuments, but the fact that Amenhotep I could not sire a living son cannot be disputed. It is possible that Amenhotep I was sterile, but the Egyptian royal family also practiced incest (and at times preferred it for political reasons); sex with his full sisters could have simply created deformed or gravely ill babies.

Incest is usually taboo, but it can be useful in the bedchambers of the powerful. In the case of ancient Egypt, it was justified by mythology. The very first god in all of creation, Atum, began existence floating weightless in the dark and infinite elements of precreation. Due to the lack of a partner beyond himself, he had sex with a part of himself (his hand[7]), thus magically producing his own birth and subsequently the first generation of male and female gods. This brother-sister pair, Shu and Tefnut, copulated with each other and produced the earth god Geb and the sky goddess Nut, another brother-sister pair who in turn produced the next generation of four children, each pairing up into brother-sister marriages: Seth married Nephthys, and Osiris married Isis. The office of the kingship descended directly from this lineage. Horus, king upon earth and the god whom the human king embodied in his palace, was the son of Osiris and Isis.

From this ancient Egyptian perspective, full brother-sister marriages were divinely inspired, and the Eighteenth Dynasty actually started with a full brother-sister marriage between King Ahmose I and Ahmes-Nefertari. The son they produced was Amenhotep I, and so perhaps we should not be surprised that the progeny of a fully incestuous relationship had trouble siring children, not only with his own sisters but also with other women. Ahmes-Nefertari, a sister-wife, was simultaneously aunt and mother to her own son. Amenhotep I may have had serious health issues throughout his life, although we cannot expect to find any mention of them in the historical record. He came to the throne quite young, perhaps as a toddler, and his mother probably acted as regent and made decisions for him during much of his reign. Later depictions of Amenhotep I always pair him with his mother instead of his sister-wife Merytamen, perhaps an apt representation of political reality for a king with no offspring of his own.

We can imagine the throne room during the early years of the reign of Amenhotep I. A boy of perhaps four or five sits on (or near) the throne, being instructed by his tutors when he really wants to be outside playing. A general who needs a decision about a Nubian military campaign or a trading expedition enters. Who answers him? The boy's mother, Ahmes-Nefertari, who is openly acknowledged to be the power behind his throne. It was common practice to assign the boy's mother as regent for a king too young to rule, relying on her to make decisions beyond the child's capabilities. It was a wise and safe practice, as even the most narcissistic mother was unlikely to betray her own son, cause his murder, or otherwise conspire against him. Such behavior would never have been in her own interest, since her power was inextricably connected to that of her child. A queen-regent would also be unlikely to alienate her son by ignoring or mistreating him, because as he grew into his power, any feelings of neglect or betrayal he harbored would only serve to ruin her. The system of queen-regent worked quite well in ancient Egypt, which was fortunate because most of the kings of the early Eighteenth Dynasty came to the throne as children, including Ahmose I and Amenhotep I.[8]

Typically, royal Egyptian women owed everything to the men to whom they were attached and only wielded power when they had a close connection to the king—as a mother, wife, daughter, or sister. The regency system worked because these women were invested with real, if temporary, power. It was a system of self-interested incentives revolving around the king.

Ahmes-Nefertari was more than just a queen-regent, however. She was one of the first royal women (perhaps the second if her mother, Queen Ahhotep,[9] was the first) to hold a newly influential religious office: the role of a priestess called the God's Wife of Amen. Like Atum or Ptah (the craftsman god of the northern city of Memphis), Amen was a creator god.[10] His regeneration, through his own agency, was the miracle that kept the Egyptian cosmos perpetually self-creating. The Egyptian temple of Karnak facilitated Amen's ongoing process of creation.[11] If the temple walls did not keep out enemies and profanity, if the offerings were not made, if the god was not fed, if the God's Wife did not facilitate his rebirth, then, it was believed, creation would stop—or at least the creation that benefited the people of Egypt would collapse. The Nile might cease to flood its banks every year, leaving no life-giving silt and mud in which to farm. The sun could fail to rise in the east every morning, depriving the crops of life-giving rays.

Egyptian texts clearly state how Amen of Thebes (or Atum of Heliopolis, who was the older manifestation of some of the same religious ideas of creation) enacted his self-creation through an act of masturbation with the God's Hand, a priestess (often the God's Wife) appointed to the temple ostensibly to provide the "activity" that a statue of a god was unable to provide for himself.[12] There were probably multiple cult statues that required such assistance, one residing in each of the Theban temples. Each statue was most likely made of solid precious metal that the Egyptians believed constituted the flesh of the gods—gold, silver, or electrum—and probably crafted with an erect penis full of potentiality and creation.

These active statues were not uncommon in ancient Egypt. In fact, the oldest known Egyptian monumental statuary, dating to before 3000 BCE, shows standing male gods performing masturbation (their display caused no end of embarrassment to Victorian museum curators and visitors).[13] But for the ancient Egyptians, this act was the most sacred moment of creation, the alpha and the omega of everything, ground zero for the continuation of this world as they knew it. These mysteries had to be facilitated and witnessed by a cadre of elites with religious training. Second in importance only to men like the First High Priest of Amen at Karnak or the First High Priest of Ptah at Memphis, the God's Wife of Amen was one of the elite few allowed into the sanctuary of the god to see him unveiled with all his vulnerable bits exposed and extended. She may have considered herself as separate from the god, protecting him, exciting him, but she must have also known the deeper mysteries of the rites: that she was part of him, an essential element of the agency that kick-started the universe every day.

Ahmes-Nefertari was getting old, which limited her ability to sexually excite Amen, and perhaps the role of God's Hand had already been given to a younger princess. But at some point, she passed the priestess position of

God's Wife on to her own daughter, Merytamen, a much younger woman and the sister-wife of Amenhotep I.[14] Ahmes-Nefertari still retained the title of God's Wife; it was her most important role—more central to her than King's Great Wife, King's Sister, or King's Mother, a trifecta of royal titles for an influential Egyptian woman and a testament to the great religious and political power she amassed in her lifetime.

Despite her great political power, she couldn't will a grandson into being. Toward the end of her son's reign, Ahmes-Nefertari must have found herself anxious about the prospects of the Ahmoside dynasty's continuation. At some point, that anxiety would have turned to fatalism, and perhaps she even aided her son in finding a successor who was not of direct lineage. Amenhotep I had no living son, but a careful decision could still be made that preserved Egypt's bright prospects. Presumably Amenhotep I had no surviving brothers, so ultimately the throne passed to a middle-aged elite man from Thebes named Thutmose (Djehutymes, "the One Born of Thoth," the moon god of Hermopolis), a man who would go on to become Aakheperkare Thutmose, whom Egyptologists call Thutmose I. This king would flourish, expanding Egypt's borders, increasing its wealth, and waging great battles in Syria-Palestine to the north and in Nubia to the south. He would begin building up Egypt's sacred temples in stone, and he would raise the status of the god Amen to an unprecedented level. This official who became king was Hatshepsut's father.

Thutmose I was not of direct royal birth. He never called himself King's Son. He probably had connections to the family of Amenhotep I but was not himself the son of a king.[15] He never once tells us who his father was—which is strange in itself—perhaps because the situation of continuing a defunct dynasty demanded his silence. Thutmose I was most likely a general before he was picked to become king. How he was chosen and why are never stated; such messy details were avoided in any formal or official Egyptian records. Kingship was a divine office, and it was not to be viewed as the subject of political haggling and horse-trading. Any real-world discussions of who would be the next king and why were kept strictly verbal. Thoughts about the royal family were whispered, obliquely discussed among a few colleagues, or kept within one's mind; they were certainly not committed to papyrus.

Perhaps Thutmose was the strongest of the strongmen in contention for the throne. Or maybe he was the one with the closest lineage of descent to the now-defunct Ahmoside dynasty. He could have been one of King Amenhotep I's tutors and part of the royal household. It's possible that he and the king were good friends from the wars in Syria-Palestine. Whatever the relationship and the circumstances, Thutmose I may have felt as if he did not belong on the throne at first, even if he was groomed for the position years in advance. It must have been a strange thing to step into such a sacred and formalized office instead of being born into its oddities and intricacies.

Regardless of any feelings of inadequacy, he would have executed his duties to the best of his ability, knowing that kingship was essential to the survival of Egypt and the Egyptian people. Politics and religion went hand in hand in Egypt: if there was no king, there was only cosmic chaos. The king supervised military, political, economic, legal, and religious affairs, all of which were imbued with ideological weight. Wars were divinely inspired and divinely won, and all spoils went to the gods as gifts. Political power was granted to the king from the time his bones were knitted together in the womb, even before his accession. Kingship was a mysterious and timeless creation.

Even a king's economic power depended on his connection to the gods: if he pleased them, they would manifest a good Nile flood, which laid down a rich layer of mud so that the seeds of wheat and barley could be sown—as opposed to a disastrously low Nile inundation or a devastatingly high flood, both of which would result in drought, disease, and conflict. For the Egyptians, wheat and barley *were* money, and essentially money grew in the rich mud the Nile inundation left behind every year. That economic wealth was a gift of the gods. Prospects were good now, but perhaps Thutmose I worried that the gods' whims would turn against him and toward devastation.

Thutmose must have keenly felt the weight of this unexpected responsibility. Any of his legal decisions as king would be wrapped up in an Egyptian religious-ethical concept called *ma'at*, meaning "order," "truth," or "justice." *Ma'at* was simply the way things were meant to function when a good king was in power, making effective, well-reasoned, fair decisions, when everyone knew their place, how to behave, and what was expected of them.

But likely nothing would have created more feelings of insecurity in the freshly chosen king than the extensive religious duties foisted upon him day and night. He acted as chief priest of every temple throughout the land. In practical terms, everyone knew that the king could not simultaneously lead rituals in Heliopolis in the north and in Thebes, some 400 miles to the south. Thus he appointed learned and intellectual chief priests to take up these duties in his stead, men who had a more profound grasp of the mysteries than the new king could ever hope to acquire, so that no temple would go without the rituals required to summon the gods into their statues: feeding them the appropriate foods in the appropriate order; performing the right kind of chanting, singing, and entertainment; offering the smell of sweet incense and maintaining the braziers; and safeguarding the golden shrines and implements on which the temple rituals depended.

Even though Thutmose worked with chief priests as surrogates in temples throughout Egypt, the religious responsibilities of the king cannot be underestimated. Not only was the intellectual preparation for such work rigorous and time-consuming, but he must have known that it was up to him to channel the goodwill of the gods to earth through complex rituals, to meditate on the mysteries of divine creation and his place within it. One can only wonder if Thutmose ever felt like a fraud because he was not brought up for this profound duty of acting as intermediary between heaven and earth, or if he worried that his inadequacies would bring about the failure of creation itself. Egypt's very well-being depended on a healthy, fit monarch, and we can picture the people's anxiety any time the king was incapacitated or unable to fulfill his sacred duties. The king should be a model specimen—a godly perfection on earth.

As every king had before him, Thutmose I would serve as the linchpin that held the created and ordered cosmos together. Whereas before his coronation he could have risen in the morning for a quick prayer at the household altar with statues of ancestors and gods to keep his family (or army) safe, he now had to rise before dawn for complex ablutions involving the bathing and shaving of his entire body, anointment with oils, and dressing in restricting kilts, corselets, and aprons. He had to don unwieldy headgear like the *atef* crown, with tall double plumes balancing a sun disk atop ram's horns, and the Double Crown of Upper and Lower Egypt, which featured a high-backed red crown joined with a white crown that looked something like a bowling pin protruding from a tall basket. His body had to be made ritually pure to enter the most sacred spaces in the state temples throughout Egypt, which meant that certain kinds of food or drink or human contact were prohibited. Priests around Thutmose I may have constantly rattled off rules for this or that, annoying him when his mind was bent toward more worldly issues. As he performed ritual after ritual for Atum of Heliopolis, Ptah of Memphis, Amen of Thebes, and dozens of other state gods throughout Egypt, were his religious obligations a constant and unending drain?

He may have even balked at some of the indignities: at the most important festivals, he was required not just to fulfill his duties inside the temple but also to lead public processions along two or three miles of hot paved surfaces lined with stone sphinxes. He had to perform ceremonial runs while clutching all kinds of unwieldy things—rowing oars, jars of liquid, thrashing live birds—as he sped on foot around a sacred circuit. One ritual involved hitting four balls with a stick in the four cardinal directions; in another he had to bash special chests with a bat of some kind. On a different day he might have to herd live, and probably uncooperative, calves into the god's presence. He was called on to strike and kill repellent animals with a spear. Along with these feats of strength or piety, he always had to go through the tedium of offering incredibly long and intricate meals to the gods, presenting courses accompanied by difficult incantations that could number over fifty. He had to accomplish all this while mastering the more subtle challenges of the rituals, such as learning to embrace a statue representing the fertile form of the god Amen, holding his arms high and away from his body so that his own nether regions did not come into contact with the massive erect phallus of the sacred god's form. In every circumstance, it was in the king's best interest to be athletic and mentally fit.

As Egypt's solar priest, Thutmose I now entered into the great mysteries of the sun god. He probably participated in a mind-numbing initiation that took place in the god's sanctuary, drinking and ingesting herbs until he was taken into the god's embrace and shown his unique place in the cosmos, finally grasping how the successful rising and setting of this ball of fire could only happen through his incantations and offerings. Thereafter, he would have woken every morning before dawn to greet the coming sun on the eastern horizon and would have communed with other manifestations of the sun god during the deepest hours of night, meditating on the mysteries of how the dead sun was able to fight off the destructive advances of Apophis, who wanted nothing more than to uncreate the universe. These solar mysteries were so meaningful to Thutmose I that he was perhaps the very first king to include excerpts from the solar temple liturgy in his own tomb decoration: scenes from the Book of Amduat[16] documenting the terrifying and perilous journey of the sun during the hours of night were carved into his burial chamber in what we now call Kings Valley 38 (KV 38).[17] Thutmose I likely believed he himself would meld with the sun god on his journey through the heavens, that his own journey into death was the rising and setting of the sun god himself.

When he became king, Thutmose I's life was turned upside down. Leaving his family's villas and lands, presumably near the town of Thebes, he would have moved to head up the palaces and campaign encampments throughout Egypt. Thutmose I's mother, Seniseneb, previously the mistress of her own home in Thebes, now became the King's Mother, with the great responsibility to watch over the newly installed harem of wives, concubines, and ornaments—all put in place to produce many sons and secure the king's dynasty.[18] Thutmose I could not have lived in one place for long; he and his entourage moved in their comfortable barges up and down the Nile or through dusty desert roads to border fortresses, as need and weather allowed. His journeys on campaigns may have seemed like second nature to him, but palace life would have demanded some psychological shifts.[19]

First off, Thutmose I needed to abandon all notions of having just one wife as was common for Egyptian men. He would have to marry again to connect himself to the family of Amenhotep I and to the mythology of masculine kingship. Assuming he had a family before his accession, we are left to wonder if his wife, sons, and daughters moved to the palace with him and what their change in status was. If his wife was still alive, she must have been anxious about being superseded by the other women to whom he bound himself upon his accession to the throne. These family details were never recorded, and we cannot expect that they ever would have been. Nonetheless, the changes in Thutmose I's life would have been a tumultuous existential shift for both himself and his family when he ascended the throne and married his new "great" royal wife.

The new wife's name was Ahmes,[20] and she would soon bear him a daughter named Hatshepsut. Thutmose I was never clear about Ahmes's origins, at least not in the formal temple inscriptions that are left to us. She is called King's Sister and King's Great Wife. The second part is easy to understand: she was now the wife of Thutmose I, and her status was higher than that of all his other women. But which King's Sister was she? Sister of Amenhotep I, the king who had just died? Or was she the sibling of his predecessor Ahmose? Or perhaps she was related to neither, because she was never named King's Daughter. Some say that Ahmes's title of King's Sister was derived from her marriage to her own brother Thutmose I. If this explanation is true, then one of Thutmose's younger, nonroyal sisters was asked to marry her own brother at his royal accession, perhaps so that he could legitimize himself as a god by sacredly connecting to his own flesh and blood as Osiris had done. This scenario would have presented a real challenge for the siblings as they carried out their duties, because they had most likely grown up in a nonroyal household, in each other's presence every day, eating meals together, arguing with each other, playing jokes, revealing secrets, sharing the love of a platonic family relation. In the palace, royal brothers and sisters were probably kept in different quarters once they had reached a certain age, which limited the closeness the siblings could share, and in any case, the sheer numbers of wives, offspring, and other relations might have been enough to discourage the close bond between a brother and sister who grew up in a patrician nuclear family. While this hypothesis may excite our imagination, most Egyptologists believe that Ahmes was not one of Thutmose's own sisters but instead related to the older Ahmoside family, even if she wasn't a daughter of a king, thus securing the place of Thutmose I (and his progeny) in a family that was not his own.[21] If Ahmes was indeed unrelated to Thutmose I, then their union to save the Egyptian kingship brought together two people who had barely, if ever, spoken to each other.[22]

If Ahmes grew up as a princess in the palaces, then marriage to the next king was expected of her. The evidence suggests that during the Eighteenth Dynasty King's Daughters and Sisters were allowed to marry *only* the reigning king, although centuries earlier and later it was quite in order for royal daughters to marry outside the royal court. But all signs point to a much stricter regime during the Eighteenth Dynasty, with royal sisters marrying their brother the king, but no one else. Royal daughters produced from such unions would then have to wait to marry the next king to take the throne, ideally their own brother. These marriage restrictions are never explicitly stated, but they are a possible explanation for the lack of marriages between princesses and commoners during the Eighteenth Dynasty.[23] These limitations might have been an effective way to keep all the wealth, power, and potential for future heirs within one family. Most important, this stricture on royal women preserved the king's funds to reward his officials for loyal service rather than waste heaps of money paying off all the expectant sons-in-law with rich dowries when they married his daughters.[24] With this Eighteenth Dynasty system, the king had no sons-in-law at all; conveniently, his own son was also his son-in-law. Any daughters sired by Thutmose I would marry the next king.

Retaining royal women in the family would have granted the king a massive amount of economic power, but it also meant that a daughter of the king could only find her place in the world within the palace. If Amenhotep I's sisters were not allowed to marry wellborn officials' sons or to move into their own villas as Mistress of the House, they could not have any children unless their destiny tied them to a brother-king of appropriate age who was able and willing to sire them. And any of their offspring were liable to bear signs of the incestuous union. In the Eighteenth Dynasty, the future of a royal woman would have been tied exclusively to the king.

If Hatshepsut's mother, Ahmes, was a younger sister of Amenhotep I, perhaps she had been too young to have sexual relations with him. Or possibly she was already married to him and was transferred to Thutmose I when he assumed the kingship. Perhaps Amenhotep I's entire harem was shifted to the incoming Thutmose I, and it was then that Ahmes was selected as the right age and bloodline to be the highest-ranking wife among them.

The female progeny of all kings, past and present, would thus have been kept in the palace, awaiting their chance to become mothers. If the king was too young or too infirm to serve as a real husband, many royal women would grow old without one. Some women would share a brother-husband with a hundred other ladies. None of these women, except perhaps the King's Great Wife, had the slightest chance of a real partnership in marriage.

Later in the Eighteenth Dynasty, there were other, even less appealing, options for King's Daughters: they could also become wives of their fathers. (The short life spans of most of the kings of the early Eighteenth Dynasty meant this did not happen to Ahmes, however.) During the reign of a later, long-lived king, Amenhotep III, a royal daughter might marry her father during her limited years of reproductive potential. Two of Amenhotep III's daughters—Sitamen and Isis—became the King's Great Wives, thereby demoting their own mother, Tiy, as the older woman reached the end of her reproductive potential. If a royal daughter did not marry her own father during a long reign, she would have no partner whatsoever, it seems, and become a childless spinster.

Presumably these royal women were conditioned to count themselves blessed to marry the king, but we can also envision the heartache and trauma produced by these limitations on relationships. Queen Ahmes was either born into this system or had to quickly adapt. Royal women likely had entourages made up of commoners—ladies who were mistresses of their own homes when they weren't at court and who were allowed to marry men other than their brothers or fathers. The royal women may have been envious of their ladies-in-waiting's freedom to run their own households and forgo competition with their own sisters for one man's attention. Admittedly, these attendants did not have the power and the money of the King's Daughters, Wives, and Sisters, but the visibility of this unattainable "normal" life must have been painful for some of the royal women.[25]

Whatever Ahmes's origins, she was now the King's Great Wife, and everyone looked to her to produce the next heir. There was no marriage ceremony that we know of. In fact, the ancient Egyptians did not seem to celebrate marriage as we do. Rather than engage in a formal, binding relationship marked by a ceremony, people merely talked about founding a household and drew up what amounted to the first prenuptial agreements in the world, legally documenting whose property was whose.[26] Marriage was more of an economic-sexual agreement in the ancient world than a romantic commitment. For kings, of course, it was also a political one. Thutmose I was already middle-aged by this point, probably around thirty or forty years old, and his current nonroyal wife and any children he had with her did not fit into this new royal circumstance. We see no record of them whatsoever. He had to start a new life full of new responsibility. As king, he was probably expected to have sexual relations every night he was in residence at the palace—either with his highest-ranking queen, Ahmes, or with one of his other women. He was considered the bull of Egypt: royal sex was linked to the ongoing creation of the cosmos itself. And sons were essential to the continuation of a divinely sanctioned dynasty.

At some point, probably even in the first year of their marriage, Ahmes faced some competition. Mutnofret, another royal wife, held the titles King's Daughter (probably the daughter of King Ahmose), King's Sister (sister of King Amenhotep I?), and after marriage to Thutmose, King's Wife as well.[27] Why she was not Thutmose I's Great Wife is unclear, because she seems to have had more obvious connections to the Ahmoside family than Queen Ahmes. Perhaps Mutnofret had been too young to be the Great Royal Wife upon his accession. Regardless, any children born by Mutnofret would display an impressive lineage that connected Thutmose I's offspring to the great Ahmoside family. She might not have been the highest-ranking wife, but she was close.

We can only imagine potential frictions between the King's Great Wife, Ahmes, and the King's Wife Mutnofret: Was Mutnofret subservient or ambitious? Was Ahmes overtly competitive? Did they behave like sisters, with real heartfelt love between them? After all, they could have been actual sisters, both married to the king.

And so the reign of Hatshepsut's father, Thutmose I, proceeded. He visited the royal women. He campaigned abroad. He rewarded his loyal officials. He ruled for thirteen or fourteen years,[28] which is not bad for a man who arrived at the kingship later in life. We can picture the dowager queen Ahmes-Nefertari lingering about the palace, encouraging more and more highborn and beautiful girls to be brought to the household for Thutmose I's enjoyment and procreation. Nobody would have wished for a crisis in the accession, nor for bloodshed and competition. All that was needed was a son to survive his father, even a very young son, for the status quo of the elite to continue as before. A king too young to rule was a problem that could be solved with a good King's Mother to act as the power behind the throne. But a king unable to sire any sons with his Great Wife was a trickier issue for the ideology of kingship to sustain. And that was looking to be the situation for Thutmose I.

Hatshepsut's birth would have been an occasion of great hope but also great anxiety. Ahmes was the King's Great Wife, and hopes for a pure and uncontested succession to the throne rested with her. She must have wanted to give birth to a son. Her labor was likely long and hard, since it seems to have been her first birth. We have no idea how old Ahmes was at this important moment, but a more mature wife, around the age of nineteen or twenty, would have had an easier time in the birthing process, at least compared with a twelve-year-old girl.

Because Ahmes was the King's Great Wife, it is likely that a special birthing pavilion was prepared for her. The Egyptians created birthing houses decorated with apotropaic images and iconography that were ostensibly set apart from the main living quarters. The pavilion may have been near a garden or a pool, a kind of birthing arbor with a roof of matting and vines supported by pillars.[29] Plastered walls were likely decorated with scenes of mothers caring for their infants and breast-feeding or having their hair done (actions that would have taken place after a successful birth) to somehow enable, if not guarantee, a positive outcome to a woman's most dangerous task. In this pavilion, Ahmes would have knelt and squatted, paced and sweated, perhaps on a cool bench of mud brick, while her baby descended the birth canal. The wise women of the household and perhaps some of her ladies-in-waiting would have helped her squat upon the birthing bricks. They might have used ancient magical implements, like ivory hippo-tusk wands or figurines, to ward off danger, death, and tragedy, creating a perimeter of safety for both the birthing mother and the coming child.

The women would have urged Ahmes on, chanting things like "Come Down! Come Down!" while placing amulets on her head and limbs, and talking among themselves about her progress between contractions, all the while murmuring incantations to the pregnant hippo goddess Taweret, "the Powerful One," whose imposing countenance of bared teeth and tongue could frighten away demons that snatched the life force of small children before they left their mother's womb. They asked Amen to keep the heart of Queen Ahmes strong and to sustain the life of the one who was coming. Or they sang songs to the lion-headed dwarf god Bes, whose maniacal grin repelled the diseases that took a child within his first few months. And the goddesses Hathor, Isis, Nephthys, Selket, and Tefnut were always in their prayers and utterances and songs. Ahmes could have pushed for many hours, and she probably hoped with each heave of her belly and hips and thighs that she would give birth to a boy. But in the end, when the moment came, she delivered a girl. The infant was placed on a little platform of mud brick: Hatshepsut, the Foremost of Noble Women.

Ahmes likely had a two-week period of purification, a time when she remained away from the palace and any acquaintances while she was passing the blood of her daughter's gestation. She would have spent time with her baby and the women of her household as her milk came in. The wise women may have rubbed her back and breasts with oil in which a Nile fish had been boiled to encourage a steady flow of milk for her new baby. Or perhaps they did not. Ahmes was the King's Great Wife, after all, and she needed to conceive another child as soon as possible. Even ancient people must have known that breast-feeding would impede the process of conception.[30]

Ahmes was probably encouraged, or simply told, or maybe just knew instinctively to give up feeding her baby so that she could be impregnated by her lord as soon as possible. After only a few months of closeness, her daughter was likely taken from her and given to a wet nurse, a noble-woman named Satre, who herself may have forgone the chance to have more children with her own husband so that she could raise and nourish this royal daughter with her own breast milk. Or perhaps the tragedy of a stillborn child had placed Satre in this position. The responsibility to hold another woman's child and nurse her was likely welcomed as a comfort. In ancient Egypt, to nurse a king's child was a great honor, not an onerous degradation. It may have been bestowed upon elite women who had just weaned their own children or, more poignantly, those who were grieving the loss of babies who had just died.[31] Who else would be lactating without a child to feed?

Satre would have been the person who gave the infant Hatshepsut most of her affection, who held her during countless hours of nursing, who cleaned her of filth and spit-up, who held the baby while she burned with fever or screamed from the pain of erupting teeth, who slept with her during the night, waking to nurse her as much as she liked, cuddling her and murmuring her love, telling her "no" when she began to get out of hand. Satre and Hatshepsut must have grown close to each other in the royal nursery. Ahmes, meanwhile, was probably back in the palace with the other royal wives, getting her figure back, grooming herself to be as alluring and beautiful as possible, so that she could receive visits from King Thutmose I as often as possible until she was pregnant again. A Great Royal Wife would ideally bear one child a year, to ensure a son who survived.

Most infants did not live long. Half of them died before their first year was finished—from fevers that burned them hotter than the desert sands, from diarrhea that parched their bodies until kissable baby-soft cheeks were parchment thin and stretched close to the skull, from coughs whose spasms wracked the small frames of children desperately seeking a clear breath, or from lung congestion that slowly drowned them until they were blue and lifeless. A baby might be bitten by a scorpion in the home or the garden and die a painful death of vomiting and convulsions from a dose of poison too powerful for such a small body.

Tragedy was so commonplace that it was just a part of Egyptian life. Royal mothers, who would have keenly felt the responsibility of keeping an infant healthy, might have responded in a number of ways. We can imagine a queen who refused to acknowledge the existence of her infant child because it might not live out the year, as such losses were too painful to take over and over again. For a mother who had already lost two or three babies, we can imagine that it might have been easier to give the baby to a wet nurse and move on, with only a small hope lurking at the back of the mother's mind that somehow the child would survive. Or as an alternative coping mechanism, a mother might smother a child with attention, monitoring his bodily activities carefully, holding him throughout the night, willing him to take another breath during the hardest nights, believing that only her constant presence kept him in this world.

The infancy of Hatshepsut must have been a scary time full of little dramas and emergencies that happened under the eyes of only a few anxious women. How much Hatshepsut's mother, Ahmes, was involved in the everyday care and feeding of the princess, we will never know. But we do know from later references that Hatshepsut and her wet nurse, Satre, were very close.[32] Like most babies in ancient Egypt, the princess would have been breast-fed for at least three years.

If a baby made it to three years of age, weaning was the next danger zone. By this time, Hatshepsut would have been able to walk, talk, even hold a brush and papyrus, or laugh and play jokes on the dozens of other palace children—many of them her half sisters and brothers born of the dozens of women married to Thutmose I. Raised in the finest palaces in the ancient world, the princess Hatshepsut was an important child—so important, in fact, that she may have been fed breast milk for a longer period of time, until she was four or even five, for the safety and nourishment it provided. In the modern world, we know that children who are not breast-fed are deprived of the many immunosuppressant factors in the body of the donor. To the Egyptians, weaning often meant death.

But Hatshepsut survived, beating the odds facing all Egyptian children, many of whom would have perished before the age of five.[33] She was able to consume and thrive on cow's and goat's milk, but also beer, wine, gruel, ducks' eggs, vegetables, and meats. Her body was probably assailed with infections, parasites, and other ailments like that of any Egyptian, rich or poor, but her own immune system was triumphant in carrying her past infancy. Hatshepsut moved on to the next stage of her life. She was three, and she was alive.

Meanwhile, Ahmes was probably intent on doing everything possible to make a son a reality. Common treatments to speed conception included consuming poppy and pomegranate seeds and burning incense and fresh fat to fumigate the air.[34] She likely prayed to the goddesses as well, asking them to make her a safe vessel for her lord's seed. Ahmes may have obsessed about her grooming—combing, braiding, anointing—so that she would be an alluring companion for her king to visit night after night, until she conceived. She knew that her future place in the palace depended on the power of her sons, and her deepest hope as a mother in a complicated and probably competitive palace environment was to bear the son who would become king—because only then could she become the King's Mother, and continue in a position of even greater power.

Not that she would be blamed if she couldn't conceive a son. In ancient Egypt, the responsibility for infertility was laid at the feet of the man. Just as Atum and Amen created the universe from their own sexual encounters with themselves, allowing their seed to propagate their own being, a human man—or a king—was believed to contain the spark of creation. Documents from ancient Egypt tell us that a woman who cannot conceive is "dry," thus empty of the semen of a man.[35] A woman—or a queen—excited her husband into action and then contained his seed, protecting it and gestating it during its transformation into a child. But she was not the creator of new life, just its container. Thus if Thutmose couldn't produce a son with Ahmes, perhaps he couldn't with any of his other wives either.

While Ahmes was attempting to make herself a fertile field for her lord, Thutmose I could not be content with one wife. His palace was filled with his women and soon with his children. He visited Mutnofret's bed as well, and all knew that any son of hers would bear powerful connections to the old royal family. Mutnofret was probably the highest-ranking wife among all the king's ladies, except for Ahmes, the King's Great Wife. There may have been a strange gestational competition between the two highborn ladies; Ahmes worried that Mutnofret's child would be a son, thus creating a rivalry with her own offspring. Ahmes witnessed Mutnofret's pregnancies, of course, watching week by week as life grew inside the woman. We cannot know how she reacted to the news that Mutnofret finally gave birth to a son, whom she named Thutmose after his father. Ahmes herself now had other children besides Hatshepsut; indeed, she probably bore the king two sons. She also bore a daughter named Neferubity.[36] And besides, Mutnofret was far from the only competition for Ahmes. It is likely that many other wives in the king's palace were also fostering his babies inside of them, and we can picture a whole palace of ladies in breeding. Births would have come hard and fast, a girl one month, a son the next, filling the ranks of the king's children, most of whom left no trace in the surviving official documentation.

As a toddler, Hatshepsut would have grown up alongside the children of her father's other wives. They were her playmates and siblings in the royal nursery. She probably saw her mother in the company of her ladies every day, but the time spent with Ahmes may have been formal and uncomfortable for her, or perhaps far too brief for a young girl in need of a loving mother's attention. Hatshepsut doubtless encountered her father's wife Mutnofret from time to time as well, perhaps in her own part of the palace, or when the lady visited her children in the nursery, but Mutnofret was not likely a daily companion for the young princess. Later memorials suggest that Hatshepsut had at least one close confidante in the royal nursery, her sister Neferubity.[37]

As for her father, around the time of Hatshepsut's birth Thutmose I was spending much of his time away from Egypt, on campaigns in Syria-Palestine and Nubia. When the king was home, his duties were to the gods' upkeep, the law courts, and the servicing of the royal wives. He would have had little time (or inclination) to cuddle and console his many toddlers. It was probably a rare moment when the king felt compelled to visit the royal nursery, with its pandemonium of small children and babies, surrounded by the women who kept them safe, fed, educated, and under control. Thus it is doubtful that Hatshepsut and her father had an affectionate relationship when she was a young child. Getting to know children under the age of four, particularly little girls, must have been very low on the king's priority list.

TWO

A Place of Her Own

As the eldest child of the highest-ranking wife in the palace, Hatshepsut must have known she was special. And experience would prove to her that she was strong. Family members and tutors may have told her so, but the knowledge that she would manifest great power likely came from deep inside her, from her quiet moments in the temple, from talking to the god Amen or the goddess Mut. We can imagine her as a serious, quiet child who carefully watched everything that happened around her, attending to the attitudes and postures of her royal mother in court rituals, or to the words spoken by her father when he read the incantations on festival days.

In the palace apartments, she likely looked on as her father's women vied for his attention by spending hours at their dressing tables fashioning fabulous wig and hair creations and smoothing their young bodies with perfumed oils and exotic scents. She would have noticed when some of these women swelled with pride and pregnancy as they made plans for a son, and seen the grief in their eyes after they had delivered a dead baby. She probably recognized the worried look of mothers whose infants were on the brink of death, about to be yanked from this world by some unnameable demon that could not be placated by even the most generous offerings.

Perhaps Hatshepsut caught a glimpse of the royal princes at their daily lessons in the House of Life—this boisterous, rowdy crowd of boys who shoved and yelled and jostled as they sat cross-legged with pens in hand, until their teacher whacked them on their backs with a switch to keep them at their scribal practice. In any case, she did not belong with the princes and their pursuits of chariot racing and archery. She may have listened as the other princesses talked about new dresses with fancy braided fringes and jewelry, but perhaps she did not share their interests; these girls were not eager to learn about the world outside.

Most likely Hatshepsut worked quietly with her tutor, who would instruct her and only her on how to see shapes in the sacred script, how to find the names of the gods and of the kings in the ornate writings, and how to form her own sacred images with a pen on her wax tablet. She also helped the God's Wife of Amen to ready rituals for the Great God in Karnak. She memorized the proper incantations and the correct gestures and movements. She yearned to please the King of the Gods and for him to find favor in her person. As the eldest child of Aakheperkare Thutmose, the Lord of the Two Lands, He of the Sedge and the Bee, and his Great Wife, Ahmes, she needed to be strong. Much was expected of her.

We have little direct knowledge of Hatshepsut's perspective on her own importance and her place in the world, but she would have grown up in a number of palaces around Egypt, most of them easily reached via the plush, luxurious royal barges that traveled up and down the Nile. The most important members of the royal family needed to be mobile. They might want to attend an important religious festival in Memphis, or stay at the southern town of Elephantine while the king was on a campaign in Nubia and Kush, or spend time in the verdant green of the Fayum while the king was hunting hippos with his noblemen. The King's Great Wife, Ahmes, and their children accompanied him on some of his travels, but most of Hatshepsut's early life would have been spent in Thebes, in the southern Nile valley, sacred to the god Amen.

Hatshepsut's immediate family included the most important people in all of Egypt if not the entire Mediterranean World. Her father was king—the link between the gods and the Egyptian people. Her mother was the king's most highly placed wife and the most sacred vessel of his fertile abilities. Hatshepsut also had two highly placed brothers, perhaps her full brothers, princes of great importance in the dynastic succession—Wadjmose and Amenmose, one of whom was destined to be the next king of Egypt and thus Hatshepsut's husband.[1] Her sister Neferubity must have been a close friend and ally.[2] Her wet nurse, Satre, was an intimate as well, because in the Egyptian mind, the bond of nursing had transformed Hatshepsut into Satre's real blood daughter. Her half brother Thutmose was nothing more than a small prince in the arms of his highly ranked mother and second King's Wife, Mutnofret. These were the essential players in Hatshepsut's family, but we must remember that the quarters of the king's women were also filled with Hatshepsut's half brothers and sisters from lesser-ranked wives.

At Thebes, the king likely had more than one palace. On the east bank, a ceremonial palace just at the entrance to Karnak bore a name that signified its importance to the king as chief priest: "I Am Not Far from Him," with "Him" referring to Amen, the Great God and lord of Thebes.[3] At this palace, Thutmose I wore the complex ceremonial attire and the tall crowns that demanded such attention and balance. Here he could meet with his chief priests and courtiers in preparation for important rituals and festivals, or to discuss temple administration. This palace was small but formal, in contrast to the sprawling and luxurious apartments occupied by his family.

The actual living residence was probably built far from the crowded and dusty town of Thebes, a good distance from its sewage, flies, and thousands of smoky cooking fires. The royal palace may have even stood on the west bank, across the river from the town of Thebes, where it was quieter and where animals and birds were abundant. The palace would have been close to the Nile and its cool waters, but not situated so low that it could be destroyed by the annual floods. Only columns, balustrades, door thresholds, and sometimes toilets were made from stone. Unbaked Nile mud bricks were used to build the other structural elements; they were the main source of building material for everyone in ancient Egypt—peasants and elites alike. In the king's palace, the walls were whitewashed and brightly painted with scenes of the flora and fauna of Egypt. Its rooms were appointed with soft, elegant furnishings. And everywhere servants moved about the complex—waving massive ostrich fans from the corner of an outdoor lounge to provide a cool breeze for the royal inhabitants, standing at the ready to fetch a cool drink or nourishment, assisting the royal family with wigs, makeup, and adornments, emptying chamber pots, and servicing the baser human needs of the royal family.

The centerpiece of the palace was the audience hall and throne room, where the king sat to discuss formal matters with his courtiers. Hatshepsut would have seen little of these areas as a young child, although she may have been expected to show herself at official court functions as she grew older. Most of her time was spent with her many brothers and sisters and the courtiers' children in the royal nursery. The children were allowed to run around naked; they played with balls, hoops, and sticks, waded in their courtyard pool, and napped in the shade of date palms. Royal children's heads were shaved, except for small locks of hair that dangled down on the side of the head. This near-shaven look was not only a marker of status but also a practical expedient against lice infestations.

As a small child, Hatshepsut was likely taught the discipline of standing still and stoic on a dais before a mass of people during formal engagements, and one wonders if she looked on with envy at the fidgeting and whining of other children. Hatshepsut must have always known the feeling of many eyes watching her, judging her bearing and expression. As the eldest King's Daughter by the King's Great Wife, Hatshepsut probably stood close to the king in important ceremonies and events in Thebes. She would have observed the king's movements and heard his words in the throne room, learning by osmosis the effective way to rule. As her father—one of the most successful warrior-kings Egypt had ever seen—relentlessly planned for campaign after campaign abroad, she received firsthand training in imperial domination. During the second year of her father's reign, after he waged a successful military operation in Nubia, the army returned to Thebes with the mutilated corpse of a conquered enemy hanging upside down from the prow of his boat. Hatshepsut may have been a witness when this body was transferred to Karnak's outer walls for a gruesome triumphal display—a real foe to enhance the symbolic images of violence and smiting carved on the exteriors of Egyptian temples. But perhaps she did not yet understand what she was seeing. She was just a baby, around a year and a half in age, and she likely did not even remember the sight. Or maybe she just imagined that she had seen it, because this triumphant moment was spoken about so often that it was formally recorded during Thutmose I's reign.[4]

As a child, Hatshepsut probably saw the young black-skinned sons of the dead Nubian chieftain at her father's court. Brought to Egypt for a kind of "reeducation," they held their heads high in proud defiance of their new master, who had killed the rest of their family before their eyes. Thutmose was following a clever and age-old tactic: abduct elite foreign children of subjugated lands, train them from a young age to love and respect their conquerors, and then return them to their own land as puppet rulers beholden to Egypt, brainwashed to obey the very king who had enslaved and murdered their families and people. For her part, Hatshepsut would have learned from infancy what constituted a successful foreign policy toward rebels in Nubia, Egypt's closest neighbor: utter destruction, brutal executions, and absolutely no mercy.

By the age of ten, Hatshepsut may well have begun her travels abroad. An inscription from Hagr el-Merwa shows Thutmose I traveling up the Nile to Kurgus in modern-day Sudan with a large entourage, including his Great Wife, Ahmes, his crown prince, Amenmose, and a princess whose name is barely legible in the inscription, but which might read Hatshepsut.[5] Journeying with her father while on campaign in Upper Nubia would have given an impressionable and smart girl direct knowledge of how a subjugated enemy should be treated, how cheap the lives of these exploited people were, and how brutally and publicly rebels needed to be punished if Egypt was to continue to prosper by extracting gold and minerals from this southern land.

Hatshepsut may have witnessed public executions and other displays of violence against the Nubian people, as they constituted the main foe during her father's reign. Indeed, there is no evidence that children were shielded from the violent realities of life, and it is likely that as King's Daughter she was well placed to witness some of the most ruthless moments of her father's imperialism. She would have been taught that violence was necessary, even righteous. Hatshepsut must have understood that Nubia's riches were Egypt's birthright, but only attained once its inhabitants had been cruelly subjugated; only the king could deliver Egypt from the dangers its enemies presented.

Hatshepsut's formal education would have begun when she was four or five. It was unusual for an ancient Egyptian girl to be trained to read and write, but Hatshepsut was not a normal girl. She was meant to hold high religious office and to marry the next king of Egypt.

First she was taught how to hold a scribe's brush and ink palette in her lap while she sat cross-legged. As her instruction advanced, she learned the difference between formal hieroglyphic and cursive hieratic writing, to draw the many hundreds of hieroglyphs, and to memorize their phonetic equivalents and symbolic meanings. Gaining more confidence, she would make lists of words categorized into types, including the gods, people and professions, and animals. To master the written language, Hatshepsut would then read and copy all kinds of Egyptian literature—mythical stories, ethical instructions, songs and hymns, and the great histories of the kings who had served Egypt before her father. The texts gave her training in leadership, ethics, religion, ritual, economics, morality, and history. In addition to copying these words onto a reusable wax tablet, Hatshepsut practiced her ink penmanship, learning how to hold the delicate brush, dip it into water, and then touch the cakes of red or black pigment to fill the brush with ink so that she could form swooping, liquid cursive script, or strictly balanced, formal, hieroglyphic images. She learned to read out loud, appreciating reading's function as a social activity with a public purpose, unlike the solitary pursuit it is today.

We don't know the details of Hatshepsut's education, only that such a highborn girl would have received the very best available. Excluded from any formal classroom instruction with her male peers, she was probably tutored in private as a young girl, spending most of her time with adults instead of children her own age. The other girls of the royal household were learning how to spin and weave linen cloth, how to create beautiful and ornate wigs and ornaments, perhaps even how to read and write a little. Whether Hatshepsut experienced her upbringing as lonely, we will never know.

The responsibilities and training shouldered by young royals must have been burdensome, but Eighteenth Dynasty court life provided some moral support. It's as if everyone knew that the king and queen would be neglectful, absent parents, as they moved through their sacred duties and political demands. Thus royal children were provided with a system of ersatz parentage—nurses and tutors from among the ranks of Egypt's courtiers and administrators who were able to teach, scold, comfort, and love the royal princes and princesses.[6] For a princess like Hatshepsut, a female nurse might have been more of a mother to her than the woman who gave birth to her. Her male tutor, Senimen, certainly provided her with more fatherly care and attention than Thutmose I, and all records show that he became a close ally and adviser to her later. The children of her nurses and tutors were meant to be like playmates or siblings with whom she could relax instead of compete.

No one needed to tell the young Hatshepsut that she was different. It was apparent to her simply because she was a royal living among non-royal courtiers, including her nurses, tutors, and their families, who likely treated her—even as a small child—with deference and respect. Such obsequious treatment kept her removed from the other inhabitants of the palace; Hatshepsut knew they were there to serve her, to be kind to her, to guide her, because she was more important than any of them and had greater responsibilities to uphold. She likely heard the daughters of her nurses talking about the men they were going to marry and the towns where they would live, the property they were taking with them into their marriage and the jewelry they were to receive. Making the right match was likely a constant topic of conversation for the wives and daughters of viziers, treasurers, stewards, and butlers who lived at the palace. Hatshepsut, however, knew that as the King's Daughter she was exclusively destined to marry the next king, bound to whichever of her brothers lived to see that day.

As she grew older, she may have witnessed some of the most beautiful and elegant of the courtiers' daughters join the ranks of the King's Wives and move into the royal harems to occasionally share the company and bed of her father. Hatshepsut might have noticed the conflicting emotions of these girls and their parents. We can only imagine the worry of a treasurer's wife who knew that her lovely daughter was destined for a life in the harem—an ambitious move to say the least, one that could vault a young woman to the very top of society if her son became the next king, but no doubt a lonely existence among many other contenders, all of whom shared the same man and whose importance rested for the most part upon their breeding capabilities.

As soon as she could walk and talk, Hatshepsut would have begun training to become the next God's Wife of Amen. She likely assisted Ahmes-Nefertari and Merytamen, both of whom had once been a wife to the king, as well as a wife to the god Amen in his temple. Hatshepsut would have learned many of the more mundane things about her role in temple activity—including the correct actions and postures to assume during temple rituals and offerings, the appropriate dresses and wigs to wear for certain rites, and the proper ways to address the god and move within his temple space. She would have learned how to effectively hold and shake a sistrum, a kind of rattle, and how to chant and sing to the god. She would have committed to memory the words of incantations and songs—by rote at first, only understanding the deeper mysteries with age, experience, and further instruction.

We don't know how old Hatshepsut was when she officially became the God's Wife of Amen, but she may have been very young.[7] Thutmose I likely wanted the influential priestess position filled by one of his own direct lineage. We have no idea if such an appointment demanded that Hatshepsut physically act as wife in reality, if she experienced menstruation and puberty before her initiation, or if she witnessed the rituals of the God's Hand priestesses before her own induction into the sacred mystery.[8] There is no evidence to suggest that the ancient Egyptians shielded children from human sexuality. On the contrary, it seems that little girls as young as eight or nine became objects of sexual attention. If Hatshepsut's destiny was to become the God's Wife of Amen herself, to connect the god's rebirth to her father's kingship, then she had to begin her training early, including knowledge of the more sexual aspects of the job.

Despite the separation enforced by palace duties and strictures, Hatshepsut's relationship with her mother and older female relations must have proved vital to the formation of her character and to the understanding of her own importance. Hatshepsut learned leadership skills from powerful women with proven track records. Ahmes-Nefertari was arguably the very first God's Wife. But Ahmes-Nefertari had also been wife to King Ahmose, whose many campaigns against the Hyksos demanded that she rule the homeland in his absence. She was also mother to King Amenhotep I, for whom she had acted as regent when he took the throne as a young boy. If nothing else, Ahmes-Nefertari knew that a highborn woman could exercise great political, ideological, military, and economic power. Merytamen, likely the acting God's Wife at the time of Hatshepsut's birth, was wife to King Amenhotep I. Despite her lack of success breeding a King's Son, she still wielded great authority as Egypt's most important high priestess.

In many ways, it was the support of these two women that linked

Hatshepsut to the older Ahmoside family, because they essentially adopted the young princess as their own daughter during the process of Hatshepsut's initiation into the priestesshood. We have no idea what Hatshepsut's relationship with these older women entailed—whether friction or gentle guidance, or great love or even cruelty—but they were her models of female power. The office of the God's Wife was second only to the High Priest of Amen within the sacred precincts of Thebes. She outranked the Second High Priest in lands and title. She owned her own estates and palaces. She commanded a powerful steward who watched over her treasury and administered her affairs.

Even if Hatshepsut's relationship with these matron priestesses was fraught with troubles, they no doubt taught Hatshepsut her worth and ability as a leader, a priestess, and an administrator. These women knew what it was like to wield power, wealth, and influence that were not connected to the health and productivity of their wombs. They fervently believed that their rites and sexuality facilitated the ongoing creation of the universe. As God's Wife of Amen, Hatshepsut was to assist the very machinery of the cosmos.

As the very first God's Wife of Amen to come from her father's Thutmoside family, Hatshepsut represented a momentous political move, positioning Thutmose I to exert direct influence over the powerful Amen priesthood. The Amen institution—with its many temples, priests, lands, and tenants—was a kind of ancient Egyptian Vatican, a force to be reckoned with, both economically and politically, and even the king needed to tread lightly.[9]

God's Wife was not an inherited position passed down the female line, despite the great power of women like Ahmes-Nefertari and Merytamen. Instead, the post always followed the king, who remained the absolute center of Egyptian society. If the kingship jumped to another family line, as it had with the accession of Thutmose I, the office of God's Wife had to move with him.[10] Thus Thutmose I's eldest daughter, Hatshepsut, assumed the office from powerful women allied with the Ahmoside family, but who saw it as their duty—and political necessity—to uphold an Egyptian kingship that was right and proper in the eyes of the gods. They undertook the training of a girl from a family not wholly their own[11] and initiated her to please the god.

As her preparation became more involved, Hatshepsut probably spent most of her time in Thebes and its holy spaces, working with her mentors and preparing herself for her initiation with the god. She was meant to become One Who Was Beautiful in the House of the Sistrum, a title that only subtly veils the sexual nature of her new position. The sistrum was a kind of rattle—a wooden handle supporting bars of metal, each piercing small rings that clanged together when the instrument was vibrated. The sistrum itself represented human sexuality—round objects penetrated by a phallic rod holding them in place. Sistra were vaginally shaped, often decorated at the top with the head of the cow goddess Hathor, a fierce protector of the sun god (her father and lover), and a violent devourer of his enemies. According to mythology, Hathor was the only one able to cheer her father, Re, when he despaired for his future. The tale reads: "Hathor, lady of the southern sycamore, came and stood before her father, the Universal Lord, and she exposed her vagina before his very eyes. Thereupon the great god laughed with her."[12]

It may be creepy for us to read about a daughter exposing her genitals to her father to make him happy, but the sun god was believed to copulate with his own mother, daughter, and wife, depending on the cycle of his daily regeneration. The familial connections with the sun god were sacred, and his daughters were meant to be lovers as well as protectors. Hathor's sexuality was a key part of her power. The sistrum decorated with Hathor's head is illustrative of what the God's Wife of Amen was meant to be doing to the god. If the sistrum was like a vagina, then her shaking it was meant to simulate sex. Part of Hatshepsut's training in the mysteries of pleasing Amen-Re involved vibrating the sistrum, and probably her body, in just the right way to create his release and rebirth. Hatshepsut was likely trained to be a lover to a god before she had ever known a man.

We can envision her initiation—the first time she beheld the statue of the Great God unveiled in his shrine. She was probably accompanied by the elder God's Wife, perhaps Merytamen, as well as the First High Priest. Hatshepsut would have been young if she ascended to the position during the reign of her father. Nine or ten years old, perhaps? She was expected at the climax of the ritual to interact with the god's statue sexually—perhaps to step forward and grasp the statue's erect member, simulating sexual activity while shaking her sistrum at the same time. The continued existence of her family, of Thebes, of Egypt, of the whole cosmos, depended on this god's continued re-creation. The moment must have been quite psychedelic for Hatshepsut and everyone else involved—full of incense, chanting, swaying, drums, sistra shaking, and primal rhythmic movements.

Hatshepsut may have even been left alone with the god in his sanctuary—a rare honor for any Egyptian—for the most sacred part of her initiation as she was revealed to his face and body for the first time, instructed to close her eyes, to listen for his words, to feel his presence. This first moment with Amen, and all her activity thereafter as the God's Wife, must have been profoundly meaningful to her, because all written documentation stresses repeatedly that Hatshepsut believed wholeheartedly in Amen's support of her power and her person, that he was personally guiding her. A later inscription of hers from Karnak states, "I acted under his command; it was he who led me. I did not plan a work without his doing. It was he who gave directions."[13] Her connection with Amen and her faith in him were ironclad, and her intimate relationship with this great Egyptian god would serve her well in her political life to come.

While Hatshepsut was learning these mysteries of the god Amen and his many manifestations, there must have been one question on everyone's mind: who would be the next king of Egypt? Thutmose I had taken the throne as a mature man. Life expectancy in ancient Egypt was in the early thirties for men, perhaps fifty for an elite who benefited from good nutrition. Thutmose I might fly to heaven at any moment. The monuments and statues left by him—all charged with political messages—tell us indirectly that he had indeed chosen a crown prince. A King's Son named Amenmose was depicted at least twice as a grown man on monuments cut during his father's reign; in year 4 he was also named a Great General of the Army.[14] In the Eighteenth Dynasty, male children of the king were generally not mentioned unless they were picked to be the next king. The absence of princes in the public eye could be seen as a canny scheme to cut down on competition among those in line for the throne. If they were denied a political platform, most princes (and their entourages) seem to have found themselves powerless to advance their own candidacy, instead passively waiting for the death of their father. Ancient Egypt was generally not plagued by the regicides and coup attempts that occurred in the courts of Syria-Palestine and Babylon, not to mention later Ptolemaic Egypt.[15]

But because the princes were denied a public stage, we know almost nothing about them during their father's rule, and even less about how the reigning king chose from among his sons (or how family members or priests might have selected from among a litter of princes at the unexpected death of the king). In the end, it seems that a particular prince was chosen to be king based on a combination of birth order, lineage, and circumstance. In other words, if you were the king's oldest son, then you would gain the throne at his death—unless of course your mother was of low rank, only one of the Beauties of the harem, instead of a highborn woman of royal lineage. If the eldest King's Son was born to a beautiful but unimportant woman, the family might move on to the next son, even if he was younger, because he contained a better lineage from a well-connected, highborn mother. Prince Amenmose's candidacy was strong. His figure was carved into sacred stone, which, for the Egyptians, magically made this outcome real. He was called Great General of the Army, a designation usually reserved for the crown prince. To depict a royal child as a functioning adult (leaving aside his actual age) was not just a political message but also a means of willing this future into existence ideologically.

Theoretically, though, each royal succession should have been blessed with many potential candidates for the throne. Each king had a mass of ladies to procreate the next heir. What could go wrong? Ideology and politics demanded at least some attempt at pure-blood unions between royal brother and royal sister, but owing to the perils of incestuous pairing, most of the kings of the Eighteenth Dynasty had mothers who were *not* of royal lineage. The ancient Egyptians might have used any number of criteria to select the next heir: age, pedigree, oracular decisions by the gods Amen, Ptah, or Atum. Whatever the requirements, Amenmose's depictions in temple stone indicate that he was meant to ascend the throne next. Such an important decision was made years in advance, likely to prepare the groundwork for a boy's accession with careful training. But even the most rigorously thought-out plans could fall through in ancient Egypt.

In addition to Amenmose, Hatshepsut had another highborn brother—Wadjmose—and both were groomed for leadership in Egypt's palaces and temples. Hatshepsut knew that it was her fate to marry one of these boys, and thus she likely observed her brothers when circumstances allowed—while they worked with their many tutors or memorized liturgies with high priests, as they suffered under the demands imposed on those of whom much is expected in the future. But it is possible that Hatshepsut, as young as she was, knew to approach life with less certainty. She had already been exposed to the practical coping mechanisms of the adults around her who were weighed down with constant anxieties and the ever-present spectres of illness and death. The ancient Egyptians knew that a sickness could sweep through a town, a region, a palace, or a military encampment like a flock of demons, taking all the small children, the elderly, even the princes of the harem, or 30 percent of the population, no matter where they lived. All the favored royal children were at risk, even those who had been chosen for great things, like Wadjmose, Amenmose, and Hatshepsut herself.

Smallpox was a particular evil. In the ancient world, smallpox was like chicken pox. Everyone got it, but tragically infants and pregnant mothers were most susceptible. A bad case settled in the face and left deep scarring in its wake. If one of the King's Beauties contracted such a case of smallpox, with thousands of pustules marring her once smooth features, her hold on power in the harem could vanish instantly. It is doubtful that the king would visit the bed of a disfigured woman, even after the disease had retreated.

Cholera epidemics were frighteningly common and violent. Few people could survive the bouts of simultaneous vomiting and diarrhea. The dehydration was so severe and so sudden that it could turn the body blue. Another scourge was the bubonic plague brought on by bites from infected fleas. Victims vomited blood and endured hard, painful swelling in the lymph nodes at the armpits, groin, and neck that left black necrotized fingers and noses in its wake. Malaria affected everyone, too, and serious cases created chronic problems. Children who survived a bad bout of malaria often suffered from severe brain damage and recurring fevers for the rest of their lives. If one survived these maladies, there were always measles, polio, typhoid, influenza, and more.

Kings and commoners alike were also forced to live with chronic diseases caused by parasites. The wasting diseases typical of tapeworm infestation were prevalent. Guinea worms expelled hundreds of thousands of new larvae through pustules in victims' feet. Hookworms voraciously drank blood from their host's intestinal walls, and the anemia they caused was a huge factor in the deaths of mothers and babies. In small children, hookworms caused mental and physical retardation. As tiny pinworms made their way through the body, the host was forced to endure the annoyance of an inflamed anus. Fatigue and bloody pink urine accompanied schistosomiasis. When life was constantly threatened by pathogens and parasites, how could succession plans be made at all? How did any dynasty survive?

Even the most basic actions of life—eating and drinking—were plagued by dangers. The Egyptians were afflicted by the ubiquitous sand, dust, and grit that got into everything, particularly bread flour. Every bite of food contained a tiny dose of quartz dust that wore down tooth enamel, until the dentin was compromised and infection could easily eat away the root of a tooth. Abscesses followed, tunneling deep into the bone of the jaw, forming hollows full of pus that would eventually burst, spreading poison throughout the bloodstream. Infected teeth killed kings as readily as commoners.

The ancient Egyptians knew that infested water was the cause of many maladies, so elites in the palace relied on wine and beer; distilled or processed products killed worms and fleas along with their larvae. The flip side, of course, was that the palace population spent day after day in a constant state of low-level intoxication. Alcoholism must have been routine in the royal palace and tolerated, although little evidence about it exists.

Hatshepsut's family lived a life that was as far removed as possible from that of a peasant who was surrounded by human and animal excrement, who warmed himself by a smoky fire fueled by dried clumps of dung, who drank from the fetid village pond when he couldn't get any beer, who worried about his empty belly and the hunger pangs of his children, who spent his nights by the fire pulling guinea worms out of an oozing wound on his foot by slowly curling the nematode around and around a stick. But the rich were not immune to parasites and sickness.

Imagine the young crown princes at dinner parties scratching their pinworm-infected rear ends, or Thutmose on his throne coughing from a newly acquired case of tuberculosis, or elegant queens like Ahmes and Mutnofret, their bellies distended by tapeworms, attending to their coiffure. In the ancient world, being healthy meant merely being alive. It may not be romantic to imagine Hatshepsut riddled with parasites, examining the bloody urine in her chamber pot or fatigued by the chronic anemia of a hookworm infestation, but it is certainly realistic. She and everyone else in the palace were afflicted by these maladies. This constant, inescapable physical suffering is the greatest difference between us and the ancients, even making allowance for the vast disparities of society, language, culture and circumstance, and it is certainly a chief obstacle when it comes to our understanding of their motivations. Perhaps if our outlook on life were shortened to twenty-five years, and if we lived in constant discomfort and anxiety over our very survival, we could know them better.

Like the dozens of other palace children, Hatshepsut and her brothers would have been particularly prone to such epidemics. Elite children were well nourished and well groomed, to be sure, and certainly their surroundings were much cleaner than the muddy alleys and mosquito-infested canals of the village children, but close proximity to one another meant that if one princess became sick, they all got sick. We have no record of what maladies Hatshepsut contracted as a child, but we do know there must have been many sleepless nights for her caretakers. And that through luck, skill, or stamina, she survived when others succumbed. We can envision the panicked behavior of the royal nurses who immediately carted the most favored royal children—Wadjmose and Amenmose in particular—onto a royal barge at the first sign of plague or cholera, hoping to keep them isolated from infection, trying to protect the future dynasty of Thutmose I. Every time the adults around Hatshepsut and her brothers acted this way, the young princess and princes would have been clued in to their own elevated worth.

What would happen if Wadjmose were to fall ill? Indeed, this crown prince disappears from historical records before his brother Amenmose, which suggests that something dire occurred.[16] Amenmose was the backup. But with such impossible odds, it was almost an act of defiant arrogance by Thutmose I to commemorate an heir into stone as an adult before he had even survived to take the crown. Early and unexpected deaths ruined many long-term plans for lineage and succession. With risks to one's health lurking everywhere, how could anyone count on anything? The harem constituted an imperfect system adapted to these impossible odds, providing the king with as many children as humanly possible. But Hatshepsut still knew that her father occupied the throne only because the previous king had sired no living sons. She must have recognized that even if the numbers were on your side, succession plans did not always work out as intended.

At around the age of eight or nine, Hatshepsut may have moved out of the royal nursery into quarters associated with the office of the God's Wife of Amen. How close she was to her mother, Ahmes, at this point is unclear, because Ahmes herself had no affiliation with the priestesses and the evidence tells us that this office was still associated with the previous ruling family. If Hatshepsut wasn't God's Wife yet, she would have been initiated soon, giving her the title, lands, and power that came with this position and vaulting her into a prominence her mother could never achieve. Ahmes was the King's Great Wife, but Hatshepsut hoped to better that by becoming God's Wife in addition to her destined pairing with the next king. After her initiation and her marriage to Amenmose, she could combine the powers of the two most important posts an Egyptian female could hold.

There is no evidence that Hatshepsut was betrothed to any particular crown prince at this point.[17] The Egyptians did not practice engagements and for good reason: Hatshepsut was intended to join the office of the kingship, whoever might occupy it. Given the health challenges in the ancient world, formal advance pairings between a particular prince and princess were probably not only impractical but even frowned upon as premature and foolhardy. No one had prior knowledge about whom Hatshepsut's husband would be, because no one knew which prince would actually survive to be king. No one knew when the current king would meet his end. And no one could tell which of the king's many sons would survive as a strong candidate—Wadjmose, Amenmose, or some other prince. There was no reason to lock in a betrothal, as happened millennia later between fragmented medieval European kingdoms. These Egyptian princes and princesses were already in the same family, and diplomatic ties were not an issue. It was better to just wait out the vagaries of fate and disease and see who made it through, rather than explicitly choose a partner.

And so Hatshepsut survives as other royal children die. She learns more and more about the intricacies of court life and ritual, as well as temple rites, and waits to find out who her future husband will be, knowing that when her father, King Thutmose I, flies to heaven, the process of succession will proceed in a whirlwind, sweeping her up into marriage with one of her brothers and the role of King's Great Wife.

Once Hatshepsut left the royal nursery, waiting to see which prince she would wed, she moved to her own palace rooms. They were likely surrounded by a meticulously maintained pool and gardens filled with birdsong and cool breezes. Instead of a space shared with many nurses and sisters, her new bedroom was more private, perhaps for her alone if she had wanted it, with a sleeping area made from a light woven material with a smooth, low, wooden headrest wrapped in soft textiles. Her bed was covered with linen sheets produced by palace Beauties, woven of the highest thread count they could manage, as many as five hundred threads per square inch. She was covered with her own soft, pashmina-like imported woolen blankets on cold winter nights when a fire made of fragrant local woods was laid on her hearth. Young naked girls wearing only girdles around their waists rushed to and fro carrying drinks, fans, and nibbles for her and her guests. A series of scribes, serving only her office, managed her day-to-day activities and the economic dealings of her now-extensive holdings, and they would have dashed about, too, waiting on the great lady's pleasure. Hatshepsut could now choose her own daily menu, or perhaps she left that domestic task to her ladies-in-waiting. Food was plentiful and beautifully prepared: beef, lamb, mutton, duck, and goose; spiced milk, fresh cheese, and goose egg custards; fragrant breads, some sweet, some savory; date and honey tarts; dishes made with green onions, leeks, greens, and garlic; smooth dipping pastes made of lentils and other beans; sweet fig cakes and delicate pistachio puddings. And there was always plenty of beer and wine, much of it sweetened with honey and laced with exotic spices that a poor villager would never taste.

No longer a little girl, though probably still a child in our eyes, Hatshepsut was now dressed as one of the highborn ladies of the palace. She likely wore a long, narrow, linen shift of the finest, most gossamer, royal fabric, enhanced with sharply pleated linen robes of diaphanous thinness that covered her arms and fastened tightly under her breasts, accentuating her femininity and her slender form. Her sandals were made from the softest leather, and her feet lay on a footstool before her high chair. She wore kohl around her eyes, which not only protected her from the glare of the harsh sun but also kept away some of the more virulent eye diseases. She was now expected to wear a wig over her own hair, and perhaps the weight of it took some getting used to—a full, structured hairpiece made of human plaits and braids cut from the heads of many peasant women who may or may not have been happy to give their locks to serve the God's Wife. A diadem of delicate filigreed stars likely adorned her wig. On her wrists and upper arms she wore solid gold bands, and her fingers bore elaborate rings, some of golden scarabs on whose undersides were embossed the names of apotropaic divinities, her father's cartouches, and images of her own name and titles.

And what did this blossoming Hatshepsut look like, as she came into her own? Her skin color was probably darker than that of most modern Egyptians, but certainly not as black as that of the sub-Saharan princes captured from Kerma whom she saw at court functions. As a princess, it was not her place to be out of doors in the full light of the sun, and so she remained as pale as her station allowed. Perhaps her hair had fully grown out from the baldness of childhood and was maintained in rows of tiny braids that would be covered with a heavy wig during formal occasions, giving her full and long tresses like today's hair extensions. She likely commissioned a collection of both summer and winter wigs for her new station in society. Her body would have been conditioned to accept the North African heat, but a brutal summer day would still demand lighter coverings.

We will never know what Hatshepsut really looked like, even if her mummy is someday identified with certainty. Later statues of her as king certainly communicate how she wanted to appear and how she envisioned herself—as a delicate girl with a charming face full of life, joy, and alertness, blessed with a tiny, straight, Barbie-doll nose, large Disney-princess eyes that opened wide in an unblinking gaze, and small, smiling lips placed into a heart-shaped face that tapered to an elegant, feminine chin. According to Hatshepsut's later portraiture, her body was slim and slight, complemented by pert breasts and the trim waist of a young woman, surmounted by the narrow shoulders of an elegant patrician who performed no manual labor in the fields. If we believe her statues and reliefs, Hatshepsut's person embodied all the ideals that most cultures hold for young women—a symmetrical, thin, shapely girl, exactly what Hatshepsut wanted to be.

She had come of age as the greatest priestess in the land, one step away from her looming marriage and transformation into the King's

Great Wife. As the God's Wife of Amen, Hatshepsut was set apart from others in the palace; perhaps she conducted her daily administrative business seated upon an inlaid wooden chair on a raised dais. She had her own steward in charge of looking after the management of her extensive real estate, making sure that the production of grain, wine, oils, honey, and beer was enriching them. An official's prosperity was inherently tied to the long-term well-being of his master, and it would have been in the best interest of Hatshepsut's steward to administer her affairs honestly. Indeed, there is no evidence that the young God's Wife was in any way a pawn of her steward, just because he was male and she was female. Her word was likely followed, and she was guided in economic and political matters by her tutors, who helped her to understand the repercussions of her decisions. But Hatshepsut certainly learned about manipulative and greedy officials along the way, and as she ascended the ranks of power, she likely grasped that it was wise to reward the loyal and true members of her staff with riches and honors, while passing over the self-interested and fickle ones.

Hatshepsut's new life was luxurious, to be sure, but it was one full of responsibilities. Her temple duties included deeply important ritual moments that demanded her presence before dawn and during the darkest hours of night. Some rites required that she leave her family and friends and travel to other temples, accompanying Amen as his statue was taken on yearly visits. She must have spent tedious hours working with the high priests of the many Amen temples in the Theban region to maintain the smooth running of the God's House. As God's Wife, she was the intermediary between two fathers—bringing communications back and forth between her earthly father, Thutmose I, and her heavenly father, Amen of Karnak.[18] The stakes were high for such a young woman. The Amen priesthood was an institution with temple lands that rivaled the king's private holdings, but all indications are that the Amen priests worked in tandem with the king during Hatshepsut's tenure as God's Wife, enriching one another in their exploitation of peasants and foreigners. Hatshepsut's bureaucratic meetings with priests and stewards and scribes were vital to keeping her own house in order, but it was also her duty to maintain the sacred connection between the king and the god Amen. In other words, her life was not her own. It belonged to her god, to her father, to her people, and soon, to her husband, the next king.

Meanwhile, Thutmose I was busy shocking the Theban elite with some of his decisions and expenses. As money poured into Egypt from his successful campaigns and tributary extractions, he was able to flaunt Egypt's wealth with visible excess. He added more stone to the God's Houses than had ever been seen: he charged his architect Ineni with constructing a sandstone enclosure wall around Karnak, adding great stone pylon gateways at the Amen temple that were unprecedented in size and material, and crafting giant monoliths of red granite excavated by tens of thousands of prisoners of war and criminals in the southern quarries at Aswan into obelisks that caught the rays of the sun, when the massive stone needles' tips were covered with hammered sheets of gold and electrum. They were the first new obelisks seen in Egypt for hundreds of years.[19]

Thutmose I blossomed as king, and perhaps because he was not brought up to follow old traditions, he was deeply interested in innovation. Ever practical, he was the first king to construct a royal tomb hidden from public view, deep in the newly consecrated and secret Valley of the Kings. Every other monarch before him, at least those who had lived during a time of prosperity, had built grand tombs for all to see, usually pyramids faced with precious white limestone so brilliant they would have caught the blinding rays of the sun, essentially turning rock into light, and thus the king inside into the sun. The pyramid was a machine of resurrection but also a beacon to potential tomb robbers. Thutmose I must have been aware of this. His predecessor Ahmose I seems to have been buried at Abydos, while Amenhotep I followed his Seventeenth Dynasty ancestors by being interred at Dra Abu el-Naga, on the Theban west bank of the Nile, facing toward Karnak.[20] Thutmose I, however, wanted something different, and he was confident enough to follow through, despite the radical nature of his burial plans.[21] He chose to be buried within the sacred mountain of western Thebes, a geological formation that resembles a massive pyramid. He selected a final resting place within the goddess, that Thebans called Hathor of the Mistress of the West, underneath the body of the great cobra goddess Meretseger, She Who Loves Silence. The goddess of the mountain would keep his body safe and hidden, and she would gestate him into a transformed sun god. He planned for a secret installation, a burial space in which his body could be placed with "no one seeing, no one hearing."[22] It was this decision of Thutmose I that forever separated the sepulcher holding the king's body from the temple space that maintained his health and happiness in the great beyond. People must have talked about these novelties and changes, especially the elites, whose education allowed them to know what had come before and what was to be expected. For everyone else, Thutmose I's excesses were nothing short of miracles, demonstrations of godly power that proved beyond a shadow of a doubt that he contained the grace of the gods.

Thutmose I was the perfect model of royal authority for Hatshepsut. She grew up seeing the economic fruits of hard military campaigning and the value of architectural and artistic creativity within Egypt's conservative cultural system. Instead of slavishly doing what kings before him had done, Thutmose I piously followed the core of established kingship, while embellishing its fringes with wonders in stone, a form of respectful progressiveness. But more than anything else, Thutmose I created a stable income of imperial tribute from vanquished foes. He made Egypt rich. Successful wars were an Egyptian king's lifeblood, at least in the early years of his reign, and Thutmose maintained that tradition through heartless exploitation of lands beyond Egypt. The money he brought back from those wars allowed him to build temples, as hundreds of kings had done before him, but Thutmose I crafted his architecture in stone, not just mud brick. Now with authority of her own, Hatshepsut would have seen the impact of his ambitious building projects. She likely heard her courtiers talking with wonder about the king's constructions at the Amen temple, and like her father before her, she understood how building programs functioned simultaneously as jobs programs, propaganda machines, and gifts to the gods. What a king did for religious reasons could prove to be of political benefit as well.

With a room of her own, so to speak, she grew as a leader in her own right. She had her own advisers and her own holdings. As servant to her father, the king, Hatshepsut was a close observer of true successful kingship, and her mind absorbed both formal and informal lessons to share with her own future husband, the next king. She likely analyzed her father's policies and agenda, and perhaps as she waited out her fate— marriage to a brother upon the death of her father—she knew she could be of profound use to her future husband. She would soon serve as Egypt's great queen. She was smart, quick, and resourceful. She had received the best possible training for her future role. She would put those qualities to virtuous use for her husband and her god.

THREE

King's Great Wife

Tragedy struck. The fate that everyone feared had come to pass: two princes dead, one after the other. Wadjmose died first, it seems, but then Amenmose, too, was taken up by the gods. The palace was in upheaval. Hushed voices alternated with the wails and lamentations of acute mourning.

The details of these events elude us. The Egyptians superstitiously avoided recounting the minutiae of tragedy in their written accounts, religious or otherwise. Perhaps the same epidemic took both brothers, or more likely Wadjmose died first, leaving Amenmose as the last prince of full blood to save his dynasty's honor. There is evidence that Amenmose lived in Memphis and hunted on the Giza plateau in the shadow of the pyramids, a convenient location to accompany his father on his Syrian campaigns. It's possible he was killed in some kind of accident, but we have no way to know. Despite the plans made for the boy—including the title of Great General of the Army and his travels to Nubia—his young life was somehow cut short. It is not clear how Thutmose I was alerted or where he was at the time. Word traveled slowly in ancient Egypt, and perhaps the news reached Thebes a fortnight later, as soon as a ship was able to complete the journey upstream by sail. Given the evidence of his investment in the boys—even recording Amenmose's name and titles on stelae as his heir—he must have felt deep anxiety at their passing.

While the details of circumstance are lost, the king did express his grief in stone. He placed the images and names of his dead sons Wadjmose and Amenmose in his own funerary temple, which was under construction at the time in western Thebes. He memorialized the princes, both once heirs to the throne, in family shrine rooms.[1] The structure was called Aakheperkare Khenemtankh, or Thutmose United with Life, and is now a very fragmentary and destroyed building near the Ramesseum. Memorializing and concretizing grief in this way was an unusual honor for princes of the Eighteenth Dynasty, most of whom went unmentioned until they became adults with their own offices and their own tomb chapels, but with little mention of their royal father. Thutmose I broke with tradition for his dead sons.

Certainly the mother of the princes grieved, but beyond this, the entire palace structure would have been paralyzed with worry; circumstances had suddenly put the royal succession, and thus their own positions as officials, in doubt. Great hopes had been placed on these princes, and the loss was palpable.[2] We can imagine the whispers, the scrutiny of the king's women, the talk of which of their sons was old enough and of the purest lineage, the discussion of the future king's mother and what kind of influence she could wield. But none of this is preserved for us. The ancient Egyptians were nothing if not discreet, particularly about court activities and intrigue. We know that this dynasty's royal succession had been jeopardized, but we are left very much in the dark about who was working to rectify the situation and how. The stakes for this new Thutmoside family were high, and elements of the old Ahmoside branch—the children of Amenhotep I's brothers—were likely waiting in the wings to step in. The human loss was keenly felt by the royal family, but the consequences of that loss were highly political. There would have been precious little time to grieve.

Hatshepsut was probably just twelve years old as she negotiated this formative moment, watching the machinations of a palace lost to uncertainty, witnessing the disquiet and bitterness of her father, the fretting and pain of her mother. She knew that she was now more important than ever to her father, as the single remaining issue of the pure and holy union of Thutmose I and Ahmes, because at some point in her early years, her sister Neferubity had also died. In her own funerary chapel at Deir el-Bahri, Hatshepsut would later memorialize the profound and lasting grief she felt over this loss: a carving in one of her most sacred sanctuaries shows Neferubity worshipping the barque of Amen.

Hatshepsut's bloodline and position were the highest of the remaining royal children, and she must have sensed the sudden weight of power and responsibility spiraling inexorably toward *her*. She was now peerless, the highest-born daughter, destined to serve the next king and save her father's dynasty with a son. But there was more to it than that, and one wonders if twelve-year-old Hatshepsut was aware of her new status: as the most mature and educated surviving child, if she were to marry one of her younger brothers, she would serve as his guide, as a decision maker, perhaps even as the power behind the throne.

King Aakheperkare Thutmose must have had doubts regarding the eldest and most wellborn of his princes left in the royal nursery, one who shared his name but apparently not his strength. If the identification of the mummy of Thutmose II is to be believed, the boy was never in good health. His skin was covered with lesions and raised pustules. He had an enlarged heart, which meant he probably suffered with arrhythmias and shortness of breath.[3] It's fair to say that Thutmose II was no athlete. And yet everyone at court depended on this boy king to continue the Thutmoside line and thus defend their own jobs and livelihoods. This prince lacked Thutmose I's endurance and vitality; he was possibly cursed with a poor constitution after surviving one of the many scourges that afflicted the royal nursery. We are not sure if there ever was a formal designation of the boy's new position, or if his mother, Mutnofret, was stunned or smug when she was singled out as the mother of the new crown prince.

The prince was so very young, a mere fledgling in the nest. Given life's hard realities, Thutmose I must have worried that a wan and unhealthy nine- or ten-year-old could hardly take the reins of Upper and Lower Egypt, let alone keep and enlarge its borders. When word spread of the king's choice of crown prince, the palace was probably filled with apprehension that everything the king had spent the last dozen years building would unravel in the blink of an eye, and Egypt might once again descend into anarchy, misfortune, and disgrace. Wrapped up in such anxieties, Thutmose I may have looked askance at Hatshepsut and wished fervently that she had been a son. Or perhaps he saw in her a solution to these problems. His eldest eligible sons had just died. At fifty years of age, he would have known that he himself was nearing the end of his time on earth. It is possible that he looked to the brightest and most capable member of his family as a salvation against political shame and ignominy before the gods, perhaps even keeping his clever daughter close, allowing her to train at his side—not to assume the throne, of course, but to provide wisdom and balance to an unready king.

And then tragedy struck the palace again, even before all the pieces of the game could be set for the next move. The great king Thutmose I, a man who had never been bred to rule, who was not the son of a king himself, died, leaving behind a boy too young to understand any of the complex political realities facing him.

Aakheperenre Thutmose (Thutmose II) indeed took the throne, but it was clear he would need a queen-regent to guide his leadership. Somehow, Thutmose I's Great Wife, Queen Ahmes, stepped in as regent, ruling for a boy who was not her own son, pushing his highly ranked mother, Mutnofret, aside.[4] With Ahmes's own daughter, Hatshepsut, soon to become the King's Great Wife, it was as if the Thutmoside women had launched a double-pronged attack of feminine political manipulation, as if they saw the threat and rose up, using their remaining influence to shore up enough support to block the new King's Mother, Mutnofret, from any real power.

The crowning of Thutmose II was probably a tedious affair, given the new boy king's constitution and inexperience. He may have been too tired to run before the god holding the golden oars, instead jogging along feebly. Perhaps he struggled to remember the proper incantations and motions due to infirmity or youth or lack of training that rendered him a poor study. Courtiers and priests might have looked on apprehensively, wondering if such a child could sire an heir, let alone live to rule effectively himself. Thutmose II's character is shielded from us, but it didn't matter if the boy was stupid or lazy or cruel or kind: Hatshepsut stood by his side and assisted with the long coronation ritual as his queen.

And so at the age of twelve or thirteen, Hatshepsut, the Foremost of Noble Women, became King's Great Wife to her younger half brother, a king no one seems to have expected or even wanted on the throne. And her own mother became regent for the boy. It's as if the two women surveyed the situation and knew it was up to them to transform a weak heir into a strong king, to create all the pillars needed to support a new Egyptian monarch. There was much to do, and it was up to these royal women to see it was done. To secure and expand the frontiers, Ahmes had to make her military ready for campaigns to put down uprisings in Nubia and Kush to the south. She also commissioned an ambitious building program that locked the new king's name in sacred stone. Using her position as God's Wife of Amen, Hatshepsut was tasked to curry the favor of Egypt's many religious institutions. But more important than these duties, Hatshepsut needed to conceive a male heir to ensure the continuation of their line. There was no room for failure.

For her part, Hatshepsut would not have seen her marriage to the next king as an honor; rather, as King's Eldest Daughter, she expected it to happen. Her rightful place was as Great Wife to the king, but she was probably as surprised as anybody that the next king turned out to be Thutmose II and not one of her other brothers. In the eyes of many elites, her attachment to young Thutmose II granted *him* legitimacy, not the other way around.

We don't know exactly when Hatshepsut married him. Marriages in Egypt were not formal affairs celebrated by revelry, feasts, and teary-eyed handfasting; they were economic contracts. And it doesn't seem as if royal marriages were formally celebrated at all, except perhaps during coronation rituals that marked the pair as king and King's Great Wife. Their wedding night was a moment for their sacred intercourse that would invite the god Amen into the physical person of the king, to impersonate him, and thus imbue the next heir with a god's holy essence. The Egyptians called the legitimate king "King of His Loins" or "King of His Body," and those loins belonged simultaneously to the previous king and to the creator god Amen-Re. We can only wonder how the night proceeded and what complications may have ensued.

Did Ahmes herself counsel the young Hatshepsut on how to excite her husband and how to effectively catch his seed? She may have been very frank with her daughter—was Hatshepsut embarrassed or not? Or maybe they did not talk about it at all, resorting instead to oblique references. Hatshepsut had been married to the god Amen for some time now, instructed at an early age in at least the mechanics of sexual congress.

Mother and daughter both knew that a son was essential to a smooth transition from one Thutmoside king to another. If Hatshepsut bore a prince, and soon, all talk of an heir from a different family might be silenced.[5]

On the wedding night, lamps would have flickered all around a sleeping platform covered with royal embroidered linens. Hatshepsut likely wore a diaphanous pleated linen garment that revealed her youthful breasts, her trim waist, and the growing hips of a thirteen-year-old girl just ready for breeding. The Egyptians knew how to dress a young girl to elicit a sexual response. How did Thutmose II, just a boy, react when his sister approached him in her seductive dress? Perhaps he giggled in embarrassment and nervousness. He and his half sister had grown up in the same royal nursery. They had seen each other in the palaces of Egypt all their lives. Now they were meant to lie together and produce the next heir, the future Golden Horus. He may have worried about performing the act as Amen intended, about being too young, impotent, or sickly.

As much as we might like to know how it all proceeded and how each party felt about the circumstances, the Egyptians never left us with such intimate particulars of kingly succession, of family intrigue, or, to say the least, of wedding nights. It is impossible to know how Hatshepsut envisioned sex with her young half brother or how she felt about becoming the King's Great Wife. Hatshepsut was probably apprehensive about the wedding night, too, but she followed through with her duty.

The half siblings, both young and inexperienced, knew only what they had seen in the palace apartments between courtiers and their wives or servants. There were no religious strictures about the sinful nature of sex in the ancient world. With no societal qualms about premarital sex or images of gods masturbating, and with many extended Egyptian families living in one-room homes with no protection of privacy, sex was simply more visible, even to a young child of the royal nursery. A short life expectancy meant that people grew up faster and started sexual activity younger than we would think appropriate or even ethical.

Hatshepsut and Thutmose may not even have been alone on their first night together. Perhaps the queen-regent was there to give practical advice, or special priestesses were invited to make the experience more erotic (that is, effective) for Thutmose and his new queen. Servants were probably present, ready to assist with disrobing and preparation for sleep afterward; the queen-regent likely interrogated them about every aspect of the act. It is unlikely that Hatshepsut and Thutmose II had a private, intimate sexual encounter. This union was not a partnership of two people; it was meant to sustain an entire land, and its biological progress was probably closely monitored by those in power.

Hatshepsut was likely older than Thutmose II, perhaps only by a year or two, just enough to give her an advantage over her brother in terms of maturity.[6] More to the point, she had likely served as God's Wife of Amen for some years before her marriage to the king, and had run a complex and wealthy household before Thutmose had even learned to string his bow and arrow effectively. She would have had a head start in experience and training, despite her gender. The evidence suggests that Hatshepsut exercised her influence over him quite early in their relationship by making her position as queen visible and powerful. She was a princess who had been sustained in her own self-worth from childhood, who was probably more self-confident and more educated than her husband, who was not awed in the presence of the public but conducted herself properly and elegantly, who had served at her father's side in complex rituals that Thutmose II was now having to learn in all their intricacies. Hatshepsut would have known her value. She could likely delegate authority with ease or put a rude noble deftly in his place. She had learned how to command an audience. Thutmose II's position as a lesser prince probably meant that he did not have the same kind of confidence in himself or his abilities.

Now that she was queen, and even though she had grown up at court and seen her mother perform alongside her father on formal occasions, Hatshepsut likely still benefited from the behind-the-scenes guidance of Ahmes. The dowager-queen's power was political and family based, less entrenched in the ideologies in which Hatshepsut had been steeped as the God's Wife of Amen. Now, as regent, Ahmes could teach Hatshepsut how to curry favor among elite clans at court as well as model the traditions and expectations of the throne room and audience hall. She could also teach Hatshepsut the nuanced ways to behave toward the king to get what she wanted, or how to discover and diffuse conspiracies in the harem before they caused any harm. Ahmes and Hatshepsut brought very different spheres of influence and training to a moment when they were needed most. These women were nothing if not survivors.

Ahmes's position as regent was only immortalized obliquely in Egypt's sacred temples, as we should expect—because the regency was always an informal post for the Egyptians, a temporary stopgap with no official titles. Since King Thutmose II was considered too young to rule on his own, it was likely Ahmes who ordered reliefs showing the king standing alongside his wife, Hatshepsut, and his mother-in-law, Ahmes. Nowhere to be seen on these new temple monuments is the king's own mother, Mutnofret. We have no idea if Mutnofret, who was obviously still alive because she gained the title King's Mother, had an adversarial relationship with the queen-regent and the King's Great Wife, but we do know that despite her highborn status she was not acting as regent for her own son as we might expect. Thus there is at least some circumstantial evidence of friction among these main players in the palace. Mutnofret had all the connections a royal woman could want: King's Daughter, King's Sister, King's Wife, and now King's Mother. But despite all this, another queen had grasped control of the Two Lands as queen-regent. It was Ahmes who was given (or claimed) the responsibility of advising young Thutmose II on the best course of action in every given circumstance. Something lay behind that choice, but the messy details are obscured from view.

Hatshepsut's mother stepped into a situation of great uncertainty, took control, and exercised more power than she had originally been given. She became a King's Great Wife par excellence. Hatshepsut must have learned a great deal from watching her mother control a throne room for Thutmose II. For Hatshepsut, her mother was a paradigm of regency just as Ahmes-Nefertari, who had acted as regent for Amenhotep I two generations before, had been the example for Ahmes (although of course this is not an exact parallel since Ahmes-Nefertari was acting on behalf of her own son). We can even picture Hatshepsut and Ahmes having closet discussions about how to deal with Thutmose II and his faction of advisers or even his mother. It was up to them to maintain the course they believed best for Egypt, and they probably thought little about their own personal glories and ambitions as they busied themselves putting the new kingship on a firm foundation. It is quite possible that Ahmes asked Hatshepsut to feed information to Thutmose II, or to misdirect him and his allies. Or perhaps the relationship between these formidable queens and the boy king was on sound footing, transparent and aboveboard, with all parties working to advance Egypt's best interests.

We wonder if Ahmes imparted to Hatshepsut, in words or in gestures, how special she was. To prepare her daughter for more ambitious steps later, she probably instilled in Hatshepsut a dignity which surpassed that of everyone around her. The exact agendas of the women remain obscure, but it is safe to presume that these two resilient queens were able to exercise great authority over their new king, even perhaps bending him to their will. Hatshepsut thus found herself in an interesting position during the reign of Thutmose II. Her own mother was running the regime, with generals and high priests alike doing her bidding; her husband likely fell far behind her in years and maturity. Was it only a matter of time before Hatshepsut took advantage of the situation and took on more power? Likely no one, not even Hatshepsut herself, suspected that the young queen had loftier ambitions than God's Wife of Amen and King's Great Wife. In the minds of Egyptian officials, priests, and courtiers, there was no higher place to which she could ascend. As much power as could be imagined was already in the hands of these two royal women.

As for Thutmose II, was he really just a puppet whose strings could be pulled at will? Ahmes's regency suggests that no one expected this particular prince to become king, and we know from the inscriptions about Wadjmose and Amenmose that others had waited in line for this great honor before him. Thutmose II was probably not just third choice for king, but fourth or even fifth. This prince was likely educated only to hold a high position as some kind of administrator, perhaps in the army, to marry an official's daughter, and to live well in a villa in the countryside, far away from the complexities of political life. He was probably trained for bureaucracy and perhaps for battle, but not for rule of the Two Lands. And he would have learned early on that his mother, Mutnofret, was always second to Ahmes, the King's Great Wife. This reality must have affected his own position among his brothers when he was growing up. The focus of the royal family had always been placed on other princes of the Thutmoside line. In all probability, no one really entertained the thought that the young Thutmose would outlive the king's other sons.

Prince Thutmose would have had little opportunity to know his father. He was a King's Son, to be sure, but he would have encountered his constantly campaigning father only in the presence of many other young princes during formal, uncomfortable affairs, and not for intimate father-son discussions. Meanwhile, Hatshepsut was the God's Wife of Amen, or at least in training to become a priestess; her work threw her into close contact with her father. Lengthy and complicated rituals needed to be performed, and on special feast days Hatshepsut and her father might have spent hours together enacting these different rites—offering up milk, then wine, then meat accompanied by the right invocations, or walking in front of a sacred procession, or perhaps watching entertainments while seated on a dais at the temple. We have little notion of the intimacy of royal father-daughter relationships in Egypt, if they ever sat or stood close enough for some whispered quotidian conversations or if lengthy rituals allowed a little down time for them to get to know each other on a more personal level. If nothing else, they were accustomed to each other's presence, and they experienced the mysteries of Amen in close proximity to one another. Perhaps Thutmose II was even jealous of this relationship as he grew up, feeling threatened by it once he and Hatshepsut married. There are no indications to that effect, but we would not expect there to be in the kinds of records the Egyptians left behind.

Was there an emotional relationship between Hatshepsut and Thutmose II? Here, again, the Egyptian sources are silent, at least concerning their affection for each other. Whether Hatshepsut was revolted by him or loved him is immaterial. They had a relationship based on politics, ritual, and sex. The ideology of kingship was central. He was chief priest and son of the sun god, and she was meant to be the vessel and protector of the next boy to hold the royal spirit in his heart. Their politics revolved around the demands of officials and priests and the nuances of foreign policy. As for the sex, well, they were probably expected to have it very often. They were told (and likely believed) that they were one step away from the gods, if not gods incarnate, and those mythologies were full of sexual creations and sacred conceptions. They desperately needed to produce an heir to save the Thutmoside dynasty. Thus, at the age of twelve, Hatshepsut found herself between two gods: the Great God Amen, who created himself and the world with his orgasm, and the

Good God Aakheperenre Thutmose, who, it was hoped, would conjure up the next living Horus falcon with his own sexual climax.

Ahmes likely advised Hatshepsut on effective pregnancy techniques that had been passed down for generations. Mother and daughter may even have gone to the temple together with prayers and offerings. One day, Hatshepsut's monthly bleeding stopped. Perhaps her attendants noticed it before she did. Hatshepsut became more aware of the growing life inside her when she felt light-headed and nauseated at palace banquets. Her condition was a great relief to most of the palace courtiers and families whose living depended on continuing the current dynasty, and she was respectfully observed under the lowered lids of her people as she moved to and fro throughout the palace and temple.

When Hatshepsut's time came to deliver, her ladies-in-waiting accompanied her to the birthing arbor and urged her on, holding her hands tightly. Hatshepsut's body felt as if it were being ripped apart by her labor pains. Ahmes was there, too, amid the blood and shit and screams of pain, to check the child's genitals, to see if it was a boy or a girl. And Ahmes's heart probably fell deep into the pit of her stomach amid the new child's cries when she saw no little penis or testicles on the royal baby, just the labia of a girl. Hatshepsut gave birth to a princess who would be called Nefrure, the Beauty of Re.

Ahmes had experienced all the same anxieties herself when she had been a young queen. She, too, had served as the King's Great Wife and felt the profound pressure to bear the next heir. Her daughter Hatshepsut had been the product of such a moment of disappointment and anguish after nine months of waiting and hours of tormented labor. Ahmes knew what it meant for Hatshepsut to have survived instead of her brothers: Ahmes was regent to a boy king who was not her own son, whose wife had just given birth to a girl. The cycle of no male heir was repeating itself. Once word of the baby's sex traveled around Egypt, a new and fresh uncertainty would settle into the hearts of the elite families of the country. Ahmes knew the stakes of such failure intimately.

Still, it is unlikely that Ahmes scolded Hatshepsut for delivering a daughter. The Egyptians believed that the husband's seed, not the woman's womb, determined the gender of a child. Thutmose II likely received the brunt of the ill will from courtiers and advisers who now had a new reason to be disappointed with him. Ahmes probably urged Hatshepsut to hand her tiny baby off to a wet nurse so that she could get her body ready for another pregnancy as soon as possible.

In the midst of all these preoccupations about sex and pregnancy and babies and heirs, these women nonetheless found a way to create a strong kingship on behalf of a young, inexperienced king. They exercised Egypt's power in foreign affairs, and they had to be merciless about it. Rebellion was dealt with swiftly, and from all accounts Ahmes granted no clemency to insurgents. Shortly after Thutmose II's accession, there was an uprising within the colonial province of Kush in southern Nubia (modern-day Sudan), a region reincorporated into the Egyptian empire by Thutmose I only a decade earlier. A military campaign against the rebel Kushites was quickly organized, with orders to slaughter all male foes, except for one son of the chieftain who would be brought back to Egypt as a captive. Did the young king order this expedition? Thutmose II was only eleven or twelve years old, and Hatshepsut was likely a girl of thirteen. Ahmes was probably the one who instigated this cruel annihilation. It was her husband, Thutmose I, who had conquered southern Nubia in the first place, his first campaign there still famous for his slaughter of their chieftain and that influential display of the bowman's corpse on the royal barge at Thebes. To her, this was sacred work.

All three key players—the king, his queen, and his regent—were perhaps in the throne room when the pronouncement of no mercy was made. Both Hatshepsut and Thutmose II would have recognized the intent behind Ahmes's decision and valued the resolution for what it was: rebellion against the king of Egypt was akin to jeopardizing the cosmos by acting against the sun god himself; such an act could never be permitted. When the Egyptian army reached Kush, they carried out their orders successfully. Egypt's riches always came upon the backs of such atrocities. War was not just compulsory; it was a gift to the gods.

Ahmes and Hatshepsut needed to add another pillar to support the new kingship: the immortalization of Thutmose II's reign in Egypt through new temple construction. The women were not content to give the young king all the credit; indeed, they included their own images in the new structures they created at Karnak Temple, an unprecedented move that hints at just how powerful they really were. On at least one of the surviving monuments, Thutmose II shares equal space with his Great Wife, Hatshepsut, and his mother-in-law, Ahmes.[7] These two women were responsible for establishing the visual ideology of the young king's reign. In other reliefs, Hatshepsut even appears without the king, standing alone before the god Amen-Re in one of his temples, perhaps the first time a King's Wife was depicted with such agency of her own, wholly removed from her husband. She is shown dressed as a traditional queen, wearing an archaic skintight linen dress that had been popular a thousand years before and a vulture headdress (which for all we know was an actual taxidermied vulture) with richly feathered wings that spread about her head like the lappets of a wig. A round crown called a modius sat atop the colorful vulture headdress, and Hatshepsut embellished the crown with two tall ostrich plumes as an extra extravagant touch. From the images on these temple blocks and stelae there is no mistaking Hatshepsut's power as queen. The reliefs depict her performing rituals that were usually the king's responsibility: Hatshepsut is shown standing before the god Amen, who is in either his clothed form or his sexualized manifestation; she is holding an offering, and the king is not present as an intermediary.[8]

In addition to these traditional trappings of a strong kingship—waging ruthless military campaigns and building monuments in the king's name—Ahmes and Hatshepsut added an unexpected twist. Something new emerged from the process of crafting this young boy's kingship: unprecedented depictions of female power, and their source is likely found in the feminine underpinnings of Thutmose II's kingship. For millennia Egyptian temples had been places of both ritual and architectural conservatism. Yet these two women not only held the reins of political power but also formally recorded that power in stone. And the remaining evidence suggests that courtiers and priests accepted these images in the most sacred temple of Thebes. Any discussions the elite may have had concerning the audacity of a woman depicted performing such sacred rituals went unrecorded, but tellingly the stone carvings from Hatshepsut's time as queen remain unmarred. Given that her supremacy on the reliefs produced during her husband's reign is so overt, many Egyptologists believe that Hatshepsut herself became a kind of regent to Thutmose II, alongside her mother; she told him what to do, ruled for him, stepped in as chief priest for some temple rituals, and used her confidence to sway his decisions. She simply overpowered him. One of the most impressive structures attributed to the king was the Great Festival Court[9] of Thutmose II. But given the circumstances, perhaps it was really Hatshepsut's plan to build this massive court at Karnak, as a gift to her lord Amen-Re. As would be expected, Hatshepsut and Ahmes were successfully establishing Thutmose II as a viable king, and whether by design or not, they were creating strong, unprecedented leadership positions for themselves in the process. But could they maintain this power that was only informally defined?

To retain their dominance, Ahmes and Hatshepsut relied on a stable of loyal officials and priests whose families had lived in Thebes for generations and who seem to have been more than happy to accept the status quo. The women had traditional nobles to support them, but they also required a new kind of lieutenant to enact their plans exactly as they wanted. Building programs and military campaigns cost money, and breaking with established traditions probably required a subtle and clever operator. Timing and political circumstance aligned to bring a new player into the political arena, a valuable asset who seemingly came from nowhere. His name was Senenmut. He had no previous palace connections, nor any links to the old Theban families, yet at some point during the reign of Thutmose II he was appointed by one woman—or perhaps both—as Overseer of the Large Hall in Thebes. (This was probably the audience hall in which the thrones of the king and queen were placed to receive visitors.) And he immediately went to work implementing the unprecedented plans of Ahmes and Hatshepsut. Somehow a nobody had managed to snag a position that put him in the company of the top decision makers of the greatest land in the Mediterranean region.[10]

In the court of Thutmose II, a savvy operator could have won favor in a number of ways. With access to the Large Hall, Senenmut likely had the opportunity to charm the women behind the throne. Or perhaps a display of tact and strategy while arranging the queens' formal meetings with courtiers left a strong impression. Whatever his method of ingress, he was favorably received by the royal court, and soon he was promoted once again to the even more powerful position of Overseer of the Two Granaries of Amen, a hugely important office that guaranteed a new source of income for Senenmut and extended his political authority in an economic direction.

Ahmes may have had her own tactics in play as well. Perhaps Senenmut was chosen by the queen-regent as her son-in-law's administrator because this was a man who had no ties to either the Thutmoside clan or the Ahmoside family, making him the ideal subordinate, one obliged only to the inner circle of the royal family. Soon after his initial appointment, he was also named steward of two more financial powerhouses: the king's palace and the queen's palace. Being entrusted with the oversight of the income and expenditures of the richest rulers in the ancient world[11] represented a massive step forward in Senenmut's career, and it was probably engineered to further the plans of Ahmes and Hatshepsut. He now had economic power in the temple as well as in the palace. He was able to wield influence in both the sphere of the king and that of the god Amen, which made him a bridge to temple bureaucracies likely valued by the royal family. Senenmut came from nothing and wound up as the most trusted adviser to the king and queen; as the years passed, he collected more titles and influence. To Hatshepsut, he would soon become indispensable and, in some ways, the closest member of her own family.

Because of Senenmut's access to the king's treasury, the queen's treasury, and, to a large extent, the Amen temple's treasuries, many people would have reached out to him for favors. It would seem he was perfectly situated to move funds between palace and temple, although there is no surviving record of this type of transaction between royal and divine purses. Ahmes and Hatshepsut likely needed an official who could influence both of these arenas, a man who understood that economic influence was the path to political control and who could exert financial power without creating too many enemies.

His appointment exemplifies the ancient Egyptian system of bureaucratic patronage: as a loyal and effective official serving the king and queen, he was handsomely rewarded, and he would have understood how to reward officials below him in kind. His own landholdings and wealth would have been expanded, and he would have gained the power to do the same for others. Later, after being named to the prestigious office of Overseer of Royal Works, he took blocks of expensive stone from the royal quarries to commission statuary of himself for placement along processional ways in temple spaces. He was able to access gold from the royal mines, probably also turquoise, carnelian, and other precious stones from royal trade routes. Although the details of how this happened are not explicit in the ancient bureaucratic records, Egyptian officials were indeed allowed to skim off the top. The tomb chapels of hundreds of Egyptian bureaucrats make it clear that their offices enriched them—royal treasurers got access to metals and riches, overseers of granaries became rich in commodities and the products of the land, and so on.[12]

There is no doubt that someone in the royal family trusted Senenmut enormously—most likely Ahmes and Hatshepsut. He was given more and more authority during the reign of Thutmose II, and he seems to have been their most effective deputy. His ability to instrument change would become vital to Hatshepsut in the years to come. But how he was brought to the palace in the first place, after having been born, as far as we can tell, to a low-level official in the backwater of Armant, some fifteen miles from Thebes, remains a mystery.[13]

Senenmut had grown up provincial and poor, not as destitute as a peasant, perhaps, but underprivileged enough to ostensibly wonder at how circumstances had transformed him into a man running the economic affairs of the royal palaces. Because he grew up without the advantages of the old elite families, he might have had great feelings of inadequacy when those around him spoke an archaic and fancy language, wrote in ancient forms of Egyptian that no one used anymore, and told tales of faraway lands that he had never visited. He must have been very intelligent to make up for the lack of highborn tutelage or to have inveigled his way into such an education as a boy. But it was not only his cleverness that brought him to the king and queen's side. We can only guess at his other abilities: proficiency in organization, mathematics, and accounting; political acumen; sharp memory; astute conversationalist; effective at persuasion—and, more than anything else, he must have been ambitious.

Did Senenmut harbor a secret anxiety that he did not fit in at the palace? Was he ashamed when a learned elite from a venerable old family said something at which he knew he should take offense, but which he did not really understand? Did he cover over that disgrace with a witty retort?

Given Senenmut's humble origins, it's all the more astounding that toward the end of Thutmose II's reign, Senenmut was appointed tutor of the king's firstborn daughter, Nefrure. Hatshepsut would have been almost sixteen years old at this point. Ahmes could have made this appointment, or perhaps Hatshepsut was more than able to see Senenmut as a man to whom she could entrust her own flesh and blood. By appointing him as tutor of her young daughter, probably less than two years old at the time, Hatshepsut was inviting Senenmut, a lowborn man, to share her, or at least her daughter's, circle, to take part in instruction, meals, and religious rituals with Nefrure, thereby creating the intimacy that a father shares with a daughter.

The title for the royal tutor in Egyptian is *mena nesut*, which essentially means "male breast for the king"; that is to say, it is the masculine version of a wet nurse whose milk provided an infant with nourishment and protection against disease. The Egyptians believed that a wet nurse became related to her charge through the milk she fed the baby—in a sense, artificially creating blood relations. The tutor "fed" his royal charge from his experience and his knowledge. His careful attention protected the child from harm when his or her parents' duties kept them away. The notion of family intimacy was meant to be the same for both the male nurse and the wet nurse.

But why was Senenmut chosen? Perhaps other officials, unlike Senenmut, were connected to the old elite families and were too embroiled in political scheming, or maybe Hatshepsut wanted to keep her little daughter close to the money that Senenmut managed. Given that Senenmut had risen to become an economic powerhouse in both temple and state, it was not only clever but also farsighted of Hatshepsut to appoint him as Nefrure's tutor. Her little girl was destined to be God's Wife of Amen and to become a great queen, just as she had.

Whether for emotional or worldly reasons, Senenmut clearly valued his relationship with Nefrure. Later he would have at least ten statues carved, each at great expense, depicting him as he cuddled the small princess in his embrace, with her little head and sweet face peeping out of his robes, or seated on his lap like a crown prince. In these statues, she looks to be two or three years of age. Her cheeks are full and cherubic. Senenmut himself looks like the kind tutor we would want him to be, young and happy, almost feminine in his visage. The images are touching and engaging, full of intimacy and notions of protection and safety.

But Senenmut was also openly displaying something else to other Egyptian elites through these statues: that only *he* had the right to touch this royal child, that only *he* belonged to this inner sphere of power and they did not, that only *he* had access to expensive granodiorite stones from the royal quarry and to the gilding that once adorned the statues. He was telling his colleagues that he now belonged to another family, a higher family than the one into which he was born. He was sending a message to his fellow elites: if you want any of these riches or this influence, then you must go through me. At first glance, these stone blocks express a bond with a precious child whom he may very well have loved, but they were also a blatant and open declaration of his royal political connections and access to great wealth. Hatshepsut would have been cognizant of what Senenmut was really doing with his statue program, publicly set up in temple courtyards and festival spaces. And she seems to have had no problem with the open display of his presumptions.

His relationship with Hatshepsut's daughter seems to have been quite intimate, even fatherly, so much so that some Egyptologists have whispered that Senenmut could have been Nefrure's real father and that the sickly Thutmose II was simply not capable of siring a child. Much ink has been spilled on conjectures about the relationship between Hatshepsut and Senenmut; however, there is no clear indication that Senenmut was anything more than Nefrure's tutor and protector, albeit a very close one.

While Senenmut was busy creating a spectacular career and working his way into the royal family, Hatshepsut may have given birth to another child; and because we have so little evidence of the baby, it was probably another daughter, one who died young.[14] There is no mention of grief, or how Hatshepsut felt about delivering another girl instead of a boy heir. If Hatshepsut ever bore a son, and there is absolutely no evidence of this, he was stillborn or too weak to survive infancy. The ancient Egyptian royal family never mentioned children in the monumental or historical record until they were a viable and useful part of their political society. If royal children died as infants, they were not declared at all. Hatshepsut likely endured many heartbreaks of which her scribes left no record. And with so much riding on the outcome of her unions with Thutmose II, she must have experienced myriad emotions—guilt, shame, anger, bitterness—none of which leave a trace in our records.

Was Hatshepsut close to Princess Nefrure? Hatshepsut would have been just thirteen or fourteen years old when she bore her. Apparently she took a strong interest in the baby, even though evidence suggests that royal child care was a duty best passed to wet nurses, especially for a woman so burdened with responsibilities. There is no indication whatsoever that she resented the girl because of her gender. In fact, Hatshepsut seems to have kept her daughter by her side, knowing that only an educated child could serve her family well. She must have been profoundly grateful that Nefrure was still alive, not a circumstance any mother could take for granted. Indeed, it is likely that Hatshepsut was training Nefrure in the temple for duties as the next God's Wife by letting the girl trail after her while she conducted rituals, so that the incantations and movements would become familiar to Nefrure, flowing into her lifeblood like osmosis.

Despite all the appearances of a close bond with her daughter, Hatshepsut had still failed to bring her most important task to completion. Anxiety within the royal palace was likely building over the king's inability to produce a son with his Great Wife, or with any of his proper wives, for that matter. We must remember that Thutmose II was just a boy himself when he became king. And if he did produce any male children they would have been just infants at this point, not substantial and tested human beings on which to pin anyone's hopes of future kingship.

Everyone in the palace depended on this boy king's virility. If a man from a different branch of the family was chosen to be the next king because of the lack of an heir—as had happened after the reign of Amenhotep I—then everything would be thrown into disarray. Officials would be sacked and lose their income and residence at court, forcing them to move back to their family lands. Other officials would take their place, creating all kinds of political and economic upheaval. A king was nothing without his own loyal stable of bureaucrats, administrators, and warriors. Egypt had seen a change in dynasty not even fifteen years earlier, and the trauma was probably fresh in everybody's memory—particularly for those who were ousted.

The need for a male heir probably encouraged Hatshepsut to visit Thutmose's bedchamber often. The queen essentially found herself in a bizarre race against not just dozens of other women, all striving to breed Egypt's royal son, but against the king's failing health as well. Thutmose would have been encouraged to lie with his wives as frequently as his stamina allowed, and his nightly activities were likely monitored and remarked upon. Earlier in the Eighteenth Dynasty, there is little evidence for large harems consisting of hundreds of wives and concubines that would later become de rigueur. But by the reign of Thutmose II, the Egyptians were moving in this direction, placing their faith in the breeding capabilities of at least a few dozen women instead of just two or three. Perhaps after Amenhotep I died without a male heir, family and palace officials became more practical about procuring ever greater numbers of fertile young women to pleasure the king.

By the Nineteenth Dynasty, these humble beginnings would develop into a massive harem characterized by a new formality of sacred sexual encounters with the king. Twentieth Dynasty temple carvings of Ramses III even formalize the religious purpose of harem sexuality, showing the sovereign playing the board game senet with naked girls or fondling the genitals of his undressed Beauties, all while he is fully dressed and seated on his throne.[15] Thutmose II almost certainly did not have hundreds of women at his disposal like the Ramesside kings, but he had enough. And one of them, a woman named Isis, produced a son for the king—once again named Thutmose.

As far as we can tell, Isis, like Senenmut, began as an absolute nobody, with no family connections worth putting on the one statue that survives of her, and with no titles showing her worth. Isis may have been one of the concubines brought to the palace to entice the king, picked for her appearance rather than her social status. In the end, this woman would make a name for herself at the palace, but only as mother to the King's Son. We have no idea if Thutmose II produced sons with other women, but there must have been some. Did these lesser sons ratchet up the pressure on Hatshepsut? Did she tell herself that she still had time to gestate another baby before her weak husband succumbed to his ill health?

For the brother-sister royal couple, there would be no more time. After just three years of rule and the production of only one viable daughter with his Great Wife, Aakheperenre Thutmose, the beneficiary of Ahmes's and Hatshepsut's tireless political maneuvering and unlikely savior of his line, succumbed to his illnesses and ascended to the sky.[16] Hatshepsut was about sixteen years old and destined to never be another man's wife; she understood that to maintain her position at court she had to hold tight to the memory of her dead husband and his living sons, even though they were only infants. She had memorial chapels built in Thutmose II's name while she prepared for the coronation of the son who would be chosen as king, a child who could not have been more than two years old; presumably everyone hoped that his health would be better than his father's.

Hatshepsut found herself in yet another moment of crisis. Caught between two kings, one a sickly boy whom she had served as the King's Great Wife, and the other a toddler monarch who would soon be in need of a regent, Hatshepsut capitalized on her religious training to manufacture a giant leap forward in her authority: she proclaimed to her people that the gods demanded it. Hatshepsut recounted a miracle that she experienced when she was just a girl, in the god Amen's presence during a public festival. She recorded this event in later documents preserved at her Red Chapel, obelisks, and funerary temple, and Egyptologists are still divided about when in her history it was supposed to have occurred.[17] The narrative tells us that the god revealed himself to her in front of the Egyptian populace and marked her for rule. It's an audacious pronouncement, and Hatshepsut is thus clear in her stance that she was destined for great power from an early age, given such authority by her god. This would be the first of many such revelations for Hatshepsut.

Hatshepsut's account of the story imparts the drama and emotion of the moment. She was in Thebes serving as daughter of the king. Karnak Temple was prepared for a great festival. The statue of the god was carried out of the sanctuary that day in a grand procession to perform *biayt*, a word usually translated as "oracle" or "miracle," but which could just as easily mean "revelation"—the moment the god expressed his opinions or ideas to the king and to the watching crowd. Festivals created the moment when the incarnation of the god (i.e., his statue) was brought out of the temple, his priests bearing the weight of his veiled shrine on two long carrying poles, to communicate with his people. These were important occasions, and many elites would have been pressed into the courtyard of the temple to watch the spectacle. But on this day, something happened that no one, not even Hatshepsut, expected.

Hatshepsut tells us that during this fateful festival, the god Amen did not perform the oracle where and when he was supposed to, which caused such anxiety that even the elites in attendance were afraid to look at the god in his portable shrine. The text says that no miracle happened in any location of the king, perhaps suggesting a kind of vacuum of ideological and political leadership. Whatever the reason behind the inaction, the god was momentarily powerless, directionless. Deep silence fell on the crowd, and people started to wonder what they should do. Palace courtiers bent their heads as in mourning. Someone there, or perhaps it was the god himself, claimed that the wise men had become ignorant. And all around the god's statue there was stunned silence and profound fear, as if the god had abandoned them utterly. Then suddenly, a great power took over the god's statue and he was moved by the priests through some miraculous force. His barque was propelled toward the river, and then, abruptly, toward the gates of the royal palace adjacent to Karnak. As the unwieldly shrine began to swing around, the god Amen unexpectedly commanded his bearers to turn back and move northward. Then, just as unpredictably, he wanted to move eastward—until finally the god passed through the western gateway of the king's palace called I Am Not Far from Him. Each sudden change of direction must have raised a gasp in the crowd of onlookers, unsure of what they were witnessing but aware that only the god could be responsible for such unprecedented motion. At last the god found himself in the forecourt of the palace adjacent to the temple. And upon seeing him, Hatshepsut appeared. Leaving the palace, she threw herself to the ground in his presence, with her arms upraised in praise. She proclaimed that the plans of his majesty were indeed great, that he was her father, the being who created everything that exists. And then, seemingly understanding the gravity of the moment, she asked him openly, "What is it that you desire to happen? I will do according to all that you have ordered." Hearing this, the god is said to have performed another miracle, one presumably witnessed by the entire populace there that day: somehow he controlled Hatshepsut's movements, communicating which way she was to go. It seems that the god placed Hatshepsut before his sacred barque, propelling her toward the Great Chapel of Truth (*ma'at*) in the temple's core. It was here, the narrative says, that she received the investiture of her majesty and her equipment of the God's Wife, granting her authority as a great queen on the one hand and as a priestess on the other.

During festival processions, the god was known to make pronouncements of importance, but nothing like this had happened before, we are told. Onlookers must have stood with mouths agape when the bearers of Amen's portable barque suddenly moved toward the palace and Hatshepsut threw her body into its path, speaking to the god directly. How Amen "answered" her is still an enigma, as is the exact political meaning of her investiture of power. But such is the mysterious nature of divine revelation. Precise details would take away its power. Perhaps Hatshepsut entered into a trancelike state that allowed only her to understand his epiphany. Or perhaps the priestly bearers of the portable shrine moved in such a way that showed Amen's support for his daughter's authority. Or was the whole oracle a stunt set up ahead of time by the priests of Amen, who were happy to have Hatshepsut's continued support? Even the timing of the oracle is uncertain—was it during the reign of her father or her brother? Hatshepsut preferred to keep the whole thing vague, using the word *king* in the oracle texts without naming anyone specifically.

The details of how any Amen oracle worked are vexing to historians.[18] We don't know how questions were put to the god, or how answers were conveyed. But perhaps we should not try to discern facts in this mystical moment, because, for Hatshepsut, this experience may well have been beyond the scope of language, a decisive instant that could not be understood in terms of worldly specifics and political agendas. It did not matter if the oracle was manufactured or authentic. What mattered was the display of her belief in and connection to the god—and that, according to Hatshepsut and the priests of Amen, her rule was decreed by nothing less than a divine revelation.[19]

The oracle text is clear on one point: Hatshepsut's claim to power came not from her own political ambition but from her deep ideological commitment and piety to the god Amen-Re, visible to all in this most public of festival ceremonies. Hatshepsut understood how to demonstrate and wield ideological power, perhaps even at a young age. She was God's Wife of Amen, yes, but this narrative clarifies that her political authority over Egypt stemmed specifically from this sacred position—not as wife of the king, not as mother of the king, not as sister of the king, but rather as wife and daughter to a god.

FOUR

Regent for a Baby King

The surviving sons of Aakheperenre Thutmose could not have been more than toddlers at the time of his death. While it is true that many earlier kings had been children when they took the throne, they were old enough to ensure that their mothers needed to act for only five or six years as de facto ruler before the boy was able to lead in his own right. The crowning of a baby would require a rare decade and a half of rule by a regent. It was a tenuous situation.

Hatshepsut likely did not care which one of Thutmose II's princes was chosen, given that all of them would have been no more than two years old and none had a mother of any standing. Her chief agenda at this most vulnerable moment was to somehow extend her dead husband's line of succession, not only to ensure her own authority but, more important, to continue the Thutmoside line of her father. All she wanted was the selection of a healthy child, given the years of anxiety she had ostensibly spent with a sickly ruler.

We don't know much about how a successor to the king was chosen in ancient Egypt, probably because it served the leadership to keep the process shrouded and exclusive. A general tenet of Egyptian society was that a man in office would be succeeded by his eldest son: it seems extremely likely that this should apply to the king as well, but the fact that a king apparently had the opportunity to formally nominate his heir (something

Hatshepsut later tells us had been done for her) suggests that some level of choice among children of equal standing might be possible. A king might also reinforce his heir by naming the son Great General of the Army, a de facto way of naming him crown prince. But, if the candidates were all too young and untried for such a decision to be made, and if the king died without having chosen an heir, then such a momentous decision was made by others. The question is: who made the selection?

A later autobiographical text of Thutmose III hints that there were a number of princes of Thutmose II to contend for the throne. Of course, the babies themselves were not competing; rather, each would have represented a particular faction of elites and officials who had a connection to the child through the mother's line. But in this case, none of the women who bore Thutmose II's sons seem to have been of any importance at all, so perhaps the political fight over their children was limited. Maybe the choice of a particular prince was immaterial, which meant that the real danger—from Hatshepsut's perspective, at least—came from groups of elites who were willing to ignore a living heir with an unconnected mother and instead push forward their own adult contenders for the throne, perhaps a man with links to the family of Amenhotep I. Although we have little evidence of such maneuvering, there must have been many far-seeing, logical men in Hatshepsut's court and throughout Egypt who were reluctant to submit themselves to the reign of a toddler, himself descended from a weak king.

If we assume that Hatshepsut was interested and involved in the decision about who would succeed her dead husband, we can imagine that she would again rely on her most trusted source of power: her connection to the gods and the inviolability of divine decision. Hatshepsut likely understood that Amen-Re had to be the one to select the prince who would rule and that such a revelation must take place in front of many eyes. If she tried to shield the selection, people might suspect that she was interfering with it. But if she opened up the succession decision for all courtiers to see within a religious oracle, she could recast a thorny political issue as the indisputable will of the god, thus enabling her to place one of the Thutmoside babies on the throne of his father and save her dynasty.

The oracle text that provides us with the basis of reconstructing what happened next is problematic because it deals with the supernatural mechanisms of divine authority. It states that Thutmose II's princes found themselves in a pillared hall of the temple, presumably brought there for this purpose, and each of them was "still a baby bird in its nest." The god appeared, his rays somehow shining into the eyes of the princes as he took on the manifestation of Horus on the horizon. Perhaps the rising sun had just slanted into the hall, moving over the floor where the princes sat and blinding them momentarily. The people present in the hypostyle hall were awestruck by the divinity before them. Next, a figure called "his majesty" appears in the written story. The identity of this figure is unclear, but presumably it refers to the king, the designation remaining vague and unnamed as happens so often in Egyptian histories of mystical experiences. Perhaps the majesty in question is meant to be Thutmose II, living or dead, but whoever he was he burned incense and made a great offering of sacrificed animals, including a bull and a calf to the god of the temple. It was at this moment that the god of the oracle makes his appearance, presumably Amen in his barque. The god is said to cross the two sides of the pillared hall, apparently an unexpected move, but part of the god's revelation. He was searching for the king who would serve him next. Suddenly, the god looked upon his choice, one of the princes before him. The prince in question threw himself to the ground on his belly and bent his arms up toward the god in veneration, dexterous movements for a toddler. Then the god, somehow, placed his chosen prince in front of "his majesty," presumably the mysterious unnamed king, and made the boy take the place of honor in the hall. Then and there, the god is said to have performed his revelation, ostensibly naming the boy as the next king before all those assembled.

We can envision the scene as it may have really happened: all the baby princes toddling around the temple, their nurses and mothers running after them, as the sacred shrine of the god, carried by a group of priests, entered the hall. For all we know, this could have been one of the next king's first memories: seeing his father Amen for the first time in his golden shrine and being plucked from among his brothers to serve. Like Hatshepsut's oracular histories, Thutmose's oracle text forgoes specifics. The Egyptians obviously believed that such a sacred event was better seen obliquely.[1] The machinations behind such selections are almost irrelevant: to the ancient Egyptians, political will and religious revelation were completely intertwined at this point in history.

The chosen prince was a boy named Thutmose, son of Isis, one of his father's lesser wives. He would become Menkheperre Thutmose, known to us as Thutmose III. Years later, Thutmose III would record this oracle in his annals. He left out many historical details, but he maintained fervently that the account was not a falsehood. To him, Amen's oracular choice was a miraculous and real event—how the god circled around the temple hall, searching for him, until he finally singled out the young prince to be the next king. Thutmose III later memorialized this event in stone in the heart of Karnak Temple, implying that Amen's revelation was ironclad and not to be doubted. Like Hatshepsut, he claimed that he was the god's choice.

The new king's mother had no special connections to either the Thutmoside or Ahmoside family. Hatshepsut considered Thutmose III to be one of her nephews, the son of her brother. But because Hatshepsut was also married to her brother, Thutmose III was a stepson to her as well. The god's choice was meaningful for Hatshepsut. Not only had the dynasty of her father been allowed to continue, but the oracle made a political decision without any indication that Hatshepsut herself was involved. The oracle also avoided the intrigue and subterfuge that would have resulted if the choice had been left to her or her courtiers.

Thutmose III's account does not include any mention of Hatshepsut, even though she must have been there at the god's revelation, perhaps acting as the God's Wife during the proceedings. It was her family dynasty that benefited most from the oracle, after all. It's possible that she even carefully organized the events with the First High Priest of Amen to lock down the succession after her husband's death. Despite the new king's Thutmoside connections, this transitional period created a problematic balancing act for Hatshepsut, who would now have no direct and formal link to the next king as sister, daughter, or wife, but who still remained as the highest-ranked and, presumably, the most capable member of the royal Thutmoside family in the palace besides her mother. In many ways, Thutmose III ruled as king only because Hatshepsut was there to make it happen. He only took the throne because she had been able to keep all other contenders and threats to her dead husband's child at bay. Had Hatshepsut not been there, it's easy to see how the crown would have passed to an experienced man from a different family, thus establishing a new dynasty. The end result was such a believable spectacle that Thutmose III himself later recorded that it was a pure and miraculous choice.

The selection process of Thutmose III was quickly (if not instantly) idealized and mythologized by the political players, but the practicalities of rule still needed a firm hand in the current delicate state of affairs. Thutmose III was a small child at best, more than a decade away from effective rule on his own; he would need a strong regent. His mother, Isis, was apparently an inappropriate choice; although we can assume that as a member of the harem she was beautiful and fertile, it is also probable that she was neither educated nor highborn. She was clearly trumped as candidate for regent by the dowager Great Wife Hatshepsut, who had already been serving as God's Wife of Amen for almost a decade.[2] When the time came to choose the hand that would guide the young king, it was Hatshepsut who took her place as regent. This fact, in and of itself, says all we hope to know about Hatshepsut's proven leadership abilities and the confidence that the priests, military, and bureaucracy had in her. They all seem to have welcomed the rule of this young queen.

In fact, an ancient biography of one important official named Ineni tells us quite clearly who took up the reins of power.

> [He (that is Thutmose II)] went to heaven, and he joined with the gods. His son stood in his place as King of the Two Lands as he ruled upon the throne of the one who begat him. His (Thutmose II's) sister, the God's Wife, Hatshepsut, was doing the affairs of the Two Lands with her plans. One worked for her; Egypt was with bowed head.[3]

Hatshepsut was no longer the wife of the reigning king, but she was still God's Wife of Amen, which was the true source of her power. She was quickly recognized as the actual ruler of Egypt by courtiers and officials, and in Ineni's text the name of the living king—the toddler Thutmose III—is not even mentioned.[4] For most elites serving in the many palaces, temples, and fortresses around Egypt, Thutmose III's mere existence cemented the royal succession from father to son, but in practical terms it didn't matter at all. In all likelihood, Hatshepsut had ruled before Thutmose II's death. She still ruled. The status quo had been maintained.[5]

If Thutmose III had been older at his accession, we can imagine him marrying Hatshepsut's daughter Nefrure at that time, allowing Hatshepsut to act as regent *and* mother-in-law, much as her mother, Ahmes, had done for Thutmose II. But marriage in Egypt was a procreative affair, and it would not do to marry two children, both no more than toddlers, as there could be no sexual union. Hatshepsut would have to devise a way to cement her power as a stepmother and an aunt, with no closer connection to her young king than that.

We have no evidence of any political rejection of this new young king by the Egyptian elite, but, again, we should not expect to see it in the official records. If an insurrection took place, Hatshepsut was able to quash it. And she wasn't one to mince words: a later text commissioned by her states, "He who will praise her, he will live. He who will speak an evil thing, ignoring her majesty, he will die."[6] What we do witness, and what makes many historians suspect that there was political disagreement at this sensitive juncture, is a concerted and systematic attempt by Hatshepsut to compensate for what this young king lacked: experience and pedigree.

Thutmose III's maternal origins were unimpressive; but his father was a king. As daughter of both a king and a Great Royal Wife, Hatshepsut had no such deficiencies. And with her priestly experience, she was able to step into the regency unimpeded. The office of queen-regent was ancient by the time Hatshepsut exercised it. Evidence for the practice of highborn, educated women ruling on behalf of their young male charges goes back to the Old Kingdom at least, almost one thousand years before, and the practice probably stems back even farther, to the Early Dynastic Period, another five hundred years before that. Many Eighteenth Dynasty kings had already come to the throne as boys in need of political guidance: Ahmose, Amenhotep I, Thutmose II, and now Thutmose III. Young kings were so common during this time period that, according to the calculations of one Egyptologist, women had ruled Egypt informally and unrecognized for almost half of the seventy years before the reign of Thutmose III, an astounding feat given Egypt's patriarchal systems of power.[7] Even so, Thutmose III seems the youngest of these kings by far, and everything depended on his coming of age and fathering male offspring. If a disease claimed him, if he was bitten by a snake, or if he took a tumble during chariot exercises, then the political maneuvering would begin again. Likely everyone was holding their breath during Thutmose III's early childhood, hoping either that he would live to secure their futures or that he would die and give someone else a chance to take the throne.[8]

Some Egyptologists suspect that Hatshepsut was too young for the crucial governance demanded in this tricky situation.[9] Although we think of adolescence as a time of teenage rebellion and irresponsibility, in the ancient world this age marked entry into adulthood, particularly for a female. Hatshepsut must have been quite a capable young woman, having already been thrust into many difficult situations and learned from strong role models of authority: her father, her mother, and probably even the dowager God's Wives. If trained and educated properly, a teenager may have been perfectly suitable to act as regent of the richest land in the ancient world and to keep dozens of scheming courtiers at bay.

During this time, Thutmose III's mother, Isis, seems to have been excluded from any exercise of authority. She had other responsibilities, anyway. The young king must have still needed his mother's close attention and care, and she was probably busy running after her toddler like any other mother. Given her lack of royal connections and titles, even Isis, mother of the king, may have behaved with great subservience in the presence of Hatshepsut. Although likely close in age to Hatshepsut, she would have been keenly aware of her own lesser abilities in Hatshepsut's company. No doubt the girl was intimidated by a woman trained in the mysteries and intellectual puzzles of Amen-Re's rebirth.[10]

As Thutmose III grew up, he would have grasped this unfavorable contrast. His mother may have paled in comparison to the great woman who ruled Egypt on his behalf, Hatshepsut who could likely control a recalcitrant official with a glance, who had intimate knowledge of the Lord of All, and who had learned leadership from his grandfather, the great Thutmose I himself. As Hatshepsut grew older, her confidence and authority seem to have been unrivaled. Thutmose III would have learned at a young age that even though his mother was insignificant and his father sickly, Amen had favored them with seed and revelation, respectively. He would have learned that not all people were meant to be powerful, even if the god had chosen them to birth the monarch, or to even serve as king. And maybe he was concerned that his father's unimpressive legacy might become his own.

Thutmose III never knew a time in his life when Hatshepsut was not in control of Egypt. To him, her rule was his constant reality. It is unlikely that he ever perceived her as an adversary, at least not during his childhood. She was doing him and Egypt a necessary service. But being the savior of the family dynasty may not have inspired her love for him. Or perhaps it did, so that Hatshepsut instructed and advised the young king as the son she never had, treating him as a mother would. No matter how she felt about him, at the beginning of his education, the young king was likely in awe of her intellectual abilities and political influence. She must have been unlike any other woman known to him.

Thutmose III was not just a figurehead, despite his age. It was believed that his kingship was developing inside him as the years passed. We can imagine Hatshepsut gently but firmly guiding her charge, a young king with a crown that was too big, through sacred and essential rituals. As the God's Wife, she occasionally acted on behalf of the king in the temple, but she would have still required his presence for many rituals. He had to learn his place in the world sooner rather than later, and she likely put him to the task of learning his ritual and political responsibilities as young as possible. Throughout it all, Thutmose III watched her interact with officials, priests, administrators, palace women, and palace children; she was his greatest role model for wielding true power.

Thutmose III's bold actions in his later reign do not give the impression that he turned into a spoiled king given to excess or narcissism. Indeed, he seems to have become a controlled and shrewd man, one who knew his own mind and trusted in his own abilities. As a boy, he was likely not given much leniency, and much was expected from him. We can assume that Thutmose III did not get his own way all the time, even though he was king. Hatshepsut must have played a role in this disciplined upbringing.

In fact, if we step back and look at the situation into which this child was thrust, we can see that the burden placed on him at such a young age was extraordinary, on par with Hatshepsut's own. Thutmose III assumed a position for which he was simultaneously training. One wonders when he recognized the profound weight of it all—that the universe's continued creation, the rising and setting of the sun in an organized fashion, the proper flooding and receding of the Nile, the safety of his land, the continued presence of the gods in their temples all depended on *him*, the rituals that *he* enacted, on *his* communication with the gods. At some point in his youth, he became aware that this burden would lay upon his shoulders forever: he was a god, and upon his death he would rise to the heavens and join with the Imperishable Stars in the northern horizon. His heavenly burdens separated him from the people around him, shrouding him in loneliness, perhaps driving him toward activities that were anchored to the dirt and reality of this world.

Or maybe he never had such a moment of panicked clarity, because Hatshepsut was always there sharing his burden of rule and making sure his officials and priests were behaving, allowing Thutmose III to learn his craft as a ruler without the threat of betrayals or insolence toward a king who was too inexperienced to thwart them. Hatshepsut saw to it that he lived in a prosperous, expanding empire, with obedient vassals and secure sources of revenue. In many ways, Hatshepsut's regency gave Thutmose III time to breathe, grow up, and foster his own skills. She was probably also the only other person in the palace who felt the depth and complexity of these responsibilities, the only other person in the entire world who could understand his anxieties.

Most of his education in kingship would have taken place at court, including a great deal of on-the-job training in the throne room or beyond Egypt's borders in the land of the subjugated enemy. There was no need to make up arithmetic problems: just present the year's tax revenue and ask him to allocate it. He didn't have to be encouraged to learn his hieratic: he could read the dispatches from Nubia that had everyone so alarmed. The necessities of execution and punishment didn't have to be explained to him in painstaking detail: he saw men impaled, staked, mutilated, or exposed firsthand, ostensibly on his orders.

Thutmose III also had formal instruction led by tutors who kept him on task. They taught him the many facets of the ancient and complicated Egyptian language. Although he likely learned no foreign languages, he was busy enough. He needed to master both hieroglyphic sacred inscriptions and hieratic cursive scripts. He learned the Middle and Old Egyptian of five hundred to one thousand years earlier. Even though no one spoke in such an archaic fashion anymore, these were the languages of the Pyramid Texts, the "Tale of Sinuhe," and the "Instruction of Ptahhotep." Mastering the oldest language forms would have been akin to learning the Greek of Plato for a Roman patrician or reading Beowulf at Oxford. He never really wrote the common vernacular that was spoken around him; even in letters, his language was formalized and archaic, befitting an immortal king who had ruled for millennia and who would continue to rule Egypt forever. He also studied ethics, as passed down through the instruction texts of his forefathers, as in "Ptahhotep," and learned to be a wise judge:

> If you are a man who leads, who controls the affairs of the many, seek out every beneficent deed that your conduct may be blameless. Great is justice, lasting in effect, unchallenged since the time of Osiris. One punishes the transgressor of laws, although the greedy one overlooks this.[11]

And he learned about the divine responsibilities of kingship from the "Instruction for King Merikare":

> Work for god, and he will work for you also—with offerings that make the altar flourish, with carvings that proclaim your name. God thinks of him who works for him. Well tended is mankind—god's cattle. He made sky and earth for their sake. He subdued the water monster. He made breath for their noses to live. They are his images who came from his body. He shines in the sky for their sake. He made for them plants and cattle, fowl and fish to feed them. He slew his foes, reduced his children when they thought of making rebellion. He makes daylight for their sake. He sails by to see them. He has built his shrine around them. When they weep he hears. He made for them rulers in the egg, leaders to raise the back of the weak. He made for them magic as weapons to ward off the blow of events, guarding them by day and by night. He has slain the traitors among them as a man beats his son for his brother's sake, for god knows every name.[12]

He also exercised his body. Thutmose would have been trained in the art of battle—in the athletics of warfare and hunting, archery, charioteering, as well as dagger and scimitar handling. Unlike Hatshepsut, Thutmose III was expected to spend time out of doors, where he wore nothing but a short kilt and allowed his skin to bronze to a dark brown, hunting game in the desert, hippos in the marshes, or fish along the river.

And, of course, he spent countless hours in the temple, memorizing the secret names of gods that were only revealed to the initiated, absorbing never-ending temple liturgies, and digesting theological treatises, as he worked toward the performance of vital and imperative rituals. He probably started this process as young as three or four years old. As he got older, Thutmose III likely began to ask his priestly instructors questions that led to vibrant theological discourse about the nature of gods and the universe, divinity's connection to this world, and the king's place in it. For this boy, temple mysteries became normal and familiar. The grand temples of Egypt, birthplaces of the gods and machines of the universe, were where Thutmose III played, literally, while lengthy festivals and rites were taking place; kind priests might have crafted toys for their young king or encouraged him to find secret passages in the pylons and the crypts. In many ways, he probably felt that the gods' abode—with its stillness, cool stone walls, inlaid gates, gilded columns, the sounds of chanting, the smell of incense, the cries of the calves, and the acrid tang of sacrificial blood—was his own beloved home as well.

We do not know how old he was at the time of his official religious initiation to the temple mysteries, but given his position as king, he was probably quite young. According to Thutmose III himself, it occurred just after his selection as king by the oracle. This is clearly an exaggeration—he was only a toddler at the time of his coronation—but the same text in which Thutmose III recollects how Amen chose him to be king tells us that after this ceremony he flew up to heaven as a divine falcon, using the body of his incarnation, Horus upon earth, to come into contact with the divine world. When he arrived in the celestial realm, the gates of heaven were thrown open for him, allowing him to cross the sky. There, he expressed his love for the gods, whose mysterious forms he contemplated. He saw the manifestation of the sun god on his descent in the west and on his rising in the east, and in between the two, in the land of the dead. He was able to understand the true nature of the universe. And then he returned to Egypt to inhabit his earthly body again, to rule Egypt as a divine Horus.[13]

This is heady stuff, at any age. From his first memories, Thutmose III knew that he was exceptional, able to commune with the gods in an intimacy and with an intricacy to which few others had access. The only other person who seemed to share those same abilities and duties was his stepmother, his aunt, his regent, the God's Wife of Amen, Hatshepsut.

During the early part of her career as regent, Hatshepsut wore the long linen gown of a queen and priestess; her

head was covered by a vulture headdress and her forehead decorated
with a cobra. Her mother, Ahmes, may still have been alive at this time,
although we have little record of her. In many ways, Hatshepsut had simply taken over where her mother had left off, acting as regent for the new
male king and relying on memories of her own mother's regency as her
best model for rule.

Yet Hatshepsut surpassed her mother and built a career not solely
connected to a man's power—because she also maintained her role as
Egypt's highest priestess. Hatshepsut continued her temple duties as God's
Wife of Amen during this time, and she quickly began to lay the groundwork for the future care and satisfaction of her god under this new king.
Hatshepsut probably trained her daughter Nefrure for the God's Wife of
Amen position personally and attentively. The young girl likely shadowed
her mother in the temple during the daily meals and all festival processions, learning the rituals at a young age just as Hatshepsut had done
before her. Nefrure was in training alongside Thutmose III—two small
children inhabiting roles much bigger than they could comprehend.

During this vulnerable and liminal time, Hatshepsut was the only
one who could build the pillars of Thutmose III's new kingship, and she
began a campaign of temple renewal throughout Egypt and Nubia. One
scene, commissioned by her at Semna temple in Nubia, shows her with
Thutmose III carved as a man, not a boy. Hatshepsut chose to show herself wearing a long gown and to name herself God's Wife of Amen and
King's Wife. Texts tell us that Thutmose III and Hatshepsut rescued this
temple from ruin. Even though Thutmose III was the king in body, it was
Hatshepsut who enacted a systematic program of monumental building to
ensure that her rule was depicted alongside his throughout the land and
that her image as a woman of authority was carved in Egypt's sacred temples.[14] Her mother, Ahmes, had done the same for herself and Hatshepsut
during the reign of Thutmose II. But now Hatshepsut went even further,
claiming more space for herself in the temples she built for her young
charge. Such depictions of a God's Wife were unprecedented, just like her
powerful regency.

As she strengthened Thutmose III's kingship with new buildings, she
also erected sacred monuments in the name of her dead husband, perhaps
reminding her people why she, and not another, served as regent. In the
temple of Khnum, the god who the Egyptians believed created the world

on his potter's wheel, located on Elephantine Island in Egypt's south, just above Nubia, Hatshepsut set up a statue of Thutmose II, with the inscription "for her brother," thus making the pious addition as much about her as about the dead monarch.[15] She also began a series of stone monuments at Karnak, now only preserved as blocks, on which the dead Thutmose II filled a prominent role. Hatshepsut seems to have been playing up her connection to Thutmose II in these monuments, perhaps with the realization that her connection to his son Thutmose III—as his aunt—was only tenuous and by no means direct. It is as if she was manipulating the monuments to rewrite history: perhaps she thought that if she focused on her relationship with the father, everyone might begin to see the son as hers, too.

Indeed, her own individual legitimacy—as regent, as priestess, as queen—was now at stake as she faced a political-religious issue of palace-temple protocol. The position of God's Wife of Amen was powerful, to be sure, but the holder of this office was meant to be closely and directly related to the current king, preferably as King's Daughter or King's Sister or King's Wife. Hatshepsut had been all of those, but only in relation to Thutmose I or II. Now, her connection as God's Wife—as the current king's aunt and stepmother—was questionable. The lineage of the priestess office needed to follow the living king; it could not move down a peripheral female line. Indeed, Hatshepsut probably hoped to finish training and appoint her daughter to the post as soon as possible. Nefrure was Thutmose III's half sister and without a doubt destined to be King's Wife at some point, if she lived to see that day. But like Thutmose III, Nefrure was only a small child. Hatshepsut played a waiting game, filling the role of Egypt's two most important positions simultaneously—effective king (as regent) and God's Wife—while both young officeholders grew up. Some decorated blocks from Karnak suggest Nefrure's transition to the office happened quite early, perhaps around her fifth or sixth year. The reliefs show Nefrure identified as God's Wife and also pictured as a grown woman, even though she must have been just a little girl, standing behind her mother dressed as a queen.[16]

Hatshepsut's life thus far was full of rich and varied experiences, as necessity led her from one vital role to another. During the first five years of Thutmose III's rule, as Hatshepsut edged closer to her twenties, she was a priestess and a politician, a mother and a widow, a dowager queen and de facto ruler of Egypt, all the while constantly scrambling to find a formally defined place in the world. She engaged in temple rituals, the training of her daughter, meetings with high priests from temples throughout Egypt, discussions with her officials—viziers, treasurers, stewards, and overseers of public works and temple construction—and gatherings with her military wing.

Her husband had been her half brother, probably her junior, and sickly to boot. Regardless of whether theirs had been a passionate love affair or if she felt him her true overlord, he was dead now. One might assume that this fact was liberating for her. Never again would there be a man to whom she was supposed to report or to whom she was meant to be subservient. There was nothing left for Hatshepsut now but to rule at the highest level. Every piece of evidence about her future actions suggests that she knew this.

But she was still a young woman, with desires and normal human tendencies, in a land where sexuality was not controlled by the same religious strictures as in much of the modern world, where royal births still needed to be managed and authenticated, but where one highborn widow's sexuality was probably not monitored or judged in the way we might expect. Sexuality was an integral part of the human experience in ancient Egypt, and Hatshepsut had no master. We should not assume her to have been chaste and nunlike. With her husband dead, she could not be accused of infidelity. She likely had no issues about faithfulness to her divine husband Amen-Re, either, because we know the God's Wives of Amen were allowed to marry at this time.[17]

Indeed, it is quite likely that Hatshepsut had lovers, affairs, trysts, whatever we want to call them. All the academic speculation about Senenmut being Hatshepsut's lover seems rather silly, as if this man were her only opportunity for an affair. Given her position of power and her lack of a husband, she could have had relationships with any number of officials, young or old, male or female. Why would we expect Hatshepsut to have embraced celibacy when she was the person to whom all looked for favor? When she took lovers, did her courtiers look the other way, or were her attachments openly acknowledged and welcomed at court meals and parties? Did she love any of her men (or women)? Did she ever have a real partner with whom she could share anxieties or talk through strategies? None are depicted in any of her formal art because there was no ideological need to record such personal details in a sovereign's life. No lovers or romantic partners are mentioned anywhere in the informal documents, either, not that we should expect them. Economic records, graffiti, and letters are devoid of any mention of Hatshepsut's (or any other ruler's) conquests.[18]

Even so, Egyptologists have often speculated whether Senenmut might have been Hatshepsut's lover, perhaps her principal one. For example, some have even suggested that a sexual graffito found in the tombs above Deir el-Bahri showing a woman being taken from behind actually represents a political satire of Hatshepsut and her submission to her lover Senenmut, even though the subservient figure in this scene is not labeled as Hatshepsut and wears no uraeus or other mark of kingship or rule.[19] There is no reason to identify these graffiti as Hatshepsut's. On the other hand, the fact that Senenmut's burial chamber would later lie within the precincts of Hatshepsut's funerary temple, and that the two owned sarcophagi seemingly designed and made as a pair means that such speculations do not easily die.

Supposing that Hatshepsut did engage in sexual activity during Thutmose III's reign, she still had to be careful. She was a young woman, and a pregnancy might cause problems politically.[20] Her husband's legacy as king was over, and any child she gave birth to at this point would have to remain unacknowledged. She had already been given the opportunity to bear the next heir, and after that failure, the next king had to be fathered by Thutmose III. We know that the Egyptians were capable of dealing with both the prevention and termination of pregnancy.[21] If necessary, Hatshepsut had these options available to her.

She knew that she could never be seen to bear or formally acknowledge another child, but how she confronted this fact emotionally eludes us. Perhaps Hatshepsut experienced profound grief at the loss of future children. Or possibly her work consumed her so that another child was the farthest thing from her mind. It could have been around this time that Hatshepsut lost a daughter,[22] a blow that would have stung this young mother. In the ancient world, the sad but common loss of one child was often ameliorated by the birth of another, but this was not to be for Hatshepsut. She may not even have allowed herself the space to grieve for the little girl, because her duties demanded a compartmentalized existence that left no room for such weaknesses.

Grief was a part of Hatshepsut's life, but her precarious position as regent demanded some creative thinking to secure a place for herself during Thutmose III's reign, and perhaps even beyond his tenure if he succumbed to an early death. There is some indication that Hatshepsut was busy building a political foundation for herself as an unattached woman standing behind the throne of Egypt's king. A series of monuments from Karnak[23] show her in the company of the new king Thutmose III, depicted not as a child but as the idealized and fully functional man he would soon become; Hatshepsut seems to be saying that this is the glorious future that will come to pass if she is allowed to continue her support. Elsewhere on this monument she is depicted accompanying the king (shown fully grown) in the presence of the gods, signifying to the Egyptian elite both that she had brought about Thutmose III's rule and that their positions of wealth and power would be in jeopardy if she were not around. Whether she held a formally defined position or not, Hatshepsut knew how to cloak herself in the legitimacy and necessity of temple ideology.

Hatshepsut was playing a cool and, some might even say, calculated game. She established an unbreakable connection to every sphere of power in Egypt, including palaces, temples, and army. She already had Thutmose III and his mother under her control; they were dependent on her for their own positions until the boy king came of age. Her trusted official Senenmut continued to run her palace finances as steward, and she was now using him for tasks beyond the sphere of her household. As for the army, there is some evidence that continued campaigns in Nubia, under her command, enriched everyone with the movable wealth of gold and minerals.[24] Her rewards to the Amen temple during the reign of her husband were significant, so much so that there is little doubt that the Amen priesthood fully supported her continued rule as regent. It is likely that other temple hierarchies, such as those in Memphis or Heliopolis, were keyed to Theban religious politics, and the evidence suggests that Hatshepsut also compensated religious institutions outside of Thebes. The documentation of her building activity in temples throughout Egypt during her regency indicates a level of construction, job creation, and income for priests and temple bureaucrats that had never been seen before in Egypt. Hatshepsut's regency for Thutmose III was probably quite popular among most Egyptians, especially if they were generals, priests, or treasurers—not bad people to have on your side.

And throughout all of this, Hatshepsut continued solidifying and expanding her influence. She never seems to have assumed more authority than she could handle or more than the Egyptians could give. But when there was an opening, Hatshepsut seized the opportunity. She made political moves incrementally, constructing her base of support slowly, as well as broadly, using many different arenas of power to engender backing and many different individuals to help her get it. In other words, Hatshepsut never favored the palace to the detriment of the army or played one side against another. And she never attempted a glorious, momentous coup, which in one bold stroke would have pushed Thutmose III from power. Hatshepsut was practical and elegant, not devious and cunning. She was intelligently ambitious.

To rule Egypt effectively, Hatshepsut needed to delegate authority to officials whom she could trust. Senenmut, her lead administrator and steward, was soon placed in charge of Nefrure's household finances as well. But even more important than Senenmut at this early point in her regency was an official with the unwieldy name of Ahmose Pennekhbet. He was part of an old and venerable family from the southern Egyptian city of el-Kab who had served the royal family for generations. Hatshepsut designated him chief treasurer.[25] Ahmose Pennekhbet controlled the finances for all of Egypt, monitoring taxes and other income, as well as all expenditures. He opened the House of Gold (in the company of the vizier) every day. He was responsible for all the state's wealth inside its treasuries, including commodities such as grain and other food stores, stone, metal, and linens. As the man who essentially bankrolled her regency, he was one of the early financial sources of Hatshepsut's power.

Men with economic authority allowed her to sustain power after the death of her husband and into the reign of Thutmose III; indeed, the continued existence of the Thutmoside line was in their best interest. Hatshepsut knew that Ahmose Pennekhbet was essential and also named him as a tutor to her eldest daughter, Nefrure. As with Senenmut, being a tutor implied a close familial relationship with one's charge; Hatshepsut seems to have wanted to keep Egypt's money in the family, so to speak.

Senenmut did not lag far behind Ahmose Pennekhbet in his own career advancement, and his ambitions began to carry him beyond the confines of the royal palace. Hatshepsut asked him to oversee the carving and transport of obelisks for Karnak Temple from the southern granite quarries at Aswan, a hundred miles south of Thebes; he recorded his efforts on a monumental relief during the job. Because much of Karnak was archaic and constructed of mud brick, Hatshepsut, like her father before her, had a desire to renew it in stone. She envisioned a pair of granite obelisks shooting up to the sky, able to catch the rays of the sun and gilded along their length.[26] She yearned to show the world wonders not seen for hundreds of years and entrusted this duty to Senenmut. He acknowledged her supremacy in turn: one of the statues he produced during her regency names only Hatshepsut as his master, noticeably and aberrantly omitting the actual ruling king, Thutmose III. As steward to the queen and her daughter during the reign of Thutmose II, Senenmut had been an essential part of Hatshepsut's palace administration in direct service to the royal family. But Hatshepsut seems to have decided during her regency to entrust him with even more responsibility, concluding that she could rely on him during this time of great political uncertainty for Egypt and for herself.

Soon after she appointed Ahmose Pennekhbet treasurer, she named Senenmut to the same post. Somehow the two men were meant to act as equal partners in the position, but the mechanics of how this worked are lost to us. And this was becoming a pattern, since she named both Ahmose Pennekhbet and Senenmut as tutor to Nefrure. It is almost as if Hatshepsut wanted Senenmut to watch over Ahmose Pennekhbet or vice versa. Regardless, she seems to have depended on this pair of officials to keep the two most sacred sources of her power safe at this early stage in her regency: her money, with which she could keep all her officials happy, and her daughter, who acted as God's Wife and who would soon be queen, finally cementing an incontrovertible connection to the new king.

The nature of each man's personal dealings with Hatshepsut remains a mystery, and we know even less about their relationship to each other. Did she appoint the two men to the same office so that neither could become overly powerful from access to all of Egypt's wealth? Had experience with competition taught the Egyptian elite to create a system of government that avoided such a concentration of power in one man? The country already had a tradition of two viziers, one for the north and one for the south. Perhaps Hatshepsut was simply continuing this approach of checks and balances among her officials.

These two men could not have had more different backgrounds. Unlike Senenmut, Ahmose Pennekhbet came from a patrician family who lived in el-Kab, a town close to Thebes, and he had served the early Eighteenth Dynasty kings in their campaigns against the fleeing Hyksos in Syria-Palestine, getting rich in the process on the spoils of war. He seems to have established his career in the military and later became ensconced in the upper echelons of palace administration and finance. The family tombs at el-Kab suggest that Ahmose Pennekhbet's wife was a wet nurse to Thutmose III, probably a move made by Hatshepsut to keep this important official close—the family's residence would have been in a palace apartment to accommodate his wife's duties.

Senenmut, in contrast, was one of Hatshepsut's "new men"; he came from more humble beginnings. And unlike his patrician colleague, he left absolutely no evidence of a wife or children. Not one of his dozens of statues, reliefs, and temple depictions records the existence of a family of his own. Without a doubt, if anything should make us wonder about the nature of his relationship with Hatshepsut, it is his lack of a wife. All Egyptian elites married. If a wife died in childbirth or from disease, an official usually married again. To not have any mention of a female partner anywhere in his extensive historical record is more than strange—it is aberrant. And so we wonder if he blatantly ignored his family to please Hatshepsut, because they were in fact lovers, or if there was something else going on. Senenmut's historical record is much more extensive than that of any other official at the time, but it seems that some of Hatshepsut's other officials also made no mention of their families on their tombs or statues.[27] Perhaps such absences were demanded by a jealous mistress, and if so then there is a lot more about Hatshepsut's character that we do not know.

Of course, homosexuality might seem another possible explanation for Senenmut's lack of a wife. The ranks of Egyptian elites undoubtedly included some men with same-sex desires, and some of these men might even have been able to talk of their sexual interests openly. But all our evidence indicates that such men would have still married in the hopes of having sons to inhabit their offices after their death. A man's future lay with his children. An official's prosperous retirement rested with his son's ability to take over his profession. Senenmut's lack of a wife (or lack of mention, at least) and the great favor Hatshepsut showed toward him do indeed raise suspicions, despite the probable twenty-year difference in their ages.[28] These are interesting conjectures, but because other officials neglected to mention their wives in their tomb chapels, Senenmut's similar omission confirms nothing about his lifestyle, let alone his relationship with Hatshepsut.

We might wonder if Thutmose III felt shut out of this close circle created by Hatshepsut, her daughter, and Senenmut. The latter's role as tutor must have fostered a tight relationship with the princess, and his many jobs for Hatshepsut certainly kept the bureaucrat in constant contact with the female king. Indeed, some of Senenmut's earliest statues created during Hatshepsut's regency,[29] when Thutmose III was a sole but infant king, include no mention of the boy at all, a not-so-subtle testament to what Senenmut thought of the new king's importance in relation to his mistress.

Most of Hatshepsut's story thus far has been tied to Thebes, not only because so many of her temples and texts have been preserved in its desert sands but also because this was, in truth, the base of her power. Hatshepsut's royal family was buried at Thebes, in what we now call the Valley of the Kings. Her priestess position as God's Wife of Amen was centered in Thebes. Amen's temple of Ipet-Sut at Karnak had grown to become one of the richest and most influential religious institutions in the land. But Egypt was a much larger political entity, essentially an oasis expanse stretched from north to south over hundreds of miles and inhabitable only where the Nile cut through and inundated its desert sands. Hatshepsut would have known that control of Thebes was not enough. She needed to ensure that she had all the provinces and local governors in line, that taxes were collected, that temples were maintained and priests were happy with their income, that government and judicial activity was happening as it should. To do this, Hatshepsut needed to contend with the dozens of governors and mayors of the forty-two regions up and down the Nile and in the delta. She thus employed numerous royal heralds who traveled throughout Egypt and abroad with authority to speak for the king and, probably, to bestow his favors upon loyal officials.

She also had to focus sharp attention on the administration of Nubia, a land of gold mines and stone quarries, but also the home of a subjugated people full of resentment and hostility. The Egyptian viceroy of Nubia bore the formal title King's Son of Kush; because of the extensive and dangerous travel required, it was a stressful position that was frequently vacant. However, the risky job promised a huge payoff in return: Nubia controlled more cold hard exchangeable wealth, in the form of gold and other minerals, than anywhere else in the known world. The vast distances between Kush and the royal court, or the Egyptian army, were temptation enough for many an administrator to take more than his due. Free access to the most fungible wealth available in the ancient world seemed to seduce many of the Egyptian men put in charge of Nubia; as a result, removal from office was common and demanded with impunity. Hatshepsut, however, seems to have handled these potential pitfalls with care and attention and kept a firm hand on the men who administered Nubia for her.[30]

In year 5 of Thutmose III's reign, Hatshepsut made a crucial appointment to her government. She designated a man called Useramen as vizier in the south.[31] The vizier acted as the king's lieutenant in all administrative, military, and economic matters. Useramen was stationed at Thebes, and Hatshepsut seems to have relied on him for her most important state business.

The vizier worked closely with the treasurers, monitoring the security of the storerooms holding all the household goods and wealth and administering the tax income that was the palace's lifeblood. Hatshepsut knew that Useramen would require strong working relationships with Senenmut and Ahmose Pennekhbet. The three men must have been thrown into one another's company a great deal, but the nature of their interactions—friendly or hostile or suspicious—remains unknown.

Useramen acted as the lieutenant of Hatshepsut, not Thutmose III. This southern vizier must have been invested in Hatshepsut's well-being, because, if someone had wanted to see Hatshepsut dead, Useramen could have easily arranged it. He also controlled Hatshepsut's communication with the rest of Egypt: he was the main conduit, through a legion of royal heralds, between the capital cities and the local rulers spread out across the Two Lands. The royal heralds reported directly to Useramen and kept him abreast of all activities throughout the country; he then distilled, filtered, and relayed this information to Hatshepsut in person. He could easily have deceived Hatshepsut on large and small matters, but there is no evidence of such subterfuge or the need for it. We can imagine the two of them together in her smaller audience hall working out plans of action for specific troubles and issues. As always, Hatshepsut continued to choose her advisers shrewdly.

Useramen also oversaw all southern military expeditions, all trade excursions, all taxes, and all royal works projects like temple building or the construction of the king's tomb in the Valley of the Kings. He may have even organized trade with Syrian and Minoan palaces and encouraged contact with peoples whose existence had never before been acknowledged by the elites in Thebes. Contact with the Keftiu of Crete, for instance, was considered so exotic and fashionable that every Theban official who kept up with the trends included a scene in his tomb chapel of these Minoan men in their colorful woolen garments, holding luxurious commodities.

Useramen must have been a close and trusted confidant and supporter of Hatshepsut. She appointed him after five years of regency, when she was probably in her early twenties, mature enough to know her own mind and abilities and experienced enough to have been betrayed more than once by undependable and self-interested officials. Useramen's loyal service was abundantly rewarded with bonuses, a fine tomb, and rich monuments. He kept her unorthodox position as regent safe. He kept her family safe. He kept her money safe. And he kept tribute and taxes flowing into the palace. In return, Hatshepsut compensated him with things more valuable than money, such as secret and, to the Egyptians, profoundly powerful texts only available to priests of the highest initiation that thus far had been inscribed only in the tombs of kings. Useramen actually had the otherwise-royal Book of Amduat painted in his burial chamber,[32] which ostensibly gave him the same access to the mysteries and powers of the solar barque as the king and chief priest. All the evidence indicates that Useramen's constancy was crucial for Hatshepsut to maintain her dominance during the early reign of Thutmose III, and she gave whatever was required to secure it.

Hatshepsut did not overlook her state temples: indeed, she put the staffing of Egypt's temples at the top of her agenda; she must have known it was a key to her success and one of the pillars of Thutmose III's young kingship. She was instrumental in professionalizing Egypt's religious arm. Temples that had previously functioned with short-term service by local elites were now staffed with full-time administrators and priests trained specifically for a life in religious service. These men had access to vast sums of cash and grain, but these were resources taken from the stores of the gods, not the wealth of the king. By all accounts, a veritable army of religious men rose under the rule of Hatshepsut, and she likely saw political wisdom in creating a legion of devoted godly supporters. Many of these priestly offices became hereditary and were passed down from father to son, thus increasing the position's long-term value. High-level priestly appointments were Hatshepsut's to give as she chose. For instance, she or her mother, Ahmes, may have appointed Hapuseneb as High Priest of Amen during the latter years of Thutmose II. He oversaw the construction projects at Karnak and Luxor, massive works funded by the hoards of gold streaming in from Nubia, and he set in motion Hatshepsut's aim to create the most lavish and awe-inspiring monuments the world had ever seen.

Hatshepsut kept her eyes on the problems of the present moment, but at the same time she had a responsibility to consider eternity. Egyptians traditionally constructed their tombs during their lifetime, and Hatshepsut was no exception. Accordingly, probably while Thutmose II was still alive or soon after his death, Hatshepsut began a tomb for herself in a remote valley (the Wadi Sikkat Taka el-Zeida) in the far south of the vast Theban necropolis.[33] To hold her body, she commissioned a precious sarcophagus of quartzite that was placed in the tomb to await her death. However, Hatshepsut would soon abandon this tomb and the priceless body container, commissioning a new, bigger, and more beautiful sarcophagus.

Hatshepsut had set all the pieces in place. She handpicked the tutors and nurses of the young king-in-training. She worked with loyal temple personnel grateful for her gifts and cognizant of the depth of her own religious capacities. She had Egypt's financiers in her pocket; some of them even served as tutor to her daughter in her own home. She now needed to co-opt the venerable families of Egypt by appointing as midlevel officials young men who would continue to support her and her ongoing rule for the king. But here she was at a disadvantage: typically a prince raised at court would have trusted childhood friends with whom he had shared lessons and beatings and with whom he had grown up to be skilled in the ways of war and administration; later, were he to become king, he could rely upon these fast and tested friends. Hatshepsut had no such intimate companions, no pool of men of known character to be handpicked to serve as new officials, and Thutmose III was obviously too young to have any of his own. Raised as a princess, Hatshepsut was likely separated from the young men who were now candidates for office, and yet she needed them to fill many positions: royal butlers, priests, overseers of stables, fan bearers (bodyguards), overseers of works, royal barbers, and physicians. Hatshepsut seems to have solved the problem with a combination of intimidation and money. Upstart lieutenants may have been kept in line with threats to their lives and livelihoods—a rare occurrence, most likely, but one visible in her later texts about disloyalty being treated with death. Spreading around money was easier than bullying. With economic co-option built into their political system and with tribute pouring in from Egypt's recently expanded empire, new officials could be assured of great payoffs in exchange for their support of this unconventional and drawn-out regency.

While Hatshepsut was shoring up her power with the appointment of trustworthy men, Thutmose III was no longer a baby. Now more than halfway through his first decade, his position as boy king had been protected by Hatshepsut, which gave him the luxury of gently growing into his position. We can imagine him hanging around the palace and watching Hatshepsut work with her loyal and well-rewarded men. He would have spent a great deal of time in the temple and throne room with her as business was being conducted, perhaps a small boy sitting on a gilded throne too big for him, next to his regent's own, smaller seat.

What was it like to be a child in these formal circumstances and with such high stakes on the line? Thutmose III must have been a healthy boy; he survived when so many died. But we have little insight into his character as a child: Did he laugh often and get into trouble in the audience chamber? Was he scolded by the High Priest of Amen during sacred temple rituals when he swiped a piece of the Great God's food for his own enjoyment? Did the vizier Useramen take him under his wing and explain complicated tax proceedings during the annual grain count, or did the treasurer Senenmut regale the young king with stories of how difficult it was to quarry stone for the obelisks of Amen's temple?

Thutmose III's relationship with all these officials must have been stimulating and constantly evolving. They knew he was king, a true son of Thutmose II and grandson of the great campaigner Thutmose I, and as such that he must be treated with respect. But a young boy can still act like a brat, a trickster, or a silly fool to be taught a lesson. As he got older and settled into more responsibility and decision making, Thutmose III must have demanded more consideration and authority from his officials. But for now, he was just a child. And it seems he did what he was told to do. Meanwhile, Hatshepsut was negotiating a few more steps forward in her own career.

At about this time, Hatshepsut was laying the delicate groundwork to relinquish the position of God's Wife of Amen, the very role that had given her access to power few women ever knew. Evidence from early Karnak monuments of this period shows Hatshepsut as the King's Great Wife offering wine vessels to the god, while behind her Nefrure, her daughter, stands as a high priestess. This is the first time we see Nefrure labeled as God's Wife of Amen.[34] It's hard to know when Hatshepsut gave up her God's Wife title, but it seems to have been within these first five years of regency; perhaps she even shared the position with her daughter during a transitional period.

Hatshepsut was in her early twenties, and strange as it may seem to us, she was probably too old to act as the sexual exciter of the god anymore. Perhaps she was expected to pass this role off to a younger female who could continue to facilitate the rebirth of the god every morning. Hatshepsut's loss of this vital position may have been the alarm inciting her call for even more power, to claim a defined and definite authority that she could never possess as regent.

Indeed, Hatshepsut's training of Nefrure may have gone hand in hand with her own future plans to maintain rule. Her choice of Nefrure as the next God's Wife was politically astute. The girl was her daughter, but she was also Thutmose III's half sister. Hatshepsut was taking another step forward by transferring the office to her own daughter, linking the holder of the God's Wife post to the current ruler, Thutmose III. But without that temple office, Hatshepsut was herself left floating in a limbo of ill-defined and poorly justified authority. With Thutmose III growing taller and more aware with every new year, Hatshepsut needed to lay the foundations for another type of power.

FIVE

The Climb
Toward Kingship

In the ancient world, having a woman at the top of the political pyramid was practically unheard of. Patriarchal systems ruled the day, and royal wives, sisters, and daughters served as members of the king's harem or as important priestesses in his temples, not as political leaders. Throughout the Mediterranean and northwest Asia, female leadership was perceived with suspicion, if not outright aversion. Mesopotamia, for example, preserves only one example of a female political powerhouse predating Hatshepsut: Kubaba, a tavern keeper, of all things, who, according to *The Sumerian King List*, consolidated power in the ancient city of Kish in the twenty-fifth century BCE during a time of never-ending war and crisis. Hatshepsut probably had little knowledge of this formidable woman, given her education's lack of focus on foreign kings. She had models of strong female leadership from her own soil.[1]

Even though Egyptian cultural and political systems sometimes tolerated women in power, at least when compared to other ancient societies, only a few women were able to climb to the very top and rule all of Egypt. One of the oldest examples was the great queen Merneith, who took charge of the political system when Egypt's kingship was new, around 2900 BCE.

A King's Mother who likely ruled on behalf of her young son, Den, Merneith was so powerful that she earned a tomb alongside the other First Dynasty kings in the royal cemetery of Abydos, complete with hundreds of human sacrifices, as was the style in those very early days of dynastic rule. She was never associated with the kingship in a formal manner that is preserved for us, but her power was so great that archaeologists uncovering her tomb assumed it belonged to a male ruler, until inscriptions proved otherwise. Merneith used her regency to take on real power, and once she had it, evidence suggests that she did not relinquish her hold on authority until her death. Merneith provided Hatshepsut with a useful case study, and we can only wonder if the Eighteenth Dynasty queen had more details of the historical reality that we lack.

Then there was Sobeknefru, daughter of King Amenemhat III of Dynasty 12, who ruled around 1800 BCE. Three hundred years before Hatshepsut was born, Sobeknefru served as the first true female king of Egypt, an astounding achievement given the odds against it. The Egyptians developed no word for "queen" in the political sense, just the phrase *hemet neswt*, "wife of the king," a title with no implications of rule or power in its own right, only a description of a woman's connection to the king as husband.[2] Thus female rulers of Egypt, like Sobeknefru, took on the masculine title of "king."

Clothing was more problematic, and Sobeknefru depicted herself wearing not only the masculine headdress of kingship but also the male royal kilt over the dress garments of a royal wife, garbing her feminine self with the trappings of a masculine office.[3] However, Sobeknefru's reign lasted a mere four years, and she was unable to save her family's lineage or establish any norms for future female kingship. After her death, Egypt descended into the weak and ephemeral kingships of the Thirteenth Dynasty.

Hatshepsut would have thus known that formally defined female rule was rare, even in Egypt where it was sometimes tolerated. And she likely learned that women in power were usually unsuccessful, born into crisis and ending their time in chaos. Hatshepsut probably did not think of such a position for herself initially. If not inconceivable, it would certainly have seemed unworkable with a king already on the throne. But against all odds, sometime around year 7 of Thutmose III's reign, the impossible happened. She was crowned as king. Hatshepsut clawed and scraped her way to that end goal, claiming royal prerogatives and powers as she went, until she realized her coronation, an expensive and overwrought affair memorializing the power that she had already amassed. As one Egyptologist describes it, her coronation was "the day on which her de jure iconography caught up with her de facto authority."[4]

The "facts" that are left to us concerning Hatshepsut's reign are far from certain. The exact timing of her ascension has been disputed by Egyptologists, some arguing that it happened as early as year 2, most claiming year 7.[5] Almost all of our surviving historical documents concerning Hatshepsut's rise to kingship are religious in nature, and many date to after her coronation, clouding our understanding of her gradual, competent, and calculating ascension. The evidence does contain clues of political realities nonetheless.

In year 2 of Thutmose III's reign, while Hatshepsut was acting only as regent, she made her first steps toward more political power. Reliefs carved at Semna temple in Nubia show her in the company of the gods, and here, the description of her actions—as an heir, as a builder, as a ritual officiate—are those of a masculine king. The goddess Satet, the guardian of the Nubian southern lands, says, "She is the daughter who has come forth from your [limbs]. With a loving heart you have raised her, for she is your bodily daughter."[6] Hatshepsut's titles of God's Wife and King's Great Wife are not overreaching; they are suitable, in all respects, for a queen. But this relief still represents a clever step forward for Hatshepsut: she shows herself performing the role of a king, without formally naming herself as such. In year 2, she was already laying the groundwork.

Around the same time, Hatshepsut ordered two grand obelisks for Karnak Temple—an operation that would demand countless man-hours. To document the start of this long-term project, Senenmut had a monumental text carved on the island of Sehel at Aswan, near the site where the stone for the massive needles would be quarried. This inscription marks a transitional moment for Hatshepsut, who was acting as a regent, with all the powers of a monarch, but unrecognized as anything more. In this text, Senenmut refers to her as "the princess, the one great of praise and charm, great of love, the one to whom Re has given the kingship in truth, among the Ennead,[7] King's Daughter, King's Sister, God's Wife, Great

King's Wife [. . .] Hatshepsut, may she live, beloved of Satet, lady of Ele-phantine, beloved of Khnum, lord of the First Cataract region."[8]

At this time, Hatshepsut's claim of a growing, nascent, and infor-mally given kingship is made only in text form, not pictorially, and thus it was accessible exclusively to learned elites and the gods. Everyone else simply saw the figure of their queen. The Sehel relief served dual agen-das, recording her power as regent—a position with no formal title of any kind—in the text and her feminine power as God's Wife in the image. Thus we have documented the moment before Hatshepsut was crowned, before she was in fact *king*, but when she was exercising all the power of the *kingship*.

Hatshepsut was busy producing an unassailable image of herself, one that further developed her divinity, a seemingly unending process for this woman. From the age of twelve to twenty, she was methodically po-sitioning herself as queen, then regent, and now she was striving for the kingship itself. Along the way, she constantly modified her depictions to support that emergent power. One of the first changes we see on her mon-uments, just a few years before she formally became king, was her deci-sion to drop the title of God's Wife of Amen and take up the title of King's Eldest Daughter. Some Egyptologists see this rejiggering of her personal relationships as the crux of her entire power grab, a shift that moved her from a queen's role to an heir's, as the rightful offspring of Thutmose I and one who could make a heritable claim to the throne despite her fe-male gender.[9]

Another block from Karnak Temple, probably carved sometime after Senenmut's Sehel inscription, makes the next leap forward.[10] It shows Hatshepsut wearing the gown of a queen on her body but the crown of a king upon her head.[11] The *atef* crown—a fabulous and extravagant amal-gamation of ram's horns and tall double plumes—was depicted atop her short masculine wig, probably to the shock of the craftsmen in charge of cutting the decoration. It was a confusing image for the Egyptian viewer to digest: a female king performing royal duties, offering jars of wine di-rectly to the god, and all before any official coronation. If we assume that she appeared at public rituals wearing this crown, it would have been the first time in history that a woman wore such a headpiece in public. With this block, Hatshepsut had finally decided to document her changing powers in pictorial—not just textual—form. And she took her display of power much further in the text, calling herself the One of the Sedge and of the Bee, or as Egyptologists translate it, King of Upper and Lower Egypt.

On this same relief, Hatshepsut also introduced a new name to encapsulate her transforming persona: Maatkare (The Soul of Re Is Truth). Hatshepsut was taking on a second name, a throne name reserved for kings and received through secret revelation. It was standard practice for a male king to do this but inconceivable for a queen with informal power. Hatshepsut was transforming her role into a strange hybrid of rule ordained before it had officially happened. Was Hatshepsut testing the waters with this relief? Or was she monumentalizing what would soon happen officially? She commissioned this scene sometime after year 5 of Thutmose III's reign, and it was probably finished just before her formal coronation. With the production of this temple relief, Hatshepsut shattered the tenets of traditional Egyptian thinking about divine rule: only the *king* can act as chief priest and doer of ritual activity. Only *he* can accept the god's prosperity on behalf of Egypt. Only *he* can wear his sacred crown of masculine virility. But here Hatshepsut—a woman—was claiming these holy duties, and all that before she was officially king.

All accounts suggest that Hatshepsut started to construct her new persona in year 2, moving swiftly, completing the process within a five-year period; but as she had done all her life, she moved deliberately, step by step, claiming new titles and names when she thought the time was right, never pushing it beyond what those around her could tolerate. And her people seem to have accepted her unparalleled presumptions.

The Amen priesthood assisted in her unprecedented ascent. We learn from a later inscribed text that she had benefited from another temple oracle from the god Amen in year 2 of an unnamed king. This time, the god foretold her impending kingship outright. The inscription is broken, but because it comes from her Red Chapel, the text must refer to her.

> Regnal year 2, month 2 of spring, day 29 the 3rd day of the Festival of Amen corresponding to the 2nd day of the offerings of Sakhmet, when foreseeing for the two lands in the wide hall of the southern Ipet-Sut (Luxor Temple). Lo, his majesty performed omens in the presence of this god. Fine of appearance is the father of his good festival, Amen in the midst of the gods.

Then he seized my majesty (ostensibly Hatshepsut) [. . .] of the beneficent king multiplying for him the miracles about me (Hatshepsut) corresponding to the entire land.[12]

The text is quite vague, as oracular texts are wont to be, and we lack the drama of the earlier revelatory inscription that invested her as God's Wife. But no matter the details, Hatshepsut was still the first Egyptian monarch to use oracular understanding to solidify and publicly declare her authority to her people, and later in the same text she claims, "He (Amen) has introduced me to be ruler of the two lands while his majesty was declaring oracles."[13]

Hatshepsut's understandings and manipulations of religious ideology were keen. She cloaked all her momentous power grabs through displays of piety. As to her kingly transformation, she tells us it was the King of the Gods himself who instructed her personally to take this step. Her later obelisk inscriptions seem a little more defensive: "He who hears it will not say 'It is a lie,' what I have said. Rather say, 'How like her it is; she is devoted to her father!' The god knew it in me. Amen, Lord of the Thrones of the Two Lands, he caused that I rule the Black and Red Lands as reward. No one rebels against me in all lands."[14] In her own mind, Hatshepsut may have seen the situations of her life—as queen, God's Wife, regent, king—through the lens of divine inspiration and planning by the gods. After all, conditions had put her in this very place and time, able to do what no woman had ever done.

It is likely that for her kingly initiation, she spent many nights and days in the heart of the temple, perhaps consuming intoxicants, suffering sleep deprivation, fasting, chanting, in an attempt to access the innermost workings of Amen's mind. She may have ascended the pylons at dawn after a long night of trancelike meditation to merge with the sun, witnessing the mysteries and miracles of its regeneration, merging with the machinations of the cosmos that made it possible. And then, exhausted but joyful, she might have appeared before her people transformed, her eyes sparkling with privileged understanding. Initiation lent her great power in the eyes of her elites, especially the priesthood, and it was something she wanted to broadcast.

After her initiation came the crowning. Perhaps she found herself on her knees in the god's sanctuary, shaking, her thin linen shift the only layer between her knees and the cold stone temple floor as she waited for the choice of the god. Perhaps when she felt the crown settle upon her brow, she began to weep, feeling the crook and scepter thrust into her hands until she grasped them closely, intimately, as if they had clutched these instruments of kingship all her life. However we might imagine the unwritten details of that first, personal moment as king, Hatshepsut herself was clear about her people's awed reaction:

> Then these officials, their hearts began to forget; their faces astounded indeed at events. Their limbs united with fatigue. They saw the enduring king and what the Lord-of-All himself had done. They placed themselves on their bellies. After this, their hearts recovered. Then the majesty of the Lord-of-All fixed the titulary of her majesty as beneficent king in the midst of Egypt.[15]

And then Hatshepsut spoke to them, claiming:

> I am beneficent king, lawgiver who judges deeds. . . . I am the wild horned bull coming from heaven that he might see her form. I am the falcon who glides over the lands, landing and dividing his borders. I am the jackal who swiftly circles the land in an instant. I am excellent of heart, one who glorifies her father, attentive of deeds to render justice to him.[16]

The reality of her coronation was likely different from the idealized version that Hatshepsut would later represent on her many monuments—particularly on her quartzite barque chapel at Karnak.[17] The first jarring jolt of reality must have been the existence of another king on the throne. Thutmose III was not yet ten years old, but he was still king. Hatshepsut's presumptions were apparently unprecedented in Egyptian political history, because she claimed a share of the throne while it was already occupied. Her decision to be formally crowned as king, while young Thutmose III still sat on the throne, smacks of great audacity, and yet it happened nonetheless.

Hatshepsut's coronation was intricate and involved, taking place within Karnak's courtyards, shrines, and sanctuaries; it was a series of complex rituals that went on for days, involving dozens of different crowns, garments, and scepters, and representing a political-religious investiture of the ultimate gravity. Hatshepsut no longer wore the headgear of a God's Wife of Amen but that of a king, essentially trading in one position of power for one infinitely higher. She tells us that the gods themselves were participants and indicates that Thutmose I himself, her dead and now-deified father, was the first to place a crown upon her head, announcing that he appointed her as king alongside himself. Hatshepsut tells us that the goddess Hathor was also present, shouting a greeting in welcome and embracing her. The god Amen-Re is said to have personally placed the double crown upon Hatshepsut's head and invested her with the crook and flail of kingship, saying that he created her specifically to rule over his holy lands, to rebuild his temples, and to perform ritual activity for him.

Because of the presence of Hatshepsut's father, not to mention Amen-Re himself, the account of Hatshepsut's coronation is automatically assumed to be fictitious by most Egyptologists. However, numerous surviving images and texts attest to similar activities by the Egyptian gods for other kings. The Egyptians did not specify in writing the exact mechanisms of the gods' participation. Nor should we expect them to have pulled the veil from such sacred goings-on. Perhaps confrontations with Amen during festivals, in the innermost sanctuaries of Karnak Temple, could only happen after sleep deprivation, inebriation, or drug use, or by some other method that allowed the participants to perceive the occurrence of a supernatural meeting, even some kind of priestly possession in which the god was believed to enter the living body of a man who took on the role. Religious mysticism created real experiences for the ancient Egyptians, and only a skeptic would say that such sacred rites were the work of cold political manipulation alone. After all, the ideology most useful for maintaining control is always the one people believe.

After the numerous crowns were positioned upon her head and the many instruments of power were placed in her hands, one after another, Amen and her father granted Hatshepsut her royal titulary—the five names with which only a king was honored. To mark her initiation into the profound mysteries of kingship, the new female king formally changed her birth name from "Hatshepsut" to "Khenemetenamen Hatshepsut," which, although unpronounceable for most of us, essentially meant "Hatshepsut, United with Amen," communicating that her spirit had mingled with the very mind of the god Amen through a divine communion. Indeed, the grammatical form is instructive, because the verb *khenem*, "to unite with," has a feminine *-t* ending here, indicating that the Egyptians were up-front about the fact that a woman had merged with the masculine god Amen.[18] There was no subterfuge about her femininity in her new royal names, but her womanly core was now linked with a masculine god through her kingship. Hatshepsut's first suggestion of sexual ambiguity was in this name change.

She had already taken on her throne name before the coronation; the precise meaning of *Maatkare* is still disputed, but it could be read as "the Soul of Re Is Truth," or even "the Soul of Re Is Ma'at," meaning that the goddess Ma'at was at the core of the sun god's essence. The name was enclosed within an oval, what Egyptologists call a cartouche, as was the name Hatshepsut. Hatshepsut was now the proud owner of not one cartouche name, as all other royal women possessed, but two, in the manner of a masculine king.

Whether Hatshepsut herself chose the throne name or it was the invention of her priests and other advisers, she was the first king to incorporate the element Ma'at into a royal name, implying that at the heart of the sun god's power was a feminine entity, Ma'at, the source that was believed to keep the cosmos straight and true. Names were believed to capture a person's essence, and with this new label Hatshepsut herself became the force of truth within the sun god, an entity that acted to maintain order in the universe. Indeed, she was not only claiming to be a manifestation of the sun's life force, as any king might, but also declaring herself to be a female expression of that solarism. Hatshepsut's throne name communicated to her people that her kingship was undoubtedly feminine, and that feminine justice was necessary to maintain life with proper order, judgment, and continuance.

This Maatkare throne name would forever be linked to Hatshepsut at her most powerful, when she was finally able to transform the unceremonious power of a regent into the formalized power of a king. She received three other throne names at her coronation, and each one clarifies that Hatshepsut was not running away from the issue of her aberrant femininity as king but standing her ground and fighting back with cleverness and theological reason. Traditionally, the Egyptians had formed royal names evocative of masculine abilities, names like Strong Bull (Ka-nakht), which tied Egypt to the sexual potential of its leader. Hatshepsut lacked the required male equipment, of course, to pull off a name like Strong Bull, but she could become Useret-kau (Powerful of Ka Spirits), as in her Horus name, using a similar-sounding word—not *ka* meaning "bull" but *ka* meaning "spirit"—to denote the mystical power of a god, if not the physical aspects of that power.

Her *nebty* name,[19] Wadjyt-renput (Green of Years, or Prosperous of Years), is essentially a theological argument that her presence would make everyone rich, but it also astutely includes another female element, the cobra goddess Wadjyt. And her last name, the Golden Horus name, Netjeret-khau (Divine of Appearances), combines her female divinity (*netjeret*) with the masculine ability to be regenerated (*khau*, "appear in glory") like the sun god himself at dawn.

If there were dissenters among the intelligentsia who had the knowledge to dissect and critique Hatshepsut's feminine kingship, they were up against some clever theologians. Whoever invented her royal names was ingenious enough to take the male elements—*ka* (spirit), *khau* (appearances), Re (the sun god)—and attach each to a feminine base. Hatshepsut's names always retained the feminine -*t*. She and her priests knew her limitations as a woman and seemed interested in flexibility rather than deceit. She became king in name and title, but she knew that she could not transform into a king's masculine body. She couldn't impregnate a harem of women with any divine seed. There was no need for her royal names to point out those deficiencies or to lie about her true nature. Instead, she and her priests focused on how her femininity could coalesce with and complement masculine powers.

An Egyptian king's masculine sexual abilities likened him to Atum, the god who, through sexual activity with himself, created his own being and the first void in which the civilized universe was placed. Kings were meant to perform the same sexual activity, and although we have no evidence that Egyptian monarchs actually did perform masturbatory rituals in the temples, we know that sexual congress with their many wives took on a similar sacred meaning. A king's masculinity was also meant to liken him to Osiris, the god who sexually re-created himself after his murder through yet another celebrated act of masturbation. What's more, the Egyptian king was also believed to be a manifestation of the sun god Re, who was thought to impregnate his own mother with his future self as he set in the west. It was this power of never-ending renewal that the Egyptian king was meant to embody in his own person, so that when one monarch died, his future self, his son, would take his place in a constant line of rule.

The king's manly loins allowed him to continue the royal line—the essence of rule for Egypt, with father following son and so on. According to Egyptian belief, a woman was not capable of such regeneration: she could contain and gestate new life, but she could not create it. She could protect her father and brother and son with all the vicious weapons in her arsenal, but, unlike a masculine creator in a harem, she could not engender her future self. Ontologically, Hatshepsut's feminine kingship was a serious theological obstacle.

From the very beginnings of her reign, Hatshepsut decided that the best defense was a good offense and conveyed to her people what she was able to do in this kingship that a man could not. She could channel the fierce protective powers of the goddesses who spewed fire at the enemies of Re and devoured the rebels, slaking their thirst with the blood of their adversaries, a fact she alluded to by incorporating these goddesses and their destructive-protective powers into her royal names. Ma'at, Wosret, and Wadjyt were all cobra goddesses who could attach to the brow of their master, ready to protect by spitting heat and poison at enemies. Perhaps these names were even meant to calm the fears of some of her priests and officials, because their meaning suggests that Hatshepsut's most important role was to safeguard her father, the sun god Re, and by extension her nephew, the boy king Thutmose III. Her names clarify that she was not progenitor, in the strict masculine sense of dynastic succession, but guardian of her family's continuance. Even dissenters could have little argument with that fact.

Why, then, did Hatshepsut take this momentous step, given all its religious impediments, if she never intended to rule on her own but only alongside another king? Why not just continue the informal regency? Thutmose III was probably under ten years of age when Hatshepsut was finally crowned. Perhaps she decided to make her move before it was too late, while her co-king was still too young to understand that her coronation meant an implicit demotion for him, cementing the relationship's inequality before he gained more maturity. Or, more likely, Hatshepsut required the formality of kingship to keep any hold on her authority.

Hatshepsut was not directly related to him. She was just his aunt. Her daughter was still not old enough for sexual congress with the young king, so there could be no marriage between them to cement her regency. Indeed, the young king still needed seven or more years until he finally reached maturity—an eternity in ancient lifetimes.

The *how* of Hatshepsut's rise to kingship can be reconstructed, at least partially; the *why* is cloaked by her own ideological depiction of it and further complicated by our own ambivalent and distrustful understandings of female power. Hatshepsut is often said to have taken steps toward the kingship out of insatiability for more power, and, in particular, for a more precisely defined power. For many Egyptologists of the last generation at least, the reason is ambition—the problematic determination of a woman attempting to take something that did not, by right, belong to her. But if we step back and look at the whole, it is possible to imagine that the Egyptian system of political-religious power itself demanded these deliberate moves. She had the support to climb this high from priests and officials who held key positions but were fearful of losing those offices if a new dynasty came to the throne; these men were apparently so troubled by Thutmose III's immature kingship that they were ready to support the most unorthodox political move possible to keep Hatshepsut in power.

We do not know the details that demanded her formal declaration of rule, but if nothing else, Hatshepsut's rise to the kingship indicates that she was a valued, essential leader, and that people were willing to rewrite the sacred rules of this highest office to accommodate her unconventional rule. She fell into the leadership role early on with the death of her husband, out of necessity, only to see it snowballing into something larger than anyone could have foreseen. She would have had no choice but to keep moving forward. Hatshepsut, and those around her, put all the pieces in place for her unprecedented authority without extravagant scheming or deal making or subterfuge. Her coronation made the change in her status irrevocable: the king died in his holy office, either naturally or unnaturally. There was no such thing as abdication in ancient Egypt.

However it was decided that Hatshepsut would actually ascend the throne, it happened. Whether it was her idea or that of someone in her retinue—the First High Priest of Amen, or Senenmut, or her own mother—all we have are oracular and ideological texts that tell us the choice was the god Amen's and that his divine image selected her at his temple at Thebes to rule. It was a radical idea for a woman to even consider, and there must have been good reason for Hatshepsut to make such a bold move. When Thutmose II died, Hatshepsut was left in a real predicament. If she gave up the God's Wife of Amen duty, she would jeopardize her access to power in Thebes and thus her regency for young Thutmose III. She would have no formal title connecting her to the current king, nothing of value that would allow her to stay in control of Egypt. We cannot forget that Hatshepsut was *not* the King's Mother. Perhaps it was at this point that she realized formal steps had to be taken. The new king was simply too young, and her familial connection to him was too indirect. The Thutmoside line was in jeopardy, and she needed to protect it—not for the boy king personally, but for her family and, by extension, for herself. Her accession would create a fixed means of locking down her Thutmoside authority on behalf of her dynasty for another decade or so, all in the hope that Thutmose III could procreate a viable son in the future (not ready himself to rule for another ten years hence, at least). Hatshepsut's kingship was an unusual solution, to be sure, but she knew there was some precedent for female rule when a family line died out. Why not anticipate the possibility that Thutmose III could also die young or childless? It had certainly happened before.

We can also entertain the notion that Hatshepsut believed she deserved the formal recognition of her power, plain and simple, that the kingship was meant to be hers. But this explanation is too easy—too dependent on the demands of one woman and too contingent on an entitled and avaricious character capable of steamrolling past all dissent in her path. It also demands that we believe the ancient Egyptian cultural system could have absorbed such a revolutionary mind-set: happy to go where no woman had gone before, simply because Hatshepsut wanted the credit. Personal self-indulgence was unlikely to be supported by so many for its own sake.

Hatshepsut's move to the throne was politically connected to many power players around Egypt, inextricably and profoundly linking her success to that of a core group of loyal courtiers and priests ready to follow her. Instead of seeing her rise to power as the willful and voracious machinations of one woman, we should reevaluate it as a clever tactic that bent, but did not break, the rules of an already millennia-old patriarchal monarchical system that saw father-to-son succession as encoded in the written law of the gods.

Realistically, Hatshepsut's kingship was not and could never have been something she planned at the start of her regency. She probably never contemplated this ultimate and immutable change in her fortunes. If we look at what she had already done in her regency—engaging in her day-to-day maintenance of Egypt's government, keeping the power centralized in the palace, making sure provincial governors and viceroys in Nubia paid into the system, cracking down on rebels abroad, forming ambitious building plans in temples throughout Egypt, acting as chief judge in the highest law court—we see that Hatshepsut was the only person who could now fill the position. The more she performed the duties of the king, the more she was led to the inevitable eventuality of kingship. In many ways, Hatshepsut was only doing what she was best at: running the richest country in the ancient world. In the end, she formally defined that role. Hatshepsut's kingship provides us with the ultimate case of merit over ambition. It was a collection of smaller, piecemeal decisions that led to the great prize, and she only became king because she was the last, best candidate to see to Egypt's well-being in a time of dynastic crisis. For Hatshepsut, it was the process of doing kingly things that led to her coronation.

And now that circumstances had prepared (or propelled) Hatshepsut to take control of Egypt in a lawfully recognized way, she would have to keep control of a more complicated situation than before, using every tool at her disposal and every official in her loyal following to justify a highly unconventional, but soon openly recognized, co-kingship between a woman and a boy. In some ways, Hatshepsut made her job that much harder by officially taking the crowns and scepters of this holy office when it was already occupied. This was a profound transitional moment for Egypt, when its power brokers stared down an abyss of uncertainty and emerged with an avant-garde solution. The entire court must have known that a Hatshepsut kingship and a coregency turned on its head would be highly unorthodox, but the priests, viziers, treasurers—everyone who was anyone—seem to have jumped on board anyway. And thus they all, Hatshepsut included, needed to shift responsibility for this crazy decision away from themselves. It was vital that this move be seen as a choice made by the gods, not by men (and certainly not by one woman). Indeed, Hatshepsut's first steps to the kingship took place in the gods' presence and with their blessing, through the oracles in the temple and through divine congress with her own dead father, Thutmose I.

We might hold a dubious view of such a strategy, to be sure, but ideology can contain both political and religious motivations simultaneously. Hatshepsut almost certainly believed in the intervention of the gods in her daily life, as well as in cosmic events, and thus she used what the Egyptians called a *biayt*, a "miracle" or a "revelation," to claim her power officially.[20] Hatshepsut created some sacred theater so that the sanctity of her rule was legitimized and witnessed before many eyes. In the coming years, she would write many more mythologies about her kingship's creation—how her father chose her personally, presented her to his courtiers, and gave her the royal names of a king—and about her divine conception through holy union between her mother and the god Amen himself, when he merged into the body of her sacred father, Thutmose I.

To cement her coronation, Hatshepsut transformed the profundity of the moment into material reality—two granite monoliths erected in Karnak Temple—proof of her god-given grace because the obelisks had been ordered years prior. Hatshepsut made it look as if she had planned her royal transformation far in advance of its occurrence, that she had long foreseen her eventual rise in formally witnessed power. In reality, these obelisks had likely been commissioned to cement the new kingship of her young charge, King Thutmose III, and were only later transferred to her when she was able to step into the kingship. When the monoliths came out of the quarry, Hatshepsut decided to have them inscribed for herself, not Thutmose III, and placed them in one of the most public locations at Egypt's grandest temple to proclaim her accomplishment.[21] It is hard for us to understand, with our rapidly evolving technology and constant invention, but in the Egyptian mind the creation of an obelisk was nothing short of a wonder, an achievement that proved beyond a doubt that the king responsible was truly blessed. Only a king thus graced by gods could have achieved such a feat, to place monoliths of the hardest granite, stone not cut by copper chisels, ten stories high, in the midst of the gods. The obelisks were evocative of masculine virility, to be sure, but also of sunlight itself. Hatshepsut and her world believed them to be shafts of light that linked their temple with the gods of heaven. These obelisks would mark her kingship—officially and publicly.

Hatshepsut did not just remake herself with her unprecedented coronation. She also transformed, and implicitly demoted, her new "co-king." Thutmose's name was changed, explicitly transferring his power from one who ruled alone to one who worked with another. Hatshepsut altered her co-king's name from Menkheperre to Menkheper*ka*Re, adding the element *ka*, or "spirit." Instead of "the Manifestation of Re Is Enduring," his name was now "the Manifestation of *the Soul* of Re Is Enduring." This move was politically and religiously brilliant, at least to the Egyptian intellectuals who could understand it. The new name implied that the boy king was now one step removed from the power of the sun, that he was no longer a direct manifestation of the sun itself but only the embodiment of part of its power, its *ka*.[22] The name change might even imply that the boy king was crowned anew alongside his mistress, a ritual procedure that demanded a downgrading in rank.

Hatshepsut may have been holding all the cards vis-à-vis her co-king, but even after her initiation into the mysteries, the coronation, the name changes, and the clever masculine-feminine arguments, she still had a problem. She was the senior king, and yet she had come to the throne second.

Hatshepsut had a clever strategy for managing this complication. Much as she co-opted traditional masculine titles by injecting a feminine element, now she cannily played with the way her co-king's reign was measured, using his established chronology—something sacred and well known to the contemporary Egyptians—to retroactively support her rule. Rather than begin a new sequence of reign dates following her coronation, she simply adopted Thutmose III's timeline as her own. Thus the date of her coronation was immaterial. His year 7 became her year 7, with the inferred meaning that she had been king even before her own recognized accession, that she had already taken the reins of power in the eyes of the gods from the moment of her husband's death. Some Egyptologists have seen her dating methods as disingenuous and deceptive—to the Egyptians, and to the gods. How could she claim royal years of rule

before her coronation? But this woman's informal power was without contest. To date the beginning of her own reign later, within the reign of the
young Thutmose III, implied a divine mistake—because, for the ancient
Egyptians, to be the king was to be the Good God. Or, put another way, the
divinity that had been inside of her since her conception had finally been
officially recognized and revealed. But it had always been there.

Hatshepsut was seated upon the throne, holding the instruments of
Egyptian kingship and acting as a true, divinely elected Horus over all of
Egypt. And Thutmose III had inexorably been transformed into a secondary co-king, a monarch who worked alongside another rather than ruling
on his own. Although he was only a boy, this sacred coronation must have
signaled to him what he already knew—that Hatshepsut ruled with the
gods' favor and was the most prepared to keep Egypt safe, prosperous, and
righteous. After the coronation, when Hatshepsut finally sat on a throne
taller than his own, in the place of honor formerly reserved for him, wearing king's crowns like his, Thutmose most likely noticed the curious and
awed looks of courtiers and priests as they entered the audience chamber;
he watched, as her majesty conducted business, and saw how his nascent
kingship was dependent on her mature authority.

Or perhaps the crowning made no difference to him and to his daily
life, except for the demands on his time; weeks of coronation rituals and
celebrations in multiple towns throughout Egypt must have annoyed the
boy. If Hatshepsut had been making all the decisions during his tenure
as king, then some formal changes in thrones and headgear and names
might have constituted only superficial changes to this child's life. But he
likely sat on the throne beside her during their first "sitting," and even
though young, he must have perceived that something important in his
life had shifted.

If he had previously been bratty and imperial in tone with his aunt,
now was the time to change his behavior. There is little indication of any
hostilities, but we do see a suggestion of increased distance between the
two monarchs. At the inception of Hatshepsut's kingship, Thutmose III
appears only occasionally on her commissioned monumental constructions. Hatshepsut was so intent on laying the ideological foundation for
her own odd kingship that she was essentially forced to exclude the king
who already occupied the throne. Did the choices visible in her building

program find a way into her policy decisions? Perhaps Thutmose III was sent off to the north to further his education in the ancient cities of Memphis and Heliopolis, away from Hatshepsut, who was busy exploiting the Amen theology of Thebes to support the weight of her new crown.

The coronation was clearly meaningful to Hatshepsut, because she ordered the exclusive and mysterious rites depicted in all their ritual detail in carved stone reliefs at Karnak and Deir el-Bahri, a first for any Egyptian king: image after image shows her kneeling before the different gods while they place the various crowns on her head and arm her with assorted regalia; speeches praising Hatshepsut's abilities and inherent worth are chiseled into the quartzite, limestone, and sandstone. Hatshepsut ordered her artisans to express her person and action in a rather bland and expected way, in line with two thousand years of royal tradition, but she knew better than anyone that the mere fact that it had happened at all—that a woman was crowned king of Egypt during a time of peace and prosperity, and that she could publicly claim it—was unequaled. Even though she tried to fit herself into previous traditions, Hatshepsut's multiple and overt representations of this moment reveal that she knew her kingship was not only absolutely unprecedented, but something that needed to be broadcast widely.[23]

As king, Hatshepsut took up her new role as dominant protector with energy, and as such she gave special attention to Egypt's goddesses. Perhaps believing that her power stemmed from the divine feminine, capable of both great destruction and soft tenderness, she embellished the temples of these goddesses, rebuilding those in ruin, and even elevating some divinities to a higher level with grand buildings and new festivals. The goddess Mut of Thebes was a beneficiary of Hatshepsut's pious devotion. *Mut* literally means "mother," but she was also believed to be the consort of the god Amen. Mut had her own temple precinct in the larger Karnak complex, and indeed, the foundations of many stone buildings in Mut's temple space were created by Hatshepsut.[24] Mut was depicted wearing the double crown, and it is likely that Hatshepsut, as Lady of the Two Lands, felt a kinship with this celestial being, enough to link her own feminine kingship with Mut's great and ferocious power. Hatshepsut

probably felt a real connection to this lioness divinity, performing countless rituals in the goddess's sanctuary, offering meals, and, most important, offering the goddess beer, getting her drunk so that she would not
unleash her ferocious power on Egypt's people.

But King Hatshepsut never neglected Amen, her father, the god
she believed had placed her in this position in the first place; and more
than to any divinity in the land, she strengthened her link to the god of
Thebes. The name "Amen" means "hidden one," and his true nature was
thought to be concealed. Hatshepsut, too, claimed obliquely that her own
true character as king had been hidden, only to be revealed as she gradu-
ally moved closer to the throne. One of her later obelisks reads that she is
"Maatkare, the shining image of Amen, whom he made appear as King
upon the throne of Horus, in front of the holies of the palace, whom the
Great Ennead nursed to be mistress of the circuit of the sun's disk."[25] She
thus claims to be the visible manifestation of the god Amen, who was believed to exist before creation itself; that is, he represented unformed potential that could become anything—mother or father, man or woman,
child or adult, animal or human. This god was thought to permeate everything and everyone. Amen's existence depended on a body created from
nothingness, from infinity, from darkness, within the primeval waters.
And he did this miraculously, from his own divine plan, from the potentiality of the universe.

The inscriptions on the surface of this same later obelisk clarify
Hatshepsut's new, divine place in the cosmos:

I have made this with a loving heart for my father, Amun, having entered
into his initiation of the First Occasion and having experienced his impressive efficacy. I have not been forgetful of any project he has decreed. For My
Majesty knows he is divine, and I have done it by his command. He is the
one who guides me. I could not have imagined the work without his acting:
he is the one who gives the directions.

Nor have I slept because of his temple. I do not stray from what he has
commanded. My heart is perceptive on behalf of my father, and I have access to his mind's knowledge. I have not turned my back on the town of the
Lord to the Limit but paid attention to it. For I know that Karnak is heaven
on earth, the sacred elevation of the First Occasion, the Eye of the Lord to

the Limit—his favorite place, which bears his perfection and gathers his
followers.[26]

Hatshepsut thus tells her people that she was able to converse personally with the creator god Amen-Re, to witness the circumstances of his
First Time—that is, to see and understand his masturbatory creation of
himself and of the universe itself. In Egypt, creation was an ongoing process, not a single origin story that happened once at the beginning of history, like the Bible's Genesis. In Egyptian belief, the king had to construct
the right conditions for the god to manifest himself and the world continuously. According to her obelisk texts, Hatshepsut's kingly transformation
allowed her to participate in and absorb mysteries that she could not before. This mystical aspect of her coronation should not be downplayed; it
provided one-to-one contact with the god.

These later obelisk inscriptions are clear: Hatshepsut wanted everyone to know that she was only doing as Amen, her father, had commanded, that she would continue to perform any work that he required,
and that she would act according to his guidance. She was advertising to
her people that she had glimpsed the will of Amen's heart. She was telling
everyone, by building this connection to the sky itself, that she was truly
in communion with the workings of the cosmos. For her, Karnak Temple
was the epicenter of Amen's creation, the place where heaven and earth
joined, the sacred structure that allowed Amen to manifest himself and
his great creative powers in the world of humanity. Hatshepsut was making some bold statements—not of martial powers or financial authority,
but of access to the innermost workings of a god's heart and to the secret
nature of the universe itself. She had tapped into the source.

This was a rich ideology that Hatshepsut could exploit. She used the
mythology of Amen to support a flexible view of her own hidden and inter-
nalized gender, lending a mythical, semidivine connotation to the adaptations demanded for her to manifest kingship. Atum-Re (of Heliopolis)
and Osiris (of Abydos) were given their due during her reign, but evidence
suggests that Hatshepsut saw in the god Amen an elasticity and an ambiguity that worked well for her own feminine rule.[27] To cement her unconventional kingship, Hatshepsut used her deep theological training to find
models that reinforced her own emerging androgyny. In some later texts,
Amen was known as a father and a mother simultaneously, and Hatshep-

sut fit herself into this indistinctness. Indeed, Amen had a feminine counterpart named Amenet, who was understood to be a kind of consort but, more correctly, was herself a feminine manifestation of the Great God.[28]

Hatshepsut was intimately aware of Amen's many forms and names, many of them invested with great masculine powers of fecundity and creation. She was able to link herself as a feminine complement to each of them, allowing her kingship to force a nuance of gendered royal divinity never seen before, as "Khenemet-Amen Hatshepsut, who lives forever, the daughter of Amen-Re, his beloved, his only one who came from him, shining image of the Lord of All, whose beauty was fashioned by the powers of Heliopolis."[29] She sometimes represented herself as a ruler with masculine/feminine powers, and in one text she is told: "They allow your borders to reach to the extent of the heavens, to the borders of deep darkness. The Two Lands are filled with the children of your children, great is the count of your seed."[30]

In keeping with her new role as caretaker of divine creation, Hatshepsut was the first known king to publish depictions and texts of the divine Opet festival. During these rites, priests carried the veiled statue of Amen-Re the two miles from Karnak to Luxor Temple to meld with the sexualized forms of the god—Amenkamutef and Amenemipet. Hatshepsut surrounded this procession with excess and embellishments.[31] Amen's connection with the sun god, Re—joined as a kind of superdivinity forming the synchronized Amen-Re at Karnak Temple—also allowed her to tap into the solar aspects of divine kingship as sun priest. Working within this solar theology, Hatshepsut worshipped and built temples for the sun god's daughters—the Eyes of Re—identifying with their ruthless violence and ferocity in protection of the sun. She underscored the ability of the female divinity to excite the sun god through laughter, love, and sexuality. Hatshepsut understood that it was the goddess who woke the god from his deathlike sleep, who fed him, and who incited him to sexual rebirth. This new, female kingship was nothing if not theological, and Hatshepsut's interpretations of its difference tapped into the elemental powers present in the Egyptian people's lives, the forces that dispel darkness, warm the skin, flood the earth, and allow the crops to grow. Her pious connection to Amen-Re allowed access to both masculine and feminine power, to both visible and hidden authority, un-like any monarch that had come before.

Hatshepsut's royal transformation was a success. She had begun her transition years before, culminating with the coronation when everyone gathered in the temple to see her blessed by the gods. Now, in the palace throne room, she presented her people with a more intimate, but still ceremonial, view of her alteration. They could see her plainly now that she was removed from the mysterious temple atmosphere filled with the haze of incense, burnt offerings, and the sharp angles of the rising or setting sun's rays. Here in the palace there were no lengthy ritual activities that shielded the object of venera-tion from the viewing audience's eyes. Within the confines of the throne room, one could address and speak to the king, assuming one used the correct formalities and conventions. Some officials of high rank were al-lowed even more intimate conversation, to the extent that they could dis-agree with the royal sovereign if the proper decorum was observed. After the overwrought ritual weight of the coronation, it was probably a relief to Hatshepsut and her officials to get down to the brass tacks of politics and finance.

At her first royal "sitting," the transformed Hatshepsut graced her throne in the presence of the most elite officials, priests, and courtiers. The gilded chair was placed upon a dais that made her higher than any-one standing in the audience hall; it may have been situated within a gilded pavilion that surrounded her person with divine imagery of ances-tor kings. She wore one of the many fabulous crowns in her arsenal and perhaps clutched her royal scepters. This was a woman who had grown up with court protocol and its accoutrements, and even in her unprecedented position as king, it is likely that she felt familiar not only with the weight of her crown and the heft of the religious instruments but also with the way she should hold her body and watch her audience with purpose.

She may have announced some of her royal policies and plans to her elites here for the first time. This formal moment would have been neces-sary for a legitimization of her new position, so that everyone could see, with their own eyes, what she had become and how she would behave among them. The Egyptians excelled in providing visual trappings that recast a normal human as an extraordinary, divinized being. Everything about this scene—from the throne and its height to the pavilion and its richness, to her crowns, kilts, sandals, and eye makeup, to the strange confluence of masculine royal regalia on an elite woman—separated her from them, making her seem superhuman and beyond their criticism.

Hatshepsut had already spent years sitting in this very room, discussing strategies with her generals, conferring over the grain tax for a specific region, or reviewing options for dealing with a troublesome new governor in the delta. But now her clothing and regalia had changed. Her names were altered and enhanced. Her place on the dais was superior. Yet these were only surface modifications. In the minds of the ancient Egyptians who served her, her very person had been revealed as a living god, a being that now had one-to-one contact with the mind of Amen. With those crowns now upon her head, it is probable that most of her officials would have treated her differently than they had before.

And the changes rippled through the court as her coronation transformed the stations of those around her. Some moved down, like Thutmose III, demoted to a junior king; others, like her daughter, moved up. Nefrure now assumed the role of God's Wife of Amen at around nine years of age, possibly just old enough to activate and formalize her sexual duties to the god and certainly old enough for improvement in her economic and political stature. With this position, Nefrure would have gained her own household, her own steward, her own income, and her own responsibilities. As the newly minted King's Daughter to Hatshepsut and King's Sister to Thutmose III, her position as God's Wife was doubly legitimized; she was directly related to both co-kings. Indeed, the young girl must have stood behind her mother during festival encounters with the god, just as Hatshepsut had done during the reign of Thutmose II. If Nefrure and her mother were close, the girl may have enjoyed the intimate company as they performed many rituals together. Or perhaps she now perceived herself to be yet another step removed from the powerful woman who was never allowed the leisure to be a devoted and doting maternal presence in the first place.

Hatshepsut's mother, Ahmes, was likely still alive to witness the miraculous transformation of the daughter she may have once wished was born a son. After Hatshepsut became king, she named Ahmes as King's Mother, a title to which the dowager queen could never previously claim ownership, thus further diminishing the authority of Thutmose III's mother, Isis. Now there were two women in the royal palaces who held the same title, which was certainly a strange reality for everyone around them; the two co-kings were close enough in age that both King's Mothers were still living. Although there is absolutely no evidence that Isis had been try-ing to wrest the regency from Hatshepsut or that she was a competitor for power, Hatshepsut seems to have been happy to demote Isis as she placed her mother, instead of Isis, in important reliefs. Perhaps the women resided in different cities or palaces, thereby limiting any unpredictable emotions—empathy, apathy, or bitterness—Isis may have felt when she beheld Ahmes's change in status and encroachment on her territory.

If we accept that Ahmes was still alive at this time, as the evidence indeed suggests,[32] then the older queen had watched as her daughter as-cended through the ranks over the years: from young princess to God's Wife of Amen to King's Great Wife during the reign of Thutmose II, to re-gent during the early years of Thutmose III. Her little girl had developed into a skilled stateswoman. Now the unprecedented had happened, and Ahmes can't have been anything but amazed. Her daughter was sitting on the throne of Egypt beside another king.

Hapuseneb, the First High Priest of Amen, must have approved Hatshepsut's kingship, given all the support she was able to garner from the Amen priesthood. For all we know, Amen's oracles were genuinely re-ceived, and Hapuseneb truly believed in his heart that the gods wanted Hatshepsut to be king, making it necessary to defy the obvious gender requirement, in order to safeguard the Thutmoside line. Or Hapuseneb may have engineered the oracles that foretold Hatshepsut's authority by providing the means for the god Amen-Re to actually speak to her and mark her for rule in public. If this high priest was willing to countenance Hatshepsut's unconventional reign, he was rewarded for doing so. Given that reality, we can imagine that the other high priests throughout the Two Lands—in Heliopolis, in Memphis, in Aswan, in Abydos—may have fallen in step as well.

Regardless of likely remuneration for their service and loyalty, Hatshepsut likely maintained an intimate working relationship with her priests, particularly at the Amen temple in Karnak. She had associ-ated with the most powerful members of the priesthood from a young age and become a king on whom they could depend absolutely. They had fostered her temple building, festival activity, and even theological questions. As God's Wife, Hatshepsut had been part of the most important creative rituals in their presence, and now that she was king, they trusted her to keep the process of creation ongoing. In return, she trusted them to form a theological means for her to maintain her authority and to create a sacred theatrical stage to display Amen's acceptance of her rule. She may have even talked with these priests about the precedent of Sobeknefru, the last woman to serve as Egypt's sovereign, a few hundred years before. Hatshepsut and her priestly supporters seem to have come to an understanding that the gods could indeed accept female power in special circumstances, and her unusual rule forced closer contact with those mysteries of a woman in power.

Palace officials like Senenmut and Ahmose Pennekhbet would have likely been pleased by Hatshepsut's kingship, despite its unorthodoxy, because their loyalty was abundantly compensated. Both of these men happened to find themselves in the right place at the right time. Senenmut had clawed his way up the social hierarchy to attain his position of authority, while Ahmose Pennekhbet was born to the life of elite officialdom and gentle responsibilities. Their mistress, Hatshepsut, was now the most powerful person in the land, and her eldest daughter and their pupil, Nefrure, was a wealthy priestess, with a palace, a treasury, and servants of her own to be managed. There was no reason for either of them to object to Hatshepsut's rule on behalf of Thutmose III or on the grounds of gender.

Harder to answer is how the elites beyond Thebes—in cities like Memphis, Heliopolis, and Aswan—who subscribed to their own protocols and cultural understandings, reacted to Hatshepsut's accession. Presumably Hatshepsut's reach was long, because apparently she was able to influence officials even hundreds of miles away by rewarding dependability and trustworthiness with prosperous positions, and by punishing dissenters and complainers with neglect and dismissal. Whatever the level of disgruntlement at this female kingship among the elites—and there may certainly have been some real displeasure because Hatshepsut repeatedly had the line "he who shall do her homage shall live, he who shall speak evil in blasphemy of her Majesty shall die"[33] carved into her later temple at Deir el-Bahri—we know that there were more than enough officials in cities around Egypt who were willing to work with this new situation and with this new mistress, certainly enough to keep the ranks of nonsupporters suppressed.

Lower-level bureaucrats may not have even understood the political intricacies of Hatshepsut's rise to power, and it was not their place to question their superiors, let alone their gods. Although many of them may have been shocked by the very notion of a woman taking the throne, none of them left any records of displeasure. Such men were scrappy survivors who aimed to please the boss above them, not the king in a palace far away. With such a young boy on the throne, even these bureaucrats would have seen the value of guaranteeing Hatshepsut's continued authority for the long years to come while waiting for Thutmose to grow into his office and produce his own new and viable heir. Everybody knew that a change in rule could mean a shake-up in palace positions.

How did the larger population of Thebes, the peasants and craftsmen, react to seeing their mistress crowned as king and appearing before them in festivals or offering to the gods with no intercession from a man? Were they shocked, or did they assume that their betters understood what was needed? Perhaps they could only catch a glimpse of her figure through the throngs of onlookers—slim and regal, wearing a long linen dress, with her crown atop a short, round wig—as she and her young co-king led religious processions of the gilded barque along the sacred pathways, accompanying the god Amen from the temple gates out to the river quay. It was certainly not a sight they were accustomed to, but in the eyes of the peasants Hatshepsut was probably just as unreachable and mystical as any other monarch. Whether she was male or female probably made little difference to them if their crops continued to thrive and they were paid for their work.

We can only scratch the surface of ancient Egyptian opinion about this unprecedented kingship by looking at the elite's actions vis-à-vis their mistress, Hatshepsut: there is absolutely no evidence of insurrection, rebellion, or coup during her reign. Without a doubt, Hatshepsut's officials cooperated to keep the royal mythology of divine kingship alive, recognizing that it was in their best interest to do so, given the political structures that rewarded them for staying in line with the program. The systems and incentives weren't in place in ancient Egypt for a wealthy landowner to raise an army, rise up as a warlord, and claim the throne by force, which cut down on enticements to plot and conspire against the royal family. Even if people were unhappy about Hatshepsut's rule, they weren't so dissatisfied that they were going to do anything about it.

Unlike the decentralized political systems in ancient Syria-Palestine, Mesopotamia, Greece, and Rome that allowed, encouraged, and even thrived on extreme—and often violent—political aggression, ancient Egyptian society did not tolerate, much less foster, discussions of their ruler's ineptitude, sexual deviance, mental instabilities, or other causes for removal. Egyptology lacks any intimate discussion of royal failures, intrigue, inter- or intra-family antagonism. Regicide happened so rarely that in the twenty-eight hundred years before the Ptolemaic period, Egyptologists can count only two verifiable cases—Amenemhet I of the Twelfth Dynasty and Ramses III of the Twentieth Dynasty—and neither was discussed nor recorded except in the most oblique of terms. And it was the same with dynastic usurpation. For example, we have no idea how Hatshepsut's father, Thutmose I, came to the throne. It is simply assumed that Amenhotep I's line petered out and that Thutmose I stepped in as a close relative to the stagnant dynastic line. But it remains in the realm of possibility that Hatshepsut's father took the throne with the backing of his armies, even if we have no evidence of it. In such cases, historians are limited to what the ancient people chose to tell, after all. And the ancient Egyptians were masters at producing selective historical accounts about an unassailable and protected kingship.

Despite all of this, some problematic evidence suggests that Hatshepsut herself may have been intending to push Thutmose III out of the picture, maybe even completely. Recovered blocks from Karnak Temple indicate that the names of the boy king were replaced with those of Hatshepsut's dead husband, Thutmose II, after she became king.[34] This is the only temple of Hatshepsut's from which Thutmose III's images were expelled, but it was located in the core of Amen's realm at Thebes. Perhaps Hatshepsut was only trying to create a clearer connection to her own political power early in her reign, telling people through stone monuments that she ruled because of her connection to her dead husband, thus removing the bothersome child who also inhabited the throne. But her erasure of his names might instead indicate something more sinister.

Here we have fascinating evidence of King Hatshepsut in a rare moment of indecision. She seems to waffle a bit—or at least explore different solutions—until, for whatever reason, not long after she had Thutmose III formally erased, she decided to put him back into her official temple reliefs. Perhaps she tried to rule without his presence for a short time, but then realized that this boy was her only political means to keeping the throne. Hatshepsut would have to find another way to solidify her base of ideological power as a female king. Her unconventional reign demanded some Egyptian conventionality. She had just embarked upon the highest-stakes move any woman had made in the history of human politics. With this novel and irregular kingship, she had arguably created more problems than she had solved. She would need to unite all her abilities in the years to come—ideological, economic, military, and political—to maintain what she had wrought.[35]

SIX

Keeping the Kingship

Temple activity had been bred into Thutmose III, and according to many temple reliefs, Hatshepsut and her co-king performed their royal rituals together in tandem. On great feast days, crowds would have stood in temple courtyards or before mighty pylons, watching aunt and nephew lead enormous processions. The divine barque belonging to Amen followed, with dozens of priests bearing the mighty weight of this sacred portable shrine made of Lebanese cedar, gold, and precious stones. Many times a year, the two monarchs were meant to walk from Karnak down the sacred processional way side by side, each with a staff surmounted by a ram's head, Amen's signature animal. Each monarch wore a tiered wig or a crown with a single uraeus on the brow and a *shendyt* (royal kilt) wrapped around his or her waist. During the sacred Opet festival, when the god was brought from his Karnak home to his place of rejuvenation at Luxor Temple, they had to stop at six different way stations along the route to allow Amen to rest.[1] Six times they performed complex rituals of healing and transformation for the gods. All of Egypt turned out to see the spectacle, which featured dancers and musicians along with hundreds of priests and chantresses, and to devour the temple-provided bread, cakes, and beer.

Nefrure, the King's Daughter, was likely in the presence of the two kings during most important religious occasions in Thebes. Even though

she was only a bit older than Thutmose III (maybe by a year), she had probably been the God's Wife of Amen for as long as the boy king could remember. Her duties were extensive and connected to his own. Perhaps he saw
that Nefrure practiced her role as priestess with great passion—talking to
the god, moving for him, and giving him his sexual pleasure. Perhaps Nefrure, like Hatshepsut before her, also believed she could speak with the
gods in the heavens and comprehend the wishes of the great ones in the
sky. Maybe everyone said she was gifted like her mother had been at this
age. But we have little record of what Thutmose III thought of Nefrure as
God's Wife, or even as his half sister. The record keeping was in the hands
of King Hatshepsut at this point, and she fashioned the public agenda to
her liking and Egyptian traditions.

In accordance with Egyptian convention, Hatshepsut did not provide many details about the nature of the relationships between any of
the major players. But we do know that the situation was more than a little
strange—a king still too young to rule and a female king now holding the
reins of power for him—and it probably elicited doubts, insecurities, and
even anger from Thutmose III when he was old enough to understand the
arrangement better. The two kings would share a working relationship
for many years to come, but it was an association that Hatshepsut started
on her own terms. By the time Hatshepsut was a king alongside him, the
eight- or nine-year-old boy was probably so used to her authority that her
kingship may have seemed rather natural to him. At first, it was all he
knew. Only later would he have questioned it.

As Thutmose III approached his teens and studied Egypt's history,
bureaucracy, and legal system, learned the more complex incantations in
the temple, and communed on a deeper level with the gods, he likely would
have pondered the strangeness of their joint rule. There is no record anywhere of Hatshepsut's political transformations having been explained or
justified to her young coregent, and so we have little clue as to how he may
have reacted (if at all) to the vulnerable state of affairs as a child when his
kingship was probably most in jeopardy.

Perhaps Hatshepsut's replacement of Thutmose III's names at Karnak at the beginning of her kingship can provide a small clue into the personal relationship between the two monarchs. At the time of the erasure,
Thutmose III was about ten years old. Even if she was only attempting to
remove Thutmose III ideologically, the action of cutting out his names

seems indicative of a hope that she be recognized as the sole king after the death of her husband. And if she had been willing to consider a kingship independent of Thutmose III, then perhaps she was not emotionally attached to her nephew, or at least not as connected to his ambitions and self-worth as she would have been if he were her own son. Maybe she really was trying to go it alone, working through a trial period, pushing to see the reaction of elites and high priests. But if this was her ultimate goal, it failed. She was never able to remove her co-king entirely. Her kingship would be forever stuck in a strange, hybrid partnership between a woman and a child king. Hatshepsut had to look for new strategies to work within this compulsory relationship, ones that could maintain her superior position as Thutmose III grew older.

Coregency, or rule by two kings, wasn't a revolutionary idea—it had long been established in ancient Egyptian politics.[2] Usually, the elder king appointed one of his sons to rule alongside him as a junior king, typically serving as the leader of treacherous campaigns in foreign lands. Thus the elder king could depend upon a coregency as a means of establishing a chosen successor and of sharing royal duties, allowing the younger king to direct the army while the senior king stayed at home away from all the risks such journeys entailed. A coregency also permitted on-the-job training of a king's son in some of the trickier aspects of political diplomacy and tactics. But most important for the coregency, the elder king always sat on the throne *first*, typically for many years, before appointing his preferred son to rule alongside him. It was a top-down, unequal relationship.

The coregency of Hatshepsut and Thutmose III, on the other hand, was essentially upside down.[3] Leaving aside the most deviant characteristic—that Hatshepsut was a woman—this coregency fits none of the customs. It was the junior king who had come to power first, only to be pushed out of the way by a senior king who ascended the throne after him. The senior king had previously acted as regent of the Two Lands during the junior king's infancy. For a regent to take such a step and rule senior to the youngster was more than anomalous. Thutmose III's situation was just as odd: he couldn't even play the traditional role of the younger co-king once the bizarre new dynamic settled down into day-to-day practice. He wasn't old enough to head up any campaigns or lead men into battle himself. He couldn't go off on his own to act as an extension of the "primary" king. What was his practical purpose? If war became a reality, Hatshepsut would have to go herself or appoint a trusted official to oversee it. All the onus of rule was on Hatshepsut, while all the legitimacy of rule lay with Thutmose III.

And so, facing problems that no Egyptian ruler had ever encountered, it fell upon Hatshepsut to manipulate this unusual situation to her own advantage and to the benefit of the Two Lands. The first practical quandary was a technical one: how to place her reign within time. For the Egyptians, counting the hours and years was not a practice of bureaucratic record keeping but of sacred ritual obligation. They were the first to invent the twenty-four-hour clock, and they used it not to record hours of labor or to organize a social calendar (dinner at eight) but to establish the exact moment that a specific incantation should be read, a sistrum rung, or a haunch of beef offered, all to keep the sun god on his onerous journey unscathed through the hours of day and night; the clock was first and foremost a religious tool. Regnal years—the length of rule for each king of Egypt—were used to measure longer stretches of sacred time. There were no absolute dates, no counting of years from the beginning of civilization; instead, time was defined by periods of divinely sanctioned rule. Thus hours of the day were measured as the sun god rose and set, and years were marked with the coming and passing of the chief ritualist—the king—on whom Egypt depended for its beneficial connection to the gods.

As we've already seen, Hatshepsut seems to have known that she could not count the years as her own, as any other Egyptian king would generally have done, and had to defer to Thutmose III's dating. Thus we see no mention of "Regnal Year 8 of Hatshepsut" or the like.[4] The Egyptians inscribed most monuments or stelae with "Year X, day Y of King So-and-So" to place the reader within an understood context. How could Hatshepsut, the senior king, have a regnal year 2 while her junior king, Thutmose III, was in regnal year 9? It was an existential problem for a semidivine ruler whose years of reign represented Egypt's past, present, and future.

Hatshepsut found a solution: she diligently circumvented inscribing her own regnal dates on any monuments, including a year date only when a monument or inscription depicted both co-kings together.[5] In other words, Hatshepsut required the presence of Thutmose III—in name and figure—on every dated monument and building she ever created. She could never have her own year dates because they did not fit the cultural requirements of the coregency, a reality that may have stung her, the senior partner, with its unfairness. We may see this omission as just a technicality, but to an Egyptian monarch it would mean that he had been removed from the counted and cumulative years of civilization itself.

Hatshepsut claimed the senior position in this coregency in terms of ability and age, but Thutmose III would always be senior where regnal years were concerned. With the existence of Thutmose III fundamental to her representation of herself as king, his year 5 became her year 5. It worked. In reality, she had only ever ruled as king in his presence. But at the same time, Hatshepsut's resolution to the problem of how to date her reign was a clever ideological argument, because joint dating implied that Hatshepsut's kingship began with the death of her husband, Thutmose II. Essentially, she grandfathered in the first seven years of her kingship by using Thutmose III's dates.

Hatshepsut was around twenty-four years old when she became king, and as far as we know she was a smart and vigorous woman who was trying to find balance within an unprecedented situation. One of her first strategies as king was to downplay the existence of Thutmose III and attach the legitimacy of her reign to that of his father, Thutmose II. She immediately ordered the alteration of all images showing her as a queen serving Thutmose III into representations of her as the senior king. Craftsmen traveled to temples throughout Egypt carving crowns onto her head, placing her in the position of honor vis-à-vis her nephew, and adding her royal names and titles. No longer would she be depicted as subordinate to Thutmose III. Every sacred space in Egypt was changed, especially in the cultic centers of power, where an image translated into reality and to write or depict something was to make it come into existence.

Hatshepsut had another unique problem: she had no female partner. According to deeply held ideological precepts and ritual demands, an Egyptian king needed a Great Wife. Obviously, Hatshepsut couldn't take another woman as a wife. She was one herself, and apparently the flexibility of gender could be stretched only so far in the eyes of the gods and her people. There would be no palace nurseries full of sons and daughters for Hatshepsut, no nightly visitations to the royal women's living quarters. Some rules could be bent, but the laws of nature were insurmountable. At the very least, Hatshepsut could engage Nefrure's services as her female counterpoint in ritual activity. And so we see Hatshepsut performing her religious duties in the temple with the God's Wife—offering up bloody haunches of freshly sacrificed calves, striking ritual chests with sacred implements, or chanting transformational spells to the sun god on the hour—just as the older woman had done for her dead husband and likely for her father before that. Also present in many of these temple scenes is Thutmose III. It is as if Hatshepsut needed the boy king's presence to add some normalcy to her own strange adaptations, or even to act as a surrogate, just as she required him to make sense of her regnal years. Hatshepsut was constantly reminded that fitting into this manly position of power in ideological terms demanded one clever adaptation after another.

Beyond the ritual challenges, Hatshepsut had to actively find ways to assert her strength and dominance; she was always trying to equal the accomplishments of past kings, most especially her father, Thutmose I, who had campaigned far away in Syria, even hunting elephants at Naharin and bringing ivory tusks back to Karnak as gifts for Amen. Hatshepsut decided against any manly pursuits that would expose her obvious femininity and instead looked back to any deeds of Egypt's most ancient and revered kings that she could emulate. Whether the idea came from her quiet moments communing with Amen or was a suggestion of an ambitious courtier, Hatshepsut decided to send men to the uncharted south on a dangerous expedition, dragging deconstructed ships from the Nile city of Coptos through the bone-dry Wadi Hammamat, 120 miles to the Red Sea, where the men would rebuild the ships and launch south along the coast, for a perilous sea journey of as many as 1,000 miles—an ancient Egyptian version of a voyage to the New World. Appropriately, she cloaked this journey in religious ideology. Before her team embarked, she asked the oracle of Amen for permission to travel; this semipublic moment was meant to create maximum drama, no doubt. The god replied—either by the movements or speech of the priests holding the god's barque—that she should "search out the ways to Punt. Open the roads to the terrace of myrrh. Lead the army at sea and on land (. . .) to bring the miracles from God's country to this god, who created her beauty."[6] After this divine revelation, she met with her council and decided to send the expedition under the organization of a northern treasurer named Nehesy, another one of Hatshepsut's "new men."[7]

Punt was located far to the southeast of Egypt, probably somewhere in modern-day Somalia, Djibouti, or Eritrea along the Red Sea coast.[8] An expedition to such a faraway land happened rarely in Egyptian history; the trip would have been talked about by every elite family in Egypt. Hatshepsut understood how to prove her kingship's worth to the people who mattered. She planned the journey not just to procure commodities but also to verify her rule. All previous expeditions to Punt had been ordered by kings thought to be blessed by the gods with good fortune and solid leadership skills: Sahure (Dynasty 5), Pepy I (Dynasty 6), Mentuhotep II (Dynasty 11), Amenemhat I (Dynasty 12), and Senwosret I (Dynasty 12). Hatshepsut was simply placing herself in their august company and using their ideological methods of political legitimization.

The expedition was a success and returned in year 9 of the joint reign with shiploads of incense trees, cargo holds full of incense gum rolled into little balls, precious ebony, and woods, flora, and fauna from the rain forest. The incense was a high-value commodity used for many things— burned in braziers in the temple for the god's enjoyment, used as a resin when mummifying the elite dead, and even chewed to dispel bad breath. The expedition members came back with amazing stories of the strange little chief of Punt and his massive and deformed wife. They described the bizarre small houses built upon stilts and the new fish and birds they had seen there.

When the ships docked to unload, it must have been an I-told-you-so moment for Hatshepsut that legitimized all her risky decisions thus far. She would later order dozens of images of the triumphant landing carved into her temple walls at Djeser Djeseru. She is shown sitting while the priceless goods are paraded and presented to her. Nehesy, the expedition leader, is there, too, monitoring the unpacking, and Senenmut stands beside him assisting Hatshepsut. The inscription informs the reader that all of these commodities were meant for her heavenly father, the god Amen, but the ideological payoff from this voyage for Hatshepsut, as his agent on earth, cannot be understated. Behind Hatshepsut in this temple relief is an image of her royal *ka*, understood as the spirit of kingship that moved from ruler to ruler, the sacred entity that allowed this woman to serve in Egypt's highest office. This royal essence was believed to have permeated her soul since conception, allowing the manifestation of her masculine power in a feminine body and determining the success of all her actions. In the minds of the Egyptians, the entire Punt voyage would have failed if she wasn't meant to be king. Hatshepsut had gambled the lives of hundreds of men, dozens of ships, and two years of preparation, plus another year or two waiting for the return of the voyage in a high-stakes public wager. If the expedition had failed, it might have given ammunition to her detractors. But the gamble paid off. Hatshepsut even commemorated the receipt of so much incense by rubbing it all over her body in a public temple ceremony: rare resins like the frankincense and myrrh of the Bible, worth their weight in gold.

> With her two hands, her majesty herself put the finest myrrh upon her entire body. Her perfume is the fragrance of the god, her odor is mixed with that of Punt, her skin gilded with fine gold, shining forth as do the stars, in the great wide festival court before the gaze of the entire land.[9]

Thutmose III would have been roughly eleven years old when the voyage came back, the perfect age to find inspiration in the spirit of adventure and fresh knowledge such an expedition spread throughout Egypt. Indeed, this trip seems to have functioned as a kind of Napoleonic voyage for Hatshepsut, as she commissioned artisans to record images of the strange people, jungle huts on posts, forest landscapes, unusual ocean fish, and exotic commodities.

The Punt mission's success confirmed that Hatshepsut was a shrewd stateswoman and businesswoman. Just two years after her formal accession, she had acquired in one stroke all kinds of exotica that she could use to pay off the Theban priests, her main source of ideological support. In return for the backing of her peculiar feminine kingship, she bestowed more incense on Amen's temple than Egypt had ever seen. She even brought back incense trees, roots and all, to be planted on temple grounds at Karnak and Deir el-Bahri and probably at temples throughout Egypt, thus ensuring a steady supply for succeeding generations. Hatshepsut had quickly mastered the art of public relations—first creating a splash with her coronation, then with the successful erection of obelisks from Aswan.

Now a voyage had returned from a mythical land overloaded with price-less goods for all to see.

Hatshepsut always kept an eye on practical matters, and a strong professional priesthood was a vital foundation of her continued authority. Her strategy included expanding the ministry of Amen to a size Egypt had never seen before. The position of Third High Priest of Amen was created; he would act as a lieutenant to the already existing First and Second High Priests. With riches pouring into her country from conquered territories, there was every reason for her to redistribute this new wealth by giving jobs to many of her elites—to keep them content and to tie her kingship even more closely to the temple cults around the land. Hatshepsut expanded the temples' economic health by hiring chiefs of the granary, chiefs of cattle, chiefs of the fields, construction supervisors, chiefs of the workshops, treasurers, and a bevy of mid- and low-level administrators, all of them now earning a steady and generous salary for their station under King Hatshepsut. If anyone benefited from her kingship, it was her priests and temple bureaucrats.

The professionalization of the priesthood had already begun under her father, Thutmose I, if not a bit before, but she continued the evolution on an unprecedented scale. Before, temple institutions had been run by only a few professional priests at the very top of the hierarchy. The rest of the personnel positions were filled by part-time priests and administrators who cycled in and out of service. By Hatshepsut's reign, this system was no longer sufficient for the growing temple machine, which now demanded a complex and extensive hierarchy of priests and administrators to support growing economic holdings, lavish daily rites, and luxurious seasonal festivals. And she was happy to pay for the expansion. Like so many rulers before and after her, Hatshepsut essentially bought her ideological and military base of power.

Hatshepsut was blessed with a keen understanding of the material and ideological sources of her power, but she also benefited from environmental and political circumstances. There is little or no evidence for famine or disastrous Nile floods during her reign (a happy coincidence from a modern perspective, but something that the ancient Egyptians would have seen as directly connected with her powers and legitimacy). What's more, her father, Thutmose I, had already established a growing empire in both the north and the south with a strong flow of income. Hatshepsut knew how to tap into established and successful systems, but she also had the acumen to improve them. As king, she managed her investments wisely and distributed high dividends to her people. Relentless and ruthless campaigning kept the mines and quarries open, flooding the land with gold and stones—the lifeblood of a strong Egyptian kingship—which not only advertised the semidivine status of the monarch but were also distributed as royal favors to loyal officials. She reopened exotic trade networks that had been closed for generations, and her courtiers could acquire luxury goods their fathers had never dreamed of: wines and olives from the Aegean, resins from sub-Saharan Africa, lapis lazuli from Afghanistan.

For Egypt's wealthy families, Hatshepsut supported bureaucratic lineages that could pass from father to son, allowing them to grow fat with dependable income, in addition to the high rents and taxation their tenants already paid on their home estates. Employing more craftsmen than ever before, she initiated massive temple projects throughout the land, relentlessly demanding work of the highest quality, which in turn created a sophisticated system of artisan training not seen for hundreds of years. Hatshepsut was responsible for a jobs program of gigantic proportions. Hatshepsut also professionalized her army, thereby enriching both the sons of elite officials and her own treasuries with the spoils of war.[10]

She relied on the growth of her administration to maintain her kingship, and Hatshepsut did not always bend to the will of her elites in so doing. In fact, she filled key spots with men who had little connection to the old families whose members usually filled the upper echelons of power. Senenmut was one of these new men, of course; Hatshepsut had been relying on him since she was queen to Thutmose II. Another new appointment but not necessarily a "new man" was Puyemre, the Second High Priest of Amen.[11] A third newly appointed administrator was Amenhotep, a man who became Overseer of Construction at the temple of Amen. None of the fathers of these officials had held an influential position; *sab*, "the honorable one," was their fathers' only title, and it was probably bestowed on them by their sons retroactively purely as an honorific.

Hatshepsut obviously needed officials without patrician agendas. We do not know how such new men, given their humble origins, were able to train for and land these positions of power, but they formed a key element in Hatshepsut's strategy of rule—a new class of elite for a new breed of king.

Whatever tensions may have existed between these new men and the old guard of respected and intellectual Theban families, the political realities made no allowances for petty behavior. All the evidence indicates that elites from established families worked with the new appointees. Patricians like the First High Priest of Amen, Hapuseneb, labored in ritual preparation and enactment alongside his second in command, Puyemre, even though Puyemre's family was not born patrician. In fact, Puyemre was married to Hapuseneb's daughter, the Divine Adoratrice Seniseneb.¹² Senenmut, his new steward, and Amenhotep, the new construction overseer, attended to temple business even though no evidence connects them to patrician families either. Given all the money pouring in for ostentatious projects and extravagant festivals at Karnak, Hapuseneb needed the men. And they were likely well paid for their accommodating demeanor.

When Hatshepsut assumed the throne, Senenmut's career took off: he was appointed Overseer of the House of Amen, which essentially made him steward of the entire Amen complex of Thebes, with economic and administrative oversight of the temples of Amen, Mut, and Khonsu and all the lands and income of these institutions.¹³ It was a huge promotion. The temples of Amen rivaled the richest palace institutions of the land and were counted among the largest landholders in Egypt. Many spoils of war, including proceeds from military occupations in Syria-Palestine and Nubia, went directly to these establishments, enriching treasuries with gold, precious stones, woven textiles, and grain.

As Overseer of the House of Amen, or Steward of Amen as many Egyptologists call the position, Senenmut oversaw not just the granaries of Amen but wealth of all kinds. He was the boss of the overseer of the houses of gold, the treasurers, the craftsmen and architects, and the overseer of works not just at Luxor but at Amen temples throughout Egypt. A number of highly placed officials in the Amen temple administration all reported to him, begged favors from him, and were probably somewhat afraid of him. Senenmut was essentially the CEO of Amen's great institution.

Senenmut apparently had to give up his work as Nefrure's tutor to take the new position, and Hatshepsut's old tutor Senimen was asked to care for the girl in his stead.[14] Senenmut still kept his title as her tutor, which gives us some idea of the importance he attached to the position, but undoubtedly his extensive duties did not allow him to focus on the training of one girl, no matter how prominent. The thousands of men in the employ of the god Amen-Re and the mass of riches in the god's treasuries were now his main priority.

Perhaps Senenmut felt it was acceptable to relinquish his close watch on Nefrure because she was growing up. Perhaps she had made a smooth transition to God's Wife of Amen and was able to occupy her position without contest and without Senenmut's overt protection. For her part, Hatshepsut must have thought it fitting to shift Senenmut's attention to more pressing matters. She had trusted him with the care of her palace economy, and now she was asking him to manage and influence the balance sheet of Amen's riches and his priesthood. Senenmut seemed to excel at both big-picture and detail-oriented organization, skills that were particularly useful for a treasurer of Egypt's most influential temple. He probably did not rock the boat too much in his new post. Hatshepsut's power relied on her continuing influence over the Amen priesthood. Who better to assign as the Amen temple's moneyman than her most trusted personal financier?

As large a role as Senenmut may have played in the lives of Hatshepsut and Nefrure, he had no formal connection to Thutmose III. Nonetheless, the young king would have seen the old man in the presence of Hatshepsut and Nefrure from the earliest moments of his childhood, conducting business in the audience hall, engaging the regent in discussions over treasury matters, or working with priests to administer Nefrure's income from her lands. Thutmose III may have even recognized Senenmut as one of the key players in Hatshepsut's concentration of power within her own palace walls.

If Senenmut was not an intimate of Thutmose III, it does not seem to have affected his career as a high official under Hatshepsut. The inscriptions Senenmut had carved on his statues during Hatshepsut's kingship bragged about his access to her. He claimed to be a "confidant of the king" and "the Chamberlain who speaks in privacy" and "one vigilant concerning what is brought to his attention, one who finds a solution every single day." The quartzite statue with this long inscription, now in the British Museum, also includes the assertion "The king made me great; the king enhanced me, so that I was advanced before the courtiers: and, having realized my excellence in her heart, she appointed me Chief Spokesman of her household."[15] On another statue, Senenmut maintained he was one "whose opinion the king has desired for himself, who pleases by means of what he says."[16]

There is every reason to believe that Hatshepsut's faith and trust in Senenmut were strong, if not absolute. According to one statue now in Berlin, he was the "judge of the gate in the entire land,"[17] thus he decided who entered the throne room and who communicated with the king. If Hatshepsut had an essential message to give to an official, Senenmut was likely the one to deliver it. Even going so far as to impinge on others' authority, Senenmut claimed control over the taxes of Upper and Lower Egypt, as well as other payments into and out of the palace treasuries. His responsibilities were similar to those of a vizier,[18] according to his own description of them, which is strange because he never actually held that title. But perhaps Senenmut worked from the precedent Hatshepsut had set for practicing the duties of an office that one did not hold. After all, she had practiced the powers of a king for seven years without being formally crowned. In exercising powers for which he did not have official authority, Senenmut seems to have made some enemies, likely including the southern vizier, Useramen, since it was his official territory upon which Senenmut was encroaching. But even if Useramen had wanted to destroy this new man, Senenmut's favor was ironclad, and all evidence suggests that Hatshepsut's reprisal would have been swift and severe. In fact, there is no evidence that anyone acted against Senenmut, at least not while Hatshepsut was alive.

Senenmut may have been an ambitious man from the start, one who was willing to step on the toes of other officials, but it could have been equally true that Hatshepsut was a clever politician who created an administration with built-in redundancies—just as during her regency she had played Ahmose Pennekhbet and Senenmut against each other. In the case of Senenmut and the vizier Useramen, Hatshepsut once again assigned multiple men to perform some of the same duties. Her officials may have encroached on one another's territory and annoyed fellow administrators, but in the end such overlap formed a system of checks and balances that prevented anyone from gaining too much power independent of the king. Hatshepsut really had been bred for palace politics.

Throughout her reign, Hatshepsut created a convoluted web of intersecting responsibilities between officials and between spheres of power that allowed her to infiltrate every aspect of temple, financial, and military activities. She even overlapped the administrations of great institutions, which permitted the commingling of resources. For example, when she appointed her most trusted palace official, Senenmut, as Overseer of the House of Amen, she automatically linked all of that temple wealth and influence back to her court and to herself. By assigning an unmarried, presumably childless man to be Steward of Amen, she was essentially diverting power away from the elite Theban families and back toward herself—almost in the same way the Ottoman Empire would rely on gelded men to hold offices during their lifetime so that they could not be passed down to the next generation.[19]

This arrangement seems to have suited Senenmut well. His economic powers gave him access to grain, gold, and a pool of skilled and unskilled labor both abroad and in Egypt. He managed hundreds of master craftsmen, and he could easily acquire anything he desired: a well-cut statue of the hardest royal stone, an intricate broad collar, an inlaid walking stick of imported ebony, or the softest and finest royal linens of the highest thread count. His landholdings must have been augmented exponentially during Hatshepsut's kingship, thereby increasing his own income in agricultural products, which were the chief commodities of payment in ancient economies. He probably had a villa in Thebes and another in Armant, where we think he grew up. Senenmut undoubtedly traveled in high style aboard his own barge, equipped with every luxury, that sailed up and down the Nile on his mistress's errands.

Neither Senenmut nor any of his early acquaintances had ever dreamed that he could achieve such a high level of influence by working directly and closely with the one woman now in charge of it all. He was not humble about advertising his success. To commemorate his rank and prestige, Senenmut started a systematic campaign to position his image in every place of honor possible: he commissioned statues, stelae, rock art, shrines, temple reliefs, a tomb chapel, and a burial chamber. No official had ever commissioned as many statues as Senenmut—not any official during the reign of the wise and relentless Senwosret III, who ruled in the Middle Kingdom, and not any administrator during the reign of Khufu, who marshaled hundreds of thousands of men to build his great pyramid during the Old Kingdom. No Egyptian administrator or general had ever deigned to proclaim his worth so publicly vis-à-vis his king, but Senenmut was fearless. He made sure his statues were strategically located in the most conspicuous spots.

His private artistic production was unprecedented, innovative, and completely devoted to establishing himself as one deserving of not just praise but awe among his peers. There were limits, though. Senenmut was apparently prohibited from showing himself in King Hatshepsut's presence in his statuary.[20] Representing himself next to the king would be placing himself on her level, as a god. But he could still show himself as tutor to her eldest offspring—even if it was only when she was a small girl. He took a liking to having himself depicted with Princess Nefrure and commissioned many three-dimensional images of himself with the child, because they broadcast his intimate connections to the royal family.

Even though the evidence suggests that Senenmut was in his fifties or beyond by this time, his statues always show him in an idealized and youthful way, with a full face, wide eyes, and a soft, smiling mouth. Some of the portraits from his tomb, however, show him as a timeworn man with a hooked nose, lines etched into the skin around his mouth, a flabby, weak chin, and fleshy lips. If these latter images are to be believed, he was not a handsome man.[21]

Whatever he really looked like, he wanted the world to know that he was not only Hatshepsut's favorite but also an innovator in his own right. He prized new ideas. His statuary included poses that Egyptians had never seen before, and not just one new form, like the squatting figure holding the princess in the folds of his garment, but multiple novel types.[22] In another innovative composition, he is kneeling behind the snake goddess Renenutet, the mistress of Armant, his hometown; her reptile coils fold in on themselves like a gathered ribbon. Another statue shows him offering a coil of surveyor's rope in homage to his pious temple-building work, a bold new design that could have elicited gasps when it was put in place along a visible temple processional way. He even created a cryptogram of Hatshepsut's name and had a statue commissioned of him holding the sign-puzzle he had invented. On another statue, he claimed to have created "images which I have made from the devising of my own heart and from my own labor; they have not been found in the writing of the ancestors."23

Such originality may not seem that astounding given his position of power, but Egyptian culture valued a certain kind of conservatism. Innovation, particularly among nonroyal elites, was practiced only sparingly. Officials were supposed to be followers of the king's lead, not fashion trendsetters. Senenmut may have been seen by some as breaking with protocol when his statuary contained more originality than that of his mistress, but Hatshepsut had her own penchant for the unusual. It seems that they both valued breaking the mold. Apparently Hatshepsut never put a stop to his displays, even though they were unprecedented in scope. The very existence of such personal monuments placed in the public sphere implies that the relationship between Senenmut and Hatshepsut was probably closer than we will ever know.

A bold and motivated pair, they were blessed by the gods with political abilities that allowed them to hold great positions of authority. Aware of his lower origins and his lack of Theban family influence at court, Hatshepsut likely relied on Senenmut exactly because he had no outside interests or private agenda to divert him from her own interests. His lack of family connections made him less likely to betray her or to overlook her wishes in favor of his own gain. With no strong ties to other elites through birth or marriage, Senenmut himself had no one else to trust besides Hatshepsut. They seem to have been mutually dependent: she took advantage of his reliance on her, and he apparently used her lack of trust in others for his own advancement.

As soon as Hatshepsut became king, Senenmut claimed prime real estate in the west Theban hills for his own tomb chapel just overlooking her Deir el-Bahri funerary temple; it was a grand space to be painted with images of himself in the company of his mother, father, and siblings, all seated before ample food, drink, and wealth for the afterlife. This tomb was also meant to link him to Hatshepsut's fortune in life and after death, because its proximity to her funerary temple allowed him to serve her in the afterlife. On its summit, he had a statue of himself carved from the live rock, with the King's Daughter Nefrure snugly in his embrace. His mother was buried under his tomb forecourt accompanied by riches she had never known as a young woman; he moved the body of his father, who had died long before Senenmut took up high office, to join his mother.[24] He even had one of his horses buried at his tomb site, on the slope of the hill just under the forecourt.[25] The horse was buried fully wrapped in a huge wooden coffin. Dragging a dead horse to the top of the Sheikh abd el-Gurna hill for burial must have involved some advance planning, not to mention a great deal of labor. Senenmut wanted his horse in the afterlife, and he found a way to make it happen.

Senenmut's preparation for death involved another extravagance. Instead of just cutting a burial chamber under his tomb chapel as most officials did, he chose a different location altogether. Not only did he lavish his funds on different localities for chapel and tomb, a privilege normally retained for kings, but he opted to have his corpse interred in the sacred Asasif valley, next to Hatshepsut's funerary temple.[26] This was perhaps the very first time a nonroyal individual separated his tomb (where his body was buried) from his tomb chapel (where relatives offered food and comfort to his soul). At this time, only kings did this: for example, Thutmose I and Thutmose II were buried deep in the Valley of the Kings while their temples for cult rituals lay in the desert fringes, near the Nile inundation. After he had done it, other officials followed his lead. Senenmut had created a new burial trend.

And Senenmut's innovations did not stop there. Within his burial chamber in the Asasif, which was made up of a series of descending staircases and chambers that were meant to remain secret after his burial, he commissioned exclusive liturgical texts for the walls that no official had previously dared to carve into stone. He also asked his craftsmen to paint on his tomb ceiling the first astrological chart ever recorded. No burial chamber of any elite had ever been so elaborate. In this way, Senenmut communicated his exclusive access to these texts to other officials and priests, broadcasting his worth in this life and the next.

Hatshepsut entrusted Senenmut with oversight of a tremendous number of building projects during her reign. No doubt he must have had architectural opinions and passions that she valued, because there is no evidence that he had any actual education in engineering. Despite this lack of formal training, he always seems to have been at the forefront of the next big thing in terms of form and design. Indeed, Hatshepsut asked him to direct construction of what was to be her greatest and most innovative temple achievement: her funerary temple at Deir el-Bahri, which was planned as an astoundingly creative, and nontraditional, tiered temple of three layers fronted by colonnades and dozens of statues of Hatshepsut as the god Osiris.[27] Its appearance was inspired by Mentuhotep II's Middle Kingdom temple in the adjacent site, but the architect, whoever he was (or she, if it was Hatshepsut's design), transformed it into a radically new structure never before seen in Egypt. Hatshepsut would call this temple Djeser Djeseru, meaning "Holy of Holies," and it was meant to promote the sanctity of her kingship. This most sacred cult place was dedicated to her depicted as an eternal Osiris king after death and as a solar falcon who traversed the heavens. It is the first surviving Temple of Millions of Years, the name the Egyptians gave to a king's funerary temple.[28] Even today, as one travels along the west bank of the Nile, amid the expected pylons and colonnaded sun courts of other great temples built centuries before and after, Deir el-Bahri is unmistakable—instantly unique, somehow modern and ancient at the same time. It stands as an unparalleled and iconic achievement.

Hatshepsut chose the site of Deir el-Bahri not only because of the dramatic half-moon of high cliffs underneath the pyramid-shaped mountain, but also because it was a popular destination for the Beautiful Feast of the Valley, a sacred procession that brought the gods' statues to Egypt's divine ancestors buried within the cliffs and beneath the hills on the west bank of Thebes. In short, this was the most public spot in western Thebes.

The Beautiful Feast of the Valley was a kind of carnival celebrated at the beginning of summer, when the Nile was at its lowest point, when the land itself seemed to be dying and families were anxious about having enough grain to make it to the next harvest.[29] In the Valley Feast, priests bore the statue of the god Amen in a gilded carrying shrine on their shoulders beyond the gates of his home temple at Karnak, placing him on his sacred Nile barge so that he could cross the river and visit the sacred ancestors on the west bank in the land of the dead. It was a means of connecting with death itself, which to the Egyptians was not a final end but a pregnant beginning to a new re-creation. Thousands of men from the army and navy accompanied the god along the way, protecting his move-

© Trustees of the British Museum

LEFT: Enclosed in the protective folds of his cloak in this innovative statue (one of many radically new statue forms that he invented), Senenmut embraces his young charge, the King's Daughter Nefrure. Senenmut was assigned to act as Nefrure's tutor, a coveted role he was more than happy to flaunt to his fellow officials. Senenmut knew he couldn't show himself in Hatshepsut's sacred presence, but including Nefrure's image was the next best way to communicate his close relationship with the royal family. And showing Nefrure as a small child granted him the superior position.

BOTTOM: Striking in its modernity, the multitiered facade of Hatshepsut's Temple of Millions of Years was positioned majestically in the most dramatic location in western Thebes. It acted as a giant stage for great festivals of divine propitiation, wild celebration, and ritual solemnity. It also linked Hatshepsut's kingship to accepted traditions, because she built it right next to the funerary temple of Mentuhotep II, the founder of Theban kingship in ancient Egypt hundreds of years before her reign.

Fly away with your imagination/© 2010 Karolina Sus

© Michelle McMahon via Getty Images

TOP: Like her father before her, Hatshepsut showed herself as the god Osiris. Here on the facade of her Temple of Millions of Years, she depicted herself with the mummified body and crossed arms of the god of regeneration after death. The first skin color she chose for these statues was yellow ocher, the traditional color of a woman. As time went on, she opted for orange, an androgynous blend. Finally, she decided to fully masculinize her imagery, and the latest statues in the series betray the red ocher of masculinity.

BOTTOM: Hatshepsut practically grew up in the sprawling temple complex dedicated to the god Amen, whom she called her father. When she became king, she dedicated a new chapel, built of deep red quartzite (the first time any king used this expensive stone to build a structure), to house the god's sacred barque, and placed it immediately in front of the holy and exclusive sanctuary where the god's statue dwelled. The walls detail her duties and achievements to the god, her coronation, and her ritual activity. The inscriptions record the oracles that marked her as the god's choice to rule all of Egypt.

© Kenneth Garrett/National Geographic via Getty Images

© Kenneth Garrett/National Geographic via Getty Images

TOP: Hatshepsut always took first position in her unorthodox coregency, even though she came to the throne second. Here, the female king and her coregent Thutmose III are in festival procession with the sacred barque of Amen. They are depicted as absolute equals—twins—communicating that both monarchs had the same access to the sacred spirit of kingship.

BOTTOM: This unfinished obelisk was likely produced during Hatshepsut's dynasty, but after her reign. It was left in the quarry at Aswan after a deep crack developed along the length of the monolith. This is the largest obelisk the Egyptians ever attempted: 42 meters in length, about thirteen stories high. Hatshepsut's obelisks, at over ten stories in height, came from the same quarries and were products of the same ancient Egyptian engineering techniques that few other civilizations have equaled. All Egyptian obelisks were sheathed (partially or fully) in precious metals.

© Yann Arthus-Bertrand/Corbis

© Vanni Archive/Corbis

TOP: Only one of Hatshepsut's obelisks still stands at Amen's temple in Karnak. Set up in celebration of her jubilee in year 16, it marked the moment when her kingship moved from carefully calculated audacity to full maturity. She had long since masculinized her images, and her co-king was now a partner in rule, leading Egypt's armies on campaign. The lengthy text places her unusual kingship within the context of religious ideology, making sure to tell her people that everything she had achieved was the will of her father, the god Amen.

Rogers Fund, 1929, Torso lent by Rijksmuseum van Oudheden, Leiden (L.1998.80), © The Metropolitan Museum of Art

LEFT: After her coronation, Hatshepsut's first moments as king likely took place in a throne room, seated on a raised dais, and she may have looked much like this red granite statue depicting her wearing a traditional, tight-fitting linen sheath dress but also the masculine *nemes* head cloth of an Egyptian king. The sight must have been strange to behold for all those accustomed to the divine system of masculine kingship.

Rogers Fund, 1929, © The Metropolitan Museum of Art

Rogers Fund, 1928, © The Metropolitan Museum of Art

LEFT: Early on in her kingship, Hatshepsut attempted to add a layer of masculinity to her feminine forms, and halfway measures resulted in strange androgyny. On this life-size limestone statue from her Temple of Millions of Years, she shows herself without a shirt, wearing only a king's kilt, but she retains her gracile shoulders, delicate facial features, and even the generous hint of feminine breasts. The statue is shocking in its blend of masculinity and femininity. It is unknown if she ever dressed this way in public rituals or in festival procession.

RIGHT: Eventually, Hatshepsut opted for a fully masculinized image in her statuary, showing herself with wide and strong shoulders, firm pectoral muscles, and no sign of breasts. Even her face is altered: the fuller cheeks and a stronger aquiline nose replaced the Barbie-doll nose of previous portraits. This change in depiction accompanied her own aging process, and we can only wonder how Hatshepsut herself dressed as she got older.

De Agostini Picture Library via Getty Images

Some twenty years after Hatshepsut's death, Thutmose III sent chisel bearers throughout the land to remove her name and images from Egypt's sacred temple monuments. Here, in the heart of Karnak temple, artisans so carefully chiseled out her human form that the shadow of her former kingship still haunts Amen's temple walls.

Anonymous gift, 1931, © The Metropolitan Museum of Art

This sketch of Hatshepsut's key lieutenant, Senenmut, looks quite different from the sweet, childlike face shown on his statuary. These portraits betray not only his age, but perhaps also a hint of his shrewd character. His was not the handsome, banal face we see in formal images, but one carved by lines of age. Many such sketches were found in Senenmut's burial chamber, and on the back of one is the inscription "a lean hairy rat with massively long whiskers," maybe referring to the reputation of the man himself and betraying the reason so many of his monuments were destroyed after his death.

© Werner Forman/Corbis

LEFT: With the King's Daughter Nefrure's tiny head peeking out of Senenmut's enfolding garments, this statue communicates warmth, love, and protective embrace; by the same token, this publicly displayed stone block constituted an unmistakable and presumptuous communication to all of Senenmut's peers that his access to Hatshepsut was unrivaled.

LEFT: Shown as a queen wearing a king's crown on this limestone block from the heart of Karnak's Temple, Hatshepsut audaciously names herself as King of Upper and Lower Egypt and includes her newly granted throne name Maatkare (The Soul of Re Is Truth), all of it, it seems, before the coronation that should grant such divine privileges.

Block discovered by Henri Chevrier at Karnak Temple in 1933, Luxor Museum, drawing by Deborah Shieh

Luc Gabolde, via IFAO

ABOVE: In this relief from a limestone temple once erected at Karnak, Hatshepsut is depicted as the God's Wife of Amen, likely when she was the Great Royal Wife of Thutmose II or at the very beginning of her regency for Thutmose III. Her ideological and political powers were clearly communicated to her people in the imagery because she stands directly before divinities without the king; she acts as her own mistress. Embraced by the goddess Hathor, she is offered life and power through her nostrils by Seth, god of violent power. Wearing feminine dress and a modius crown, this image was not a target of Thutmose III's later destruction because here she is not claiming the kingship, only her role as high priestess of Thebes.

ments and reveling in his triumph. Everyone drank too much and partied too hard. Musicians played the lute and banged the drums. Young girls wearing only small girdles around their hips danced, and acrobats performed backbends and flips, all for the god's erotic enjoyment. It was a time when the Egyptians pondered the shortness and unpredictability of life and celebrated the possibility of new beginnings. One of Hatshepsut's first and most ambitious projects, her funerary temple, was constructed at a Valley Festival site. Clearly from the earliest years of her reign, she understood the value she could gain from these religious celebrations.

A temple here in the Asasif would set her up for maximum visibility among the people who mattered most, not to mention the gods of Thebes. The place was already sacred to the deified king Mentuhotep II, who, some five hundred years before, had reunified Egypt after a long period of civil war. Its cliff faces were also thought to be the realm of the goddess Hathor, the mistress of the western mountains, a daughter of the sun god known for her sexuality and violent protection. An ancient and sacred spot for centuries, the location was well chosen. Hatshepsut would project her most profound political-religious claims in the text and relief planned for this structure.

Hatshepsut began construction at Deir el-Bahri immediately after her coronation (although many argue it started even before).[30] The project was ambitious, and the temple work would continue until the end of her reign. The plan of the structure—the ramps leading the participant ever higher, the massive platforms on which thousands of spectators could stand, the colonnaded porticoes serving as stages visible to the crowds below—was meant to showcase Hatshepsut's highly visible annual festival celebrations to further broadcast her unassailable kingship.[31] She would use the city of Thebes as a giant stage to display her piety to the Egyptian world.

During Hatshepsut's coregency with Thutmose III, the money, time, and labor spent on festival activity exploded. It may be hard for us to understand why this investment was necessary, but in a world where seasons of planting, harvest, and inundation ruled life and death, it was imperative to bring the gods into daily life to help things along. The more a king invested in festivals of cyclical renewal, the more prosperity the gods bestowed. But if the gods were ignored, bad floods would result, and that meant meager planting and poor harvest, which led in turn to drought, pestilence, disease, and death. Festivals were viewed as a way to physically invite the gods into public spaces where the people could appease them and give them gifts of food, music, and incense, as much as was needed. The statues of the gods were taken out of their sanctuaries and placed into mobile shrines that were carried aloft beyond their temple walls and out of doors, so that the gods could visit other temples and family members, engage in sexual activity, and revel in the adoration of the pious Egyptian people. Such intensification of festivals would have been a drain on earlier New Kingdom treasuries, but apparently Hatshepsut could afford it. The power of kingship was renewed in the process of many such celebrations, another reason, perhaps, for Hatshepsut to emphasize such ritual activity.

The whole population stopped their work to witness the movement of the gods and to participate in the revelry, drinking and eating to excess, dancing and singing, communing with divinity. For example, in the Beautiful Feast of the Valley, the god Amen crossed the Nile to visit the tombs of kings, ancestors, and dead gods, so that he could link with that most sacred potentiality of rebirth after death. Thebans followed the procession, partaking in massive feasts at the tombs of their own ancestors, in a weeklong banquet akin to Mexico's Día de los Muertos.

Across the river, during the Opet festival,[32] the god Amen left his sanctuary at Karnak to visit the temple at Luxor and thus meld with a manifestation of himself linked to sexuality and self-creation. It was during Hatshepsut's reign that we see the first evidence of the Opet festival, also known as the Festival of the Residence, when the sexualized manifestation of the god Amen left his temple of Ipet-Sut at Karnak for his enclosure at Ipet Resut, his residence to the south. Opet was celebrated at the beginning of fall, after the Nile inundation waters had receded and planting had begun. According to the people of Thebes, the success of their crops depended on Amen's renewed sexual potency.

The festival was shrouded in mystery; no priest or king ever explicitly recorded the rituals that took place inside of the temple, but they appear to have been definitely sexual in nature. Hatshepsut and Thutmose III would have been initiated in such secret knowledge and might have facilitated the strange mysteries of Amen-Bull-of-His-Mother's mounting and impregnating his own mother with his own future self.

During the later public procession, crowds followed along and watched with rapt attention the god's regenerative journey and thus the renewal of their own crops and livelihoods. By injecting her presence into these festivals, Hatshepsut was essentially saying that her rule was necessary to keep the sun rising and setting and the Nile flooding. During her reign, these religious occasions lasted for more days, included more participants, and grew in overall importance. Just the architectural evidence alone proves that she spent more money on these events than all previous New Kingdom kings combined.

Hatshepsut enacted her festival rituals in stone buildings of great size and opulence instead of the temporary or mud-brick structures used before her reign. She thought in terms of a broad plan, not single buildings. Her ambitious constructions created massive festival processions that stretched for many miles along ways now paved in stone. It took more than a dozen years of continuous dusty and noisy construction work that was halted probably only to celebrate religious ceremonies, but Hatshepsut essentially turned Thebes into one giant stone ritual space stamped repeatedly with her names and imagery.

She was the first king to build extensively in sandstone, and its hardness allowed her to construct larger and taller buildings than ever before, bridging wider spans than had been possible with the limestone used by previous kings. Sandstone also had its religious associations. The quarries of Gebel el-Silsila were located south of Thebes,[33] directly adjacent to the river, and were bathed by the Nile when it flooded its banks every summer. Sandstone cut from these banks was thought to be connected to the source of new life, of creation from nothing, and any temples built of this precious resource would be imbued with the hallowed powers of the annual inundation.

Although Hatshepsut's most innovative (and lasting) structures were built at Thebes, she was systematic in her construction efforts and injected her divine presence into religious activities all over Egypt, from north to south—temples for Ptah at Memphis, for Thoth at Hermopolis, her Speos Artemidos shrine for Pakhet at Beni Hasan in Middle Egypt, temples for Khnum and Satet at Elephantine, Monthu at Armant, Ptah at Thebes, and numerous constructions in Nubia.[34] But in the end, Thebes was her base of ideological power, and some of her most vital constructions for the legitimization of her kingship were erected at Karnak in the heart of Amen's domain, where Amen had picked her to rule all those years ago, actualizing the event in stone to make it ritually real for her people.

Her funerary temple at Deir el-Bahri—Djeser Djeseru—was the centerpiece of her overall scheme at Thebes. Its sightline connected to a new pylon gateway she was constructing on the north side of Karnak Temple. Standing on the topmost terrace of her funerary temple and looking east, one could see her obelisks and pylons at Karnak directly across the river. Everything at Deir el-Bahri was planned on this axis, including the sanctuary of her funerary temple. In fact, the sanctuary was precisely oriented so that on the winter solstice the sunlight streamed through a window to bathe the statue of Amen, the hidden one, inside.[35]

Farther north, Hatshepsut had a rock-cut shrine built to the goddess Pakhet, "the one who scratches," a lioness and fierce protector of her father, the sun god. Inside, Hatshepsut left a lengthy and radical treatise on her kingship. The temple, now called the Speos Artemidos by Egyptologists, gives us some idea of why Hatshepsut spent so much time and money building ritual spaces out of stone; she was of one mind with the gods.

> My divine mind is looking out for posterity, the king's heart has thought of eternal continuity, because of the utterance of him who parts the *ished*-tree, Amun, lord of millions, and I have magnified the Order he has desired. For it is known to me that he lives on it: it is my bread, and it is of its dew that I drink. I was in one body with him, and he has brought me up to make the awe of him powerful in this land. I am one whom Atum-Khepri, who made what is—made know[ledgeable], one whom the Sun has fated as established for him.

She continues with a section on how temple building is akin to marking herself as the chosen one.

> The temple of the mistress of Qusae, which had (completely) fallen into dissolution—the earth having swallowed its noble sanctuary, children dancing on its roof(s), no tutelary goddess causing fear, the lowly reckoning defenselessness in (her) absence, nor her days of appearance having ever (be)en experienced—I hallowed it, built anew, fashioning its Leading Ser-

pent of gold [. . .] in order to defend its town in the processional bark. . . .
My incarnation gives clarity of vision to those who shoulder the god.

Next, the text includes a rare claim that links Hatshepsut's success with
the creator god himself.

Every [god] says to himself: "One who will achieve eternal continuity has
come, whom Amun has caused to appear as king of eternity on Horus's
throne." So listen all you elite and multitude of commoners. I have done this
by the plan of my mind. I do not sleep forgetting, (but) have made firm what
is ruined. For I have raised up what was dismembered beginning from the
time when Asiatics were in the midst of the Delta (in) Avaris, with vagrants
in their midst toppling what had been made. They ruled without the Sun,
and he did not act by god's decree down to my (own) uraeus-incarnation.
(Now) I am set on the Sun's thrones, having been foretold from ages of years
as one born to take possession. I am come as Horus, the sole uraeus spitting fire at my enemies. I have banished the gods' abomination, the earth
removing their footprints.[36]

Hatshepsut used all of her ingenuity to negotiate a difficult path as
a female king. She was approaching thirty years of age, was ruler of the
most powerful land in the Mediterranean and Africa, and shared the
throne with a boy who would soon grow into a man. She had triumphantly
received a successful expedition from Punt. The Nubian and Eastern Desert mines were creating a steady stream of gold at the expense of indige-
nous populations and society's unwanted. Trade with Syria-Palestine was
booming, with timber from Lebanon, wine from Crete, poppy products
from Persia and beyond, and luxury goods brought in from places as far
off as Babylon, Anatolia, and Afghanistan. The quarries were churning
out stone for new statuary. All over Egypt, hammers and chisels rang out
as they met stone; men were laboring in her name and building temples
that would forever link Hatshepsut's reign to Egypt's current prosperity. In
temples north and south, people saw new priests hired and old, neglected
festivals reinstated. By all appearances, everything seemed in order and
on track for Hatshepsut.

Except that it wasn't. Her nephew and co-king Thutmose III was
now thirteen or fourteen years of age and acquiring more knowledge

and confidence every day. Hatshepsut's mother, Ahmes, may have died around this time, leaving her motherless and with no ties to her old life as princess and queen. And her daughter Nefrure would soon grow into a young woman ready to conceive an heir. Changes were coming. Hatshepsut would need to adapt to an extent that she had never imagined when she was scurrying around the royal nurseries as a small girl. Something would soon oblige her to take extraordinary steps with regard to how she depicted her feminine self.

SEVEN

The King
Becomes a Man

Around Thutmose III's fourteenth birthday, some of the wives in his harem were likely beginning to grow with child. Thutmose probably married Nefrure around this time as well. As a King's Daughter and King's Sister, Nefrure was expected to join with him and no other man. This union was his sacred duty, as it was her privilege. She was a royal daughter, and their son would be of the purest blood, destined to rule Egypt as his father and grandfather had done before him.

Hatshepsut's risky plan to keep the Thutmoside family in power was paying off. Thutmose III had turned out to be a vigorous young man, able not only to sire children, but to participate in military campaigns. Hatshepsut's reign with Thutmose III included several foreign wars to the south of Egypt,[1] and Thutmose III probably accompanied such campaigns. No matter what his precise role at this young age, he was growing into a mighty warrior-king before the eyes of his people.

There is no evidence that her femininity made Hatshepsut soft toward her traditional enemies. To the contrary: she knew that foreign suppression was Egypt's lifeblood, a key source of her country's great wealth. Nubia's subjugation was not just to Hatshepsut's advantage as king but to the economic advantage of her military elite. The notion entertained by some Egyptologists[2] that she was a pacifist just because she was a woman is simply wrong. Hatshepsut may have traveled personally with her troops to Kush,[3] and there was every reason to bring Thutmose along.[4] Hatshepsut likely organized four campaigns to Kush, and Thutmose III may have participated in all of them.

Hatshepsut did not campaign in the north, but that was probably because she was able to maintain active and effective diplomatic connections there. Her father, Thutmose I, had already campaigned in Syria-Palestine, which raised awareness of Egypt's growing military presence among the kings beyond the Sinai. With no evidence that any kings in northwest Asia decided to become aggressive just because a woman was on the throne, it seems that her gender made little difference in the politics of the region. Egypt's position in the north, in Syria-Palestine, remained largely unchanged throughout her reign, and Hatshepsut never brought troops there—either because she did not have the strength to do it, or because the mere threat of her military power maintained some tribute payments. Possibly her campaigns to Nubia kept her men busy and rich without the complications of constant war on two fronts. Hatshepsut was smart enough to establish a steady stream of wealth from Nubia and Kerma in the south early in her reign; these were certainly much easier conquests than the urban Syrian centers of Kadesh and Megiddo to the north.

Hatshepsut knew that it was in Egypt's and her own best interest for her co-king to be trained as a skilled general. There is reason to believe that she sent Thutmose III to the north of Egypt to learn about the system of border fortresses along the Sinai road and to train with the army at the ancient military stronghold of Perunefer, modern-day Tell el-Daba.[5] While he was there, his privileged training and military contacts likely helped him appreciate Egypt's place in the Mediterranean and Near Eastern worlds. He would have met leaders from Babylon, Susa, Phoenicia, Anatolia, Canaan, and Crete. The Egyptians called the Cretans Keftiu and depicted them wearing colorful woolen garments and fabulous high looping hairstyles. In fact, everything Cretan was all the rage in Egypt during Thutmose's adolescence. Artisans from Crete were invited to the royal palace at Perunefer to create frescoes in the colorful style of their people, and bull-leaping demonstrations were likely incorporated into the royal court entertainment.

Thutmose III probably met with the ambassadors sent by kings of the city-states of Phoenicia; these kings were much older than he was, and unlike his, their dynastic lines stretched back many generations. Although they held far less territory than Thutmose, the Phoenicians counted as Egypt's best trading partners. It was a time of possibilities, at the height of Bronze Age globalization and prosperity, and the young king likely watched the lands to the north of Egypt with a calculating eye, weighing the potential benefits of including some of them in an expanding Egyptian empire of his own. None of these northern territories were under Egypt's control while he was growing up. He would have known, however, that control of Syria-Palestine implied an imperial force to be reckoned with, allowing him to demand tribute from numerous subjugated vassals even farther afield. Perhaps Thutmose recognized that it fell to him to conquer Syria-Palestine and re-create Egypt's empire in the north. If Hatshepsut felt threatened by her co-king's ambitions, she did not betray it. Instead, she seems to have welcomed any future improvements of Egypt's empire and offered him the most sophisticated military training imaginable, even inspiring in him the lofty goal of fulfilling Egypt's manifest destiny of hegemony over its traditional enemies.[6]

Hatshepsut's young co-king was almost a man. As the king reached fifteen or sixteen years old, we can imagine that his opinions were not only more forcefully expressed but reasoned and educated. His bearing was manly, no longer boyish. He was probably now taller than his female co-king.[7] And here Hatshepsut had another problem to put to right, one that good fortune and careful planning had thankfully allowed. It was quickly becoming unseemly for her to stand next to Thutmose III in the senior position during sacred rituals and at court. A woman could outrank a boy but not a man. If she was to continue her dominance in this unequal partnership, something had to change.

Hatshepsut began experimenting in earnest with how to represent her own sexual identity, negotiating between her actual feminine self and the masculine kingship she inhabited, striving to find a more acceptable way to present her unusual rule. Images from the first years of her reign typically depicted her wearing the long dress of a woman and the crown of a king. At some point, Hatshepsut recognized that this honest and obvious depiction had lost its efficacy. Whether it was in the new context of a young man rather than a boy standing beside her, or some other factor, it seems that ultimately a feminine king was too jarring in the context of this coregency, even to the relatively liberated Egyptian mind. Egyptian female kings were rare, ephemeral, temporary solutions to a political crisis, not a long-lasting ideal.

In her early twenties, Hatshepsut had already taken the first steps in a manly direction by ordering her craftsmen to add some masculine elements to her feminine figures. They widened her shoulders and extended the stance of her legs, even in figures wearing a queen's long dress, to give her the active pose of a king striding forth for duty. At this point in her reign, Hatshepsut was probably only conceding to add a masculine veneer to what was, at its core, a visibly feminine depiction of herself.

Hatshepsut chose the same blended male-female depictions in her statuary; it seems clear that she wanted to retain her female core at first. Her earliest three-dimensional images show a woman wearing a dress but the headgear of a king. Later she showed herself shirtless, ostensibly bare-chested like a man, but her incongruous retention of female breasts on the naked chest makes for a shocking image. The most famous example shows her wearing a masculine kilt and kingly headscarf with a completely bare chest, accentuated by small, but clearly feminine, breasts. The statue's body shape betrays a slight and slim woman, not the typical strong shoulders of a masculine king. Most Egyptologists doubt that Hatshepsut wandered about the palace in such attire, with her pert breasts bared for all her courtiers to see, and it should come as no surprise that this statue type, such an experiment in hybrid sexuality, was not replicated, nor displayed openly before the populace, but only kept in the innermost rooms of Hatshepsut's Djeser Djeseru temple, where the mysteries of Hatshepsut's female kingship could be appreciated by those intellectual enough to understand it and by the gods who had ordained it.[8] This openly feminine representation was deemed too problematic. Soon Hatshepsut would shift all her images to a broad-shouldered man's body accentuated by strong pectoral muscles and wide shoulders—with no visible breasts.

Her earliest constructions at her Temple of Millions of Years at Djeser

Djeseru show the same combinations of masculine and feminine traits. In the first years of her reign, she commissioned dozens of statues showing herself as Osiris, the mummiform god of rebirth. On the whole, the image was a masculine one: a god with crossed arms with Hatshepsut's portrait. But a closer look revealed the feminine elements on the earliest such statues: her skin tone was rendered in the yellow traditionally employed to depict an elite woman who stayed indoors, not the deep red ocher of a man who was part of the wider world. Her face included feminine aspects, too, such as a small smiling mouth and a delicate, heart-shaped visage with a dainty chin.

Ultimately, such a frank combination of fine womanly features on Osiris's figure seems to have been insupportable, and Hatshepsut had to further masculinize the next series of images. The ensuing Osiris statues at Deir el-Bahri were painted with both yellow and red pigment, resulting in a strange hybrid orange skin color—not at all a part of the established color scheme for Egyptian art. The statue faces were carved with new masculine features, including a stronger chin, nose, and brow. This image was more in line with expectations, but Hatshepsut still made an undeniable attempt to retain some femininity. One can almost feel the underlying anxiety on her part, an uncertainty about how she should look to please the gods and her people, how much of her own self she could show and how much she had to transform. She may have been king, the most powerful person in the ancient world, but beliefs and expectations greater than she was forced her to perform unending ideological gymnastics to satisfy the sacred role. In the end, Hatshepsut had no choice but to change her outward appearance.

All the evidence suggests that Hatshepsut's transformation toward masculinity was a process, not a sudden event, squarely in line with her modus operandi in claiming the kingship. It seems she opportunistically waited for the precise moment to move toward masculinity in her imagery. Just as her transition to kingship was careful and calculated, she did not suddenly appear as a man before her people or in her art. Hatshepsut only went as far as was needed at the time. She constantly negotiated ways to stay in power, and in this case she did whatever it took—eventually showing herself not as a female ruler or a strange hybrid, but simply as a man.

Hatshepsut did not manipulate her depictions because she lacked manly courage in leading military campaigns or because she was losing the confidence of her generals. Hatshepsut had no problem with subjugating enemies, destroying rebels, and extending the borders of Egypt, and there is no evidence to suggest that her political clout was fading. Hatshepsut's ongoing gender shifts thus seem to have had little to do with realpolitik or external political pressures and must have been motivated by deeper understandings of kingship and, in particular, her relationship with her co-king.

Whom did the changes in representation serve? The modifications probably appealed less to Hatshepsut than to others. She began her reign showing her sex, and this first imagery may have been her truest inclination. As the years went on, however, we see doubt creeping in. Her masculinization does not seem to appeal to any narcissistic desire on the part of Hatshepsut, some inner need to claim all aspects of masculine rule no matter the costs. Instead, she was obliging the ritual needs of her gods and allowing a precious and tenuously balanced co-kingship to continue without shaming the junior partner. She was fitting herself to her co-king's changing agenda. Hatshepsut's makeover has as much to do with Thutmose III as with anybody else. He no longer needed a motherly figure to watch over him—in life or in temple imagery. Now that he was older, Hatshepsut had to remake herself into something that did not threaten his authority or legitimacy. The public may have demanded her alterations; ideology certainly did. Thutmose III himself may have insisted on it as well, although we cannot know definitively. Because there was no mechanism in place for Hatshepsut to produce the next heir (the question of with whom being the greatest problem), the continuation of her dynasty now depended on Thutmose III's growing cooperation and acceptance of this ongoing rule.[9]

With no mention of her makeover in ancient texts, we have only her changing depictions to tell the story. Hatshepsut soon decided to go all in. As time went on, her images were completely masculinized in face and body, which suggests that even in real life she may have worn a king's kilt and either bound her breasts or included no shirt at all, at least during temple rituals. Hatshepsut could not force Egyptian kingship to fit her unconventional gender; instead, she had to conform to its sacred tenets. This was not a woman who demanded that the system mold itself to her. All the evidence shows an unusual monarch who continuously fretted about and experimented with her place in the world. Masculinity was a key component of Egyptian kingship, and step by step, as her years of royal authority accrued, she concealed her feminine aspects until there was almost no woman left, except in the sacred texts alongside the pictures that continued referring to "she" and "her."

Only in these labels, hieroglyphic texts associated with her depictions, do we see a stubborn refusal to give up her feminine self; she decided on a confusing combination of masculine and feminine markers in the accompanying inscriptions so that sometimes she was called "he" and sometimes "she." She was on occasion entitled "Son of Re" but more often called "Daughter of Re." Occasionally she was labeled the "good god," but in most places, even next to an image that was totally masculine, she was the "good goddess." Usually Hatshepsut was named with a masculine Horus bird, but sometimes she even feminized this divine element, creating an extraordinary, unprecedented, and abstract feminine version of the god Horus, thus turning herself into a female heir to the gods.

One title that she never feminized was King of Upper and Lower Egypt, which in Egyptian literally translates as "He Who Belongs to the Sedge Plant and the Bee," with the sedge being emblematic of Upper Egypt and the bee of Lower Egypt. Likely it was considered too theologically fraught to feminize such an archaic royal title. When Hatshepsut bore this label at the beginning of her reign, she always included some masculine elements in her depiction, even if it was only a king's wig and headgear. As her kingship continued, she accompanied the title King of Upper and Lower Egypt with a fully masculine figure.

In inscriptions from Hatshepsut's reign, we also see a new use of the word for palace (per-aa, which meant "great house") in association with the king's authority. This way of referring to the king as "the palace" would later be taken up in the Bible as "pharaoh," but perhaps Hatshepsut's advisers created the new meaning expressly to create an easy way out of a complicated situation in which no one knew which king in this strange coregency was responsible for which message or which opinion. Or perhaps Hatshepsut herself invented the new meaning to veil her femininity.

Her given name, Hatshepsut, was more of a problem when it came to her masculine transformation: "the Foremost of Noble Women" was not an easy name to masculinize. Nonetheless, Hatshepsut and her advisers had already hit upon an ingenious solution. Just after her accession, she had added the phrase "the One United with Amen" to her birth name.

When Hatshepsut said she was "united" with Amen, she meant that she had actually joined her feminine self with his essence, taking on Amen's aspects of divinity, his mind, his intentions, and even, to some extent, his abilities. This particular name modification also suggests that Hatshepsut did not undergo her gender transformation manipulatively or cynically, but piously. It is quite possible that she actually believed Amen had allowed her to transcend her own human body to become an entity greater than herself. In fact, Hatshepsut actually feminized the word *khenem,* "to unite," in her inscriptions by adding a *-t,* so that her name read "Hatshepsut the Female One Who Unites with Amen."

She had already found an intellectual solution for her feminine kingship that was much more elegant than just putting on masculine garb. The texts betrayed Hatshepsut's femininity even when the associated images showed her as a man. It is almost as if she knew the sacred inscriptions had to carry her true nature, while her depictions could cloak and transform it when necessary. Just as she did during her regency when she was depicted as God's Wife but referred to herself as a ruler in the text, Hatshepsut was broadcasting different messages to different sets of people. To those elites who could read hieroglyphic text and participate in complex theological discourse, she presented the full complexity of gender-ambiguous kingship. There was no need to hide her feminine self from these learned men and women anyway because of their close access to her and her palace. But for the common man or woman who could not read and who might not understand such academic explanations, Hatshepsut presented a simplified and unassailable image of idealized and youthful masculine kingship. For them, she became what everyone expected to see—a strong man able to protect Egypt's borders and a virile king able to build temples and perform the cult rituals for the gods.

Hatshepsut was a realist at her very core, a negotiator. Despite the innovations implicit in her very existence as a ruler, she does not seem to have been a romantic idealist willing to break rules and destroy relationships just to forward her own interests. She masculinized herself when expectations for it were insurmountable. And she never tried officially, before god and all the people of Egypt, to remove Thut-

mose III from the throne. She always, throughout her whole reign, ruled
with him, *alongside* him, not *instead of* him. Her monuments and images
may have ignored his existence when he was a young child, but through
all of that indecision about how to proceed, Hatshepsut never attempted
to rule on her own, in her own right. This woman had learned that she
couldn't change the system; she had to work with it. Thutmose III's manhood could have been perceived as a threat to her kingship, but only if she
had intended to have it all for herself. Apparently Hatshepsut was skilled
enough to see the eventuality of Thutmose III's coming adulthood, and
there's every reason to believe that she engineered this situation so that
Thutmose III could become an asset to her rather than competition. This
was the way that Hatshepsut worked. Thutmose III the infant king had
lived, against all odds, saving the Thutmoside line. She modified herself
partly to fit his growing abilities—because, one day, his son would carry
on her proud legacy.

Now that her cohort was ready to become a full partner, Hatshepsut
hit upon an age-old strategy to cement her new role with Thutmose III: the
oldest festival in the Egyptian arsenal, the Sed festival, a rare renewal of
kingship that occurred only after thirty years of continuous rule.[10] Preparations including extensive temple construction were ordered years in advance of a king's jubilee. Courtiers and villagers alike would receive gifts
of the king's favor. The royal palaces spent inordinate amounts of money
brewing beer and fermenting wine from their vineyards. It would be a time
of ongoing revelry and celebration. Most Egyptian kings did not reign
long enough to celebrate a jubilee; indeed, none of Hatshepsut's or Thutmose III's subjects could remember a jubilee in their lifetime. But Hatshepsut was going forward with the Sed festival, even though she had only
ruled for fifteen years as regent and king. Granted, the timing was off. But
she probably needed the legitimacy of the Sed now, and she may have engaged in some tricky calculations to justify such an early date for her jubilee: Hatshepsut combined the thirteen or so years of her father's reign
with the two to three years of her husband's with the seven years of her
regency on behalf of Thutmose III with the seven years of her own reign
as king, which totaled thirty years, the ideal and traditional number.[11]
Her Sed festival was thus held at the thirty-year anniversary of Thutmose I's accession. Hatshepsut marked thirty years of Thutmoside rule

with the biggest celebration Egypt had seen in generations.[12] She organized the jubilee not just for herself but for her family's lineage and her place in it. Hatshepsut's Sed festival was part of a larger political agenda.

Hatshepsut's jubilee still confuses Egyptologists: many think that her claim to a Sed festival is a fabrication manufactured to support an illegitimate kingship or that her inscriptions could be interpreted as the *hope* to celebrate a jubilee in the future, not as a record of actual festivities.[13] But if we take her at her word, this Sed festival becomes another part of Hatshepsut's innovative methodology of maintaining balance in an unprecedented kingship and publicly claiming god-given providence within it. If nothing else, the decision to hold a jubilee was a clever political move.

The Sed festival rituals themselves must have been long and overwrought affairs, their archaic incantations barely understandable to the New Kingdom public: never-ending processions of divine standards, which showed that the many gods and geographical regions of Egypt supported the king's rule; presentation of dozens of different garments, crowns, staffs, and weapons, which invested the king with their nuanced and varied kinds of sacred power; and the formal seating on the thrones of both Upper Egypt and Lower Egypt, which demonstrated the king's ability to unify these different lands. Rituals of running displayed the king's renewed energy, and both Hatshepsut and Thutmose III would have had to sprint in distinctive races while holding a variety of strange and ritually charged objects, such as vases, live birds, oars, rudders, document chests, staffs, and flails. One scene even shows Hatshepsut running alongside the sacred Apis bull as if in a sacred rodeo. Hatshepsut's celebrations also included the erection of another pair of obelisks.[14]

During the jubilee, the king was the lead actor in a complex and sacred stage production that continued for weeks, if not months, and required a number of supporters. It seems the ever-present Senenmut performed the duties of the "stolist" of Horus, a title denoting the purification and adornment of statues and even of the king herself, a title he was proud enough to incise onto multiple statues. He was also named as the One Who Covered the Double Crown with Red Linen,[15] which suggests that he was part of the coronation rituals and handled the sacred crowns before and after they were placed on the head of the king.

Hatshepsut's inscriptions plainly state that she celebrated the Sed in year 16 of her joint rule, and all the evidence tells us that she spent massive amounts of capital in preparation for the sacred rituals before her people and her gods. She ordered new temple structures at Karnak, including a massive gateway of stone (later called the eighth pylon by Egyptologists)

an Egyptian temple. She had
elisks from the Aswan granite
d she had now finished most of
astounding building program
ne.

nally seen as a renewal of king-
resh start, a kind of religious
e. The Sed's sacred rituals were
youthful vigor and, by placing
god's support for the kingship.
icient rituals to take on a fixed
no temple image ever shows her
self behind. In her imagery, she

lls us something about how she
she had indeed been the power
l-brother, Thutmose II, and her
ds verify that Hatshepsut's rule
tmose II's death; thus she likely
ng died. But we learn something
me, she was also linking her rule
explicitly before. She was essen-
lling her people that his years of
as well. The Sed festival therefore
Thutmose I, designating her as

it was in year 16 of her joint rule
an to change the story of her king-
nd and concentrating instead on
chosen her to rule alongside him
in the tradition of the father-son
othing else, it demonstrated to her
nd elites, that Thutmose I was the
reason she occupied this throne. For the first time, Hatshepsut claimed

Place

-638

Pick Up By:
3/1/2018

The woman who would be King

0112410075231

Place items on hold for programs at Sorensen

Please take this item to a self-check station or staff member for check out.

Visit us on the web at colapublib.org

that she was the rightful successor as the eldest child of Thutmose I, essentially pushing her husband-brother, Thutmose II, out of the picture entirely and giving herself a clean linear succession. While depicting herself as a son, not a daughter, to Thutmose I, and wearing a king's kilt, beard, and wig, she used the jubilee to redefine her person to fit the patriarchal system of succession alongside Thutmose III.

Hatshepsut also modified the jubilee to remake her public image as a father figure to Thutmose III. Styled as a man in formal depictions and rituals, she now pivoted 180 degrees from her start as his regent and mother figure when he was a toddler king. The jubilee cemented her role as the senior king in a royal partnership, thereby creating the foundation for further rule in the next generation, as a father would do for his son, and as she claims Thutmose I did for her. Hatshepsut used the festival to maintain her closer ties to the patriarch of their Thutmoside line; after the jubilee, Thutmose III was linked to his grandfather Thutmose I through Hatshepsut, as her heir. She was doing her best to safeguard her family's legacy by bringing up a co-king from infancy, training him in ritual and war, and, ostensibly, marrying him to her daughter to create an heir. The jubilee demonstrated that Hatshepsut and Thutmose III were not only useful but also necessary to each other. Knowing that she would not rule forever and that Thutmose III would someday be king alone, Hatshepsut was investing her energy in precisely defining the nature of her dynasty, for her co-king and for future Thutmoside kings. Her unusual and aberrant rise to power instantly fit into a classic, well-established mold of continuous royal stability.

But Hatshepsut was not martyring herself for the good of her dynasty; she used her Sed festival to broadcast the miraculousness of her own strange kingship by publishing a number of narratives after the jubilee. Craftsmen carved them onto the stone walls of her temples in sacred areas beyond the public gateways, locations to which only elites would have access. One of these royal narratives, already quite ancient before Hatshepsut included it in her program of jubilee decoration, recounted her divine conception and birth in picture and text.[17] It supported the well-accepted mythology that the king's body and soul derived from the god's essence, claiming that Hatshepsut's authority

was predestined even before her physical creation. In this narrative, the
god Amen-Re is shown visiting the bedchamber of Hatshepsut's mother,
Ahmes. The moment of Hatshepsut's conception is sweetly and benignly
depicted as god and wife sitting across from one another touching hands
and gazing into each other's eyes. Their meeting is more evocative in the
text:

> He found her taking her pleasure in the harem of her palace. She awoke
> because of the fragrance of the god. She smiled at his majesty. And he went
> right up to her, desiring her and loving her. He let her see him in his form
> of a god, after which he came with her. She was exultant at seeing his beau-
> ties, and love of him overtook her body. The palace was flooded with the
> fragrance of the god, all his pleasant odors from Punt [. . .] The majesty of
> this god did all that he wanted with regard to her. She placed his body upon
> hers. She kissed him.[18]

In a later scene, the pregnant Ahmes walks calmly to the birthing
room for her labor. When the baby is born, her royal spirit accompanies
her. This spark of divinity was what allowed her to rule, and Hatshepsut
claims in this account that the royal spirit had always been with her, from
her first moment of existence in her mother's womb.

Egyptologists once thought that Hatshepsut was the first to depict
such a divine birth mythology and that she had created it expressly to justify her extraordinary female kingship, but we now know that Hatshepsut
was adapting older narratives of divine connection for her own use.[19] She
was placing herself in the culturally accepted framework manipulated by
Egyptian kings for millennia and explaining how her kingship was indeed a miracle blessed by the gods.

Also probably derived from older forms were claims that when her
father, Thutmose I, was still alive, he had personally introduced her to his
courtiers when she was just a child and told them that he had chosen her
to rule and selected her royal names himself. A similar narrative survives
relating to Ramses II, thus suggesting that such a "presentation" formed
part of the usual rituals of nominating an heir to the throne. One wonders
if Hatshepsut did indeed attend such a ceremony before her father died—
but one at which one of her brothers received his nomination as heir
instead.

Hatshepsut never claimed that Thutmose II's kingship did not happen, but in her stone monuments with their inscribed histories, she simply ignored her dead husband's existence and made her link to kingship directly through her father, claiming that she was king in the eyes of the gods even before that kingship was officially recognized by the populace. It was a claim of predestination, a fait accompli from the moment of her conception. Some historians have viewed Hatshepsut's justification for her kingship as a bald fabrication and the manufacture of ideological fiction to support her selfish whims. However, if viewed from a more practical real-world perspective of Egyptian divine power, Hatshepsut was only recording the political realities and responsibilities with which she had been saddled since childhood. She was relaying a great mystery to her courtiers: a child could be chosen to rule even before it had formally been named king; a girl could contain the royal spirit; and, in her current situation, a woman could be named king alongside a boy. When Hatshepsut celebrated her Sed festival eight years after she officially took the throne, she created a significant vehicle to display and communicate this foreordained kingship.

Perhaps we should accept that Hatshepsut was intent on telling her unusual story as she knew it to be. She must have truly believed that her father had chosen her to be king and that the gods had placed her in the position of saving her family dynasty. Or maybe, in her mind, the faith her father had placed in her when she was named God's Wife of Amen and Great Wife of Thutmose II was akin to his personally appointing her for great authority.

Hatshepsut's glorification of Thutmose I was an essential tool in her redefinition of her kingship. He was still remembered as the king who pulled Egypt out of a defensive, survivalist mind-set and back toward the riches of expansionist empire building. Any prominence afforded to Thutmose II instead might encourage people to ask why Hatshepsut, wife to a dead king, was still on the throne when that king's son was successful, vigorous, and able. Albeit now dwelling in the afterlife, Thutmose I was the only linchpin who had ostensibly marked Hatshepsut as chosen by the gods. The fact that Thutmose I was dead made no difference to the Egyptians. As a king reborn, his deified spirit was now more powerful than ever, able to carry good fortune and messages back from the source of creation to the living world. Hatshepsut capitalized on her place as chief communicator with this divinized spirit and built a temple dedicated to him within her Djeser Djeseru temple, where cult activity inside paid homage to a sacred living statue channeling his powers.

Hatshepsut now styled herself not only as the heir of her superhuman father, Thutmose I, but also as the divine offspring of Amen-Re, King of All the Gods, everywhere that she could—on her obelisks, on her sacred shrine at Karnak, on her new pylon gateway at Karnak, and at her funerary temple of Djeser Djeseru. This was no different from what other kings did, but Hatshepsut's plan was more concentrated on the powers of the sun god than earlier examples. She definitively linked her kingship to the worship of Re in all his manifestations. She erected more pairs of red granite obelisks in Karnak Temple than any known Egyptian king, all of them partly covered with electrum (beaten silver-gold sheets that were attached to the top halves of the monoliths). In fact, Hatshepsut's devotion to the Egyptian solar cult was something that later New Kingdom monarchs would model and follow,[20] and for good reason. Association with Egypt's powerful solar rays granted the king a new and impressive public display in temple spaces. When the early morning or late afternoon sun hit these colossal objects, they were thought to channel the powers of the sun god over her graven images on each obelisk and into the core of Karnak Temple, pulling the solar divine essence into the temple where the god's statues dwelled. On these obelisks, Hatshepsut associated herself with the rising sun as "the one who has forms like Khepri (scarab beetle representative of dawn sun), who rises like Horakhty (Horus of the Horizon, representative of noon sun), pure egg, splendid seed, whom the Two Magicians nursed; the one whom Amen himself made appear on the throne of Southern Heliopolis (Thebes)."[21] In public ceremonies, Hatshepsut may have appeared between her obelisk pairs when they shone in the most dramatic and blinding sunlight, displaying herself as a golden god to her people, an offspring of divinity, a superhuman being like her father. If she appeared between these obelisks as a man, complete with kilt, beard, wig, and crown, holding her crooks and staves, her gender transformation could be considered blessed and facilitated by the sun god himself.

When she wasn't claiming to be a god with solar manifestations, she styled herself as a sun priest who welcomed, worshipped, and aided the sun god's many forms, calling herself "the one who knows"—the only human capable of fathoming and facilitating the sun's mysteries. She modeled her family's native city of Thebes on the ancient city of Heliopolis, up north, building obelisks and associating her worship of Amen with the sun god Atum-Re.[22] Heliopolis was believed to be where the world was first created. Hatshepsut was turning her beloved hometown of Thebes into an originator of creation itself. And everywhere we see her ability to connect with divinity in a way that normal human beings could not. At Djeser Djeseru, she created an open-air altar to the sun god with texts expressing her ability to join the solar orb as he traveled through the day and night sky. Spells that granted Hatshepsut authority over time itself and allowed her to rise and set with the sun for eternity were carved into the walls, including one example in which Hatshepsut joins the ranks of the solar baboons, who were believed to speak the secret language of the sun god, greeting his triumphant movements through night and day. She likely chanted the following in Egyptian:

> "The baboons who announce Re, when this great god is born at the sixth hour of the underworld. They appear for him only after they have taken on their form. They are at both sides of this god and appear to him until he takes his place in heaven. They dance for him and leap in the air. They sing for him, make music and create 'joyful sound.'"[23]

Because Hatshepsut was such a force to be reckoned with, we often have to remind ourselves that she never ruled alone. At the jubilee celebration, her co-king, Thutmose III, would have been roughly seventeen years old. He had come of age, and the Sed festival would have been the best way for Hatshepsut to formally include him in the kingship as an active power. Even if Hatshepsut had tried to remove Thutmose III from the throne during the early years or, at the very least, ignored his existence, she could no longer behave this way. After the jubilee, the coregency was openly acknowledged and celebrated in monuments around Egypt. This Sed festival elevated the status of Thutmose III at the same time that Hatshepsut cemented her image as a masculine king. It may actually have represented an open acknowledgment and acceptance of real joint rule, with Thutmose III now responsible for decision making in the temple and palace.

Hatshepsut knew how to put on a good show. She went out of her way to create the most expensive, time-consuming, and innovative stone temples Egypt had ever seen as a backdrop for her jubilee. All around Thebes, construction projects commissioned at the start of her reign were nearing completion. At Karnak, she created the first monumental sandstone structure in Egypt: a massive pylon (the eighth), connecting Amen's temple with the axis of the temples of Mut and Luxor, that was 21 meters high, almost 48 meters wide, and 10 meters thick—so broad that a staircase fit inside.[24] The first of the enormous pylons built on the north-south avenue of festival movement, it probably replaced the previous mud-brick version. Just next to her funerary temple she constructed a chapel to the goddess Hathor that played a part in both the Valley Festival and her Sed festival. Hathor was a cow goddess, mistress of the western mountain, simultaneously mother and daughter of the sun god, a violent protector of the king, and goddess of sexuality and beauty. On some of the column capitals, Hatshepsut carved images of herself as a masculine king running in the Sed festival ritual race. These images follow the main temple axis, which suggests that Hatshepsut actually performed some of those running rituals here before the goddess. Other scenes show Hatshepsut interacting with the cow goddess directly, and it is even possible that Hatshepsut visited a worldly manifestation of the goddess Hathor in animal form as a cow here or somewhere nearby. One image shows the sacred animal licking the hand of the enthroned king; in another, a male Hatshepsut kneels underneath the cow goddess's udders and drinks the divine milk promised only to kings. Hathor was thought to be the mother of the sun god, and to show Hatshepsut suckling from her was to show the king feeding from divinity itself as the predestined son of Re.

At the nearby small temple at Medinet Habu on the west bank,[25] Hatshepsut built a shrine for the eight gods of precreation, male-female pairs of divinities representing darkness, infinity, primeval matter, and hiddenness. Hatshepsut knew the importance of the site. (In Dynasty 20, Ramses III would choose the same location for his grand funerary temple in an attempt to connect with the festival locality.) The god Amen, hiddenness itself, was thought to be buried here in his sexualized form, full of potentiality for new creation of himself and the world. One rite depicted at this sacred burial spot shows Hatshepsut embracing the statue of a god with a massive erect penis. She had to lean in from a distance so as not to come into contact with his enormous manhood peeking out of the god's mummiform wrappings. For the Egyptians, such an embrace was not sexual, but channeled prosperity through the king by facilitating the king's connection with the god Amen.

Back across the river in the realm of Karnak Temple, Hatshepsut paid homage to another ferocious and beautiful goddess: Mut, Mistress of Isheru and consort to the god Amen-Re. A series of sandstone column drums recently uncovered bear the inscription: "[She made it as a monument for her mother Mut] Mistress of Isheru, making for her a columned porch of drunkenness anew, so that she might do [as] one who is given life [forever]." Hatshepsut built a stone portico for an extraordinary ritual during the Valley Festival in which a ferocious and bloodthirsty goddess was given beer colored with red pigment. Rituals encouraged the goddess Mut to drink what she thought was the blood of Egypt's rebels until her violent temper was calmed. Her worshippers drank alongside the goddess during this feast, purposefully becoming so inebriated that they passed out in the temple space or engaged in sexual activity amid the sounds of priests and priestesses singing and dancing for the goddess.[26] There is even the suggestion that the beer was laced with opium, which gave the participants a mystical, hallucinogenic connection with the goddess.[27] The entire ritual was meant to break down the barriers of normal human behavior, which would allow divinity to creep into the world and pave the way for the god's release in the form of the great Nile flood. Hatshepsut built a stone temple (ostensibly tearing down the old mud-brick structure that was there previously) to facilitate Mut's appearance on the porch of drunkenness—calm, propitiated, sexualized, and beautiful.

Hatshepsut and her co-king would have been very busy during such state festivals. The offering of the god's meal was especially time-consuming and tedious on the great feast days. They presented dozens of different foods and drinks to the god's statue in the right order accompanied by the correct invocations to strengthen him. Other rituals were more challenging and probably required some training. In one rite, the king had to sprint before the god while holding two tall vases for libations. In another, the king had to dash about holding two heavy ship's oars in each hand. Another ritual had the king driving four live calves before the god Amen in his erect manifestation. The king had to perform all of these rituals while wearing unwieldy and awkward headgear and holding royal instruments, with the ever-present bull's tail hanging between his legs. If

Thutmose was available, Hatshepsut may have asked him to perform the more athletic rituals.

Hatshepsut's jubilee preparations gave her old cohort Senenmut even more opportunity to display his close connection to his mistress, because as new temples were ordered, he always found a way to fit himself into the building program. At Hatshepsut's Djeser Djeseru temple, Senenmut commissioned dozens of small carved images of himself on the walls hidden behind door leaves or in other overlooked places, an act that shocks modern Egyptologists, and presumably shocked the ancient Egyptians, with its audacity. For a private person to inject his own personal presence into some of the most sacred locations in Egypt seems somehow underhanded and immoral. The carving of his name and image in these temples was an extraordinary and unprecedented privilege unlike anything other officials had ever claimed from a king before.

There is no evidence that Senenmut was Hatshepsut's lover, but he was certainly someone who was able to ask for unparalleled dispensations, and this set him apart from her other supporters. Always part lawyer and part entrepreneur, he seems to have foreseen our consternation and made sure to state in the accompanying inscriptions that Hatshepsut gave him explicit permission to carve himself into her temples. Even his tomb chapel copied the tiered facade of his mistress's funerary temple, Djeser Djeseru, and was located at the top of a steep slope with one of the finest views in the necropolis, meant to be the culmination of his own mini–festival procession at his eventual death. His massive stone sarcophagus was made of the yellow quartzite stone used, as far as we know, only by royalty. It precisely matched the style, design, and workmanship of Hatshepsut's own final sarcophagus (she commissioned three as her career progressed). As time passed, there would be repercussions to Senenmut's boldness.

Depictions of Hatshepsut's daughter Nefrure on her mother's now-extensive temple reliefs or stelae show her to be one of her dynasty's most significant royal women.[28] Images of Nefrure focus on her priestess duties as God's Wife of Amen more than her role as King's Wife to Thutmose III. The details of Nefrure's life are almost impossible to elucidate because someone would later attack her name and images, viciously removing almost all trace of her from the many temples and shrines created during this period. Many of these monuments displaying a queen of Thutmose III were later recarved, but some traces of a name underneath—maybe Nefrure's—remain. If nothing else, circumstantial evidence points to a marriage between Thutmose III and Nefrure.[29] For Nefrure, it was likely a decision between marriage to Thutmose III or spinsterhood. She probably had no real choice at all.

Because she was erased from a number of monuments, Nefrure's history is fragmentary, but generations of Egyptological detective work have given us the veiled outlines of her life. The story may go something like this: Nefrure was married to her brother Thutmose III (in the Egyptian sense—that is, for procreation). Nefrure was his highest-ranking wife. Her life story mirrored that of her mother, Hatshepsut, who was also God's Wife as a young girl and then Great Wife to her own half brother, Thutmose II. Hatshepsut and courtiers alike hoped that Nefrure would be blessed with a strong and healthy son so that she could someday gain the title King's Mother and avoid all the dynastic trouble that had been plaguing the court since the early death of Thutmose II.

We also know that Nefrure was put into the strange position of acting as her own *mother's* wife, at least for ritual purposes, in temple rites and in public processions.[30] Perhaps it was even Hatshepsut who forbid any inscriptions calling Nefrure King's Great Wife because she needed the girl for her own political purposes. It would make sense that Hatshepsut, as senior king, would want to play down Nefrure's union to Thutmose III, thus highlighting her own connection with the God's Wife. We are left with a very interesting situation: if Nefrure was married to Thutmose III, and there is good reason to believe that she was, then she was also acting as wife to her mother simultaneously, at least for ritual events. Poor Thutmose III: he had to share absolutely everything with his aunt Hatshepsut, even his own Great Royal Wife.

If this was the reality, the royal family formed a unique political ménage à trois—aunt and nephew both tied to the same girl who, when acting as a consort in either a ritual or a spousal sense, was daughter to one and sister to the other. Nefrure probably had no illusions about her own importance as the only living princess born to Thutmose II and Hatshepsut. She was a key player for both monarchs: she allowed her mother to have a highborn King's Daughter playing the female role in temple rituals and gave her brother the opportunity to produce offspring of pure royal blood. Nefrure had become the bearer of sacred female sexuality in the royal palace in every sense.

Nefrure was a formidable presence; even as a girl, she had courtiers and a household of her own as God's Wife of Amen. An inscription placed in the Sinai in year 11, when she was around thirteen years old, shows her offering directly to the goddess Hathor—this level of cultic access was typically reserved for kings.[31] Some have even suggested that Nefrure was encouraged to transcend her roles as priestess and queen so that she could emulate the female sovereign her mother had become. One statue found in Rome in 1856 that now resides in the Museo Barracco depicts a female sphinx with a curled wig. It was probably produced during the joint reign of Hatshepsut and Thutmose III and is the largest sphinx that can be attributed to this period. The name of the woman for whom it was cut has been lost, but some Egyptologists make a convincing argument that it depicts Nefrure at the height of her power.[32]

Even if she was a wife to her half brother Thutmose III,[33] Nefrure may have preferred to use her title God's Wife of Amen, just as her mother before her had, because of the power associated with it. Or perhaps it was understood that every God's Wife was also a King's Wife, given that there is no evidence the royal women could marry anyone else. Or maybe Hatshepsut demanded that Nefrure only be named God's Wife to keep the powers of this priestly office in her camp instead of under the influence of her co-king and his entourage. Confusion continues to swirl around Nefrure: What was her place in the family? How important was she to both Hatshepsut and Thutmose III? What motivated her: power, religious duty, loyalty to her mother? Our bewilderment is compounded by Nefrure's later obliteration from temple reliefs: an indication that darker days lay ahead for the female caretakers of the Thutmoside family.

EIGHT

The Setting Sun

Now in her late thirties, Hatshepsut seems to have devoted her time as king to cult activity, either by building temples or by celebrating festivals. She was still the senior monarch, but Thutmose III had emerged as an energetic co-king. New temple scenes were ordered to show and name the junior monarch—if not to put him on equal footing with his senior king, then at least to raise his status. Now in his twenties, Thutmose III ruled as commander of the army. If he had wanted to get rid of his aunt, this would have been the time to do it, but there is no evidence that he made any such move. What did he think about being the only male king in Egypt's fifteen-hundred-year pharaonic history to rule as the junior of a woman monarch? Did he prepare for the day when he would finally rule alone? We can only wonder. The evidence suggests that Hatshepsut and Thutmose III worked within a partnership of mutual dependence because of the strange way in which their joint rule had been formed at its outset.

The year 16 Sed festival had already changed their relationship irrevocably, and to Thutmose III's benefit, by elevating the nature of his kingship, finally making him a visible partner. He seems to have kept his altered throne name at the jubilee—which had been changed from the original Menkheperre to Menkheperkare with Hatshepsut's accession, but in just four short years, around year 20,[1] he would have the agency to change it back, moving from "the Manifestation of *the Soul* of Re Is Enduring" to "the Manifestation of Re Is Enduring," no longer separating him from the true embodiments of the sun god.

After the Sed festival, Hatshepsut began work on the artistic master-piece of her reign: a small chapel of sparkling deep red quartzite built in the heart of Karnak Temple, which is fittingly called the Red Chapel by Egyptologists. The reliefs and texts found here represent the culmina-tion of Hatshepsut's conception of divine kingship. Nowhere is she rep-resented as a woman; rather, she is always fashioned with a masculine kingly form—broad shoulders, narrow hips, muscular legs, and a mascu-line nose and chin—that makes her depiction on this monument almost indistinguishable from her nephew's. Apparently the artisans who carved their figures side by side into the red stone were instructed to make the co-kings look exactly alike, as if they were replicas of the same king. There are more figures of Hatshepsut than Thutmose III in the Red Chapel, and she was still given the primary position in each scene, but something about their relationship had changed. Only her names and pronouns distin-guish her from her nephew and betray her feminine nature. Thutmose III and Hatshepsut are placed symmetrically—as partners—in the relief scenes on many of the carved blocks: both oversee countless festivals and religious rites and act in concert to keep Egypt in the gods' good graces.

Hatshepsut had to relocate the barque shrine that was standing where she intended to build her Red Chapel; it was a shrine at which she had performed countless rituals.[2] All of this work to disassemble struc-tures and construct new ones demonstrates how vital Hatshepsut felt it was to inject her presence—through the carving of her images and names—into the very core of Karnak Temple where the great god Amen dwelt and was transformed. Perhaps she was looking forward to her leg-acy after death, when future kings would perform cultic rituals to Amen while lamplight flickered over *her* many images, just as she had made of-ferings in the sanctuary of her forefathers. Hatshepsut wanted to leave an indelible mark on Karnak's most sacred heart, and near her new barque shrine[3] she built a suite of rooms called the Palace of Truth that was deco-rated with her introduction into the gods' presence and highlighted by a scene of purification by two gods who poured streams of holy water over her head and welcomed her into their holy midst.[4]

She called her new barque chapel "the Place in the Heart of Amen." Some of the blocks were so dark red they appeared to be purple, the perfect color to evoke the sun as he expired and slipped below the western horizon full of the potentiality of rebirth. It was a fitting construction for the last years of Hatshepsut's pious reign: it exemplified her claims to supernatural abilities and characteristics,[5] and by representing her heir Thutmose III, it promoted her Thutmoside dynasty in the future on her terms. On this structure, she explained how and why her kingship was supported by the gods and highlighted her support of Thutmose III's junior leadership. The walls featured a list of the king's duties, with an emphasis on the obligations of being chief priest: how she stocked the altars with food and drink, tended the temple and palace lands, relegated duties to her priests, created and implemented laws and regulations, built temples of sandstone and granite, created statuary of herself and her co-king, constructed a proper homelike setting for each and every god according to his or her requirements (Mut liked beer, Amen needed his wife's sexual abilities, etc.), and created the appropriate conditions for each god's "primeval time," or sexual rebirth. Finally, like a good ruler, she sought out economic growth to increase her empire and expand her treasuries to support the Egyptian deities.[6]

The Red Chapel was a culmination of what Hatshepsut believed her kingship to be, and to Hatshepsut that meant unceasing and untiring activity, always being there when the gods needed her. She used the Red Chapel blocks to highlight her piety by showing the daily meal for the god Amen in his sanctuary (perhaps this was something that she enjoyed doing, like a daily meditation that calmed her and cleared out her head): awakening the statue of the god, purifying and anointing him, changing his clothing, offering food and drink, then resealing and veiling the gilded shrine. Upon leaving, she would have erased all traces of having been there; a scene from the Red Chapel shows Hatshepsut herself sweeping the floor of her footprints as she backs out of the sanctuary.

Another scene from the Red Chapel suggests that such rituals were performed for statues of the living king, a new hallmark of the New Kingdom seemingly started by Hatshepsut and continued by the likes of Amenhotep III and Ramses II.[7] Thutmose III is depicted offering in front of a statue of Hatshepsut as Osiris at one of the way-station chapels on the processional avenue between Karnak and Luxor Temples. In another scene, Hatshepsut herself is represented performing rituals before her own Osirian statue. Such ritual activity reinforced the mysteries of the Egyptian monarchy at the most profound level, with the living king offering to the larger kingship, of which he was a part but still simultaneously served.

Given that cult activity was so time-consuming, particularly for a pious monarch like Hatshepsut, the female king needed support in the form of priests or priestesses in temples throughout the land.[8] The royal family could not spend all their time in the temple. Instead, Thutmose III and Hatshepsut probably passed most of their days and nights in the plastered and painted mud-brick palaces along the Nile and scattered around the delta, shaded by palm trees and near pools of cool water. The junior king probably went wherever important administrative or military duties pulled him, while Hatshepsut likely preferred her beloved hometown of Thebes.

Apparently Thutmose III was constantly in transit, whether visiting the harem palace at Medinet el-Gurob at the mouth of the Fayum oasis, working with venerable elites at Memphis, celebrating Atum's creation at Heliopolis, or inspecting the fortresses along the northwest border from his base at Perunefer. He was fulfilling the duties of the junior king, to the benefit of both himself and Hatshepsut, becoming the Thutmoside heir Hatshepsut needed. Evidence suggests that sporting activities—like hunting, archery, rowing, running, and charioteering—were important to Thutmose III and his entourage. We can only imagine the Egyptians energetically relating the zeal of their young, fit king and his manly exploits on the battlefield or hunting grounds. The previous years under Hatshepsut's leadership had been rather thin in the area of royal sport, what with the partnership of a woman and a child king, and before that with the short-lived Thutmose II and the older Thutmose I. These last years of the joint reign must have been an exciting time for the young king to display his physical prowess. The Egyptians had not had a vigorous young man on the Egyptian throne for generations. Thutmose III fit the ideals and expectations of the royal hymns of old.

Thutmose III's eldest son was named Amenemhat, and Nefrure—if indeed she was married to the king—was most likely to have been the boy's mother; Amenemhat would have been seven or eight years old in Hatshepsut's last years.[9] But this child is hard to find in the ancient sources, and uncertainty swirls about him. It remains unclear how many times Nefrure became pregnant, if ever; how many times she brought a child to term; how many miscarriages or stillbirths she suffered; or any other details about her ability to bear children. Thutmose III had many other wives, most of them unnamed and unrecorded—though some, like Queen Satiah, the daughter of the treasurer and tutor Ahmose-Pennekhbet, came from the families of powerful officials—and they all would have been engaged in a high-stakes race to produce sons. Viable successors were always a necessary commodity. A king wasn't truly accomplished until his heir was securely placed on the throne after him. Perhaps Hatshepsut dwelled upon this fact and was anxious to fill in this last remaining gap.

Hatshepsut was now an androgynous, mature, and unmarried female king, and the long-term possibilities of claiming future rule for her direct lineage (via Nefrure) were fated to fail. Everything would have depended on the political success of just one girl. But there is indeed evidence that Nefrure, like her mother, reached a status higher than that of the typical Egyptian queen and God's Wife of Amen. In the reliefs on the upper terrace of Hatshepsut's funerary temple, Egyptian artisans were ordered to carve a large-scale female figure (whose name is now erased but who many think was once Nefrure); she is shown standing directly before a goddess, a kingly presumption not fit for a queen and proof for some that Nefrure was indeed raised as her mother's heir to take over some kind of shared kingship with Thutmose III.[10] Perhaps Hatshepsut was now considering Nefrure as a kind of female heir. At this point in Hatshepsut's reign, Nefrure was labeled on a Sinai inscription as Mistress of the Two Lands and Mistress of Upper and Lower Egypt—titles used by the female king Hatshepsut herself.[11] The stela from the Sinai seems to be dated to Nefrure's own regnal year, an audacity in itself—"year 11 of the majesty of the God's Wife Nefrure"—as if she were a king in her own right.[12] On the same Sinai stela, her name was followed by royal epithets like "living forever" or "stability and power like Re," which should only follow the name or image of a king, not of a woman, no matter how highly born. All of this hints that Hatshepsut really did intend for Nefrure to become some kind of coruler to Thutmose III. It was an indication that she trusted her daughter more than anyone else to keep her legacy secure: Hatshepsut continually placed her in powerful positions, set her up for more authority in the future, and depended upon her to keep the family dynasty thriving.

Between years 18 and 21, Hatshepsut ordered craftsmen to create another such image of Nefrure, this time at her Djeser Djeseru temple in Thebes, where everyone would see it, and with the title Mistress of the Two Lands, which was reserved only for the highest-ranked queens capable of political leadership.[13] Whatever the real intentions of this scene, it seems to have been too much for some to take. Nefrure's names were later removed and changed to those of Hatshepsut's mother, Ahmes, long since dead, suggesting that depicting Nefrure in such a powerful position was considered inappropriate by influential power players. There is further evidence to the same effect: in the Upper Chapel of Anubis at the same temple, Nefrure's images were replaced by carvings of Thutmose I, Hatshepsut's father, modifications many believe were made during Hatshepsut's lifetime.[14] It is possible that Hatshepsut had wanted her daughter to attain a status approaching her own, a level of power that neared that of a king, but she was ultimately forced to change her plans. It is likely that Thutmose III, or the Amen priesthood, or some faction of elites resisted, fearing the creation of another strange male-female coregency, this time beyond the justification of necessity and dynastic security. Hatshepsut apparently relented, bowing to political or religious pressures and ordering the removal of all such images from her funerary temple. Or maybe no one dared speak against the senior king at all. Nefrure might have died during her mother's reign, ruining all such hopes for an heir of her own lineage.

If Hatshepsut was really considering the elevation of Nefrure to co-king, then it suggests that there was more to her own rule than selfless protection of her dynasty; perhaps her power had developed beyond a need to serve the gods and the country. Or it raises the possibility that by the time Thutmose III had become an active co-king, she now saw this arrangement of elevating Nefrure as preferable to just letting Thutmose pass the kingship on to an heir of his choice. If she was really attempting to give Nefrure unprecedented power as God's Wife and queen (or even co-king) alongside Thutmose III, then she was meddling with affairs of succession after her death, trying to force the selection of an heir from her chosen wife. If all of these hypotheses bear out, then Hatshepsut did finally become a revolutionary thinker, a romantic idealist who believed she could permanently change the nature of the kingship, by appending a queen, in the modern sense of the word, as a coruler. This may have been Hatshepsut's last, best attempt to institutionalize the ongoing power of a woman, a decision she could make only after years of authority had changed her character. When she began her rise to power, it was in a mad scramble to save her dynasty. When she claimed the kingship, there is every suggestion that she was constantly negotiating and adapting her femininity to accepted traditions. But then, finally, in her last years, secure upon her throne and possibly lost in anxious ruminations, she acted on her own personal investments, attempting to institute a significant change in Egypt's system of kingship on behalf of her daughter. The details are murky, but Hatshepsut's orders toward the end of her reign suggest her modus operandi had shifted.

Despite Hatshepsut's maneuvering (perceived or real) to ensure her daughter the best possible political and religious positions, all we see today are hints of Nefrure's name, and the clear evidence of a systematic campaign to remove her from the record. Why? Nefrure was also born to Thutmose II, making her a sibling of Thutmose III. Who would harm the King's Sister, ordering an assault on the girl most closely connected to Hatshepsut? If Nefrure's execrations happened during her mother's lifetime, it could indicate that the God's Wife had fallen out of favor with one or both of the ruling kings. If her names were removed after Nefrure's death, after another woman took over as chief queen of Thutmose III and God's Wife of Amen, it is likely that people suffered her aspirations and presumptions only while she was alive and gladly removed any trace in her absence. But in the end, the destruction of her names implies that Nefrure's claims to kingly power—at least in the way she was depicted as standing directly before divinities, offering to them as a king, and calling herself Mistress of the Two Lands—were seen as overreaching and something that needed to be expunged.

Hatshepsut lost all ambitions for her daughter when Nefrure's names were erased. If the execrations happened in these last years of Hatshepsut's life, this massive political defeat must have been a devastating end to all the female king's plans and ambitions, perhaps even hastening an early death. Indeed, Nefrure's presumptive claims of royal titles are enough for some Egyptologists to whisper that Hatshepsut did not die a natural death at all[15] but was helped to a premature end because her presumptions for Nefrure were made out of personal ambitions that were likely antithetical to the agenda of her partner on the throne.

Senenmut's role in Nefrure's fall is unknown. According to the sources, Senenmut was the overseer of the ongoing work at Djeser Djeseru, and ostensibly he was the one who supervised the creation of Nefrure's images and possibly even the one who subsequently had to see to their removal. Because Nefrure had the potential to be a great future patron to Senenmut, just as her mother had been, he may not only have protected her but also actively promoted her interests. If she were to fall from grace, Senenmut would have tumbled as well.

A few circumstantial clues point to tensions during the later years of Hatshepsut's reign. Carved repeatedly at her temple of Djeser Djeseru is the phrase "he who shall do her homage shall live, he who shall speak evil in blasphemy of her Majesty shall die."[16] This statement is not typically found on a New Kingdom funerary temple, leading us to wonder what criticisms people were actually whispering about Hatshepsut's reign. Despite such a warning, there is no evidence that Hatshepsut killed any of her officials for noncompliance. To the contrary, the fact that Nefrure's names may have been replaced during Hatshepsut's reign indicates that she was not able to get her way all the time, and that she may have bent to the will of the majority who longed for traditional models of kingship.

There can be no doubt that Hatshepsut's unprecedented power came at a price, literally, and during her reign officials were well compensated, spending more money on conspicuous displays of statuary and tombs than during any previous period in the New Kingdom. The number and size of the elites' tomb chapels in western Thebes testify to the rapid uptick in wealth among her officials, riches they could only have earned under her watch. Officials commissioned numerous temple statues of themselves and competed with one another for the most unusual and impressive tomb chapel paintings and secret religious inscriptions.[17] To be sure, Hatshepsut ruled over a time of prosperity and expansion for Egypt, but this boom of nonroyal construction represented something more. The elites understood the unusual nature of the current kingship, as well as the affluence of the nation's financial situation; they combined the two to create a perfect recipe for their personal enrichment, one that verged on bureaucratic blackmail. This new breed of king was dependent upon their approval, and collectively they seem to have taken advantage of their clout, asking for more tombs, more statues, more sacred texts—more than previous officials ever felt they could demand. These men formulated new rules of style and convention and reveled in their creativity and one-upmanship.[18] Hatshepsut likely created her own monsters—nobles she bought off and had to keep compensating and elevating.[19]

Luckily for Hatshepsut, Egypt's current state of prosperity could support such payoffs to loyal men. Without gold from Nubia and the Eastern Desert, sacred stones from her quarries, turquoise from the Sinai, cedar from Lebanon, ebony from sub-Saharan Africa, electrum from the Eastern Desert, ivory, and panther skins from Punt, stores of grain from rich harvests, and trade with Phoenicians and Cretans of the Aegean, it is unlikely that Hatshepsut ever could have gained as much power as she did. She did not create her position as female king through bullying or charm; she bought it.

Hatshepsut also commodified her ability to talk to the gods. Many officials had their pious monarch painted into their tomb chapels because she could speak to divinity on their behalf.[20] These "loyalist" depictions provide some clue as to the coercions and inducements that transpired during Hatshepsut's reign, implying that there was something material and political to be gained from having a figure of Hatshepsut in one's tomb and that an individual would thrive from showing the king such respect and demonstrate his favored status at court. There is no evidence that any officials refused to display such loyalty or, on the other end of the spectrum, that they were compelled to do so by force or threat; rather, it seems an oft-deployed tactic, and royally bestowed honor, to win and keep the king's favor. Her officials knew that they needed to stay on her good side, or at the very least everyone was happy to ride the gravy train and toe the line.

For her part, Hatshepsut seemed eager to stay in the gods' good graces. The empire was growing—extending from parts of Palestine to the Fourth Cataract of the Nile in modern-day Sudan—and its products were designated by Hatshepsut to be the gods' bounty. Prisoners of war were plentiful, and the institution of slavery had recently been revived as a more significant part of the Egyptian economy. Spoils from the campaigns in Kerma had been extensive.[21] Egypt was so prosperous that temples of mud brick, which had previously been periodically rebuilt when the unbaked bricks denuded, were now being constructed entirely of stone. Now, instead of growing vertically as time went on, temples grew horizontally in giant sprawls of stone, at Hatshepsut's command. With each passing reign, kings continued to add structures and elements to Karnak Temple, eventually turning it into the largest surviving religious complex in the world.

It is a happy coincidence that Thebes, the best-preserved site for archaeology, was also Hatshepsut's ancestral home, her most favored holy city, and the focus of most of her building projects. Elite families swirled about in a cheerful concoction of co-option and payoffs; they endorsed Hatshepsut's nontraditional coregency because it benefited them in the here and now, but ostensibly had no intention of continuing such female kingships in the future. However, during her reign, her courtiers were more than happy to bow to her demands in exchange for jewels, tombs, statues, homes, livestock, lands, and the marriage of their daughters to her male counterpart, the junior king. She communicated her message to her elites—through endless reliefs and obelisks, through her trading expedition to Punt, through celebrations such as the Valley Festival, the Opet festival, the Sed festival—and it was a simple one: I am god, and thus I am also money. Follow me, and you will be rich.

Many men did follow her. Hapuseneb, the First High Priest of Amen, did not even feel compelled to include the image or name of Thutmose III in his tomb, keeping all his displays of loyalty to Hatshepsut alone.[22] Senenmut also focused on his service to Hatshepsut and was allowed to have his image carved into many of her temples, thus displaying to everyone his intimate level of access.[23] Her vizier Useramen was granted the privilege of the secret incantations from the Amduat for his burial chamber, a text that the kings after Hatshepsut jealously reserved only for their own use. [24]

It was time for Hatshepsut to prepare for her own final end in the eternal west, and she opted for the grandeur and innovation that we've come to expect from the female king. She had long ago abandoned her tomb as King's Daughter and King's Wife in the inconspicuous Wadi Sikkat Taka el-Zeida, choosing instead to be buried as a king in the majestic royal cemetery established by her father, Thutmose I. Not only did she follow him to the hidden Valley of the Kings, but in keeping with her father's creative example, she also separated her tomb from her funerary temple; each was built in a different Theban location. Until the late Seventeenth Dynasty, kings had buried themselves in richly marked graves that were usually topped with gold-capped pyramids, and the temple structures for the cult of the dead king were directly attached to that grave.[25] Hatshepsut's father, however, had hit upon an ingenious solution ostensibly meant to ward off tomb robbery or to create another layer of secrecy and mystery around the king's tomb. Thutmose I had decided to inter his body in a secret cliff-side tomb within the huge, naturally pyramid-shaped mountain at western Thebes—today we know it as the Valley of the Kings. It was a bold plan conceived by a confident monarch. His son Thutmose II followed suit, it seems, and King Hatshepsut also adopted this new burial scheme. There remains debate over whether she cut a tomb of her own or simply added a new burial chamber to that of Thutmose I.[26] Either way, it was in an Amduat-adorned[27] burial hall that Hatshepsut intended to share eternity with her father. His coffin would be placed inside the first sarcophagus she had commissioned for herself on becoming king; she had it almost entirely reinscribed for Thutmose. Having so carefully reworked the piece, it must have been a terrible shock when Thutmose's coffin turned out to be too big to fit inside: the scars of the hurried hacking-out of additional stone to make more space can still be seen. Hatshepsut ordered another sarcophagus for her own ultimate interment alongside Thutmose I, and a near-duplicate was ordered for Senenmut.[28]

Her funerary temple of Djeser Djeseru was also finished during her lifetime, so she had the luxury of adding elements that were not completely necessary, little embellishments that she (or Senenmut, the building's architect) enjoyed. At the foot of the long avenue leading from the funerary temple to the edge of the desert, Hatshepsut added a valley temple to receive her body before it was to be carried to the funerary temple itself. This valley temple was one of the last structures built by Hatshepsut, and work appears to have been ongoing when she died. Archaeologists found tools lying in the fill, seemingly left by their owners, who abandoned the site the moment they found out that the king had flown to heaven, perhaps sensing that the valley temple would not be finished by Thutmose III.[29]

Work on Egyptian royal tombs and temples always seems to have continued to the very last moment of a ruler's death. It was almost as if the Egyptians thought the process of preparing for the afterlife could stave off the end itself. And when a monarch died, the next king typically did little more than ensure that the previous king's sepulcher was capable of housing a body—any other outstanding details were left unfinished. The new king's interests, along with his predecessor's funds, were now directed toward the new king's tomb and the new king's temples. Egyptians were not troubled by the idea of burying a king in an incomplete tomb—that was the last guy's problem—so the unfinished elements of Hatshepsut's tomb or temple alone should not make us suspect she met a bad end.

The truth is that we have no idea how Hatshepsut died. Maybe she fell ill. Perhaps her daughter Nefrure sat with her as she lay prone in her royal bedchamber, burning with fever, attempting to calm her mother's spirits during this final transformation. Because all the evidence suggests that Hatshepsut was quite pious, she probably believed that the gods were calling for her to ascend to them, to fly up to the solar barque of millions of years and journey with Re through the heavens of day and night. Perhaps her deathwatch was accompanied by solar spells of mourning marking the moment of the sun god's passing into the west and the underworld:

> They adore the great god after he has reached them. It is their voices which guide them to him. It is their wailing which accompanies him. . . . They are those who bring the ba-souls to their sleep. What they have to do is to care for the bringing of deep night and to perform sacrifices according to their hours. It is they who guard the day and bring the night until this great god has come out from the Unified Darkness to settle in the gateway of the eastern horizon of the sky. They wail because of this great god. They mourn him after he has passed by them. Whoever knows them will go forth by day and by night. He will be carried off to the trees of the Greatest City.[30]

And so, after almost twenty-two years as regent and then as king, ruling from approximately 1479 to 1458 BCE, the woman who started as a King's Daughter and God's Wife, who went on to become the greatest female ruler Egypt would ever see, who transformed mud-brick temples into sprawling complexes of stone, who professionalized the priesthood of her gods and the army of her people, was dead. All her plans, all her anxieties, her obsession with succession and political stability—it all was finally out of her hands, and in the firm control of another.

There is no record of Thutmose III's emotions at the death of his aunt and co-king. Presumably he visited her on her deathbed, perhaps covering his nose with a linen cloth against the overwhelming stench of coming mortality. Throughout Thebes and beyond, to the priests and elites of Memphis and Heliopolis, word would have spread that Egypt's mistress was near her end. All of Egypt would have waited until finally the air left her lungs and her body deflated, leaving her lying prone, not in the stillness of sleep but in death. Priests and servants would have chanted and wailed around her, aiding her passage into the beyond.

We can imagine Nefrure (if she was still alive) directing the servants to bathe Hatshepsut for the last time and to wash and plait her mother's hair before the royal embalmers arrived to take her to the place of purity within the temple. Once in the house of embalming, Hatshepsut's body (the extremities perhaps already turning black) would have been laid on a tall bed with legs fashioned to resemble a lion's, a symbol of kingship, for a long night of incantations and spells. The priests likely chanted out the mechanisms for a successful journey through the heavens, intoning sacred words and phrases that would give her sustenance and strength for the long road ahead, protection against demons along the way, and transformation when she ultimately became an everlasting golden Osiris.

At one point in the ritual, Nefrure may have stood at her mother's feet, in the place of the goddess Isis, through the long night, wailing and lamenting. During these rituals, Nefrure would have performed as a Daughter of Re, a ferocious protector against any who might do the king harm. And in her grief, Nefrure likely tore at her linen garments, baring her breasts, ripping and tangling her hair so that when daylight came and the embalmers readied themselves to carry away Hatshepsut's corpse for mummification, Nefrure had to be restrained, still screaming and crying out for her dead mother. Such was the grief we see depicted in some Eighteenth Dynasty paintings of mourning. Or perhaps Nefrure stood there stoically, watching over her mother, knowing that her circumstances had instantly and irrevocably changed.

The royal place of embalming was likely filled with a haze of incense, a cacophony of priestly incantations and muttered orders among the mummifiers going about their business. The first incision into the royal corpse would have been made with a razor-sharp ritual knife of flaked obsidian—a cut just below the belly on the body's left side, just long enough for the flesh to gape open and pull away from itself, creating a hole that likely released a puff of methane, hydrogen sulfide, and ammonia gases with a slow hiss. The other embalmers would then turn to the priest who had dared to cut the royal body, and, as was traditionally expected in the ritual, curse him with invectives and throw potsherds at the poor man, driving the priest out of the room under a hail of broken bits of crockery until he himself could undergo a purifying ritual.

Another embalmer would have then stepped forward and carefully fit his hand into the seam in Hatshepsut's belly. He probably took his time feeling about until his fingers found the body part he wanted. Perhaps he started with the bowels, slowly pulling the length of Hatshepsut's intestines out of the cavity, lest they break, snaking the shiny wet mass into a large bronze bowl held up by one of his colleagues. The work was likely slow and smelly. The putrid stench of death would have collided with the sweet, rich fragrance of incense in the room, probably produced from the very same pellets procured on her trading expedition to Punt more than ten years before.

When the embalming priest inserted his hand into the cavity yet again, he would have reached farther into the corpse to pull out the king's stomach. Hatshepsut's last meal of gruel and broth may have still sloshed about inside. When he reached into her abdomen again, he would have had to thrust his entire forearm inside the body of the king. Perhaps he closed his eyes to concentrate as he broke some of the tissue connections, and then, with one hand on top of her belly to guide his movement, the other still inside, he shifted the liver toward the incision. With great care and with the help of more colleagues, he must have stretched the incision by applying lubricating oils so that he could remove the quivering, dark brown-red mass without damage to the body or the organ. Only with skill and patience could the liver be removed in one piece.

The lungs were always tricky. The embalming priest's arm would have been thrust beyond his elbow at this point, and maybe with intense concentration and incantations on his lips invoking the gods in protection of the lungs, he could carefully detach the right lung with his fingertips, never able to see what he was doing, but knowing the places where the organ might burst if prodded or where he might snap the tissue holding the mass to her body. The priest had to work around the heart muscle; it had to remain in the body undisturbed as the seat of the king's soul, a measure of Hatshepsut's goodness, and the physical tether holding her spirit to her corpse. Once the lobe was free, he could maneuver the lung around the heart with one hand inside the body, the other pressed against her breast, until the organ reached the mouth of the incision. With practiced skill, the organ was removed and placed in a bowl for curing in a dedicated room in the embalming house.

Throughout the process, men assisted with basins of water to allow the chief embalmer to wash his bloody hands. Priests would have chanted spells and kept the incense pellets burning until a new set of instruments was brought. At this point, the embalmer would have selected a long metal hooked tool and approached Hatshepsut's head, leaning down so that he was face-to-face with the mighty king, his chin at her forehead, before carefully inserting the tool into the nose of the corpse. He likely reached for another tool from the tray—a small mallet, which he could use to smack the metal stick sharply until he heard the crunch of the ethmoid bone giving way. After repeating this gesture on the other nostril, he would have inserted a long-handled spoon into the skull cavity and scooped out bit after bit of brain through the nose, trying to remove large chunks to speed the work, but not so large that his actions would harm the nostrils, certainly knowing that any impatience would result in a dilated and deformed nose.

When the spoon no longer pushed easily through soft, fatty brain matter but collided with the back of the skull, Hatshepsut's corpse would have been turned facedown and tilted feet up so that the rest of the brain matter could slide toward the nostrils for removal. With no way to take out the brain in one piece, its removal was laborious and time-consuming. Hatshepsut's brain tissue was thus not embalmed, but likely saved for burial in a mummification cache, a collection of used embalming materials and bits of human tissue. One did not just throw away the remnants of a pharaoh's putrefaction; this was a god's body, after all.

The body cavity would then have been packed inside and out with natron salts to draw out the moisture, the salts either held in linen bags or left loose like sand. Hatshepsut's naked body, rounded with middle age, was likely covered by these salts for weeks; when the natron became soaked with liquids after a few days, the embalming priests would apply a fresh salt treatment, slowly and carefully drawing all the moisture from Hatshepsut's body. This curing process lasted for more than a month, during which time the corpse was never left unattended. The king's body was believed to be like the god's statue in a sanctuary; it was meant to be safeguarded and cared for, while priests chanted spells, made offerings, and burned incense night and day. Hatshepsut herself was finally receiving the ritual attention that she had been trained to perform as a girl and had done for countless gods in countless sanctuaries as king. As a mummy, she was transformed into a god, clothed, anointed, and revered.

When the body was finally cured, it would have appeared brittle and brown, with its hair and toenails in danger of falling away; Hatshepsut's face contracted to the skull; her eye cavities sunken under closed eyelids; her body shed of its fat and lifelike fullness; and her ribs protruding through slack folds of grayish-brown skin. To rectify this, the embalmers would have dipped their hands into precious oils and fats, which they carefully poured over and massaged into the royal corpse, granting it pliability and flexibility. They used fatty unguents and fragrant tree resins to treat every part of the king's body. A funnel was likely placed into the nostrils, and aromatic resins were even poured into the empty skull cavity.

When the body was ready for wrapping, embalmers would have worked closely with priests who chanted transformative spells while the first layers of sacred temple linens—specially woven for the occasion—were wound about the corpse. Necklaces and collars were placed around Hatshepsut's neck, rings on fingers and toes, belts around her waist, and a golden diadem upon her head. Each finger and toe was likely individually wrapped over the jewelry, adding layer after layer of finely woven temple linen, restoring fullness to the corpse and lending sacred protection to the sanctity of this holy body. When the embalming was finally complete, after about two and a half months, the Egyptians believed the corpse of Hatshepsut had become Osiris, ready to be interred into his tomb.

Thutmose III would have received word when the embalming was done—it was his responsibility to act as chief priest at the funerary rituals of his aunt and co-king. He may have even visited the house of embalming to ensure that the wrapped body was properly prepared for the transformation rituals.[31] It was his duty to bring the body of Maatkare Hatshepsut to the temple of Djeser Djeseru for the last time.

The procession from the temple to the river was orchestrated to be a demonstration of grief: some priests beat drums as they walked, officials and other priests dressed in their finest white linen with bowed, freshly shaved heads followed behind, and elites in their wigs and finery made a more stoic march. Hatshepsut's women would have provided a stark contrast, ripping at their clothing and beating their breasts, throwing sand and dirt upon their heads. The royal children may have trailed along, their eyes wide at seeing their first royal funeral. Nefrure may have paced in the procession as God's Wife of Amen, behind her king and husband, Thutmose III.

Oxen would have dragged the prepared corpse and gilded coffins on sleds toward Djeser Djeseru on Thebes's west bank in Hatshepsut's last sacred festival procession. Her canopic chest—containing her stomach, liver, lungs, and intestines, each in its own cylindrical container—followed on another sled. Servants would have carried stools, tables, chests, boxes with wigs and clothing, sheets and food, makeup, and sandals. Priests likely bore shrines containing the statues of divinities, sacred papyri, and boxes containing mummified meats. Others brought amphorae of beer and wine. This long and opulent procession wound its way to the quay where all of these necessary commodities were loaded on a Nile boat for the king's last journey to the west.[32]

The rituals inside Hatshepsut's funerary temple must have lasted for many days, if not weeks. Thutmose III, now the sole living king, would have acted as her son and heir in the Opening of the Mouth rite when her mummy was placed upon its feet so the living king could touch different parts of the body with sacred instruments, thus enlivening her mouth and eyes, opening her ears, and enabling her arms and hands to be cut loose from their bonds of death, so they might reach out and touch and take again. Food was offered in a lengthy ritual meal. Drums banged. Sistra shook. Chanting filled the room.

Hatshepsut's death rites visited all of the cult spaces within her funerary temple, connecting the dead Hatshepsut with a series of divinities, including Amen, Hathor, Re-Horakhty, Anubis, Ptah-Sokar-Osiris (an amalgamation of mummiform gods who have the power to resurrect themselves), and even her deified father, Thutmose I. The cult space dedicated to Hatshepsut as a woman was inscribed with the Book of Hours[33] and chapter 148 from the Book of the Dead.[34] Here Thutmose III probably enacted hourly incantations connecting Hatshepsut's transformations with the sun god's movement. Her mummy was probably set up like a cult statue in this consecrated sanctuary, as rituals enabled a sacred transfer of power from Hatshepsut to her nephew.

Now believed transformed in her Temple of Millions of Years, Hatshepsut's mummy would have been placed back into the coffin, loaded on the sacred sled once again, and dragged over the dirt and sand roads in yet another stately procession. Attended by all of Thebes along the way, her revitalized corpse was eventually brought to the valley hidden behind the cliff face of her funerary temple, its entrance nestled high in the western mountain sacred to the goddess Hathor. The crowd was not allowed into this mysterious valley, home of the Thutmoside kings.

Hatshepsut was probably less than forty when she died. Despite the claims of a Discovery Channel television show *The Lost Queen*, her mummy has still not been firmly identified. Given that there is no direct evidence for any kind of foul play,[35] Hatshepsut probably died the same way most people did in her day: from a viral or bacterial inflammation of some kind. She must have already suffered her share of infections and survived—perhaps tuberculosis or malaria or eye maladies—but each would have taken a toll on her health. With a steady supply of rich palace food, malnourishment wasn't an issue, but her diet also meant she would not have kept the trim shape of a young woman into middle age. Still, as a woman required to be on her feet for much of her daily duties, walking before processions and performing cult rituals in temples throughout Egypt, it's unlikely that she was the indolent, lazy monarch some claim she was.[36]

Hatshepsut seems to have been treated with care and respect at her death. Indeed, objects recovered from western Thebes indicate that she was buried as the king she claimed to be.[37] As Hatshepsut's corpse was transported to her sacred tomb, the procession would have thinned to less than a dozen people, not counting the craftsmen and laborers pulling the corpse and all the funerary objects. Only those initiated in the mysteries of royal burial and transformation could enter and perform the necessary rituals, including another Opening of the Mouth. It is possible that Nefrure, as God's Wife of Amen, was able to accompany her mother's body into the tomb, ready to act as a grieving goddess for the king, a sacred bird who spread her wings over the deceased in protection. There is no reason, however, to believe that Senenmut, a highly placed bureaucrat, would have been allowed to take part in such a hallowed procession.

By the time Hatshepsut was placed into her sarcophagus in her tomb, she had been dead for almost three months. Her mummy may have been covered with a shroud similar to the decorated cloth that was later placed over the body of her nephew Thutmose III. The words on the surface of his linen linked the king inextricably with the sun god: "His ba soul is your ba soul. His corpse is your corpse. Re says to Menkheperre: You are like me, my own second self." This total identification of the king with the sun god was included in the Litany of Re, which listed the seventy-four different manifestations of the sun god.[38] The series of nested coffins containing Hatshepsut's mummy was then placed in a quartzite sarcophagus. The coffins are now lost (apart from some fragments found elsewhere in the Valley of the Kings), but the sarcophagus in which she was buried lies today in the Egyptian Museum in Cairo.

Despite the Egyptians' obsession with dates and regnal years, the actual date of Hatshepsut's death is also a mystery. We know that Thutmose III left for his great Syrian campaign in year 22, and because there was no mention of Hatshepsut in the inscriptions recording those battles, Egyptologists assume that Hatshepsut died in or just before year 22, probably just shy of forty years of age. She had spent her childhood as the God's Wife of Amen during the reign of her father, Thutmose I, a few years as chief queen to a short-lived king, seven years as a regent to a child king, and fifteen years in a coregency with her nephew-king, Thutmose III. Neither she nor her daughter had sons who survived to take kingly office. Despite not having an heir herself, Hatshepsut had trained Thutmose III, creating the conditions for him and his offspring to continue what she had created. Her legacy thus lived on through the Thutmoside line she had scratched and clawed and fought to maintain, against all the odds. She may have died aware of her unprecedented achievements, knowing that all was in place for her legacy to be celebrated for millennia after. Hatshepsut died as king, and she was buried as such—serving forever as this ancient land's longest-lived and most successful female monarch. Egypt would not be ruled by another such woman for fifteen hundred years.

But if Hatshepsut had hoped to be buried alongside her father, Thutmose III had other ideas. The dead do not bury themselves, after all. He seems to have moved the mummy of his grandfather from Hatshepsut's tomb and into KV 38, which was either Thutmose I's original tomb or a new tomb made especially for his grandfather by Thutmose III. In any case, the dedicatory inscriptions on the sarcophagus and canopic chest that came to house Thutmose I in KV 38 show that they were made for the reinterment by Thutmose III. Poor Thutmose I could not rest in peace, his mummy moved first by Hatshepsut and then by his grandson. Everyone wanted to claim lineage from this great man to form a royal dynastic mythology. Thutmose III's future kingship depended on creating his own direct connection to his grandfather.

Whether Nefrure lived on after her mother's death is still a matter of debate, as is the fate of Senenmut. If they were still alive, how they reacted to Hatshepsut's end is not known, but her death must have devastated both of them, if in different ways. Nefrure lost more than a mother; Hatshepsut had been her best means to acquire further political power. Without Hatshepsut there, Nefrure's position as highest-ranking wife was likely threatened; indeed, Satiah, the daughter of treasurer Ahmose Pennekhbet, seems to have been promoted to chief wife after Hatshepsut's death. As for Senenmut, Hatshepsut had provided the only means for him to gain and keep economic power. After she was gone, not only did he never climb another rung of the Theban social ladder, but he fell off completely.

Unfortunately, her choice of a hidden burial chamber in the Valley of the Kings did not have the desired effect. Hatshepsut's tomb in the grand valley was robbed when all the other New Kingdom tombs were opened—five hundred years after her burial, at the end of the Twentieth Dynasty and in the beginning of the Twenty-First, when Egypt entered a deep economic and political crisis. Only a few tombs survived unscathed, and those owing to the good fortune of virulent flash floods or later construction that had obliterated their entrances shortly after they were sealed.[39] Hatshepsut's tomb was a tomb-robber's prize, filled as it was with gilded objects and statuary, furniture, precious woods and gems, and linens. Thieves took items that were valuable or could be exchanged and they left behind wooden, ceramic, or stone objects that had no fungible worth.

There is no evidence of her body having survived in the two known caches of royal mummies.[40] The heretic king Akhenaten was another monarch tellingly missing from the royal caches.[41] It's tempting to think that her corpse may have been purposefully discarded by Amen priests during the reburial of the royal mummies at the end of the New Kingdom, but Hatshepsut was no heretic. She wasn't even a rule breaker. Even the body of Thutmose I—a universally venerated king—remains missing. Perhaps Hatshepsut is still waiting for archaeologists to find her body, fittingly, alongside her father's.[42]

NINE

The King Is Dead; Long Live the King

Hatshepsut was gone; Menkheperre Thutmose was now the sole king. He had no one to answer to; no one he needed to consult about his campaigns; no one to keep apprised of his location; no one chiding him to share Nefrure's bed that night; no one to whom he must defer. It was year 22 of his reign, time to make a statement and show the world how his rule would be shaped.

His first move was a massive assault on Syria. The campaign came hard upon the passing of his co-king, so much so that he had probably been meeting with army generals and strategists while Hatshepsut was on her deathbed. Thutmose's reign-defining action was to be taken against Syrian cities that had refused to send their annual tribute payments. An Egyptian account of these events has been preserved, and one adviser is said to have proclaimed dramatically, "From Yerdi to the ends of the earth, there is rebellion against his majesty."[1]

Perhaps Syrian strongholds were resisting Egyptian hegemony because they thought Thutmose III was weak without his co-king, Hatshepsut. Or perhaps they had already stopped the onerous payments to their Egyptian overlord during the latter reign of Hatshepsut. No matter the reason for his timing, Thutmose III communicates in his historical records that these vile rebels needed to be brought to heel now.

At the end of his twenty-second year of kingship, Menkheperre Thutmose set out at the head of his men, perhaps as many as ten thousand strong, as they marched from their northern Sinai fortress up into Syria. He would have felt the dust in his nostrils and the grit on his palms, and his heart was likely joyful to be traveling with his men instead of leading another endless funerary ritual or temple ceremony. They were heading to the town of Megiddo where a coalition of Syrian princes had organized a defense against the invading Egyptians.

Thutmose III and his commanders were vexed over a vital strategic decision: there were three roads to the great city of Megiddo. Two of them circled the highlands and were well traveled and watched from on high, depriving the Egyptians of the advantages of speed and surprise. Their enemy would be waiting in large numbers for them where the roads opened up into the valley. But there was another way, a narrow path that no one would expect them to take, from the small town of Aruna, through the crags of the highlands, eventually spilling out into the valley just before Megiddo. It was the most direct path; his army would be able to reach the city quickly. But there was great risk in this choice. His army would have to travel in a single-file line—spreading his forces too thin to engage in battle once the first regiments arrived on the plain. If enemy forces were waiting for them, they would be cut down instantly, unable to mass a defense as they exited the pass.

Thutmose III was intent on taking the mountain pass. The story tells us that his generals questioned his decision openly, to his face. Perhaps they worried that Thutmose's newly won power had gone to his head or that ruling under a woman had put a chip on his shoulder, forcing him into an impulsive decision that would destroy the Egyptian army in one stroke. Thutmose, on the other hand, was not interested in limiting his losses. He clearly desired one bold strategic move whose audaciousness would shock the world—military action that people would talk about on all three sides of the Great Green Sea.[2] He likely also believed that victory was Amen's will, and that with such divine protection he was invincible. Whatever Thutmose III's motives were in such risky decision making, he no longer had to consult Hatshepsut. It was his time.

When they entered the mountain pass the next day, his majesty was in the lead, riding over rocky paths. His elite fighters followed their young king, their eyes probably looking up to the right and left constantly for the ambush they all expected. But they met not a single enemy. When Thutmose finally came through the pass into the Qena valley below, regiment after regiment followed behind, slowly filling up the mouth of the valley, one by one, until all three divisions were there, organized and in formation. Scouts returned to tell the king that the city of Megiddo was only lightly protected—the Syrian army had split its divisions between the other two roads, leaving only a small force at the city itself. The Syrian coalition had no time to move its great army back to protect the city.

His majesty led the center column of the three divisions, and they quickly broke the enemy line. Panic broke out among the coalition forces left to defend Megiddo. The routed Syrians ran back to their walled city. We can imagine the scene vividly: Thutmose knew that victory was imminent as he cut down men right and left, his gilded armor shining in glory, his gleaming weapon catching Amen's first morning rays.

But the king failed to see what was happening behind him until it was too late. Instead of reorganizing themselves to take the city, his men had already begun to claim their booty—chariots and horses left behind by the fleeing enemy.

Most of the enemy had reached the gates and were now shutting the great doors behind them. Those Syrians who arrived too late were hoisted up on garments and rags dangled out by the inhabitants. When he heard the gates shut with a thud, Thutmose must have known that the only option was siege.

Thutmose III's annals tell the story with precise detail: if his troops had not set their hearts to plundering the possessions of the enemy, they would have captured Megiddo in that one moment. But it seems likely that his soldiers were more accustomed to the Nubian campaigns, much crueler affairs meant to utterly destroy and pillage, than to the tough battles in the northeast that demanded patience and careful strategy. Thutmose's disappointment at the pillaging is recorded; he was cognizant of how difficult it was to take and hold a Syrian city.

But the war was not lost; there was simply more work to be done. Engineers measured the town by walking around its perimeter, and ordered the infantry to dig a great ditch encircling the city walls. Thutmose ordered the surrounding fruit orchards to be felled, and he used the timber to reinforce the ditch. He then returned to the comfort of his tent to wait while the people inside the city starved.

The Syrians, however, were not interested in any heroic stands. After some months, they chose negotiation. The gates were opened, and the assembled Syrian princes showed their submission, likely crawling out on their bellies and begging the great Egyptian king's forgiveness. In their arms, they held out tribute for Egypt—gold and silver, perhaps lapis lazuli and turquoise, definitely wine and beer. Servants behind them led out cattle, goats, and sheep. Thutmose listened to their pleas. He granted them leave to continue their rule—for a price.

As the real cost of rebellion, Thutmose carried eighty-four children of the enemy elites back to Egypt, probably forcibly separating them from distraught and desperate mothers whom they would never see again. Raised in his palaces as friends of Egypt and as future loyal vassals, these children were essential to the success of a growing empire. The Syrian populace left behind would fail to rebuild a successful coalition against Egypt while Thutmose III was alive.

Thutmose III started his reign off with a bold attack on foreign soil. Some historians have suggested that the rumor of Hatshepsut's death may have been all that the Mitannians, who lived in Anatolia and northern Syria, were waiting for to form a coalition with the Syrians against the young, untested king.[3]

This first campaign took place when Thutmose III was in his early twenties. He had probably been active on the battlefield for some time during his joint reign with Hatshepsut, leading campaigns to Nubia long before his triumph in Syria.[4] Based on the record he kept in his annals, he had apparently trained for such a war his whole life.

The Megiddo campaign occurred at the end of Thutmose III's twenty-second regnal year and lasted into the first part of the twenty-third, when he had only been ruling solo for one or two years at most. The young king wasted no time in earning himself a reputation as a warrior-king. As the only king in Egyptian history to rule subservient to a female king, he likely felt conflicted about how his kingship was perceived. During the last few years of Hatshepsut's reign, he may have been biding his time: planning and training, pondering this Syrian campaign as a defining declaration of his kingship. The Megiddo suppression was so successful that Thutmose III quickly became addicted to yearly military sojourns abroad; his fight for wealth, fame, and political influence never ended. During his thirty-two years of rule following Hatshepsut's death, he would lead his Egyptian army on an astounding eighteen military campaigns to Nubia and Syria, quelling rebellions and gaining spoils for the gods in obscene quantities. Apparently he did have something to prove.

These risky ventures were still moneymakers. The army survived on the products of enemy lands[5] and returned with extraordinary amounts of plunder: tens of thousands of prisoners of war to serve as slaves in elite households or temples; masses of luxury objects like exotic woods, metals, perfumes, and jewels; and commodities of daily life, including foodstuffs and livestock of various kinds. In Egypt, the prestige of all things Syrian began to soar among the elites at court. The rich competed with one another over fashionable products from the northeast, such as vessels made by wrapping molten columns of glass around a solid core, a technique that was improved upon in Egyptian glass factories.[6]

The Egyptians had long since developed an incentive system for these wars based on redistribution of plunder: men gave their takings to the king, who in turn granted some slaves and livestock as their due; the most successful warriors received additional prizes, such as solid gold neck ornaments in the shape of the flies that feasted on the corpses of the enemy dead. In the campaigns of Ahmose I and Amenhotep I, generations before Thutmose III, men boasted of winning the gold of honor in exchange for the hands they cut off the dead enemy, which they sometimes gruesomely displayed in strings around their necks.

Thutmose III's intensive campaigning brought more riches to Egypt than ever before. He put the funds to good use with temple construction. One of the first things he did was finish Hatshepsut's Red Chapel in Karnak. His own figures and names were already cut into many of the blocks of the structure, and during the early years of his sole reign, he completed the top courses of blocks in the two-room sanctuary. Thutmose III thus monumentalized Hatshepsut's role in supporting his own kingship. Some historians argue that he felt compelled to show piety toward the dead aunt and former co-king who had supported his candidacy as prince.[7] But there is the more pragmatic argument that finishing what was already under way was a much faster way to create monuments throughout Egypt instead of starting everything from scratch.

Some Egyptologists suggest that Thutmose III was actually an insecure king who needed to continue his connection to Hatshepsut, at least in the temples, to gain support among Egypt's political factions.[8] If this was the case, it's no wonder that the young king started his reign off with a massive moneymaking invasion of Syria.

But the Theban monuments tell a more complicated story than that of a desperately vulnerable and self-doubting king who was hoping to prolong the goodwill given to his dead aunt: at the same time that he was finishing Hatshepsut's Red Chapel hidden deep inside Karnak, where few had access, he may have already removed Hatshepsut's image from the most public parts of that same temple. In front of her eighth pylon, which was located where all could see—right at the front gate of the north-south axis of Karnak, where the Opet festival procession passed by—Hatshepsut had erected two colossal limestone statues of herself as a masculine king. Ordering chisel to stone, Thutmose III reassigned these statues to his father, Thutmose II, and to the Eighteenth Dynasty ancestor, King Amenhotep I. Inscriptions on both of these statues say they were "perfected" (*senefer*) or, in a sense, "made good" in year 22 of Thutmose III. By turning one of the statues into Thutmose II, Thutmose III was making a direct claim to the throne for himself, as the son of that king. The Egyptian kingship wasn't meant to pass from aunt to nephew, after all. Perhaps to stake his claim as the divinely chosen king, Thutmose III had to make some changes to this very public space by inserting a figure of the father he had hardly known and whom Hatshepsut had erased to affirm his own legitimacy. If these statues were changed in year 22 (and there is some disagreement about the date),[9] then it stands as our earliest evidence of Thutmose III's removing Hatshepsut's image from the temple landscape in favor of his own father's. But it was far from the last.

In a much more private part of Karnak Temple, Thutmose III began his own masterpiece—the Akhmenu, "Effective of Monuments"—a structure featuring rows of grand columns in the shape of his beloved war campaign tent poles, a building he called his Temple of Millions of Years, in which he intended to celebrate and renew his kingship. Just after the Megiddo campaign, and likely using funds from it,[10] he began building this grand structure at the eastern end of Karnak with an entrance through a small gateway hidden behind the bulk of the temple on the south side. It was year 24; Thutmose III was already planning ahead for his Sed festival in year 30 by creating a protected but grand space for his coronation renewal. Statuary was ordered specifically for the Akhmenu temple at Karnak. The artisans carving the statues had spent years executing monumental works for Hatshepsut, so at first they delivered statues of Thutmose that continued to resemble Hatshepsut's facial features in her masculine guise.[11] When we remember how similar the faces of the two monarchs appear on the Red Chapel, it makes sense that at the beginning of his sole reign Thutmose III used a portrait that resembled his aunt's. There were practical reasons for keeping this public face for new statues: it was almost certainly the same portrait he had been using during the last five years of joint reign with Hatshepsut.

Within this Akhmenu temple, he built a small chapel dedicated to his royal ancestors, including reliefs showing sixty-two seated kings who had served Egypt previously (now relocated in its entirety to the Louvre in Paris).[12] Because this temple was to serve as a space for his sacred jubilee when he would be transformed into all kings past, present, and future, he filled the chapel with images of ancestor kings, placating and pleasing their spirits and eternally linking his kingship to their powerful presence. His father was almost certainly depicted in the list of previous monarchs, but the image is now lost. Most historians assume that Thutmose III decided not to include Hatshepsut with his other ancestors, but this is debatable since the ancestor list is not completely preserved.[13] If he did leave her out, it would be a stark indication that Thutmose III did not think her worthy of the title of king anymore, and something had changed in the few years between his completion of her Red Chapel and his construction of the Hall of Ancestors. By the time this latter relief was carved, Thutmose III may no longer have wanted to continue his association with Hatshepsut.

This is clearly the case when, five years or so into his reign, he had Hatshepsut's beloved Red Chapel, her triumphal display of kingship and legacy, dismantled block by block.[14] After putting his own time and money into finishing a structure celebrating the coregency, he now decided to sever all visible ties to Hatshepsut. The blocks ended up in a haphazard pile somewhere within the Karnak precinct, inside the walls but beyond the sacred confines of the temple proper. All of those images of Hatshepsut—as a man on the throne, running with oars, offering incense to the god, leading processions, acting in ritual with her co-king—lay strewn about the Karnak work area awaiting their fate. In place of the Red Chapel, Thutmose III commissioned a granodiorite chapel devoid of his former co-king.[15] From that point on, Thutmose III would not order a single monument, text, statue, or papyrus that mentioned, or even visualized, his aunt Hatshepsut.

After the first five years of his reign, Thutmose III created new monuments that laid down a foundation for his own kingship wholly disconnected from his former coregent. Perhaps he was ashamed that his kingship had been sullied by a woman and that he had been weak (i.e., young) enough to need her help. Perhaps political elements from Hatshepsut's side of the family, or even Nefrure herself, were asserting themselves, and he needed to deny them any connection to his crowns. Or maybe such negative emotions and strategies played no part, and he was only following every other king's lead by linking the place where cosmic regeneration happened with the names and body of the currently reigning king.

Thutmose III nonetheless saw Hatshepsut in the temples all around him. Because she had built so much in so many places, her images were inescapable. At this point of his sole reign, around five to seven years in, images of Hatshepsut abounded all over Egypt: reliefs on the eighth pylon on Karnak's south side, reliefs and statuary in the Great Festival Court of Thutmose II, her porch of drunkenness and main temple gateway in the Mut precinct, reliefs at the Amen-Kamutef temple nearby, dozens of reliefs from the Ma'at suite surrounding the barque shrine, not to mention her grand funerary temple of Djeser Djeseru at Deir el-Bahri, easily visible from the Karnak Temple quay where his boat alighted each morning from the royal palace during his stays in Thebes and still a highlight of the great Valley Festival every year. Why he took apart Hatshepsut's Red Chapel while leaving untouched most of her other structures remains shrouded in mystery. Confident in his own divinely inspired place as Egypt's unassailable leader, Thutmose III may have been content to rule with his aunt's images looking over him from Karnak, Luxor, and temples throughout the kingdom. Or perhaps he did not want to waste precious time and money destroying when he could be making his mark building and campaigning.

Around this time, Thutmose III commissioned (or composed

himself) his Text of Youth, describing how he had been named king as a child.[16] The text betrays a profound need to communicate to his people that he had been the god Amen's specific choice as king even though he had been just a small, helpless boy. He describes his young age honestly, but highlights how he was chosen despite it. He dwells on his mystical encounters with the gods who called him to heaven as a divine falcon to see the secret forms in the sky and to adore the sun god in his own realm, presumably referring to his later initiation in which he was meant to confront divinity face-to-face in a transcendental moment of celestial contact. Nowhere in this text does he mention Hatshepsut—even though we know she facilitated his early kingship. This inscription focuses on his own extraordinary and innate characteristics, his ability to connect with the gods suggesting that Thutmose III needed to legitimize his reign on his own terms after Hatshepsut's death.

Perhaps Thutmose III was finally able to assert his own will, independently of his now dead aunt, only after his successful campaign at Megiddo. It was his decision to make war that brought him his first solo income with which to placate, pay off, and otherwise reward officials, priests, and bureaucrats, autonomous of Hatshepsut's already established economic systems. Only then, perhaps, was he able to defy her memory by dismantling the Red Chapel and changing his portrait to resemble his grandfather. Some Egyptologists go so far as to suggest that Thutmose III's building program indicates a past hostility between the two rulers.[17] If nothing else, Thutmose III's decisions during the first five years of his sole reign laid a foundation for increasing separation between his kingship and that of Hatshepsut.

It is not clear how such decisions affected Nefrure. Some Egyptologists doubt she was still alive at this point, although others point toward documentation showing that she outlived her mother by at least two years and perhaps more.[18] She disappeared from the archaeological record at some point after her mother's death, in any case. Without Hapshepsut her value as queen and priestess was obviously gone. Thutmose III erased Nefrure's name from temples and stelae, inserting the names of other royal women in her place. It was an irrevocable move. Up to this point, Thutmose III's life had been inextricably linked with Hatshepsut and her daughter. Now he was shifting to a life that included neither of them, even denying their memory in carved temple reliefs.

If Thutmose III excised Nefrure while she was still alive, he had plenty of wives to keep him company or serve as priestesses in her stead. His harem seems to have been one of the largest of any New Kingdom monarch thus far,[19] in part due to the number of foreign women he brought back to Egypt from his campaigns. Daughters of vassal kings were given to Thutmose III and treated gently as hostages and tokens of their fathers' loyalty, guarantees that these men would not align with another coalition. Egyptian documentation names Syrian wives of Thutmose III, including Menhet, Mertit, and Menway, all of whom cemented international alliances.[20]

In addition, Thutmose III promoted lesser royal wives to serve alongside his Great Wife instead of having them act only as informal companions. He himself had been the product of a union between a king and a lower-status woman, and we cannot discount the political problems of legitimation that this may have created for his own kingship. After all, his early years on the throne were shared with a woman ruler, which was unprecedented in Egyptian history. Something must have threatened the security of this boy king's ascension to allow Hatshepsut to take the unparalleled step of kingship—possibly something connected to his own lowborn mother, Isis.

Now that he was established as the sole king, Thutmose III officially recognized many lower-born women as King's Wives, thus easing the problem of legitimacy for one of his own sons in the future. Or maybe the king did not want Nefrure's offspring to assume power, and by naming other women as legitimate queens he ensured that any offspring from these later unions would be seen as viable future kings. Perhaps Thutmose III was a kind of ancient Henry VIII of England—figuring out a way to create the succession that he wanted without any dependence on the highborn women around him and the unpredictable circumstances of their wombs.

Thutmose III's chief wife probably resided in her own apartments in the royal palace, but most of the other wives, ornaments, and beauties lived in lavish palaces dedicated specifically to their comfort and upkeep. Harem palaces existed at Memphis, Thebes, and Medinet el-Gurob, the latter founded by Thutmose III himself in a secluded but fertile location near the Fayum. Amazingly, we read nowhere of the men serving in such places (most likely *not* eunuchs) or of the drama of the women trying to leverage their children for a spot at the top of their limited social spectrum. There is no suggestion of political intrigue among the women or descriptions of the king's visit to remote locations populated by women whose only masculine company was that of their young sons and bureaucratic minders. We can imagine that some of these women only shared a bed with the king for one or two nights of their lives before he moved on to the next girl, or the next palace, or the next campaign.

Thutmose III's harems housed not only many women but also many children. The boys not chosen to be crown prince who came of age during the king's lifetime seemingly left all trace of their royal parentage behind; when they left the nursery, they married nonroyal women and raised families of their own supported by positions in the king's administration. As for the royal girls, who likely were only allowed to marry the next king during the Eighteenth Dynasty, there is no evidence that the long-lived Thutmose III ever married any of his own sisters or daughters. On the other hand, there is no evidence that the king relented and let some of these women marry nonroyal men. The King's Wives stayed busy by creating the most intricate and sumptuous royal textiles, bolts of linen cloth with a thread count so high that their softness was a marvel. The cemetery of Medinet el-Gurob indicates that these royal women and offspring were honored with fine burials.

During the early Eighteenth Dynasty, the role of King's Great Wife was a singular position held by a woman of royal blood, usually the king's sister. However, Satiah, Thutmose III's best-known Great Wife, whom he married around the time of Hatshepsut's death, had no royal blood at all. She was the daughter of the official Ahmose Pennekhbet.[21] One of his stelae even named Satiah as God's Wife of Amen, suggesting that Thutmose III also took this most precious office away from Nefrure and gave it to a woman with no bloodline connection to himself. Many Egyptologists, however, point out that Satiah is only named God's Wife once and in a place where Nefrure's name may have originally appeared. If Satiah did serve as God's Wife, she held the office only until Thutmose III's daughter Merytamen was old enough to replace her.[22]

Another of Thutmose III's wives who was given the honor of being im-

mortalized on temple walls was Merytre-Hatshepsut, almost certainly not
a daughter of Hatshepsut, because she never held the title King's Daughter. Likely one of the many Ornaments of the King brought into the palace
for his pleasure, this girl would soon realize her importance as the mother
of many boys who managed to live through scourges and epidemics and
who might grow up to be rulers.

The most highborn son of Thutmose III
seems to have been Amenemhat, the possible offspring of Nefrure. The
child may have been eight to ten years old at this point, and he was named
an overseer of cattle in year 23 of Thutmose III's reign, likely administering that position with help from royal agents and tutors.[23] Thutmose III
had produced a son who had survived the perils of childhood and was ready
for his training to become a viable king, ensuring the future of the Thutmoside dynasty. Nefrure was never explicitly named as the boy's mother,
or the mother of any sons in fact, but such an omission does not necessarily discount her. It suggests that we are now dealing with a wary king who
was unwilling to give any of his wives political power by marking them as
mothers of princes on his monuments. If Nefrure wasn't the mother, there
were other candidates, such as Thutmose III's wife Satiah.[24] Or perhaps
Nefrure is never mentioned as the mother because now that Thutmose III
was trying to distance himself from his dead aunt, he had to cut out her
daughter as well.

Almost all of the women and children in the king's harem remain
unnamed—vexing historians who want to know the method used to
choose Thutmose III's successor. During the Eighteenth Dynasty especially, it was not considered appropriate to show children in any formal
reliefs or statuary because these royal children were all potential heirs,
queens, and priestesses, and until they were fully indoctrinated in an office, there was no reason to formally inscribe their names anywhere.[25]
Daughters were more likely to be named on formal monuments than sons.
After all, daughters could officially act for the king as ritual protectors and
sexual exciters; no such ritual role existed for sons during their father's
reign.

Such a gender disparity in the representation of royal offspring
shouldn't be surprising. The Egyptians seem to have understood that it

was politically threatening to show male royal family members on their sacred monuments, because it may have provided them with a religious claim to political power. Royal women, on the other hand, were largely cut out of administrative office, and thus they could be included in the king's public life. It was the assumed innocuousness of such women that allowed them to be represented. Only rarely could King's Daughters like Hatshepsut and Nefrure break out of such strictures and find a platform for real governmental rule.

Thus the carving of Thutmose III's eldest son Amenemhat into the stone blocks of Karnak Temple must have been a significant move for the Egyptians, a testament to the plans that were being made for him. The fact that his name was incised into a sacred space dedicated to the eternal continuity of kingship from father to son is even more telling, encouraging the presumption that he was to be the next king. But, as was so often the case in the ancient world, the boy disappeared before he could fulfill these royal plans. If he died, there is no record of the circumstances in Egyptian documents. It is also possible that Thutmose III decided, for reasons unknown, that Amenemhat was not fit to serve as the next king. This last point highlights how little we know about the royal succession or about how the living king chose his heir from among his sons. In the end, all of that investment in the boy did not amount to anything. He disappeared from the historical record, leaving his father, Thutmose III, without his chosen son and with the anxiety of having to groom another crown prince.

Either way, Thutmose III had to make do with the offspring of his lesser wives, knowing that boys who resulted from these unions would not have a bloodline hearkening back to the old kings or linked to the higher-born queens in his harem. And this genealogical deficiency seems to have been the tipping point for Thutmose III and his formal relationship with his dead aunt. At some point, he must have realized that just the mere remembrance of Hatshepsut's legitimate ancestry was a severe liability to him, something he needed to erase utterly from Egypt's sacred temples. If he was going to have to pick a future king from the harem of lesser wives anyway, then he had to find alternative ways of bolstering such a son's rights to the throne by changing the system of royal succession in his favor. Since he himself had likely been such a lesser son, the claim for legitimate kingship had to begin with him and his own lineage, direct from his grandfather, Thutmose I, and down to his own chosen son and heir.

In true Egyptian fashion, Thutmose III started with the temple, tying the legitimacy of his successor to that of his own ideologically grounded, public image. If his portrait still resembled Hatshepsut, then his kingship would be perceived as dependent on her support. Now that he knew his heir would come from a lesser wife, just like he himself had, perhaps he worried that the boy might suffer from the same doubts of lineage. Thutmose decided that he needed a makeover, and during the next decade he crafted his public representations to differentiate himself from Hatshepsut as much as possible. He worked to create the perfect portrait of himself, and the surviving texts suggest he actually gave personal instructions to his sculptors so that they got it right.[26] Around year 42, almost twenty years after his Megiddo campaign, he officially changed his portrait to resemble that of his father and grandfather. Most Egyptologists agree that his father, Thutmose II, had only been able to order a few statues to grace the halls of Egypt's temples because his reign had been so short. But images of his grandfather, Thutmose I, were much more commonplace, and the grandson now chose to emulate the portrait of his grandfather, connecting himself with Thutmose I's Osirian statues from Karnak's wadjyt hall and from the old king's relief imagery in the heart of Karnak.

Then, a few years later, Thutmose III started construction on a new temple on the west bank at Deir el-Bahri that could compete in innovation, magnificence, and visibility with Hatshepsut's funerary temple at Djeser Djeseru. He called it Djeser Akhet, "Holy of Horizon," and he built it right next to his aunt's looming masterpiece. Strangely, in his zeal to best Hatshepsut, he ended up copying both her architecture (mimicking the multiple tiers and ramps) and her choice of placement (locating his temple in the same sacred bay of cliffs across from Karnak Temple). His structure was smaller, but he placed it higher up on the cliff side—so high that an earthquake eventually caused its collapse, probably not that long after his reign was over. The construction of this temple so close to Hatshepsut's most visible monument may seem surprising if he was really trying to distance himself from the dead female king. Even the choice of name, Djeser Akhet, seems derivative of Hatshepsut's Djeser Djeseru, and indeed it came from the name of the solar altar within Hatshepsut's temple. It seems he felt that Djeser Djeseru's holiness transcended the identity of the person who built it. Hatshepsut's temple was considered so beloved and so sacred that his best choice was to associate himself with its prominence.

He kept her temple, even embellishing it, despite the presence of his aunt that haunted its colonnades and shrines.

While Hatshepsut's nephew was working to establish his legacy, her greatest supporter was scrambling. Senenmut, old as he was, may have lived into the reign of Thutmose III, and while the nature of his relationship with the new administration is unclear, he was likely doing his best to stay in the court's good graces. During the early years of Hatshepsut's regency and reign, Senenmut had mentioned only her and her daughter in the hieroglyphic texts on his statues and monuments, but in the last years of her reign, he obviously felt the need to start lauding Thutmose III, too,[27] a decision that was probably connected to the year 16 jubilee and the larger part Thutmose III took in Egypt's rule as he came of age. Whatever the exact political reasons, it represents a shift away from Senenmut's earlier thinking that loyalty to Hatshepsut was all he required. By all accounts, Senenmut possessed a calculating mind, and he had probably been trying to find inroads into Thutmose III's entourage and court even before Hatshepsut's death.

When Hatshepsut died, Senenmut lost his most important link to power and influence. And he suffered as a result. His monuments dwindled in number during Thutmose III's sole reign, most likely because he did not have the same unfettered access to high-quality stone and craftsmen that he had enjoyed during Hatshepsut's kingship. His images were no longer carved into the king's funerary temple, or into any of the niches of Thutmose III's state temple structures. Nor was he named tutor to any of Thutmose III's children as he had been with Hatshepsut's. Instead, Senenmut was only able to scrape together the resources to commission a few statues, which at the very least suggests that he was a survivor, able to stay visible on the political-religious scene even without his patron Hatshepsut. But it also signals that Thutmose III's sole kingship marked the beginning of Senenmut's downfall.

Some of Senenmut's statues were found by archaeologists in situ at Thutmose III's Djeser Akhet temple, and one statue fragment includes hieroglyphic text specifically mentioning this later temple at Deir el-Bahri. Because this temple was not started until year 43 of Thutmose III's reign, this provides evidence that Senenmut lived to a venerable old age, perhaps into his late sixties or early seventies, continuing on in public service for about twenty years after his mistress's death.[28]

Work on his tomb construction was stopped suddenly while the chambers were still quite incomplete. His tomb chapel (Theban Tomb 71) included the unusual touch of a block statue atop the structure depicting the tomb owner as a tutor, squatting with his cloak wrapped around his young pupil, Princess Nefrure, as she would have appeared as a small child. It was carved out of the live rock on the summit above the tomb—a visible transmission to all his fellow elites of his close connection to Hatshepsut's family. This statue was never completed even though the limestone from which it was cut was quite soft and easy to carve. Something or somebody stopped it from being finished.

Senenmut's extensive burial chamber (Theban Tomb 353) was not located underneath his tomb chapel as was the norm. Instead, he followed his king and located the burial chamber near Hatshepsut's temple Djeser Djeseru, probably so that his body would always be near her eternal cult and the pioneering temple he had labored so hard to create. His underground burial chamber was crafted as a series of rooms and staircases that descended to the west, toward Hatshepsut's temple enclosure and the Valley of the Kings where his mistress was buried. Only the first of Senenmut's burial chambers had decorated walls, and these were not fully finished. More strangely still, this first chamber was filled with limestone rubble cut from the lower two chambers, themselves only roughly carved and completely undecorated. The fill in the burial chambers was never cleared, which leads us to believe that Senenmut's body was never interred here. The tomb was sealed without his corpse inside it.

We can only speculate as to why work stopped on this tomb. Perhaps Senenmut died, and the workmen quit in the absence of payment. Or maybe the project was disrupted during Thutmose III's sole reign when Senenmut lost most of his influence, leaving him with no access to the workers and funds needed to continue construction on his extensive tomb. If so, Senenmut ceased work on his sepulchers during his own lifetime, content to use them in their incomplete state for his eventual burial.

His ostensible lack of a wife or a son to bury him might explain why his body was never interred in his burial chamber at Theban Tomb 353, but it does not help us understand the greatest mystery about Senenmut. Inexplicably, his quartzite sarcophagus was dragged up the steep slope to his tomb chapel on the top of Gurna hill. Not only was Senenmut's sar-cophagus in the wrong place—located in the corridor of his accessible tomb chapel and not in a sealed burial chamber underground—but there is no evidence that he was ever buried in the priceless quartzite object: no linens, mummy parts, amulets, remains of embalming resins, or any of the detritus of death that is so common in the western hills of Thebes.

And Senenmut's final end is even more peculiar. At some point, the sarcophagus was completely destroyed, smashed into hundreds of pieces. Usually when an individual died while his tomb was still in progress, the structure was simply left unfinished while the owner was buried in a shaft beneath the chapel. But this is not what happened to Senenmut. There is absolutely no evidence that he was interred underneath his tomb cha-pel, which has no burial chambers at all—they were all far away at Deir el-Bahri. His final resting place and the circumstances of his burial re-main a mystery. The information we do have speaks only to a bad ending for poor Senenmut, alone and friendless, lacking the great resources that he had once amassed during his lifetime under Hatshepsut.

Archaeological evidence indicates that Senenmut's statuary, tomb chapel, and even his sarcophagus, the priceless quartzite body container he received as a gift from his patroness the king, were all defaced and de-stroyed. The assault on Senenmut's tomb chapels and burial chambers—and even the intentional defacement of his names and images—seems to have happened either around year 40 of Thutmose III's reign[29] or perhaps later, around year 43, when Thutmose III was building his new temple of Djeser Akhet. It is even possible that Senenmut was still alive to witness his own annihilation. The Egyptologist Peter Dorman has argued that the pattern of attack suggests opportunistic enemies of Senenmut rather than the king's agents. In other words, Thutmose III probably did not order the destruction of Senenmut's names and images because the attacks were neither systematic nor thorough. People seem to have taken the matter into their own hands and fulfilled their personal vendettas against this man who had angered so many. Using a number of different methods, from careful chiseling to rough hacking, they erased his legacy when they found the time and energy. Whatever the justification, the destruction of a hard quartzite sarcophagus would have required extensive labor and considerable expense. Someone really wanted him disgraced.

For the ancient Egyptians, violence against the images of the dead—

particularly in a tomb context—was not just a defacement of the deceased's memory but action meant to harm the spirit for eternity in the afterlife. Without names or images for Senenmut's spirit to recognize, he would forever be separated from the wealth of his tomb chapel and from the connections to the royal family that he had so carefully fostered. His tomb chapel suffered the most. Hardly any of the painted imagery remains. His statues scattered about Egypt's temples were also attacked, but not with as much ferocity as his tomb chapel walls. His name was removed from only nine of his twenty-five statues.[30] Presumably the priests of Amen did not appreciate it when enemies of Senenmut came to their temples to destroy statues in their sacred midst, so most of these depictions survive intact. The images Senenmut had carved into Djeser Djeseru were more systematically removed, probably by agents of Thutmose III.

The attacks against Senenmut even extended to his sealed and unmarked burial chamber, but here only a few representations were destroyed, probably because the space was largely inaccessible owing to the rubble cluttering the rooms. However, his tomb chapel on Gurna hill was intended to be a public space for the cult to his spirit; all those who wanted to give him offerings and connect with his spirit would be free to enter. Located within the community graveyard, it was ostensibly passed every week by officials who had been harmed by Senenmut's power grabs during Hatshepsut's reign. One's tomb chapel was the place where an official chose to record his greatest personal and career exploits, and here Senenmut documented his close relationship to Nefrure as tutor and his responsibilities as Steward of Amen; he even listed all the different kinds of statuary Hatshepsut had granted him, down to the exact stone type and pose. As a record of his life's work, his tomb chapel was a prime target for personal vendettas and attacks. It seems many wished him ill.

We can find irony in one of his tomb inscriptions: "As for any man who will cause damage to my image, he will not follow the king of his time; he will not be buried in the western cemetery; he will not be given any lifetime on earth."[31] Senenmut's paranoia was obviously valid, and without Hatshepsut to protect him or his memory, he was powerless to stop such destruction. Because Senenmut was likely unsuccessful in finding a place in the new administration, his funerary monuments were left not only unfinished but also unfunded, unused, and unprotected. He likely lost the right to any funerary foundations he may have set up to pay for regular priestly visits, a common elite method to provide economic support for ongoing mortuary cult activity. Even in death, the Theban people around him did not wish him well.

Similar acts of desecration were carried out against some of the other "new men" of Hatshepsut's administration—particularly against those who had no links to the old and admired Theban families and had come from nothing to climb to the very pinnacle of the Egyptian government. The tombs of the royal steward Amenhotep and Nehesy, who had organized the great expedition to Punt, were also defaced, though not to the same extent as Senenmut's, their names and images removed and hacked away. Amenhotep and Nehesy hadn't commissioned as many monuments as Senenmut had, so there weren't as many targets to hit.

Such a fate did not await every high official who worked under Hatshepsut, most of whom were retained under Thutmose III.[32] The young king wasn't intent on a revenge campaign or the upheaval of a completely new administration. Most officials stayed in their posts, facilitating a smooth transition of power.[33] Senenmut's ordeal related to his unique origins, or his methods of taking power, or his means of exercising it. Some believe that Senenmut's fall was linked to a larger phenomenon: the propensity of overseers of the royal household to gain too much authority, thus creating an imbalance in the distribution of power away from the traditional sources, including the king himself and the elite Theban families.[34] While the images of Senenmut, Amenhotep, and Nehesy were destroyed, Hatshepsut's remained largely untouched.[35] But not for long. She, too, would pay for her ambitions.

TEN

Lost Legacy

After forty-two years of rule, Thutmose III was now faced with the same problems of succession that had plagued his own accession. If he chose a son from a queen of great lineage, she might feel empowered by recent precedent to involve herself in government affairs, as Hatshepsut had done. Thutmose had learned his lesson, it seems, and he was already in the process of curtailing the office of God's Wife of Amen, stripping its power little by little, handing the title off to one of his daughters so that he could better wield control. Soon the God's Wife would be nothing more than a ritualist, without income, lands, personnel, or political influence.

If he chose the son of a lesser wife, however, there was the worry of legitimacy because the child would have no other ties to the old kings and no links to Egypt's great families. His own lineage from Isis had been problematic enough to cause Hatshepsut to step in as king, when many elites ostensibly complained that her young nephew lacked a pure and lofty descent.[1] Passing over any sons of Nefrure or other highly placed wives would be a bold move. It may be that Thutmose III was carefully laying the groundwork for the acceptance of a successor who had no maternal connection to Egypt's ancient bloodline. He chose to demonstrate that it was the king's lineage *alone* that mattered; the queen's origins had to be made inconsequential. He was looking forward to the future—to the support of his heir and to his legacy—but in so doing, he had to go back to the past and rewrite history so that it followed his desired patriarchal succession. Thus, for the remainder of his reign, Thutmose III systematically removed all of Hatshepsut's images and substituted the names and figures of his male line of descent for hers. Hatshepsut was now treated like an intercessor.

Despite all the time Hatshepsut had invested in her co-king, all the political support she had built for him, all the elites she had empowered, all the bureaucratic systems she had legitimized, and all the timeless monuments she had built, none of it mattered. Many of her supporters had already lost favor and were powerless to stop this machine of destruction that Thutmose III was now rolling out against her. Her legacy would soon be erased. Her monuments had been built to stand for centuries, as the temples and chapels of her predecessors had. But nothing could stop a king who was given the power to both build monuments and destroy them. It had taken almost no time for the legacy of Hatshepsut's supporters—Nefrure, Senenmut, Amenhotep, Nehesy—to be swept away. Now the time had come for the most powerful woman in Egypt's history to suffer the same fate.

Hatshepsut's Red Chapel had already been dismantled, its quartzite blocks lying in a jumbled pile somewhere on the grounds of Karnak Temple. Her Djeser Djeseru temple was apparently still the main focus of the Beautiful Feast of the Valley, providing the context for the revelry, drinking, and sacred processions that took place over a week every summer in Thebes. But Thutmose III's building program in Thebes was finally catching up with his aunt's. His west bank funerary temple was probably complete at this point. His Akhmenu jubilee temple at Karnak had been finished, and his other modifications at Karnak would have been extensive and visible to many.

Something happened to change his perception of Hatshepsut, causing him to abandon any protection of her legacy in stone. He decided to eradicate her from every temple in Egypt. Between his years 43 or 44 and 46 or 47, when he was fast approaching fifty years of age, an astounding twenty-five years after her death, Thutmose III decided to embark on an official and systematic campaign to destroy the images and names of his aunt and former coruler, Hatshepsut.[2] All around Egypt, but in Thebes especially, Thutmose sent chisel bearers to demolish what she had labored so long to build. The boy she had raised and trained as her partner and heir for all of those years had become a man who, after twenty-five years of waiting, had finally come to the momentous decision to wipe all trace of her as king off the face of the earth.

At the beginning of Thutmose III's reign, he had actually ordered his craftsmen to *finish* her monuments and piously add his name and likeness to Hatshepsut's sacred structures where appropriate. Now he adopted the diametrically opposite approach by removing hundreds, if not thousands, of Hatshepsut's images and replacing them with depictions of his father and grandfather. Dozens of life-size statues and Osirian monuments from Djeser Djeseru were attacked with hammer, mallet, and chisel until they were nothing more than fragments of their former splendor, fit only to be thrown into pits close to the temple site, to be buried and kept away from view. Those carved of hard stones like red granite or granodiorite required tremendous investments of labor and time to destroy. Any effort diverted toward this cause was costly and slowed the progress of Thutmose's own extensive building program. Yet despite his advanced age and the urgency of the work on his own funerary temples and tombs, he obviously felt he had no choice but to allocate workmen and resources for such an important task. The woman who had paved his way to a stable and legitimate kingship now had to be obliterated from the Egyptian temple landscape. His own legacy demanded it.

Thutmose III never wrote down any explanations for his removal of Hatshepsut from the Egyptian temples, but he had already been distancing himself from her for some time before he diverted precious resources to destroy her images. He had already changed his own portrait to give it a unique visage apart from his aunt's stylistic legacy. He chose a likeness that resembled the faces of his father and grandfather instead, visibly aligning himself with the male ancestors with whom he wanted to be associated. Statue after statue featured Thutmose's new portrait; it was an inevitable development to distinguish his face from what he was now having demolished.

The erasure of his former coruler was methodical and calculating. He removed her from the public spots that served as settings for particular festivals and from the innermost shrines where the gods dwelled. Nearly every image of Hatshepsut as king was affected. Sometimes craftsmen were clearly ordered to leave the reliefs of her face and body alone but to cut down the raised carving of her names, so that they could quickly and easily replace them with the hieroglyphic names of Thutmose I or II. But this strategy proved more troublesome than expected because many of the texts surrounding her figure included remnants of her femininity. Every .*s* of "she" had to be replaced with .*f* for "he." The -*t* after *sat*, for "daughter," had to be removed so that the label read only *sa*, for "son."

Hatshepsut's nuanced use of pronouns often tripped up Thutmose III's craftsmen. For instance, on the gateway to the upper terrace of Djeser Djeseru they changed the name of the king from Hatshepsut to Thutmose III but neglected to change "her" to "his," so one inscription about him incongruously reads, "Amen is satisfied by her monuments."

The sheer volume of monuments to destroy, coupled with the painstaking attention to detail required to complete the erasure work, meant that Thutmose III's men couldn't always get around to creating new images to fill the blanks. Sometimes he substituted a tall offering table of food for Hatshepsut's image, which left the god standing before a meal instead of interacting with the king. This solution removed most of the ritual activity and movement from the temple walls, so it was not always a satisfying fix. Instead of seeing the king burning incense in a brazier before the god, now the viewer observed the god standing inexplicably still before his offering table. Instead of the female king running before the god, now the god was simply standing before another offering table.

The banality of such fixes was probably disappointing to both the craftsmen and the king, but in many other places nothing at all was added to beautify or clean up the destroyed reliefs. We see only the rough shape of a human body formed by overlapping chisel marks, as if Hatshepsut's crisply cut concrete form had been supplanted by an unlabeled and blurry shadow of her former self.

Interestingly, images of Hatshepsut as queen—from before her claim to the throne—were left untouched. Only reliefs and statuary that supported the presumption of her kingship were revised. Thutmose III was attacking only Hatshepsut's kingly ambitions and actions, not her soul as a woman or a human being. In fact, he seems to have been content to coexist with her depictions as God's Wife, King's Daughter, and King's Wife. But portraits and texts showing her as king caused him grief, enough to create an ideological purge twenty-five years after her death. Most Egyptians only lived thirty years. It's important to remember that Thutmose III waited an entire lifetime before he attacked his aunt's monuments. Something must have shifted in his political landscape, something that hadn't been a problem before, something that kings worry about at the end of their reigns, not the beginning. After twenty-five years of coexisting with the memory of his aunt—the extraordinary woman with whom he had once reigned and worked, perhaps even argued with and loved—he now removed her from his presence.

He even ordered his men to erase her from the dismantled blocks of her Red Chapel at Karnak, even though they were not being used in any current structure. A disassembled monument with images of Hatshepsut as king was enough to vex Thutmose III. Leaving the great heap of heavy blocks where they lay, the craftsmen chiseled away her name and images only from those stones that proved to be easily accessible in the massive pile.[3] And so, after all visible traces of Hatshepsut had been removed from the quartzite, the blocks would remain there for a few generations until they were salvaged as rubble fill for the construction of a new pylon. Eventually they were discovered inside of a Karnak pylon by archaeologists quite confused at the haphazard pattern of Hatshepsut's removal.

Near where the Red Chapel had once stood and around his own new barque shrine of gray granodiorite, Thutmose III ordered Hatshepsut erased from the surrounding suite of rooms.[4] Perhaps since so few people saw these rooms, he never replaced these images with anything at all; the raw chisel marks remain as an open wound on these most sacred and intimate spaces in Karnak Temple.[5] He was already distracting his elites with new monuments nearby, so perhaps no one really noticed. Around his new barque shrine he carved his own historical annals, which documented his feats, campaigns, and successes as king.[6]

Thutmose III never took down Hatshepsut's obelisks, perhaps because that would have been seen as an affront to the gods or because the intense labor would have drawn more attention to his destructions than his constructions. She had already covered up the lower section of one pair of obelisks, building walls between the fourth and fifth pylons, which concealed the pertinent inscriptions and saved them from Thutmose III's chisels.[7] Apparently Thutmose III wasn't worried about leaving the ideological essence of Hatshepsut's names and images—and thus, in the Egyptian mind-set, her spirit—in the temple of Karnak. He simply wanted to prevent people from *seeing* and *interacting* with her as king. He did attack the other obelisks more visible to the public; craftsmen were sent to the very top of these six-story shafts with rigging and rappelling equipment so that they could remove any figures of Hatshepsut and replace them with offering tables.[8]

On the southern face of the eighth pylon, where her monumental statuary had already been reassigned to earlier kings, Thutmose III completely defaced the reliefs of Hatshepsut; the entire pylon was essentially left blank, with only violent chisel marks as decoration. A temple pylon was meant to introduce the king as the protector of his people and was typically decorated with images of him grasping his vile enemies by the scruff of the hair, ready to smash their skulls with a stone mace. The king's violence was thought to protect the temple space, creating a kind of force field between the profanity of the outside world and the sacred, clean, undefiled space inside the temple walls. Thutmose III had just such an image—smiting his eastern foes—carved on the seventh pylon, but because this pylon was hidden behind the eighth (Karnak was essentially a series of pylon gateways with shrines and colonnades in between), the public standing outside the temple entrance saw only undecorated surfaces, not images of their heroic king. Perhaps Thutmose III's seventh pylon reliefs sufficed for the festival activity that took place in this part of Karnak Temple. Indeed, it wasn't until the reign of his son that the eighth pylon was recarved with any new reliefs.[9]

Across the river, the defacement of Hatshepsut's monuments on the west bank was also under way. Thutmose III wasn't intent on dismantling the entire temple of Djeser Djeseru, probably because the site was intensely sacred, not only to Hathor but also to Amen and to deified kingship in general. Instead, he decided to transform this structure from a funerary temple dedicated to Hatshepsut into one dedicated to his father and grandfather. He converted every possible relief image into one of these kings, and because Hatshepsut was depicted as masculine here anyway, it was relatively easy work. Some of the images at Djeser Djeseru already represented Thutmose III, and thus the structure was altered into a confirmation of how kingship could move through three generations, ending at the rightful heir—himself. Hatshepsut did not fit into this story of masculine linear succession, nor did her daughter Nefrure. They were both removed from the temple walls, although Nefrure's images were probably already long erased by this point.

Hatshepsut's divine birth narrative claiming godly ancestry had to be removed entirely, but the chiseling was so superficial that the text and imagery could still be easily read by any who cared to visit. The reliefs of Hatshepsut's expedition to Punt and her obelisk scenes—some of Hatshepsut's proudest achievements as king—were likewise only shaved down and never entirely erased. If Thutmose III redecorated these walls, he relied heavily on plaster, none of which remains today.

At Hatshepsut's sacred funerary temple, all the ritual activity for Amen-Re, Hathor, Anubis, Re-Horakhty, and Osiris, all the incense offering, running, libation pouring, embracing, and other rites were assigned to different kings. It was now Thutmose I, Thutmose II, and Thutmose III who facilitated these most sacred rites as depicted in the reliefs. It must be said that Thutmose III may not have viewed his activities as destruction but rather as a transformation, *senefer*, "making good." Regardless of any rationalized justification, Hatshepsut was still deprived of an eternal afterlife as chief priest and king in these temples; she was relegated to a few images in Karnak and elsewhere as queen, wife, and mother. As king she had merely been a placeholder.

It was the Djeser Akhet, Thutmose III's new temple just south of Hatshepsut's, that saved Djeser Djeseru from complete obliteration, because it created an architectural complex unifying all the buildings at the site, a visible manifestation in stone of three generations of kings.[10] After Thutmose's recarving, the bay of cliffs at Deir el-Bahri could be seen as containing an orderly progression of structures dedicated to the kingship of the Theban ancestors (Mentuhotep II's funerary complex), to his father and his grandfather (Djeser Djeseru), and to his own cult (Djeser Akhet).

The statues from Hatshepsut's funerary temple were probably a great annoyance for Thutmose III, as they could not be converted into other kings without extensive recarving of the face and sometimes of the body as well. Despite the expense of stones like red granite, which other later New Kingdom kings (like Ramses II) would have been more than happy to reuse rather than throw away, Thutmose III decided that the best course of action was the removal and complete destruction of all of Hatshepsut's statuary. Crews of men pulled down and smashed the dozens of colossal limestone statues of Hatshepsut as Osiris that fronted the temple colonnades. A row of standing Osiris-Hatshepsut divinities fronting each colonnade was renovated into a row of plain rectangular columns, which lent Deir el-Bahri a more austere, and perhaps less Egyptian, air.

Thutmose III ordered any freestanding statues of his aunt utterly destroyed—one depicted her wearing a dress in combination with the king's *nemes* headdress; another showed her wearing a masculine kilt but with girlish breasts on her bare chest. Most of the statues from Djeser Djeseru, however, depicted her in an orthodox fashion, as a strong man kneeling before the gods in the act of offering jars, vessels, or insignia. But all of these statues, too, even though they could have been easily re-assigned like the colossi in front of the eighth pylon, were dragged down the ramps of the temple from their sanctuaries or processional avenues and into the courtyards below, where they were brutally smashed.[11]

The ancient Egyptians believed that harming a statue or removing a name could provoke the dead. Angry ghosts could visit considerable dev-astation upon the living. Hatshepsut had been a formidable personality in life and remained a force to be reckoned with after her death. The priests must have tried to calm Hatshepsut's spirit during all of this destruction by performing spells and incantations or placating her with food and drink offerings. We don't know how the Egyptians justified this destruction in their own minds. All we have is the devastation they left behind.

Thutmose III's craftsmen were instructed in how to best annihilate these statues, presumably so that they could deactivate them and break the link between Hatshepsut and the kingship. Every statue was pur-posefully and directly struck at the uraeus cobra on her forehead, sever-ing the queen from her kingly rule in one swift blow. And each one had erasures or strikes where Hatshepsut had been named king, thus cutting the owner from the royal titulary. These explicitly destructive ritual ac-tions were likely performed first, and then the statues were haphazardly struck to pieces. Workmen used an old limestone quarry near the Djeser Djeseru temple causeway—ignominiously termed the "Hatshepsut Hole" by twentieth-century archaeologists—as a dumping ground for the frag-ments of Hatshepsut's once grand statuary.

Some officials seem to have followed their king's lead. For example, Puyemre, the Second High Priest of Amen, perhaps worried about his close professional connections to the former female king, removed all her names and images from his tomb and modified scenes to include Thutmose III instead. He was able to keep his position when Thutmose III became sole king, but his son Menkheperre never rose in rank as high as his father. His family's political associations with Hatshepsut may have been to blame for his son's stunted career.[12]

Despite the breadth and organization of the destruction, Hatshepsut had simply built too much and embellished Egypt too widely for Thutmose III to destroy it all. He did not start his methodical removal of Hatshepsut until the last decade of his reign, and ten years was, astoundingly, not enough time for him to complete it. Destruction fatigue seems to have set in for him and for his workmen.[13] Perhaps his architects and engineers became anxious about the time and expense of these side activities and encouraged their crewmen to focus on the living king's construction work so that they could finish vital building before his death. Thutmose III's successor would have to continue the removal of Hatshepsut, but history would show that he lacked the necessary zeal for the work, eventually dropping the chisel, as it were, a few years into his own reign.

When Egyptologists first considered the destruction of Hatshepsut's monuments, it was easy to write a simplistic story about a woman who took what was not hers and got what was coming to her in the end, a tale of the rightful heir taking revenge on an aunt who had deigned to claim his crown for herself. Narratives full of loathing and retaliation were written with impunity. It wasn't until 1966 that the Egyptologist Charles Nims concluded that the systematic erasure of her names and images did not happen until after year 42 of Thutmose III, at least twenty years after her death.[14] Other Egyptologists have since pushed the date even further.[15] It seems that Thutmose III's campaign of destruction was done more for complex political reasons than personal hatred and vendettas. Hatshepsut's erasure does not seem to have been a campaign driven by Thutmose's narcissism, either, since he replaced most of her images with those of his ancestors, not himself. Her defacement wasn't about the status and perception of his own kingship but about something larger: how the office of kingship was transferred from one generation to the next. Thutmose III was repairing the ideology of succession to fit his current needs, and each modification he made to a relief or a statue was ostensibly to show how the sacred office had been passed from Thutmose I through Thutmose II to him—and eventually to his own son.[16] Thutmose III waited until the end of his reign to erase Hatshepsut's presence because it was only then that he needed to shore up the legitimate kingship for a son who had no genealogical connection to Hatshepsut's side of the family. By removing his aunt, whose lofty and pure family connections sullied the aspirations of his own chosen son, Thutmose III was strengthening the history of *his* dynasty.

Some Egyptologists have theorized the existence of two rival family lines: one descended from Hatshepsut's family and the other from Thutmose III's, both vying for the throne.[17] Unfortunately, no direct evidence speaks to any claims to the kingship by men descended from Thutmose I and Ahmes, but there is no doubt that this calculated destruction of Hatshepsut's images would have sent a powerful message that Thutmose III would brook no upheavals among his courtiers and family members, or against his chosen heir.

As expected, the Egyptians left little information in the historical record about the sons of Thutmose III, but there are clues. There is the evidence of Prince Amenemhat, who had been named as Overseer of Cattle earlier in his reign, and we also hear of another boy named Siamen, who lived long enough to have his name recorded on Egypt's sacred monuments. If either of these princes had lived or been deemed suitable for the throne, then perhaps Thutmose III would never have destroyed Hatshepsut's monuments.[18] Each of these sons may have had strong connections to both their powerful father and a well-bred mother, lineage enough to allow some influential families at court real power. Both also would have been old enough to rule out any need for a regent even if Thutmose III had died in his fourth or fifth decade. But it seems likely that both of these boys died before their father did.

Or perhaps we shouldn't discount the possibility that Amenemhat and Siamen were still alive when the campaign against Hatshepsut began. Maybe they were born to women too powerful for Thutmose III's tastes or had family connections that proved too problematic for his current political agenda. We know too little about Egyptian rules of royal succession to say with certainty that the kingship always went to the eldest son or that these princes were definitely dead. While it is clear that Thutmose III was making an ideological statement with his destruction of Hatshepsut's images, we still don't know the exact nature of the political problems that made him expend so many of his resources on her ruin. But the best explanation, using all the available evidence, is that he was anxious about his succession, his dynasty, and the legitimacy of his chosen heir.

Either by choice or by necessity, Thutmose III picked Amenhotep, a very young prince who was probably no older than eight. He made his choice around the same time as he embarked on his campaign of destruction against Hatshepsut. The boy's mother, Merytre-Hatshepsut, certainly does not seem to have been a woman educated to rule. Although her parents were never named on any monuments, her mother was almost certainly a royal nurse named Huy. Merytre-Hatshepsut was not a high-ranking queen; her titles were unimpressive until she was named King's Mother. Prince Amenhotep may have been born as late as year 37 of Thutmose III's reign, and his father assigned him as many tutors and nurses as possible, not just one as was conventional, but two male tutors and at least nine nurses.[19] He was making sure that his son had plenty of political supporters at his disposal, in case his own unexpected death left a young boy on the throne, who would be just as vulnerable to the ambitious and the power hungry as he had once been.

When Prince Amenhotep was crowned as Aakheperure Amenhotep, thus becoming Amenhotep II, his father was still alive. Amenhotep II was crowned as a coregent, ruling alongside Thutmose III, just as the elder king had reigned with his aunt Hatshepsut so many years ago. Once this coregency was in place, the destruction of Hatshepsut's monuments largely stopped, and Egypt's craftsmen returned to building rather than dismantling.[20] So it appears that Hatshepsut's destruction was only necessary when Amenhotep's future was uncertain. Once he was crowned, once he was king, its usefulness had passed.[21]

By erasing Hatshepsut from the landscape, Thutmose III was probably helping his son to avoid all the problems that he himself had faced: kingship while too young to rule; an overbearing regent who took his power before he was even aware of what it was; a lack of strong advisers who could speak up on his behalf; a mother too weak or politically marginal to help him succeed as king; and humble origins on his maternal side. Like so many parents who want their children to avoid their own missteps and misfortunes, Thutmose III actively worked to create a better life for Amenhotep than he had had himself by paving the way for a reign unhindered by doubt and insecurity.

Amazingly, the campaign of destruction suggests that Thutmose III's own complicated origins and succession still haunted him as he prepared to pass the kingship to his son.[22] But if he corrected the perception that his rule was somehow less valid or legitimate than Hatshepsut's, then Amenhotep stood a better chance of ruling unmolested. According to some Egyptologists, Thutmose III was essentially dissolving Hatshepsut's reign into his own and into that of her father and her husband.[23] And after he did so, before he died during his fifty-fourth regnal year, when he was in his midfifties, it was as if she had never existed at all. Hatshepsut was gone.

Thutmose III's actions suggest that he worried about the threats posed to the Egyptian government by women with power and influence, particularly the God's Wife of Amen, an office that both Hatshepsut and Nefrure had occupied. He systematically and ruthlessly gutted the authority of the position; first he bestowed it on his daughter Merytamen, a girl who was under his control, and after her on Amenhotep II's mother, Merytre-Hatshepsut, a woman of no royal blood and of no apparent talents or ambitions. Later in the Eighteenth Dynasty, kings usually decided that the safest people to trust with such a powerful position were their own mothers, women who ostensibly would do nothing to jeopardize the ambitions of their own sons.[24] After Thutmose III, the office of God's Wife was forever weakened.[25] And after the reign of Thutmose IV, all record of the God's Wife of Amen disappears for hundreds of years.

Amenhotep II apparently learned the lessons warning against wives who were too influential, at his father's knee. He never named or depicted any of his wives, not even his Great Wife, depriving her of any platform for authority during his reign. Without titles and offices these women had no political place at court. And so it went with Amenhotep's son Thutmose IV. Both kings focused on their mothers at the expense of their wives, presumably because a mother was much less likely to become overly ambitious on her own behalf. Amenhotep II actually relied on his own mother, Merytre-Hatshepsut, to serve in the official role of wife in religious activities. These kings shied away from including their queens in any public rituals. Hatshepsut had left a legacy indeed—of keeping women from power. Everything she had built and fought for—to empower herself and her daughter—seems to have pushed the liberal Egyptian allowance of female rule to the breaking point. If anything, Hatshepsut's kingship would eventually drive influential women out of positions of authority for generations to come.

Most likely the ambitions of Hatshepsut and Nefrure pushed these kings to forbid their women a public persona and, in turn, to undermine the importance of maternal lineage. With the royal succession restricted to the paternal line and the queen's line of descent deemed irrelevant, the King's Wife truly became just a vessel for the king's sacred seed. And interestingly, none of the women we know about from this time period—generally just King's Mothers—had any royal lineage. These royal women were not King's Daughters or King's Wives.[26] Later Eighteenth Dynasty kings ruthlessly cracked down on their women's power; female genealogy was simply ignored—certainly not the legacy Hatshepsut would have wished on the women of her dynasty.

Although we might assume that Hatshepsut was completely forgotten by the people she had once ruled, her existence and achievements lived on in the shadows of Egyptians' historical memory. During the Twenty-First Dynasty, the priest-king of Thebes, Panedjem I, named a daughter Maatkare and a son Menkheperre—clearly in memory of Hatshepsut and Thutmose III—thus showing that even some four centuries later they were still remembered as a family partnership in royal authority. Indeed, Panedjem seems to have been something of a Thutmoside enthusiast: for his own burial he took over and redecorated Thutmose I's coffin. Maatkare went on to become God's Wife of Amen; one wonders whether Panedjem had an eye to Hatshepsut's occupancy of the role when choosing which daughter to invest with that honor.

Thutmose III may have removed Hatshepsut's images as king from formal temple inscriptions, but the Egyptians kept a record of her reign in a different, less public set of texts meant for the learned and intellectual to consult. The fourth century BCE Egyptian historian-priest named Manetho—the same man who first recorded Egypt's system of thirty dynasties as a king list for posterity—included a woman named Amessis in his history.[27] His text was written in Greek, which was common for scholars of the time, so we should expect her name to be different. This female king was said to be the sister of a king named Amenophis (instead of Thutmosis). Some of the details don't fit with the story Egyptology has reconstructed, but this woman was recorded to rule for twenty-one years and nine months, which corresponds quite well with Hatshepsut's last attested regnal year of 22. Manetho also mentions a great deal of military campaigning after the death of this female king, which aligns with our information about Megiddo and later conflicts of Thutmose III. Thus, almost a millennium after Hatshepsut was erased from the temple landscape, her name, rule, and deeds were still remembered by historians. Egypt has always maintained two narratives, the ideological and the real: temple reliefs were religiously driven and represented a cleaned-up and idealized version of history, while historical papyri recorded what was actually known to have happened, even if it did not accord with the orthodox expectations of the gods or the political agenda of the ruling king. Present-day knowledge about ancient Egypt is largely based on the ideologically driven story, the one inscribed on massive blocks of stone meant to survive through the ages, because stone lasts longer than fragile papyrus or vellum rolls.

But Hatshepsut had another legacy, too; her architectural innovations and royal theologies remained meaningful to the kings who came after her. Even though her names and images were removed from Egyptian temples, the royal and priestly libraries seem to have been full of information about her creations and successes as king. Perhaps later Egyptian rulers perceived her to be a pious leader, but one their people couldn't understand or appreciate. Egyptologists have pointed out that Amenhotep III—a king unrivaled in exquisite temple building and known for extraordinary innovations, who arguably outbuilt Ramses the Great—used Hatshepsut as a model for his own kingship.[28] As a child, this Eighteenth Dynasty monarch was instructed in various styles of leadership, including that of Hatshepsut, and apparently he was strongly affected by her ideologies, particularly her interest in divine revelations. Thutmose III and Amenhotep II fostered an image of themselves as warrior-kings—with multiple ruthless campaigns and records of athletic and hunting exploits—but Amenhotep III strove to be more like Hatshepsut: a pious child of the gods who was ready to accept their oracles and act on their behalf, a builder of sacred monuments, and a participant in profound mysteries. By the time Amenhotep III came to the throne, no one alive in

Egypt remembered Hatshepsut's rule, but her methodology of leadership, her platforms, and maybe even her own letters and communications must have been accessible to Amenhotep III and his agents. She was preserved in the written and unwritten memories of the Egyptian people—in temple libraries, in the craftsmen's songs, or in the stories heard by the oldest Amen priests.

There was much in Hatshepsut's innovative reign to impress a king like Amenhotep III. She systematized the Opet festival by creating a stone stage for the Theban ritual that stretched from Karnak Temple to Luxor Temple. She solarized the monuments of her kingship—dedicating them to the mysterious workings of the sun god. She resurrected the practice of populating Egypt's temples with obelisks, rays of the sun set in stone. Her use of stone was unprecedented: she built the southern axis of Karnak Temple in stone for the first time, added stone elements to Luxor Temple, constructed the temple of Amen Kamutef and the temple in the Mut precinct in stone. And she dedicated her workmen to building temples for goddesses all over Egypt—female divinities who devoted their viciousness and their sexuality to their father, the sun god.

During her reign, we see evidence for the first codified and large-scale Beautiful Feast of the Valley. Hatshepsut took esoteric valley celebrations of renewal and firmly linked them to the politics of her own kingship—in her capacity as a high priest who could understand the mysteries of life after death—to her benefit and that of every king who followed her. She styled herself as a sun priest, and she was initiated into the secrets of that cult. In her open sun chapel at Djeser Djeseru, she recorded the journey of the sun through its hourly manifestations, probably a first for any New Kingdom monarch.

Hatshepsut was the first known Egyptian king to choose divine revelation as the chief justification for her kingship. In accordance with her deep piety, everything she did was in service to the gods, and to Amen of Thebes in particular. She used sacred festivals, when the god went forth from his sanctuary and communed with the people, as a public setting to demonstrate the gods' support of her rule. Even the wealth she collected on Nubian campaigns was described as the gods' due, and every bureaucratic or priestly position created was said to be for the gods' glory. Hatshepsut needed to intertwine her kingship with the religious structures that meant so much to people, the rituals and traditions on which they depended to make their crops grow and their children healthy, to facilitate her unprecedented political and economic control.

In keeping with Hatshepsut's model, her officials and priests sought more immersion in religious mysteries and wider access to sacred books, which led to the first extensive papyri inscribed with the Book of the Dead. She instituted an intellectual theological renaissance in Thebes. Before that time, extracts of sacred books had appeared on funerary pieces like coffins or canopic jars, but now for the first time elites were being buried with lengthy and personalized papyri, which provided evidence of participation in the mysteries of divine renewal at a broader, abstracter, level than ever before. During her reign, people were writing new things down on papyrus and carving inscriptions into stone that they hadn't ever recorded before.

In the end, Hatshepsut's greatest accomplishment and most daring innovation was her methodical and calculated creation of the only truly successful female kingship in the ancient world. Historians can find almost no evidence of effective, formally defined, long-term female leadership from antiquity—not from the Mediterranean, the Near East, Africa, Central Asia, or the New World. These societies—city-states, regional states, or vast empires—were inherently based on masculine dominance because of their reliance on kingship and dynastic succession. A woman could take the throne only when regional or imperial aggressions had removed all men from the centers of power or when a dynasty was at its end and all appropriate males in the royal family were dead. The only rivals to Hatshepsut's models of female power would come later, from imperial China.[29]

In the ancient world, female power was made possible only in times of crisis; catastrophe was seemingly a prerequisite to a woman's participation in an exclusively male system. Queen Tawosret of the Nineteenth Dynasty claimed the kingship alone for a mere two years after she had no son to continue her lineage; however, the only thing her reign brought about was the beginning of a new ruling family. Boudicca led her Britons against the aggressions of Rome around 60 CE, but only after that relentless imperial force had all but swallowed up her fiercest and most noble kinsmen. A few decades later, Cleopatra used her great wealth, intelligence, and sexuality to tie herself to not one but two of Rome's greatest warlords, just as Egypt was on the brink of provincial servitude. She bore offspring to Julius Caesar and Marc Antony in the hope that her children would bond Egypt's dynastic succession to the fortunes of a victorious Roman warlord. Boudicca and Cleopatra gained power only once the Roman Empire threatened their people's sovereignty and only because there were no remaining male candidates to lead the defense. Both women saw the destruction of their dynasty, their independence, their very way of life, and ultimately their own selves during the crises that defined their rule.

Not until the development of the modern nation-state did women like Elizabeth I or Catherine the Great take on long-lasting mantles of power. The post–Roman Empire, Christian reconfiguration of a fragmented Europe depended on a delicate balance of intertwined dynastic bloodlines that always preferred the person, male or female, who had the clearest claim of descent. In other words, in an ethnically and linguistically divided Europe, when no man could be found to continue a ruling house's bloodline, a female representative of the ruling family was generally preferred over handing the kingdom over to a "foreigner."

Through all of antiquity, however, history records only one female ruler who successfully negotiated a systematic rise to power—without assassinations or coups—during a time of peace, who formally labeled herself with the highest position known in government, and who ruled for a significant stretch of time: Hatshepsut. She should have been no exception to the biological rules that stymied ancient women's ability to hold political power—the vulnerabilities of their wombs, their childbearing abilities, their hormonal changes, their physical weakness. The ancient Egyptians themselves conceived of the Egyptian goddess not only as a womb for the regenerating god but also as an unstable and fickle feminine force—sometimes kind, other times vicious—that could decide on a whim to destroy or to safeguard. Feminine power was a dangerous energy that needed to be contained and placated, not encouraged or expanded. As a rule, women in ancient Egypt were only allowed to rule as a regent on behalf of a man, as Ahmes-Nefertari did for her young son, or as the last living member of a ruling family, as Sobeknefru did on behalf of her dying dynasty. Given more latitude than in most other places in the ancient world, women in Egypt assumed leadership roles in the household and palace and every so often popped up on the political landscape as king of all Egypt: Nitocris of Dynasty 6 (if Herodotus is to be believed), Sobeknefru of Dynasty 12, Hatshepsut of Dynasty 18, Nefertiti of Dynasty 18, Tawosret of Dynasty 19, and Cleopatra VII of the Ptolemaic dynasty, all of them, with the exception of Hatshepsut (and Nefertiti), the last gasp of their dynastic lineage (although Tawosret was not of royal blood and may have come to the kingship by murdering the young king for whom she was acting as regent: she showed none of Hatshepsut's compassion, elegance, or political acuity).

In the eyes of the Egyptologist Betsy Bryan, Egyptian women fulfilled an important role: they were a reliable means of transferring elite lineage within a dynasty. Kings often married their highborn sisters because those elite women were connected to the people and families who were meant to be in power and thus could serve as receptacles to breed the next king.

Bryan describes female power as analogous to the spokes of a wheel radiating out from the king, the hub of the political system. The king required unions with multiple women to continue the royal lineage from himself to a son, but when that son did not materialize, a woman could—albeit rarely—become ruler of Egypt. As Bryan puts it, "Females were guarantors of dynasty continuity."[30] Thus, in a few cases, the desire to protect the interests of the ruling family could trump the imperative to have a male king rule Egypt, but usually only at the end of the line.

And so, as Bryan argues, royal women were sometimes essential in moments of great political uncertainty, when the ruling family needed a monarch with ironclad and uncontested connections to the family lineage. But once power returned to a man, all evidence of that woman's rule was stifled, which explains why we have so little information about female kings of Egypt or anywhere else in the ancient world.[31]

Hatshepsut learned firsthand that a female leader could not transmit succession through her own womb. As a queen, if she had produced a son, the boy could have acted as the next ruler. But as king, Hatshepsut was not, it seems, allowed to hand the reins of power to any of her own offspring, including her daughter. She may have tried to place the girl next in line for power, just as a man would do with his son. Her attempts to position Nefrure ultimately failed, and she may have even lived to see them collapse. Since Hatshepsut was essentially acting as a placeholder for Thutmose III, any male child of her womb at this point in her reign would have produced a reaction even stronger than that against Nefrure. She was ruling alongside a masculine ruler as coregent. *He* was the spoke of the political wheel. She was just the insurance policy against the young king's unexpected death and an interim solution to his temporary youth and inexperience.

Hatshepsut ruled Egypt in her own right, to be sure, and she ruled until her life ended. She was the ultimate working mother, hiring wet nurses and nannies to care for her offspring during those vulnerable years before her children reached the age of five. She may have even felt the ancient version of "mommy guilt" for relegating her precious daughter Nefrure to the care of others while she saw to the leadership of Egypt. But in the long term, Hatshepsut's authority was finite and severely limited. A man could pass down rule to his male progeny in the ancient world whereas a woman could not—because when considering men as an economic construct, the male body will always outproduce the female body. He can create multiple children simultaneously, using the wombs of many women, but women can only depend on their one womb, with one (or, rarely, two) offspring in a given year. In a system dependent on royal succession, it was in *no* dynasty's best interest to place a woman at the center of the wheel of political power. Evolutionarily speaking, this was tremendously inefficient. Even if she was surrounded by a series of men, a female ruler still could not secure the succession of her dynasty because her production of offspring would always be limited. Thus no female monarch could expect her rule to last long in any ancient complex society or, if she reigned until her death, to continue after her through her own female progeny. Her leadership would always conclude with a man resuming the throne.

All of this biological reality only makes Hatshepsut's achievements that much more extraordinary. She was only twenty years old when she methodically consolidated power and catapulted herself into the highest office in the land. She stepped into the position of king during the Eighteenth Dynasty, when the Egyptian empire was experiencing a renaissance—imperialism made everyone rich, and new building projects were under way, including the sprawling temples of Karnak and Luxor. Hatshepsut remains the only ancient woman who claimed absolute authority on a firm foundation when her civilization was at its most robust.

Her femininity was really the only strange part of her rule. In many ways, Hatshepsut's unconventional kingship was an exercise in conformity. Apparently it was too much to expect the kingship to adapt to her womanhood. Instead, she fit herself into the patterns of kingship with which she had grown up, at least those in which a woman could conceivably participate. Like any successful male king, she waged imperial warfare and ruthlessly exploited the population of Nubia to enrich her gods and her people. She participated in the respected system of coregency in which an elder king fostered a junior king in a divinely inspired partnership, thus protecting the future kingship of Thutmose III. She created a masculine identity for herself so that she could perform and participate in religious rituals that demanded a male presence. She constructed temples and obelisks according to accepted traditions and left behind more stone temples and monuments than any previous Egyptian king. Her innovation was directed at sustaining a successful, if unusual and unprecedented, kingship. She wreaked no havoc on the economic and political systems around her; she led no insurrections. She made no revolutionary breaks with tradition but attempted to link herself to the unending line of masculine kings who had come before her. Hatshepsut's kingship was a fantastic and unbelievable aberration, but little more than a necessity of the moment. Her feminine kingship was always to be perceived as a negative complication by the ancient Egyptians, a problem that could only be reconciled publicly and formally through its obliteration. After all her great accomplishments, despite her unique triumph, her fate was to be erased, expunged, silenced.

Thousands of years later, when archaeologists began to find traces of her rule, historians disparaged her character, saying little about her success and a great deal about how she had stolen the throne from its rightful heir, Thutmose III. They commented on her torrid affair with Senenmut and her audacity to make the ridiculous and scheming claim to be a man, or to celebrate a Sed festival, or to be the offspring of the gods. The chisel marks and smashed statues were seen by some as indications of some kind of transgression on her part, proof that she really was a bad woman in need of a beating. When historians began to correct the simplistic mis-

conception of Hatshepsut as an overreaching witch, some ended up turning her into a selfless, first-wave feminist, willing to sacrifice her sexuality
for her career, dynasty, and family, paving the way for her nephew's future
success as king. And as for academia, most Egyptologists became so mired
in the thousands of monuments, statues, and inscriptions she left behind
that many forgot Hatshepsut was human at all.

Through the millennia, we have called powerful women many
things—bitches, witches, regents, seductresses. And we have demanded
that women relinquish their sexuality to assume authority, including the
God's Wives of Amen of the Twenty-Fifth and Twenty-Sixth Dynasties, ves-
tal virgins of ancient Rome, Catholic nuns, and countless women of the
1970s and '80s in business or government or academia. In the ancient
world (and in many places today), women who made decisions about their
own bodies were at first seen as threatening to systems of power and were
usually considered nothing more than immoral sluts. The women of antiquity who held political and military power can be counted on the fingers of one hand—women like Boudicca, Empress Lü, Cleopatra, and
Hatshepsut. Hatshepsut's story can help us appreciate why authoritative
women are still often considered to be dangerous beings who need to be
controlled, monitored, contained, and watched.

Hatshepsut had to carve out her own niche in a society that identified
power with masculinity. To do this, she had to explore what feats a woman
could accomplish: commission obelisks the likes of which Egypt had never
seen or trade with far-flung lands like Punt. She recorded a step-by-step
account of her divine origins from Amen-Re and how the god's statue revealed that she was chosen to rule all of Egypt. The challenges Hatshepsut
faced and the sacrifices she made are familiar to powerful women of the
twenty-first century: balancing the personal and the political, overcom-
ing stereotypes of hysterical and unbalanced femininity, and making
compromises never asked of powerful men. For Hatshepsut, her unprecedented success was rewarded with a short memory, while the failures of
other female leaders from antiquity will be forever immortalized in our
cultural consciousness.

ACKNOWLEDGMENTS

This book was started when my son was just a few months old and finished at his fourth birthday. No woman should write a book during those years. No one. And yet I am glad that Hatshepsut picked me at this time in my life. The hard edges of sleep deprivation and the complexities of breast-feeding and child care demanded that I not forget the biological and economic truths of womanhood. Thank you, Julian, for providing hard realities that I had blithely ignored (and denied) in my twenties and early thirties. I could not have understood Hatshepsut then.

The idea for this book came from *Out of Egypt*, a comparative archaeology television series I developed and produced with my husband, Neil Crawford. We never did do an episode on women in power, but Hatshepsut remained on my brain. Thus when book agent Marc Gerald suggested I write a biography on Hatshepsut (and after I had initially replied, "I can't write a biography about Hatshepsut"), I took on the task with enthusiasm. If he hadn't asked, I wouldn't have written the book. Thank you, Marc, for telling me what you wanted to read (instead of accepting what I thought a young academic should write).

I am deeply (and profoundly) grateful to my husband, Neil Crawford, for reading the manuscript multiple times with relentless attention. If there is any narrative life in this biography, it is because of him. Neil is always my sounding board for ideas about human systems and personal motivations, and I am grateful for the time he gave to these discussions and revisions. I was never more nervous than when he was reading the manuscript for the first time. I'm thankful that my most honest critic also loves me so much. He also took Julian to Disneyland, the park, Fast

Taco, etc., while I wrote. I will always be grateful that my life has been shaped by his considerable influence.

I'm indebted to Betsy Bryan, my dear *Doktormutter* from Johns Hopkins University, who provided a profound role model of a woman in power. While I was at graduate school, I had no idea how hard it must have been for her to balance a growing career and family; now I can't believe she came through unscathed. I couldn't have written this book—with its unorthodox interest in human emotions and intents—without her blessing. She is more a master of the Eighteenth Dynasty than I will ever be.

Thanks are also due to old friends JJ Shirley and Violaine Chauvet, both alums of Johns Hopkins, for reading the manuscript, providing bibliography, talking over ideas, and for encouraging me to write a readable and smart biography of Hatshepsut. I owe much to our conversations (and some frantic e-mails about sources and facts). I will return the favor.

My dear friend Rebecca Peabody at the Getty Research Institute has been a confidante from the proposal stage to publication. Like me, she always has a gig on the side. Rebecca is knowledgeable and skilled in the ways of publishing, and I benefited from her experience. She was the first to read anything from the manuscript, and her support encouraged me when I needed it most. To have the encouragement of a fellow academic (and non-Egyptologist!) while writing a nontraditional book delivered me from many anxieties along the way.

Aidan Dodson, an Egyptologist who knows his Eighteenth Dynasty history much better than I do, read the manuscript, alerting me to red flags and potential problems. Although we didn't always agree (as I'm sure he'd want me to point out), I am grateful for his attention to this biography.

Deborah Shieh acted as my research assistant. Her drawings of Karnak and of temple blocks were skillfully and patiently done. She also kindly fetched books, scanned countless images, worked on bibliographies, and performed other technical tasks. I could not have completed this project without her help.

My colleagues and students at UCLA have been patient listening to me talk about women and power for years upon years. My course on the subject at UCLA is now taken by many enthusiastic undergraduates (not all women, I might add), and whether they like it or not, they will soon be reading this book.

My family—my mother and father, sisters and brother—have all supported me throughout the writing of this book, always simultaneously confused by and proud of my intense interest in the ancient world. In particular, I need to thank my mother, Pamela Cooney, who provided me with my first model of a woman with authority. She helped me write this book in more ways than she knows. My sister Erin Cooney also threw her considerable attention and energies my (and Julian's) way, as did Jim and Kelli Cooney whenever I was in New York.

I thank Vanessa Mobley, my editor at Crown, who understands my preoccupation with women and power deep in her own soul. Because this book was written while both our children were very young, we always understood, without ever having to communicate it outright, the panicked inability to finish a project with any kind of elegance or timeliness. I am grateful for her patience with my messy process.

Finally, much of this book was written at a Mexican joint across the street from me, and I owe thanks to Martin, Mario, Carmen, Rosendo, Sandra, Manuel, Erick, and many more whose names I don't know but whose faces I recognize. All of them facilitated my concentrated work, even on Taco Tuesday.

NOTES

Preface

1. My thoughts on this subject have been informed by a class I recently developed at UCLA called Women and Power in the Ancient World, in which we examine biological and social motivators for women's lesser place in politics in complex society, including R. D. Masters and F. de Waal, "Gender and Political Cognition: Integrating Evolutionary Biology and Political Science," *Politics and the Life Sciences* 8, no. 1 (1989): 3–39; M. Ingalhalikar et al., "Sex Differences in the Structural Connectome of the Human Brain," *Proceedings of the National Academy of Sciences* (2013); Carol R. Ember, "The Relative Decline in Women's Contribution to Agriculture," *American Anthropologist* 85, no. 2 (1983): 285–304; Ernestine Friedl, "Society and Sex Roles," *Human Nature* (April 1978), reprinted in *Anthropology 94/95* (Guilford, CT: Dushkin Publishing, 1994), 124–29; Bella Vivante, *Women's Roles in Ancient Civilizations: A Reference Guide* (Westport, CT: Greenwood Press, 1999).

Chapter One: Divine Origins

1. There are no texts from Hatshepsut's time—historical, administrative, religious, or otherwise—that betray openly expressed negative feelings toward the ruling king or political activities of officials. We do have veiled references from earlier Middle Kingdom literary texts that obliquely discuss the regicide of Amenemhat I, the instability of the times, and the royal family's inability to trust any of the courtiers and officials. See Miriam Lichtheim, *Ancient Egyptian Literature*, vol. 1, *The Old and Middle Kingdoms* (Berkeley: University of California Press, 1975), 135–38. Later legal texts will point toward another regicide, that of Ramses III in Dynasty 20, and the involvement of the royal harem. See Susan Redford, *The Harem Conspiracy: The Murder of Ramesses III* (DeKalb: Northern Illinois University Press, 2002). The Tale of Wenamen, a text from the end of Dynasty 20 that belongs to both the literary and historical genres, reveals the opinion that the Egyptian king had lost his power over foreign lands and even his own country. See

Miriam Lichtheim, *Ancient Egyptian Literature*, vol. 2, *The New Kingdom* (Berkeley: University of California Press, 1976), 224–30.

2.   The length of Thutmose II's reign is disputed, but most historians think he ruled for only three years. See Erik Hornung, Rolf Krauss, and David A. Warburton, eds., *Ancient Egyptian Chronology*, Handbook of Oriental Studies, sec. 1, The Near and Middle East (Leiden and Boston: Brill, 2006), 200–201; Luc Gabolde, "La chronologie de règne de Thoutmosis II, ses consequences sur la datation des momies royales et leurs repercutions sur l'histoire du development de la Vallée des Rois," *Studien zur Altägyptischen Kultur* 14 (1987): 61–82. For the argument for a longer reign, see J. von Beckerath, "Noch einmals zur Regierung Tuthmosis' II," *Studien zur Altägyptischen Kultur* 17 (1990): 70–71. Betsy M. Bryan, "The Eighteenth Dynasty Before the Amarna Period," in *The Oxford History of Ancient Egypt*, ed. Ian Shaw (Oxford: Oxford University Press, 2000), 235–36. Circumstantially, it could be argued that Hatshepsut's kingship was only possible with a short reign for Thutmose II, because it was this king's death that put Egypt into the hands of a toddler king, unable to rule for a dozen years at least.

3.   For a possible identification of Hatshepsut's mummy, see Zahi Hawass, "The Quest for Hatshepsut—Discovering the Mummy of Egypt's Greatest Female Pharaoh," http://www.drhawass.com/events/quest-hatshepsut-discovering -mummy-egypts-greatest-female-pharaoh, and Zahi Hawass, Yehia Z. Gad, and Somaia Ismail, "Ancestry and Pathology in King Tutankhamun's Family," *Journal of the American Medical Association* 303, no. 7 (2010). Many are of the opinion, however, that Zahi Hawass's identification of Hatshepsut as mummy KV 60A is not sound and certainly not backed up by DNA evidence. See Erhart Graefe, "Der angebliche Zahn der angeblich krebskranken Diabetikerin Königin Hatschepsut, oder: Die Mumie der Hatschepsut bleibt unbekannt," *Göttinger Miszellen* 231 (2011). There is also the problem that both coffins in KV 60 bear only the title of Royal Wet Nurse. Despite the lack of evidence for Hatshepsut's mummy, there is no reason to believe that Hatshepsut's body was not prepared as a queen and God's Wife, at the very least, and possibly even as a king. I did appear as an expert in the Discovery Channel's *Secrets of Egypt's Lost Queen* (2007), but I was not part of the mummy identification.

4.   If Hatshepsut's rule lasted from 1473 to 1458 BCE, and if she started her kingship after her twentieth year, then she was born around year 1500 BCE. See Ian Shaw, ed., *The Oxford History of Ancient Egypt* (Oxford: Oxford University Press, 2000), 481. Also see Hornung, Krauss, and Warburton, *Ancient Egyptian Chronology*, 201, 492.

5.   The word *Hyksos* comes from the Egyptian *Heka khasut*, meaning "rulers of foreign lands." See Janine Bourriau, "The Second Intermediate Period," in Shaw, *Oxford History of Ancient Egypt*, 184–217.

6.   Some historians have argued that he had a son named Amenemhat, whose mummy bore a pectoral with the name of Amenhotep I on it; see W. C. Hayes,

Scepter of Egypt II (New York: Metropolitan Museum of Art, 1953), 419. However, because the pectoral probably dates from the Twentieth or Twenty-First Dynasty and because Amenhotep I was deified in later reigns, the pectoral is not evidence that Amenhotep I sired any children; see David Aston, *Burial Assemblages of Dynasties 21–25: Chronology, Typology, Developments* (Vienna: Österreichische Akademie der Wissenschaften, 2009), 231.

7.   In Egyptian, the word for hand is *djeret*, a feminine word. Atum thus had sex with the feminine element of his person. See J. P. Allen, *Genesis in Egypt: The Philosophy of Ancient Egyptian Creation Accounts*, Yale Egyptological Studies (San Antonio, TX: Van Siclen Books for Yale Egyptological Seminar, Yale University, 1988).

8.   Indeed, back in the pioneering days of the First Dynasty, fifteen hundred years earlier, with Egypt newly minted out of hostile principalities, Merneith ruled the country in the name of her young son, Den, after the premature death of her husband, Djet. As such, she was granted a tomb among the kings of her time, of the same size and grandeur as theirs.

9.   Ahhotep I has the title of God's Wife of Amen on her coffin in the royal cache of Theban Tomb 320, but nowhere else. Evidence for Ahmes-Nefertari's priesteshood, on the other hand, is ample and comes from contemporaneous documents, in particular the Donation Stela of Ahmose, now in the Luxor Museum, on which King Ahmose documents his purchase of her priestly office from the Amen Priesthood at Karnak. Identifying Ahhotep I as the first God's Wife of Amen is therefore problematic. For more, see Gay Robins, *Women in Ancient Egypt* (Cambridge, MA: Harvard University Press, 1993), chap. 8, and Anne K. Capel and Glenn E. Markoe, eds., *Mistress of House, Mistress of Heaven: Women in Ancient Egypt* (New York: Hudson Hills Press, 1996), 91–120.

10.   Amen is also known as Amen-Re in his manifestation as King of the Gods. *Amen* literally means "hidden." To unite that which is hidden and thus permeates everything with that which is visible—the sun god Re—creates a powerful new divine manifestation as Amen-Re. Amen's other manifestations include Amen-Min, the sexually excited form of the god who can engender his own rebirth; Amen Kamutef, or "Amen Bull of His Mother," who can impregnate his own mother with the essence of his own future self; and Amen-djeser-a, meaning "Amen Sacred of Arm," a clear allusion to his ability to create himself from nothing. For more on the god Amen, see Kurt Heinrich Sethe, *Amun und die acht Urgötter von Hermopolis, eine Untersuchung über Ursprung und Wesen des aegyptischen Götterkönigs* (Berlin: Verlag der Akademie der Wissenschaften, 1929), and Jan Assmann, *Egyptian Solar Religion in the New Kingdom: Re, Amun and the Crisis of Polytheism*, Studies in Egyptology (London: Kegan Paul International, 1995).

11.   For more on Karnak, see Elizabeth Blyth, *Karnak: Evolution of a Temple* (London: Routledge, 2006), and Diane Favro, Willeke Wendrich, and Elaine Sullivan, "Digital Karnak," University of California, Los Angeles, http://dlib.etc.ucla.edu/projects/Karnak/.

12.   For more on the God's Wife of Amen, see Erhart Graefe, *Untersuchungen zur Verwaltung und Geschichte der Institution der Gottesgemahlin des Amun vom Beginn des neuen Reiches bis zur Spätzeit* (Wiesbaden: Harrassowitz, 1981), and Robins, *Women in Ancient Egypt*, 149–56. For more on the political and economic powers of the God's Wife office, see Betsy Bryan, "Property and the God's Wives of Amun," in *Women and Property*, a conference with The Center for Hellenic Studies, Harvard. Deborah Lyons and Raymond Westbrook, eds. Published online at www.chs.harvard.edu/.

13.   For the statues of Min, see Barry Kemp, *Ancient Egypt: Anatomy of a Civilization* (London: Routledge, 1991), 79–85, fig. 28.

14.   This analysis isn't completely accepted by scholars who see little evidence of Merytamen serving as God's Wife, but see Lana Troy, *Patterns of Queenship*, Acta Universitatis Upsaliensus Boreas 14 (Uppsala: University of Uppsala, 1986), 162–63. For a brief history of the God's Wives of Amen in the early Eighteenth Dynasty, see Bryan, "Eighteenth Dynasty Before the Amarna Period," 226–30, and Robins, *Women in Ancient Egypt*, 149–56.

15.   It has been suggested that Thutmose I's mother was married to Ahmose-Sipairi, making him the grandson of Seventeenth Dynasty king Seqenenre Taa. See Aidan Dodson and Dyan Hilton, *The Complete Royal Families of Ancient Egypt* (London: Thames and Hudson, 2004), 126. The mummy from the royal cache at Theban Tomb 320 that is usually identified as Thutmose I is most certainly not him. See Salima Ikram and Aidan Dodson, *The Mummy in Ancient Egypt: Equipping the Dead for Eternity* (London: Thames and Hudson, 1998), 320–30.

16.   The Amduat was the first of the Underworld Books, a series of magical incantations and descriptions of the underworld space inside of the sky, through which the dead sun god was believed to travel after his setting in the west. The Amduat came to be used only for kings' burials, but curiously the vizier Useramen, a contemporary of Hatshepsut and Thutmose III, had the text inscribed in his private tomb. Some Egyptologists believe the Amduat was composed from scratch during the Eighteenth Dynasty, while others believe that these texts were parts of older temple liturgies that tied the king's afterlife journey to the successful passage of the sun through the hours of night. See Erik Hornung, *The Ancient Egyptian Books of the Afterlife*, trans. David Lorton (Ithaca, NY: Cornell University Press, 1999), 27–53.

17.   There is a debate over whether KV 38 was Thutmose I's original tomb, or whether it had been made for him by his grandson Thutmose III after his mummy's removal from Hatshepsut's burial chamber in KV 20. It is also possible that even if the tomb was made during his lifetime, the decoration was added at the time of the move from KV 20 and that the latter was decorated with the Amduat by Hatshepsut. For more on the debate about these royal tombs, see Catharine H. Roehrig, "The Building Activities of Thutmose III in the Valley of the Kings," in *Thutmose III: A New Biography*, ed. Eric H. Cline and David O'Connor (Ann Arbor: University of Michigan Press, 2006), 238–59.

18.   For more on the Egyptian harem, see Silke Roth, "Harem," *UCLA Encyclopedia of Egyptology*, 2012, http://escholarship.org/uc/item/1k3663r3?query=harem.

19.   For a discussion of ancient Egyptian palaces, see in particular Manfred Bietak, ed., *House and Palace in Ancient Egypt*, Denkschriften der Gesamtakademie 14 (Vienna: Austrian Academy of Sciences, 1996).

20.   I have chosen to use the name Ahmes instead of Ahmose for Hatshepsut's mother, to avoid confusion with King Ahmose. Both names mean "The moon is born" and are spelled with the same hieroglyphs, except for the determinative (the explanatory sign at the end of a word); however, the pronunciation for each sex would have likely been different. Most think Thutmose I did not marry Ahmes until his accession; see Bryan,"Eighteenth Dynasty Before the Amarna Period," 231. Some Egyptologists argue that Ahmes may have married Thutmose I before his accession to the throne, which would mean Hatshepsut was many years older when she married Thutmose II. See Ann Macy Roth, "Models of Authority: Hatshepsut's Predecessors in Power," in *Hatshepsut: From Queen to Pharaoh*, ed. Catharine H. Roehrig (New Haven, CT: Yale University Press, 2006), 11, and Peter F. Dorman, "The Early Reign of Thutmose III: An Unorthodox Mantle of Coregency," in Cline and O'Connor, *Thutmose III: A New Biography*, 60. This is unlikely, however, given the many ostensible barriers for the King's Sisters and Daughters to marry anyone other than the king. It is also unlikely that a nonroyal man would have been allowed to marry a King's Sister before his accession to the throne, and there is no evidence of such a thing taking place in the early Eighteenth Dynasty.

21.   This is not to say that I argue for any kind of "heiress theory" that the new and unrelated king was required to marry a specific female member of the old family to secure his place. I do suggest, however, that a new king with no relation to the old dynastic line would have been expected to take on one or more of that older family's women as wives, to ensure that his offspring also be related to that original family. For more on the importance of royal women in the Eighteenth Dynasty, see Bryan, "Eighteenth Dynasty Before the Amarna Period," 226–30. Also see Gay Robins, "A Critical Examination of the Theory That the Right to the Throne of Ancient Egypt Passed Through the Female Line in the 18th Dynasty," *Göttinger Miszellen* 62 (1983): 68–69.

22.   The historical information about Ahmes is unclear. She has the title of King's Sister but not King's Daughter. See Troy, *Patterns of Queenship*, 163. In *L'Égypte et la vallée du Nil*, vol. 2, *De la fin de l'ancient empire à la fin du nouvel empire* (Paris: PUF, 1995), Claude Vandersleyen argues that she was Thutmose I's own sister. But according to Betsy Bryan ("Eighteenth Dynasty Before the Amarna Period," 231), Ahmes's name suggests that she was a member of Amenhotep I's family, perhaps a daughter of Prince Ahmose-ankh, a son of Ahmose and Ahmes-Nefertari and a brother of Amenhotep I.

Even though we do see Ahmes's title of King's Sister only after the marriage, there is no evidence of a woman named Ahmes at all before the reign of Thutmose I. Before her marriage to the king, she was essentially invisible, as so many royal women were when they had no political or ideological use. Based on the fact that Ahmes was named King's Sister but not King's Daughter, we might conclude that she was sister to Amenhotep I or another early Eighteenth Dynasty king and that Amenhotep I could not produce male or female heirs. If Ahmes was the sister of Amenhotep's father, Ahmose, the previous king, then she must have been one of his much younger sisters, given that Ahmose's son, Amenhotep I, ruled for twenty years.

In any event, the lack of an heir made Ahmes very important. This royal woman's connections to the Ahmoside family may have been essential for Thutmose to create a convincing claim to the throne, because only with Queen Ahmes could this general produce children with a link to the kings who began the Eighteenth Dynasty. The dynastic succession had been broken on the male side, but an appropriate royal woman could create some kind of continuation. Their children, at least, would have the royal blood that Thutmose I did not have.

23.   There has been the suggestion that royal women "gave up" their titles of King's Daughter or King's Sister to marry outside the royal family, thus providing an explanation for why we never see these women anywhere but married to the king at Hatshepsut's time. However, there is little, if any, evidence for this happening during the Eighteenth Dynasty. See Roth, "Models of Authority," 11.

24.   Bryan, "Eighteenth Dynasty Before the Amarna Period," 227–28.

25.   I have to be clear that there is no explicit evidence that marrying the king was a formal "rule" for royal women, only that there is no evidence of royal sisters or daughters marrying anyone but the king in the early Eighteenth Dynasty. Such strict control over royal women was not characteristic of all time periods. Back in the Old Kingdom and later in the Third Intermediate Period, royal daughters regularly married outside the royal family. Although some historians argue that there are simply not enough definite sister-wives during the New Kingdom to be able to infer this kind of endogamous "rule" (see Dodson and Hilton, *Complete Royal Families of Ancient Egypt*, 122–41), I conclude that King's Daughters and King's Sisters were expected to marry the current or next king, at least during the early Eighteenth Dynasty, and that there were important political and economic benefits for this practice.

26.   For more about marriage in ancient Egypt, see Robins, *Women in Ancient Egypt*, and J. Toivari-Viitala, *Women at Deir el-Medina: A Study of the Status and Roles of the Female Inhabitants in the Workmen's Community During the Ramesside Period* (Leiden: Nederlands Instituut voor het Nabije Oosten, 2001).

27.   Some Egyptologists see no reason to date the marriage of Thutmose and Mutnofret to his accession as king, leaving room for an earlier date. Aidan Dodson, for instance, believes that Mutnofret could have been Thutmose I's wife for many years before he became king and that their relationship would provide an excellent

argument against a ban on royal women "marrying out" (Dodson, personal communication, 2013; also see Peter Dorman, "Early Reign of Thutmose III" in Cline and O'Connor, *Thutmose III: A New Biography*, 59n7). However, because the only evidence for their marriage comes from after his accession and because there is no other evidence of royal daughters marrying nonroyal men, I prefer the hypothesis that Mutnofret married Thutmose I after his ascension.

28.   Thutmose I reigned for thirteen or fourteen years. See Hornung, Krauss, and Warburton, *Ancient Egyptian Chronology*, 199–200; Dorman, "Early Reign of Thutmose III," 39; and Bryan, "Eighteenth Dynasty Before the Amarna Period," 230–35.

For related discussions of Hatshepsut's age at queenship, regency, and kingship, see F. Maruéjol, *Thoutmosis III et la corégence avec Hatchepsout* (Paris: Pygmalion, 2008), 22–25, and David A. Warburton, *Architecture, Power, and Religion: Hatshepsut, Amun & Karnak in Context*, Beiträge zur Archäologie 7 (Zurich: LIT Verlag, 2012), 239–40.

29.   For details on childbirth and childhood in ancient Egypt, see J. J. Janssen and Rosalind Janssen, *Growing Up in Ancient Egypt* (London: Rubicon Press, 1990); Robins, *Women in Ancient Egypt*; and Toivari-Viitala, *Women at Deir el-Medina*.

30.   For proof that hunter-gatherers understand the link between breast-feeding and conception, see M. Konner and C. Worthman, "Nursing Frequency, Gonadal Function, and Birth Spacing Among !Kung Hunter-Gatherers," *Science* 207 (1980). For evidence of knowledge of this link in the ancient world, see V. Flides, *Breasts, Bottle and Babies: A History of Infant Feeding* (Edinburgh: Edinburgh University Press, 1986). Egyptians must have known about breast-feeding and its immunity and contraception benefits. See Erika Feucht, "Women," in *The Egyptians*, ed. Sergio Donadoni (Chicago: University of Chicago Press, 1997), 315–46.

31.   There is little research on wet-nursing in ancient Egypt, but see Keith R. Bradley, "Wet-Nursing at Rome: A Study in Social Relations," in *The Family in Ancient Rome*, ed. Beryl Rawson (Ithaca, NY: Cornell University Press, 1986), 201–29.

32.   A poorly preserved sandstone statue of a small adult King Hatshepsut sitting on the lap of her wet nurse, Satre, also known as Inet, was placed in her funerary temple at Deir el-Bahri after Satre's death. The statue is currently in Cairo's Egyptian Museum (JdÉ 56264) and was found by Winlock during excavations at Deir el-Bahri. See Herbert E. Winlock, "The Museum's Excavation at Thebes," *Metropolitan Museum of Art Bulletin* 27, no. 3 (1932). Amazingly, the inscription on an ostracon in the Ambras Collection in Vienna matches the broken text on the statue, allowing a better understanding of the piece. Winlock translated it as follows: "May the king Maatkare [Hatshepsut] and Osiris, first of the Westerners, [the great god] Lord of Abydos, be gracious and give a mortuary offering [of cakes and beer, beef and fowl, and everything] good and pure, and the sweet breath of

the north wind to the spirit of the chief nurse who suckled the Mistress of the Two Lands, Sit-Re, called Yen [Inet], justified."

One of the bodies found in the undecorated KV 60 may represent Hatshepsut's wet nurse. Two bodies were found in KV 60, one body in a coffin, another on the floor. The coffin holding the body was inscribed with the name of In, or Inet, and it seems possible that the wet nurse was given the privilege of burial in the Valley of the Kings by Hatshepsut.

33.   Evidence for infant mortality rates is spotty. For estimated ages at death of individuals from the predynastic cemetery of Naga ed Deir, see P. V. Podzorski, *Their Bones Shall Not Perish: An Examination of Predynastic Human Skeletal Remains from Naga-ed-Der in Egypt* (New Malden, UK: SIA Publishing, 1990). Also see Janssen and Janssen, *Growing Up in Ancient Egypt*.

34.   See the Kahun Gynecological Papyrus published by F. L. Griffith and W. M. Flinders Petrie, *The Petrie Papyri: Hieratic Papyri from Kahun and Gurob (Principally of the Middle Kingdom)* (London: B. Quaritch, 1898). For more specific information about how women aided conception and pregnancy in New Kingdom, see Toivari-Viitala, *Women at Deir el-Medina*, 168–82.

35.   Later Ramesside texts from western Thebes indicate that fertility was the man's responsibility. See Toivari-Viitala, *Women at Deir el-Medina*, 161. For ideological notions of fertility in ancient Egypt, see Ann Macy Roth, "Father Earth, Mother Sky: Ancient Egyptian Beliefs About Conception and Fertility," in *Reading the Body: Representations and Remains in the Archaeological Record*, ed. Alison E. Rautman, Regendering the Past (Philadelphia: University of Pennsylvania Press, 2000).

36.   Most Egyptologists see Neferubity as a daughter of Ahmes, making her Hatshepsut's full sister. See Troy, *Patterns of Queenship*, 164; Bryan, "Eighteenth Dynasty Before the Amarna Period," 231; and Dodson and Hilton, *Complete Royal Families of Ancient Egypt*, 132.

37.   Neferubity would later be depicted in the Amen sanctuary of Hatshepsut's Temple of Millions of Years at Deir el-Bahri, a great honor and evidence of their bond.

Chapter Two: A Place of Her Own

1.   Wadjmose and Amenmose appear in the tomb of Paheri at el-Kab, because the official Paheri acted as tutor for the princes; see J. J. Tylor and F. L. Griffith, *The Tomb of Paheri at El Kab* (London: Egypt Exploration Fund, 1894), 11. Amazingly, we don't know who was the mother of these sons, and Egyptologists' opinions are divided among Ahmes, Mutnofret, and a third wife, perhaps one who was married to Thutmose in his youth. Not knowing the full parentage of a prince is not surprising. Given Egypt's patriarchal system, a prince's masculine parent was the most essential part of his creation to document formally, and his connection with his mother might have only been stressed upon his succession to the

throne, as an honor to her. Some historians believe that Amenmose was actually one of Thutmose I's sons from his first marriage, because by the fourth year of his father's reign Amenmose had already been named as a general in the army on a broken naos shrine that documents his hunting activities on the Giza plateau— unlikely activities for a three-year-old child (now in the Louvre, accession no. E 8074). However, the title of Great General of the Army was also used to designate the crown prince in ancient Egypt, so why not use it for a three-year-old Amenmose if he was the chosen heir to the throne? The noas also labels him as the king's eldest son. For more on this discussion, see Christiane Zivie-Coche, *Giza au deuxième millénaire: Bibliothèque d'étude* (Cairo: Institut Français d'Archéologie Orientale, 1976), 52–55, plate 4; Dodson and Hilton, *Complete Royal Families of Ancient Egypt*, 130; and Bryan, "Eighteenth Dynasty Before the Amarna Period," 230–31.

2.   Hatshepsut's sister was later memorialized at Deir el-Bahri in the Amen sanctuary. See Édouard Naville, *The Temple of Deir el Bahari*, vol. 5, *The Upper Court and Sanctuary* (London: Egypt Exploration Fund, 1895), Plates CXIX–CL.

3.   This palace was built by Thutmose I at right angles to the Karnak Temple entrance on the north side. See Blyth, *Karnak*, 65–66, and David O'Connor, "Thutmose III: An Enigmatic Pharaoh," in Cline and O'Connor, *Thutmose III: A New Biography*, 18.

4.   We learn about this moment from an autobiography recorded in the tomb of the official Ahmose son of Ibana at el-Kab. After the battle, "his Majesty sailed northward, all countries in his grasp, with that defeated Nubian bowman being hanged head down at the [front] of the [boat] of his Majesty, and landed at Karnak." This translation is based on Bryan, "Eighteenth Dynasty Before the Amarna Period," 234. Bryan identifies the bowman with the leader of the Kerma insurrection. For the text of Ahmose son of Ibana, see Kurt Sethe, *Urkunden der 18. Dynastie*, *Band 1*, ed. Georg Steindorff, Urkunden des ägyptischen Altertums 4 (Leipzig: J. C. Hinrichs'sche Buchhandlung, 1906), 1–13.

5.   For the inscription from Hagr el-Merwa, see two works by Vivian W. Davies: "Kurgus 2002: The Inscriptions and Rock-Drawings," *Sudan and Nubia* 7 (2003): 55–57, and "Egypt and Nubia: Conflict with the Kingdom of Kush," in Roehrig, *Hatshepsut: From Queen to Pharaoh*, 52.

6.   Although in English it is better to differentiate between "nurse" and "tutor," in ancient Egyptian the word was almost the same: *mena* for "tutor" and *menat* for "nurse." Both had the breast determinative, and both were associated with the idea of nursing, or feeding a baby nourishment from the breast. Conceptually, this nourishment could take the form of education and support, and thus it could be provided by a male nurse as well as a female. For more on this topic, see Catharine H. Roehrig, "The Eighteenth Dynasty Titles Royal Nurse (mn't nswt), Royal Tutor (mn' nswt), and Foster Brother/Sister of the Lord of the Two Lands (sn/snt mn' n nb t3wy)" (PhD diss., University of California, Berkeley, 1990).

7.   Hatshepsut's position as God's Wife probably predated the reign of Thutmose II; in "Eighteenth Dynasty Before the Amarna Period," 236–37, Bryan states: "A stele of Thutmose II's reign shows the king followed by Ahmose and Hatshepsut. Apparently the latter was already 'god's wife of Amun' in the reign of Thutmose I, following Ahmose-Nefertari's death." Hatshepsut was definitely God's Wife of Amen and queen during the reign of Thutmose II, according to remains of a limestone structure from Karnak that is now in the Open Air Museum in Luxor, showing her with her daughter Nefrure behind her. See Betsy M. Bryan, "In Women Good and Bad Fortune Are on Earth: Status and Roles of Women in Egyptian Culture," in Capel and Markoe, *Mistress of the House, Mistress of Heaven*, 31–32, and Luc Gabolde, *Monuments décorés en bas relief aux noms de Thoutmosis II et Hatchepsout à Karnak*, Mémoires publiés par les membres de l'Institut Français d'Archéologie Orientale du Caire, t. 123 (Cairo: Institut Français d'Archéologie Orientale, 2005). Some Egyptologists think that Hatshepsut was not God's Wife of Amen until as late as Thutmose III; see Dmitri Laboury, "How and Why Did Hatshepsut Invent the Image of Her Royal Power?" in *Theban Symposium: Creativity and Innovation in the Reign of Hatshepsut*, Occasional Proceedings of the Theban Workshop, ed. José M. Galán, Betsy M. Bryan, and Peter F. Dorman (Chicago: Oriental Institute, University of Chicago, forthcoming). However, Bryan thinks it is quite possible that Hatshepsut took on this priestess role as early as her father's reign because Ahmes-Nefertari and Merytamen, the previous God's Wives of Amen, died during the reign of Thutmose I and were likely replaced by Hatshepsut. If we follow the idea that the reigning king had political motivations to place one of his closest female blood relatives in the position, Hatshepsut would have been the ideal candidate. Furthermore, Hatshepsut was probably just old enough to be trained by Ahmes-Nefertari before she was officially placed. Hatshepsut was therefore the first member of the Thutmoside family to act as God's Wife. See Troy, *Patterns of Queenship*, 91–114.

8.   Some Egyptologists deny actual sexual manipulation of sacred statuary by human hands, concluding that only verbalization was necessary to evoke sexual movements and subsequent creative actions. If we look at the many surviving texts about these divine transformations meant to occur in Egyptian temple spaces, it seems more appropriate to take the Egyptians at their word and understand titles like God's Hand or God's Wife literally rather than figuratively. The actual mechanisms for such sacred sexual rites remain, as we would expect, veiled.

9.   Bryan, "Administration in the Reign of Thutmose III"; JJ Shirley, "Viceroys, Viziers and the Amun Precinct: The Power of Hereditary and Strategic Marriage in the Early 18th Dynasty," *Journal of Egyptian History* 3.1 (2010): 73–113.

10.   Egyptologists once connected the God's Wife of Amen to a kind of heiress system, in that the God's Wife produced the future kings. But for sound refutation, see Robins, "Critical Examination of the Theory That the Right to the Throne of

Ancient Egypt Passed Through the Female Line in the 18th Dynasty," *Göttinger Miszellen* 62 (1983).

11.   If Ahmes-Nefertari was grandmother to Hatshepsut through her mother, the choice of Hatshepsut to be God's Wife was likely influenced by her Ahmoside family line. See Bryan, "Eighteenth Dynasty Before the Amarna Period."

12.   For this text, "The Contendings of Horus and Seth," see Lichtheim, *Ancient Egyptian Literature*, 2:197–99.

13.   Ibid., 27. This text comes from one of Hatshepsut's later obelisks, which is still standing at Karnak Temple.

14.   Zivie-Coche, *Giza au deuxième millénaire*, 52–55, plate 4. There is even still some disagreement about the parentage of Amenmose and doubt that he was even a son of Thutmose I. See H. Hohneck, "Hatte Thutmosis I wirklich einen Sohn namens Amenmose?," *Göttinger Miszellen* 210 (2006): 59–68.

15.   Thutmose IV, who attained the throne by bypassing his elder brothers, mutilating their monuments, and publicly ascribing his accession to the favor of a god, is one Eighteenth Dynasty exception. See Betsy Bryan, *The Reign of Thutmose IV* (Baltimore: Johns Hopkins University Press, 1991).

16.   Wadjmose appears in a memorial chapel near the Ramesseum at Thebes (B. Porter and R. Moss, *Topographical Bibliography of Ancient Egypt: Hieroglyphic Texts, Reliefs, and Paintings*, 2nd ed. [revised by J. Malek from 1974 onward], Oxford: Griffith Institute, 444–46) and in the tomb of Paheri, a court official buried at El Kab, as a little boy on his tutor Itruri's lap (Tylor and Griffith, *Tomb of Paheri at El Kab*).

17.   Even if marriage was imminent, there is no evidence of a betrothal to seal the deal. Both parties ostensibly waited until they were sexually ready and able. For instance, Ann Macy Roth suggests that Nefrure could not be married to Thutmose III at his accession, when Hatshepsut would have needed this link most, because both were too young ("Models of Authority: Hatshepsut's Predecessors in Power," 13).

18.   For more on Hatshepsut's depictions as God's Wife of Amen, see Christina Gil Paneque, "The Official Image of Hatshepsut During the Regency: A Political Approximation to the Office of God's Wife," *Trabajos de Egiptologa* 2 (2003): 83–98.

19.   For more on the obelisks in Karnak Temple, see the reconstructions on the UCLA Digital Karnak website at http://dlib.etc.ucla.edu/projects/Karnak/archive/query?type=obelisk.

20.   See two works by Aidan Dodson: "The Burials of Ahmose I," in *Thebes and Beyond: Studies in Honour of Kent R. Weeks*, ed. Zahi Hawass and Salima Ikram (Cairo: Conseil Supréme des Antiquités, 2010), 25–33, and "On the Burials and Re-burials of Ahmose I and Amenhotep I," *Göttinger Miszellen* 238 (2013): 19–24.

21.   For a discussion of Thutmose I's tomb, see J. Romer, "Tuthmosis I and the Bibân el-Molûk: Some Problems of Attribution," *Journal of Egyptian Archaeology* 60 (1974): 119–33; Roehrig, "Building Activities of Thutmose III," 246;

Catharine H. Roehrig, "The Two Tombs of Hatshepsut," in Roehrig, *Hatshepsut: From Queen to Pharaoh*, 184–86.

22.   This is from an inscription in the tomb chapel of Ineni. James Henry Breasted, *Ancient Records of Egypt*, vol. 2, *The Eighteenth Dynasty* (Chicago: University of Chicago Press, 1906), 38.

Chapter Three: King's Great Wife

1.   There is disagreement about this funerary temple: was it built specifically for the sons, or were the sons added to the king's funerary temple later? See the two reports by G. Lecuyot and A. M. Loyrette, "La Chapelle de Ouadjmès: Rapport préliminaire I," *Memnonia* 6 (1995): 85–93 and "La Chapelle de Ouadjmès: Rapport préliminaire II," *Memnonia* 7 (1996): 111–22.

2.   The family maintained their memory as the two princes were revered in later generations as part of Theban ancestor cults, including their insertion into the 19th Dynasty ancestor list preserved in the Theban craftsman Khabekhnet's tomb at Deir el-Medina. See Dorman, "Early Reign of Thutmose III," 40. For the text from Theban Tomb 2 of Khabekhnet, see Kenneth Kitchen, *Ramesside Inscriptions: Historical and Biographical*, 8 vols. (Oxford: Blackwell, 1969–90), 3:806–7.

3.   The mummy identified as Thutmose II was just over 5 feet 6 inches tall (168 centimeters) and had extremely good teeth, a sign that he died young. See G. Elliot Smith, *The Royal Mummies, Catalogue général des antiquités égyptiennes du Musée du Caire*, nos. *61051–61100* (Cairo: Institut Français d'Archéologie Orientale, 1912), 28–30. Determining the age of ancient remains is problematic, because modern aging criteria may not be fully applicable to ancient times; however, teeth-wear patterns present useful criteria. See T. Molleson and M. Cox, *The Spitalfields Project*, vol. 2, *The Anthropology: The Middling Sort* (York, UK: Council for British Archaeology, 1993), 169. Even though mummy research usually focuses on the cause of death, rather than overall health, or lack thereof, thus limiting results for social studies, the mummy of Thutmose II shows evidence for a life plagued by physical ailments.

4.   There is disagreement about whether Ahmes served as Thutmose II's regent, but her placement on Egypt's monuments does suggest that she, instead of the boy's mother, was the highly placed woman who acted as regent over all official and administrative management. For a stela of Thutmose II with his wife Hatshepsut and his mother-in-law Ahmes, see the Berlin stela with accession number 15699 in D. Wildung, "Zwei Stelen aus Hatschepsuts Frühzeit," in *Festschrift zum 150 jährigen Bestehen des Berliner ägyptischen Museums* (Berlin: Staatliche Museen zu Berlin, 1974), 255–68, plate 34; also see Troy, *Patterns of Queenship*, 110. It is still not clear why Mutnofret did not act as regent for her young son, given her patrician origins. Was she politically disconnected even though she was a King's Daughter?

5.   Some Egyptologists suggest that Ahmoside elements from the family of Amenhotep I were waiting in the wings to take over the kingship, although there is

no hard evidence for such an Ahmoside threat. See in particular Dimitri Laboury, "Royal Portrait and Ideology: Evolution and Signification of the Statuary of Thutmose III," in Cline and O'Connor, *Thutmose III: A New Biography*, 266.

6.   The relative ages of Hatshepsut and her husband-brother Thutmose II are debated. If Ahmes married Thutmose I first, as expected for the highest-ranking royal wife, then Hatshepsut may have been born before Thutmose II. Mutnofret was a secondary wife, and thus likely married Thutmose I later. And because Thutmose II was positioned lower in the rankings for kingship, we can assume he was a younger brother of not only his older brothers Wadjmose and Amenmose, but also of his sister Hatshepsut. Of course, if Thutmose I married Ahmes before his accession (for which there is no evidence), none of this accounting can stand. Or, if Mutnofret was married to Thutmose I before his accession, as his primary wife before he became king (for which there is also no evidence), then Thutmose II may have been older than Hatshepsut. See Dorman, "The Early Reign of Thutmose III," 59n7.

7.   The most well-known monument showing Thutmose II with his wife Hatshepsut and his mother-in-law Ahmes is a stela from ancient Thebes.

8.   For monuments from Hatshepsut's time as queen and regent, see Gabolde, *Monuments décorés en bas relief*, and Troy, *Patterns of Queenship*, 108–14.

9.   For a digital reconstruction of this festival court, see the UCLA Digital Karnak website at http://dlib.etc.ucla.edu/projects/Karnak/feature/PylonAnd FestivalCourtOfThutmoseII.

10.   Senenmut's beginnings were humble. His father had no title of significance, and his mother had a rich burial only because by the time of her death Senenmut had attained a high enough status to bury his mother with costly goods. See Peter F. Dorman, *The Monuments of Senenmut: Problems in Historical Methodology* (New York: Kegan Paul International, 1988).

11.   The titles are Overseer of the King's Great House and Overseer of the House of the King's Great Wife; see ibid.

12.   Bryan demonstrates how these bureaucrats benefited from their positions in "Administration in the Reign of Thutmose III."

13.   Some Egyptologists suggest that he started his professional life in the army, an institution known to allow quick changes in social status, but there is little evidence for this conclusion. Theban Tomb 71 of Senenmut mentions gold armbands in association with battle or plunder, but this provides no evidence that he himself served in the army. Senenmut's titles are administrative, and none of his plentiful monuments mention any affiliation with the army. See Dorman, *Monuments of Senenmut*, 7–13.

14.   The biography of Ahmose Pennekhbet, one of Hatshepsut's later trusted officials, refers to Nefrure as "the eldest daughter," implying that there was a younger daughter, as does a statue of Senenmut now in the Chicago Field Museum (Acc. No. 173800). See Sethe, *Urkunden der 18. Dynastie, Band 1*, 34.

15.   These scenes are from the tower gate at the funerary temple of Ramses III

at Medinet Habu. See Oriental Institute Epigraphic Survey, ed., *Medinet Habu*, vol. 7, *The Eastern High Gate* (Chicago: University of Chicago Press, 1970), plates 630–54.

16.   The ancient Egyptian historian Manetho claims that Thutmose II ruled for thirteen years, but this assertion is not widely accepted. For a discussion of this longer reign, see Jürgen von Beckerath, *Chronologie des pharaonischen Ägypten: die Zeitbestimmung der ägyptischen Geschichte von der Vorzeit bis 332 v. Chr.*, Münchener Universitätsschriften; Philosophische Fakultät.; Münchner ägyptologische Studien, 46 (Mainz am Rhein: Verlag Philipp von Zabern, 1997), 201. A thirteen-year reign would add almost ten years to Hatshepsut's ages put forth in this book. Thus she would have been around twenty-five when she served as regent for Thutmose III at the death of her husband, and then in her thirties at her own accession as king.

17.   The text is recorded on her Red Chapel barque shrine at Karnak. See N. Grimal, F. Burgos, and F. Larché, *La chapelle rouge: Le sanctuaire de barque d'Hatshepsout* (Paris: Centre Franco-Égyptien, 2006). For a translation of these texts, see Warburton, *Architecture, Power, and Religion*, 226–33. The recorded information about the mechanics of the oracle is very vague, partly because we are dealing with a divinely inspired moment, and partly because the text was purposefully destroyed, leaving Egyptologists with only traces to reconstruct the full inscription. The festival was said to occur in year 2, but the reign of which king is not stated. If it was the second year of Thutmose I's reign, Hatshepsut would, ostensibly, have been a mere infant then. Perhaps it was meant to occur in year 2 of Thutmose II, even though at this point Hatshepsut may have already been acting as God's Wife of Amen and the King's Great Wife.

18.   We do not know if this oracle really happened in a way that everyone in the audience could understand, or if this revelation was shared only with Hatshepsut, who then communicated it to her people. There is another oracle recorded on the Red Chapel, also ascribed to Hatshepsut, with another first-person text talking about another year 2 of an unidentified king, which took place at Luxor Temple, not Karnak, and referring to the god marking her as the next king. David Warburton treats these oracles together, and they are connected in the same narrative stream; see *Architecture, Power, and Religion*, 226–33. The description of events, however, suggests two separate oracles at two different times—the first when she was marked as God's Wife and the second when she was marked as king. Both are said to have happened in year 2 of an unspecified king, however, and it seems we are meant to see these events as happening in quick succession of one another.

19.   Pascal Vernus, "La grande mutation idéologique du Nouvel Empire," *Bulletin de la Société d'égyptologie Genève* 19 (1995): 69–95. In his book on Hatshepsut's architecture, Warburton cites Vernus when he says, "The use of oracles to legitimate the inheritance of kingship by Hatshepsut and Thutmose III was an ideological innovation. It can also be related to a change in the understanding of

the authority behind kingship, as Hatshepsut appeals to Amun rather than Re"
(*Architecture, Power, and Religion*, 42). Warburton continues with the argument
that in tying her legitimacy to Amen rather than her own "accomplishment of
justice as the successor of Re," as he puts it, Hatshepsut forever weakened Egyptian kingship, transforming it into an institution that was hereafter looking to
the heavens for its justification rather than to its own kingly ideology of power on
earth (ibid., 49).

Chapter Four: Regent for a Baby King

1.   For the oracle marking Thutmose III as king, also known as the Texte
de la Jeunesse, see Sethe, *Urkunden der 18. Dynastie, Band 1*, 155–76, and Piotr
Laskowski, "Monumental Architecture and the Royal Building Program of Thutmose III," in Cline and O'Connor, *Thutmose III: A New Biography*, 184. For the idea
that this oracle text may have Middle Kingdom origins, see Donald Redford, "The
Northern Wars of Thutmose III," in Cline and O'Connor, *Thutmose III: A New Biography*, 340. To take just one issue that is unclear in this oracle text: was Thutmose II actually present when the new king was chosen, as the text suggests but
never overtly states, or was "the majesty" referred to in the text meant to be the god
Amen? Perhaps "the majesty" is referred to obliquely because he wasn't there in
person. Perhaps the reigning king was ill, and a choice needed to be made about
his heir. Or maybe he wasn't there at all in body but only in spirit because he had
just died, and the oracular choice was made in haste.

2.   This is, of course, assuming that Hatshepsut was indeed God's Wife of
Amen during the reign of her father, Thutmose I, for which there is no direct evidence, but for which the circumstances of dynastic rule—and having a God's Wife
related to the reigning king—make a strong case. The new Thutmoside dynasty
would almost certainly have wanted a God's Wife from its own family. See Bryan,
"Eighteenth Dynasty Before the Amarna Period," 231.

3.   Sethe, *Urkunden der 18. Dynastie, Band 1*, 59–60. Although some Egyptologists argue that the biography of Ineni would have been written down long after
the reign of Hatshepsut (see Laboury, "How and Why Did Hatshepsut Invent the
Image of Her Royal Power?," in Galán, Bryan, and Dorman, *Theban Symposium*),
there is evidence that Ineni's inscription finds its origins in the early reign of Thutmose III and thus is a remnant of the insecurity of that very moment in history
when a baby was sitting on the throne of Egypt and a woman was making all the
decisions. Bryan, for example, thinks that Ineni's biography represents how Egyptians perceived Hatshepsut's regency in its contemporary historical moment. See
Betsy M. Bryan, "Hatshepsut and Cultic Revelries in the New Kingdom," in Galán,
Bryan, and Dorman, *Theban Symposium*.

4.   Marianne Schnittger entertains the possibility that it was Ahmes who
acted as the regent for the baby king until her own demise, leaving the role to
Hatshepsut. This discounts the evidence for Ahmes living into the reign of her

daughter Hatshepsut, however. See *Hatschepsut: Eine Frau als König von Ägypten* (Mainz am Rhein: Verlag Philipp von Zabern , 2008), 26.

5.   Another one of Hatshepsut's trusted officials—Ahmose Pennekhbet, whose daughter became one of Thutmose III's most important wives—also recorded his autobiography on the walls of his tomb, listing all the kings under whom he had served: "I have accompanied the kings of Upper and Lower Egypt, the Gods (deceased kings), under which I lived, on their campaigns in southern and northern foreign countries, at each place, to which they have gone, the King of Upper and Lower Egypt 'Nebpehtyre' (Ahmose I), the blessed one, the King of Upper and Lower Egypt 'Djeserkare' (Amenhotep I), the blessed one, the King of Upper and Lower Egypt 'Aakheperkare' (Thutmosis I), the blessed one, the King of Upper and Lower Egypt 'Aakheperenre' (Thutmosis II), the blessed one, down to this good God, the King of Upper and Lower Egypt, 'Menkheperre' (Thutmosis III), given life for ever. The God's Wife repeated favors for me, the Great King's Wife 'Maatkare' (Hatshepsut), justified; I educated her eldest daughter, Neferure, justified, when she was a child at the breast." The translation is based on Dorman, *Monuments of Senenmut*, 37–38.

Egyptologists have long used this text to prove that Hatshepsut was—just a few years after her death—posthumously demoted, no longer remembered as king but only as the God's Wife and King's Wife. However, new work on Ahmose Pennekhbet's tomb suggests that this text is actually a copy from his original family tomb, which was decorated during Hatshepsut's regency for Thutmose III. This new information indicates that Ahmose Pennekhbet was recording the rank of Hatshepsut as regent, from a time before she was officially king, rather than demoting the monarch in his tomb inscriptions after her death. For this new understanding, see Vivian W. Davies, "A View from Elkab: The Tomb and Statues of Ahmose-Pennekhbet," in Galán, Bryan, and Dorman, *Theban Symposium*.

6.   See Boyo Ockinga, "Hatshepsut's Appointment as Crown Prince and the Egyptian Background to Isaiah 9:5," in *Egypt, Canaan and Israel: History, Imperialism, Ideology and Literature; Proceedings of a Conference at the University of Haifa, 3–7 May 2009*, ed. S. Bar, D. Kahn, and JJ Shirley (Leiden: Brill, 2011).

7.   Roth, "Models of Authority," 11.

8.   Indeed, there is evidence that the elites of Thebes were very worried about the possible death of their infant king. Children were named Menkheperreseneb, meaning "May Menkheperre (Thutmose III) be healthy!" One such child would grow up to become High Priest of Amen during the sole reign of Thutmose III.

9.   Some Egyptologists suggest a longer reign for Thutmose II to alleviate the perceived problem of Hatshepsut's age and inexperience. See Dorman, "Early Reign of Thutmose III," 61. Donald Redford solves this problem by suggesting that Amenhotep I and Thutmose I had a coregency and arguing that toward the end of the reign of Amenhotep I, the king chose one of his generals, Thutmose, to succeed him and that he married him off to Ahmes and elevated him to the level of

king. See Donald B. Redford, *History and Chronology of the Eighteenth Dynasty of Egypt: Seven Studies* (New York: University of Toronto Press, 1967), 73. However, Murnane includes no evidence of a coregency for these kings. See William J. Murnane, *Ancient Egyptian Coregencies* (Chicago: Oriental Institute of the University of Chicago, 1977), 115.

10.   The only surviving statue of Thutmose III's mother, Isis, is in the Cairo Museum (JdÉ 37417; CG 42072).

11.   This passage is from the "Instruction of Ptahhotep"; my translation is based on Lichtheim, *Ancient Egyptian Literature*, 1:64.

12.   This passage is from the "Instruction for King Merikare," which dates from the First Intermediate Period; my translation is based on ibid., 106.

13.   See Sethe, *Urkunden der 18. Dynastie, Band 1*, 159.

14.   Only scraps of this building activity remain. Depictions of Hatshepsut as queen regent were found at Karnak. See Gabolde, *Monuments décorés en bas relief*, and the Karnak Temple page on the webpage of Karl H. Leser, "Maat-ka-Ra Hatshepsut," http://www.maat-ka-ra.de/english/start_e.htm.

15.   Peter F. Dorman, "Hatshepsut: Princess to Queen to Co-Ruler," in Roehrig, *Hatshepsut: From Queen to Pharaoh*, 88.

16.   See Gabolde, *Monuments décorés en bas relief*, plates XI, XLII.

17.   This was not always the case; the evidence suggests that during later Dynasties 25 and 26 these priestesses were unmarried and, it seems, also celibate. See Mariam F. Ayad, *God's Wife, God's Servant: The God's Wife of Amun (c. 740–525 BC)* (London: Routledge, 2009).

18.   Ancient Egyptian letters do not usually contain gossip, unless there was a legal issue at the core, and they certainly do not include discussions of the king's (or regent's) romantic engagements. See Edward F. Wente, *Letters from Ancient Egypt* (Atlanta: Scholars Press, 1990).

19.   For the erroneous hypothesis that these graffiti represent Hatshepsut and Senenmut, see Edward F. Wente, "Some Graffiti from the Reign of Hatshepsut," *Journal of Near Eastern Studies* 43, no. 1 (1984), and John Romer, *People of the Nile: Everyday Life in Ancient Egypt* (New York: Crown, 1985), 156–59. For a much-needed corrective, see Bryan, "In Women Good and Bad Fortune Are on Earth," 35: "Surely more caution is demanded. The tolerance for female rulers exhibited throughout Egypt's first eighteen dynasties must be taken into account before we espouse such unsubstantiated opinions."

20.   Consider the parallel of Catherine II (the Great) of Russia, who bore two children with one of her lovers, having taken the throne after the overthrow and subsequent murder of her husband, Emperor Peter III.

21.   Toivari-Viitala, *Women at Deir el-Medina*, 168–70.

22.   Some Egyptologists once believed that Neferubity was Hatshepsut's second daughter, born after Nefrure, but most would now argue that Neferubity was Hatshepsut's sister instead. See Dodson and Hilton, *Complete Royal Families of*

Ancient Egypt, 140. Nonetheless, it is completely within the realm of possibility that Hatshepsut bore another daughter to Thutmose II during his three-year reign and that the girl died in childhood, leaving us with little evidence of her existence beyond the mention that Nefrure was Hatshepsut's "eldest" child in the tomb of Ahmose Pennekhbet.

23.   From the Netjery Menu temple at East Karnak. See Gabolde, *Monuments décorés en bas relief,* and Blyth, *Karnak,* 65.

24.   Anthony J. Spalinger, "Covetous Eyes South: The Background to Egypt's Domination of Nubia by the Reign of Thutmose III," in Cline and O'Connor, *Thutmose III: A New Biography,* 344–69.

25.   It is also possible that Thutmose II appointed Senenmut as chief treasurer before Hatshepsut became regent and during his own reign. The Egyptian name for the treasurer was Overseer of the Seal, which meant that he was in charge of the seal placed on the doors of the treasury and thus monitored everything that came in and everything that went out. See Bryan, "Administration in the Reign of Thutmose III," 77–81.

26.   These obelisks were placed in East Karnak, at what the Egyptians called the "Upper Gateway." See Blyth, *Karnak,* 55. For a reconstruction, see the contra temple obelisks on the UCLA Digital Karnak website at http://dlib.etc.ucla.edu/projects/Karnak/feature/ObelisksAtContraTemple. It is possible that the limestone temple Netjery Menu, which was constructed during Hatshepsut's regency, was also here at East Karnak. See Gabolde, *Monuments décorés en bas relief,* 26.

27.   Judith Weingarten, "Hatshepsut and the Tomb Beneath the Tomb," http://judithweingarten.blogspot.com/2009/03/hatshepsut-and-tomb-beneath-tomb.html; José M. Galán, "The Tombs of Djehuty and Hery (TT 11–12) at Dra Abu el-Naga," in *Proceedings of the Ninth International Congress of Egyptologists,* ed. J.-C. Goyon and C. Cardin, *Orientalia Lovaniensia Analecta* (Leuven: Peeters, 2007), 777–88. For Egyptian tombs without mention of a husband or wife, see Ann Macy Roth, "The Absent Spouse: Patterns and Taboos in Egyptian Tomb Decoration," *Journal of the American Research Center in Egypt* 36 (1999): 37–53.

28.   His family seem to have been low- to mid-level elites from Armant. If we hypothesize that Senenmut started his palace career around age twenty, serving in an administrative post in the royal treasury during the reign of Hatshepsut's father, Thutmose I, then he would have been thirty-four at the accession of Thutmose II and almost forty when Thutmose III took the throne, when Hatshepsut was around sixteen.

29.   None of Senenmut's many statues are dated with certainty to the reign of Thutmose II. Most come from the joint reign of Thutmose III and Hatshepsut. See Dorman, "Early Reign of Thutmose III," 63.

30.   For more on the position of King's Son of Kush, also known as the Viceroy, during the reign of Hatshepsut, see Spalinger, "Covetous Eyes South," in Cline and O'Connor, *Thutmose III: A New Biography,* 344–69.

31.   Useramen's father had been vizier from Thutmose I onwards, and his son's appointment as vizier by Hatshepsut is a testament to the family's strength. Hatshepsut likely had no political choice. JJ Shirley, personal communication, 2014. For more on the officials who served during the reign of Hatshepsut and Thutmose III, particularly in the vizierate, see Bryan, "Administration in the Reign of Thutmose III."

32.   E. Dziobek, "Denkmäler des vezirs User-Amun." *Studien Zur Archäologie and Geschlchte Altägyptens* 18 (Heidelberg: Heidelberger Orient-verlag, 1998). Userhat's tomb decoration has much in common with Thutmose III's own tomb decoration and may have been done later.

33.   H. Carter, "A Tomb Prepared for the Queen Hatshepsuit," *Annales du Service des Antiquités de l'Égypte* 16 (1917): 179–82.

34.   For depictions of Nefrure as the God's Wife of Amen, see Paneque, "Official Image of Hatshepsut," 83–98.

Chapter Five: The Climb Toward Kingship

1.   I have not mentioned Nitocris in this summary because sources for her are so problematic. This Egyptian woman may have ruled at the end of Dynasty 6, but there are no contemporary Egyptian sources about the queen, only a possible and disputed mention in the Turin Kinglist, a papyrus from the reign of Ramses II that preserves a canon of Egyptian rulers, which may actually refer to a male ruler; stories from Herodotus; and a mention in Manetho. For more about ancient Egyptian female leaders in general, see Bryan, "In Women Good and Bad Fortune Are on Earth."

2.   Troy, *Patterns of Queenship*, 2.

3.   A broken statue of Sobeknefru is preserved in the Louvre (Louvre E 27135). See ibid., 30, and Elisabeth Delange, *Catalogue des statues égyptiennes du Moyen Empire, 2060–1560 avant J.-C.* (Paris: Musée du Louvre, 1987). Most of the head is missing, but it is still clear that the female king is wearing the traditional dress of a queen in combination with a *nemes* headdress and a king's kilt over the female dress. It is disputed whether Sobeknefru was a sister of Amenemhat IV (and thus whether Amenemhat IV was even of royal blood at all), because she lacks the title King's Sister; however, she does bear the title of King's Daughter (of Amenemhat III). See Bryan, "In Women Good and Bad Fortune Are on Earth," 29; Dodson and Hilton, *Complete Royal Families*, 95. For this history and the ensuing decline after the fall of the Twelfth Dynasty, see K. Ryholt, *The Political Situation in Egypt During the Second Intermediate Period, c. 1800–1550 BC* (Copenhagen: Museum Tusculanum Press, 1997).

4.   Dorman, "Early Reign of Thutmose III," 53.

5.   The dating of Hatshepsut's accession depends on an ostracon found buried in the fill in front of Senenmut's tomb at Sheikh abd el-Gurna, Theban Tomb 71, when the tomb of his mother and father was scaled. The ostracon reads

"Year 7, month 4 of sprouting, day 2," and this is understood to have been the date when the tomb was closed. Inside the tomb were inscribed materials, including one marked with "the Good Goddess Maat-ka-Ra" testifying that by this point Hatshepsut had formally been named king. The Semna inscription, another text used to date the formal beginning of Hatshepsut's reign, is problematic because it was recarved at least twice in antiquity. For a thorough discussion of the dating of Hatshepsut's accession, see Dorman, *Monuments of Senenmut.*

6.   For the translation, see Dorman, "Early Reign of Thutmose III," 41.

7.   The Ennead simply means "The Nine" and refers to the first generations of divinities after the first creation: Atum, Shu, and Tefnut; Geb and Nut; Osiris and Isis; Seth and Nephthys. These are the nine gods of the Helipolitian creation, since the god Atum created his First Time at Iunu, the city of the sun, called Heliopolis by the Greeks. For more, see Erik Hornung, *Conceptions of God in Ancient Egypt: The One and the Many* (London: Routledge, 1983).

8.   The Sehel text is published in Labib Habachi, "Two Graffiti at Sehēl from the Reign of Queen Hatshepsut," *Journal of Near Eastern Studies* 16, no. 2 (1957): 88–104. The translation follows his.

9.   Dorman, "Early Reign of Thutmose III," 48.

10.   For this important block, now located in Luxor Museum, see H. Chevrier, "Rapport sur les Travaux de Karnak (1933–1934)," *Annales du Service des Antiquités de l'Égypte* 34 (1934): 172, plate 4; Abeer el-Shahawy, *Luxor Museum: The Glory of Ancient Thebes* (Cairo: Farid Atiya Press, 2005), 116–17; and Peter F. Dorman, "Hatshepsut: Princess to Queen to Co-Ruler," in Roehrig, *Hatshepsut: From Queen to Pharaoh*, 88.

11.   This limestone block was found in 1930 by the French archaeologist Henri Chevrier at Karnak, and it belongs to a chapel dismantled toward the end of her reign or after. It is now displayed in the Luxor Museum. See Chevrier, "Rapport sur les Travaux de Karnak (1933–1934)," plate 4. For a discussion of the image, see Karl Leser's Karnak page on his website at http://maat-ka-ra.de/.

12.   The translation is based on Warburton, *Architecture, Power, and Religion*, 231–32. The mention of "his majesty" is confusing and unclarified, and although Warburton sees this as referring to the god "Amen," I am not convinced because the god is referenced later in the text. Also see Dorman, *Monuments of Senenmut*, 22. For a description and image of block 287 with the Luxor oracle, see Schnittger, Hatschepsut: Eine Frau als König von Ägypten, 42.

13.   The translation is based on Warburton, *Architecture, Power, and Religion*, 232.

14.   The translation is based on Lichtheim, *Ancient Egyptian Literature*, 2:28.

15.   This text appears on Hatshepsut's Red Chapel and is in reference to the coronation. The translation is based on Warburton, *Architecture, Power, and Religion*, 229.

16.   Ibid., 230.

17.   For these scenes, see Franck Burgos and François Larché, *La chapelle Rouge: Le sanctuaire de barque d'Hatshepsout*, vol. 1 (Paris: Éditions Recherche sur les Civilisations, 2006). Her coronation is also depicted at her Deir el-Bahri Temple of Millions of Years as well as at Buhen Temple (now reconstructed at the National Museum of Sudan in Khartoum since the creation of Lake Nasser).

18.   Although some might argue that this merging with Amen is meant to be sexual in nature, it is doubtful this is what is meant by this new prenomen. She melded her essence with his and took on his powers and abilities through that process of royal initiation.

19.   The *nebty* name was the Two Mistresses name, and the writing shows the goddesses Nekhbet and Wadjyt. For more on the titulary of ancient Egyptian kings, see Peter A. Clayton, *Chronicle of the Pharaohs: The Reign-by-Reign Record of the Rulers and Dynasties of Ancient Egypt* (London: Thames and Hudson, 1994), and Jürgen von Beckerath, *Handbuch der ägyptischen Königsnamen*, 2nd ed. (Mainz am Rhein: Verlag Philipp von Zabern), 1999. For a discussion of the titulary of Hatshepsut, see Gay Robins, "The Names of Hatshepsut as King," *Journal of Egyptian Archaeology* 85 (1999): 103–12.

20.   Murnane, for example, argues that the oracular events promoted Hatshepsut's claim to the throne by expressing Amen's doubts concerning Thutmose III's ability to rule (*Ancient Egyptian Coregencies*, 33–34).

21.   These first obelisks were placed at East Karnak. Her second pair commemorated her Sed festival in year 16 and were placed in the Wadjyt hall of her father, Thutmose I, or in front of the fifth pylon. See Blyth, *Karnak*, 55. For a digital reconstruction of the obelisks in the Wadjyt hall, see the UCLA Digital Karnak website at http://dlib.etc.ucla.edu/projects/Karnak/feature/ObelisksOfWadjetHall.

22.   The addition of the element of *ka*, or "soul," does seem to move Thutmose III one step from the source of active creation, but why was this particular element added to the boy king's name? Did the *ka* denote a masculine element that Hatshepsut lacked? Perhaps the change was orchestrated by an oracle of Amen to validate Hatshepsut as the leading king in a feminine-masculine pair. Or was the *ka* linked to Maatkare and therefore Hatshepsut's place on the throne, thus making the claim that Thutmose III was dependent on her rule for his own? Hatshepsut never explains why the name was altered, but she obviously felt that it was necessary: Thutmose III's kingship had to change to fit her rule.

23.   No previous king documented his coronation so extensively. This was another one of those exclusionary and secret moments that Hatshepsut felt she had to publish; the reasons for this documentation are not stated, but it likely was done to justify her insecure kingship. Thutmose III would follow suit with such published imagery of his crowning, probably because the origins of his own kingship were also perilous. See Schnittger, *Hatschepsut*, 44–45.

24.   Betsy M. Bryan, "The Temple of Mut: New Evidence on Hatshepsut's Building Activity," in Roehrig, *Hatshepsut: From Queen to Pharaoh*, 181–83.

25.   The translation is based on Lichtheim, *Ancient Egyptian Literature*, 2:26.

26.   The translation follows James P. Allen, "The Role of Amun," in Roehrig, *Hatshepsut: From Queen to Pharaoh*, 84.

27.   For more on the mythological foundations of divine androgyny in connection with female rule, see Troy, *Patterns of Queenship*, 12–32.

28.   For Amen and Amenet, see Sethe, *Amun und die acht Urgötter*; Assmann, *Egyptian Solar Religion*; and Richard H. Wilkinson, *The Complete Gods and Goddesses of Ancient Egypt* (London: Thames and Hudson, 2003), 136–37.

29.   The translation is based on Lichtheim, *Ancient Egyptian Literature*, 2:26.

30.   The passage is from Hatshepsut's birth mythology. See Sethe, *Urkunden der 18. Dynastie, Band 1*, 248–50.

31.   The first clear evidence for the Opet festival is from Hatshepsut's reign, and some suggest it was during her rule that the festival actually began. See William J. Murnane, "Opetfest," in *Lexikon der Ägyptologie*, vol. 4, ed. W. Helck and E. Otto (Wiesbaden: Harrasowitz, 1982), 574–79; John C. Darnell, "Opet Festival," *UCLA Encyclopedia of Egyptology*, 2010, http://escholarship.org/uc/item/4739r3fr; and Blyth, *Karnak*, 53. I, however, prefer to see in her reliefs the first open publication of the Opet Festival.

32.   An alabaster kohl jar found at the Ramesseum includes Ahmes's name with both Thutmose I and Thutmose II, indicating that she lived into the latter's reign at least and probably longer. See J. E. Quibell, *The Ramesseum* (London: B. Quaritch, 1898).

33.   This translation matches Bryan, "The Eighteenth Dynasty Before the Amarna Period," 242.

34.   Gabolde, *Monuments décorés en bas relief*, 164–79. The removal of Thutmose III's names suggests that she may even have been plotting his ultimate removal, although there is no direct evidence of any such plans. If Hatshepsut ever conceived of such a coup, there is no confirmation of it or its failure.

35.   These four types of social power are discussed in Michael Mann, *The Sources of Social Power*, vol. 1, *A History of Power from the Beginning to A.D. 1760* (Cambridge: Cambridge University Press, 1986).

Chapter Six: Keeping the Kingship

1.   Blyth, *Karnak*, 60–62.

2.   See Murnane, *Ancient Egyptian Coregencies*.

3.   The same could be said of the later coregency of Neferneferuaten (probably formerly known as Nefertiti) with her husband Akhenaten and (probably later) her son Tutankhaten. See Aidan Dodson, *Amarna Sunset: Nefertiti, Tutankhamun, Ay, Horemheb, and the Egyptian Counter-Reformation* (Cairo: American University in Cairo Press, 2009), 33–52.

4.   Although new coregents often began their own year count on appointment—so that one might see Year X of Regent A; Year Y of Regent B (Murnane, *An-*

cient Egyptian Coregencies)—this seems not always to have been the case in the New Kingdom. Hatshepsut does have one date assigned just to her, without mention of Thutmose III, and it was fittingly found at Karnak, one of her main foundations of power. See Hornung, Krauss, and Warburton, *Ancient Egyptian Chronology*, 201.

5.   According to Dorman, a "general avoidance of attaching a specific reg-nal date to Hatshepsut alone, noticeable even on the monuments for which she took primary responsibility, is part and parcel of the etiquette of coregency that Hatshepsut devised in order to bring historical reality into concord with her ideo-logical claims" ("Early Reign of Thutmose III," 54).

6.   For the Punt inscriptions, see Kurt Sethe, *Urkunden der 18. Dynastie, Band 2*, ed. Georg Steindorff, Urkunden des ägyptischen Altertums 4 (Leipzig: J. C. Hinrichssche Buchhandlung, 1906), 319–21.

7.   Nehesy's tomb was constructed at the northern necropolis of Saqqara. Bryan therefore suggests that he was carrying out the Punt mission under direct orders from a northern vizier, perhaps Neferweben, and not the southern vizier, Useramen ("Administration in the Reign of Thutmose III," 77).

8.   For more information about the land of Punt, see Louise Bradbury, "Re-flections on Travelling to 'God's Land' and Punt in the Middle Kingdom," *Journal of the American Research Center in Egypt* 25 (1988): 127–56, Rolf Herzog, *Punt*, Abhandlungen des Deutsches Archäologischen Instituts Kairo, Ägyptische Reihe 6 (Glückstadt: Verlag J. J. Augustin, 1968); Kenneth Kitchen, "The Land of Punt," in *The Archaeology of Africa*, ed. Thurstan Shaw et al. (London: Routledge, 1993); and Dimitri Meeks, "Locating Punt," in *Mysterious Lands*, Encounters with Ancient Egypt 5, ed. David B. O'Connor and Stephen G. J. Quirke (London: University Col-lege London Press, Institute of Archaeology, 2003), 53–80. Officials connected to Hatshepsut's Punt expedition placed great value on it, mentioning it in their statue and tomb inscriptions. Many promotions were made just after year 9. JJ Shirley, personal communication, 2014.

9.   Sethe, *Urkunden der 18. Dynastie, Band 2*, 339–40. Also see Warburton, *Architecture, Power, and Religion*, 247.

10.   War led to new sources of income; indeed, in the ancient world, getting rich was the chief reason to wage war. See Spalinger, "Covetous Eyes South," in Cline and O'Connor, *Thutmose III: A New Biography*, 344–69; for the men en-riched by military campaigns during the reign of Hatshepsut and Thutmose III, see Bryan, "Administration in the Reign of Thutmose III," 101–7.

11.   Puyemre's may have only been "new" on his father's side. His mother was a wet nurse to Thutmose II, and thus he grew up in the palace. Puyemre was mar-ried to Seniseneb, a Divine Adoratrice and daughter of Hapuseneb, the First High Priest of Amen. Both of these men were connected to the Thutmoside family, which allowed them to consolidate power within the Amen priesthood by giving offices to friends of the Thutmosides. See Bryan, "Administration in the Reign of Thutmose III," 70, 109–10.

12.   Bryan, "Administration in the Reign of Thutmose III," 109–10.

13.   His seal with this title is on page 111 of Roehrig, *Hatshepsut: From Queen to Pharaoh.*

14.   Bryan, "Administration in the Reign of Thutmose III," 98. However, new work suggests that Senimen was instead appointed as tutor by Thutmose II with Senenmut taking over as tutor after him. JJ Shirley, personal communication, 2014.

15.   Roehrig, *Hatshepsut: From Queen to Pharaoh,* 121.

16.   The statue is currently in the Cairo Museum (JdÉ 47278). See Dorman, *Monuments of Senenmut,* 124.

17.   Bryan, "Administration in the Reign of Thutmose III," 94.

18.   Bryan suggests that the new description of the duties of the vizier written during the reign of Thutmose III may have been a reaction to Senenmut's over-reaching: "This last title (that is, judge of the gate in the entire land) suggests that Senenmut could usurp the authority of the vizier's office" (ibid., 93–94).

19.   Shaun Tougher, *The Eunuch in Byzantine History and Society* (London: Routledge, 2008).

20.   This proscription gives us an idea of how important the nurse Satre was to Hatshepsut, because in this statue (in the Cairo Museum, JdÉ 56264), the older woman was able to show herself holding a figure of Hatshepsut as king sitting on her lap.

21.   Indeed, an inscription on the back of one of these ostraca reads "a lean, hairy rat with prodigiously long whiskers"; see W. C. Hayes, *The Scepter of Egypt,* vol. 2 (New York: Metropolitan Museum of Art, 1959), 110. This description may refer to Senenmut, and perhaps he was a wiry, ratlike man who was overly obsequious to Hatshepsut. There are four such drawings of Senenmut's face: three ostraca are in the Metropolitan Museum of Art in New York; the other example is drawn directly onto his limestone tomb wall in Theban Tomb 353.

22.   Senenmut claims the earliest tutor statue, the earliest statue of someone holding a shrine, the first statue of someone holding a coiled surveyor's rope, and the first statue of someone holding a votive emblem (in this case, Hatshepsut's rebus name of a snake wearing a horned sun disk on *ka* arms). He also owned his own quartzite sarcophagus in the manner of the royal sarcophagi, and he was honored with his own devotional reliefs at Hatshepsut's funerary temple. See Roehrig, *Hatshepsut: From Queen to Pharaoh,* 107–33.

23.   Keller, "Statuary of Hatshepsut," 117.

24.   Senenmut had both of his parents buried in a chamber just in front of his own grand tomb chapel (Theban Tomb 71), a showplace that he was building in western Thebes for his high rank. He was able to purchase a painted coffin and gilded mummy mask for his mother, Hatnefer, probably in advance of her death. Senenmut also commissioned funerary papyri, canopic equipment, silver pitchers, a silver bowl, and a precious heart scarab set in a gold bezel for his mother. He

made sure that she was carefully mummified with the highest-quality linens from Hatshepsut's royal workshops, and he included funerary offerings of wine, beer, and foodstuffs, much of it marked with Hatshepsut's name as king.

Senenmut even had his father, Ramose, reburied to accompany his mother in death. Senenmut had the unmummified corpse sent to the embalming house for treatment, even though his father had died more than a decade before. There it was rewrapped in fine linen. When ready for reburial, it was placed in a simple painted coffin without any gilding. The body of his father had not previously been embalmed for burial, which suggested that neither Senenmut nor his family had access to extra income for elite burial extravagances at the time of Ramose's death. But now cash was not a problem for Senenmut: he made sure that his mother and father could dwell next to each other for eternity, their bodies imperishable. See Dorman, *Monuments of Senenmut*, 86–97, and *The Tombs of Senenmut: The Architecture and Decoration of Tombs 71 and 353* (New York: Metropolitan Museum of Art, 1991), 168–73.

25.   For the publication of the discovery of the tomb of Senenmut's parents, Ramose and Hatnofer, see A. Lansing and W. Hayes, "The Egyptian Expedition 1935–1936," *Metropolitan Museum of Art Bulletin* 32 (January 1937, sec. 2): 5–39.

26.   See Dorman, *Tombs of Senenmut.*

27.   Betsy Bryan believes these architectural Osirian statues are inspired by similar statues of Hatshepsut's father, Thutmose I, carved out of sandstone and installed at Karnak on the east bank of Thebes; see Bryan, "Eighteenth Dynasty Before the Amarna Period," 241.

28.   Egyptologists are still debating how to understand and define the Temple of Millions of Years. Such a funerary temple is differentiated from state temples like Karnak and Luxor by the fact that it was usually built by one king for his own functional cult and was meant to link his being and royal rule with the gods Osiris, Re, and Amen. For more on temples in ancient Egypt, see B. E. Shafer, ed, *Temples of Ancient Egypt* (Ithaca, NY: Cornell University Press, 1997), and M. Ullmann, "König für die Ewigkeit: die Häuser der Millionen von Jahren," *Ägypten und Altes Testament* 51 (Wiesbaden: Harrassowitz Verlag, 2002).

29.   This festival is discussed in Elaine Sullivan, "Processional Routes and Festivals," 2008, UCLA Digital Karnak, http://dlib.etc.ucla.edu/projects/Karnak/assets/media/resources/ProcessionalRoutesAndFestivals/guide.pdf.

30.   It is possible that Hatshepsut's funerary temple at Deir el-Bahri was begun for Thutmose II, as his Temple of Millions of Years, during the reign of her husband, but that she had it reassigned to herself. After all, she did not include a funerary temple of Thutmose II in her Red Chapel list, alongside the funerary temples of Thutmose I and III. See Zygmunt Wysocki, "The Temple of Queen Hatshepsut at Deir el Bahari: The Raising of the Structure in View of Architectural Studies," *Mitteilungen des Deutschen Archäologischen Instituts Abteilung Kairo* 48 (1992): 234–54.

31.　For the idea that these temples acted as stages for festival activity, see Jadwiga Lipínska, "The Temple of Thutmose III at Deir el-Bahari," in Roehrig, *Hatshepsut: From Queen to Pharaoh*, 285–86.

32.　For more on the Opet festival, see Darnell, "Opet Festival," *UCLA Encyclopedia of Egyptology.* http://escholarship.org/uc/item/4739r3fr.

33.　For this place, see R. A. Caminos and T. G. H. James, *Gebel el Silsilah* (London, 1963).

34.　Hatshepsut built temples or shrines at Elephantine, Kom Ombo, Hierakonpolis (el-Kab), Gebel el-Silsila, Meir (Cusae), Batn el-Baqqara, Speos Artemidos, Hermopolis, Armant, Nubia, and the Sinai, according to Cathleen A. Keller, "The Joint Reign of Hatshepsut and Thutmose III," in Roehrig, *Hatshepsut: From Queen to Pharaoh*, 97. For a survey of Hatshepsut's monuments, see Karl Leser's webpage at http://maat-ka-ra.de/.

35.　This precise orientation has since been shifted by earthquakes, but the sun does still enter the sanctuary on the winter solstice. It just does not hit the statues anymore. See J. Karkowski, "The Decoration of the Temple of Hatshepsut at Deir el-Bahari," in *Queen Hatshepsut and Her Temple 3500 Years Later*, ed. Z. Szafrañskj (Cairo: Warsaw University Polish Centre of Mediterranean Archaeology in Cairo, 2001): 99–157.

36.　The translation of all sections of this extraordinary text is after James P. Allen, "The Speos Artemidos Inscription of Hatshepsut," *Bulletin of the Egyptological Seminar* 16 (2002): 1–17. Warburton points out that Hatshepsut was likely using Middle Kingdom monarchs as her inspiration when she claimed she was only doing what the god wanted and commanded (*Architecture, Power, and Religion*, 128).

Chapter Seven: The King Becomes a Man

1.　Spalinger, "Covetous Eyes South," in Cline and O'Connor, *Thutmose III: A New Biography*, 344–69, esp. 354.

2.　For example, see A. H. Gardiner, *Egypt of the Pharaohs: An Introduction* (Oxford: Clarendon Press, 1961), 189, and H. E. Winlock, "The Egyptian Expedition 1925–1927: The Museum's Excavations at Thebes," *Metropolitan Museum of Art Bulletin* 23, no. 2 (1928): 52. For a discussion of such patriarchal scholarship, see Joyce Tyldesley, *Hatchepsut: The Female Pharaoh* (London: Viking, 1996), 137–40.

3.　In year 12 we see evidence of another campaign to Kerma on a rock inscription at Tangur. See Davies, "Egypt and Nubia," 52. Another campaign, which is undated but likely earlier, was led by Hatshepsut herself according to a biographical inscription at Sehel belonging to the royal chancellor Ty. Redford says there is reliable evidence to prove at least four campaigns during Hatshepsut's rule and perhaps as many as six if the different campaigns mentioned in some Deir el-Bahri inscriptions are included (*History and Chronology of the Eighteenth Dynasty*, 62). According to another account by Overseer of the Treasury Djehuty in Theban Tomb 11, Hatshepsut accompanied her troops to Kush. Djehuty records that the queen engaged in the collection of booty personally. See Habachi, "Two Graffiti at Sehēl," 88–104. But compare the more conservative view taken by Spalinger, "Covetous Eyes South," in Cline and O'Connor, *Thutmose III: A New Biography*, 344–69.

4.   O'Connor, "Thutmose III: An Enigmatic Pharaoh," 6.

5.   See Manfred Bietak, "Egypt and the Aegean: Cultural Convergence in a Thutmoside Palace at Avaris," in Roehrig, *Hatshepsut: From Queen to Pharaoh*, 75–81.

6.   For this idea of manifest destiny in Egyptian imperialism, see Bryan, "Administration in the Reign of Thutmose III," 103.

7.   Tyldesley notes that "the Thutmosides evidently had a family tendency towards shortness" (*Hatchepsut: The Female Pharaoh*, 125). Elliot G. Smith (*The Royal Mummies, Catalogue général des antiquités égyptiennes du Musée du Caire, nos. 61051-61100* [Cairo: Institut Français d'Archéologie Orientale, 1912], 34) found the mummy of Thutmose III to be only 1.615 meters (5'3"), but some have argued that he was measured without his feet (Dennis C. Forbes, *Tombs, Treasures, Mummies: Seven Great Discoveries of Egyptian Archaeology* [Santa Rosa, CA: Kmt Communications, 1998], 631), indicating he was actually taller, maybe 5'6". The most recent examination of Thutmose III's mummy found it to be 175 centimeters (Z. Hawass, "Quest for the Mummy of Hatschepsut," *Kmt: A Modern Journal of Ancient Egypt* 17, no. 2 (2006).

8.   Roth points out that Hatshepsut is shown with a feminized male body (with breasts and narrow shoulders but no shirt or dress) only in the innermost sacred areas at Deir el-Bahri, in the sanctuaries of Amen and Hathor ("Models of Authority," 13n2).

9.   See Dorman's summation in "The Early Reign of Thutmose III," 52.

10.   For the Egyptological study that lists all the known attestations of Sed festivals throughout history, see Erik Hornung and Elisabeth Staehelin, *Studien zum Sedfest*, Aegyptiaca Helvetica (Basel: Edition de Belles Lettres, 1974).

11.   Another dating scheme might work for the jubilee; perhaps she celebrated her thirtieth year of life as thirty years of reign. No matter what, her priests were engaged in some serious numerology to justify the Sed. See Tyldesley, *Hatchepsut: The Female Pharaoh*, 110.

12.   Some Egyptologists have suggested that she started her idealized reign with the death of Thutmose I, and thus this year 15 was really year 30, but the calculation only works if Thutmose II ruled for thirteen years or more ($13 + 15 = 28$). For discussion, see Jürgen von Beckerath, *Chronologie des ägyptischen Neuen Reiches*, HÄB 39 (Hildesheim: Gerstenberg, 1994), 111, and Dorman, "The Early Reign of Thutmose III," 39–68, especially 60n2.

13.   For information about and scenes from the Sed festival, see E. P. Uphill, "A Joint Sed-Festival of Thutmose III and Queen Hatshepsut," *Journal of Near Eastern*

Studies 20, no. 4 (1961), and Hermann Kees, *Der Opfertanz des Ägyptischen Königs* (Leipzig: J. C. Hinrichs, 1912).

14.   One obelisk from this pair still stands, and I have included extensive translations from it already. For the inscriptions on the base and shaft, see Lichtheim, *Ancient Egyptian Literature*, 2:25–29.

15.   Dorman, *Monuments of Senenmut*, 129–30.

16.   Laboury, "Royal Portrait and Ideology," 274–75.

17.   For a discussion of such scenes, see H. Brunner, *Die Geburt des Gottkönigs: Studien zur Überlieferung eines altägyptischen Mythos* (Wiesbaden: Harrassowitz, 1986). For a discussion online, go to the Second Portico of the Djeser-Djeseru section on Karl Leser's website at http://maat-ka-ra.de/.

18.   The translation is based on Warburton, *Architecture, Power, and Religion*, 229.

19.   For recently uncovered fragments showing similar divine birth scenes from the mortuary temple of Senwosret III of the Middle Kingdom, see Dieter Arnold, "Neue architektonische Erkenntnisse von der Pyramide Sesostris III in Dashur," *Sokar: Geschichte und Archäologie Ägyptens* 23, no. 2 (2011), and Adela Oppenheim, "The Early Life of Pharaoh: Divine Birth and Adolescence Scenes in the Causeway of Senwosret III at Dahshur," in *Abusir and Saqqara in the Year 2010*, ed. Miroslav Bárta, Filip Coppens, and Jaromír Krejčí (Prague: Czech Institute of Egyptology, Faculty of Arts, Charles University, 2011).

20.   Assmann, *Egyptian Solar Religion* (London: Kegan Paul International, 1995), 102–32, and Arielle P. Kozloff and Betsy M. Bryan, *Egypt's Dazzling Sun: Amenhotep III and His World* (Cleveland: Cleveland Museum of Art; Bloomington: Indiana University Press, 1992), 96–97.

21.   This translation is based on Lichtheim, *Ancient Egyptian Literature*, vol. 2, 26.

22.   Lana Troy, "Religion and Cult During the Time of Thutmose III," in Cline and O'Connor, *Thutmose III: A New Biography*, 131, 138–39. Also see Jan Assmann, *Der König als Sonnenpriester: Ein kosmographischer Begleittext zur kultischen Sonnenhymnik in thebanischen Tempeln und Gräbern*, Ägyptologische Reihe Bd. 7 (Kairo: Abhandlungen des Deutschen Archäologischen Instituts Kairo, 1970), 102–32.

23.   The text is from Hatshepsut's solar chapel at Deir el-Bahri. See J. Karkowski, *The Temple of Hatshepsut: The Solar Complex* (Warsaw, 2003). The translation is based on Assmann, *Egyptian Solar Religion*, 24.

24.   For imagery, digital modeling, and a bibliography on the eighth pylon, see the UCLA Digital Karnak website at http://dlib.etc.ucla.edu/projects/Karnak/feature/PylonVIII.

25.   For this site, see Oriental Institute Epigraphic Survey, ed., *Medinet Habu*, vol. 9, *The Eighteenth Dynasty Temple*, pt. 1, *The Inner Sanctuaries*, Oriental Institute Publications 136 (Chicago: Oriental Institute of Chicago, 2009).

26.   There is evidence that such rituals already existed in the Middle Kingdom, but they do not consistently show up in Egyptian temple architecture until Ptolemaic and Roman periods. Hatshepsut included these rituals in texts at her funerary temple at Deir el-Bahri and at the Mut precinct at Karnak. They seem to be associated with Valley Festival activities. See Bryan, "Temple of Mut," 182.

27.   Betsy M. Bryan, "Hatshepsut and Cultic Revelries in the New Kingdom," in Galán, Bryan, and Dorman, *Theban Symposium*.

28.   In the Eighteenth Dynasty, kings had multiple wives, although their harems were likely relatively small, at least at the start of the dynasty and in comparison to later Ramesside harems. We know who some of their royal wives were from private monuments of their family members, nurses, tutors, and officials, as well as from funerary objects. Royal wives were usually not depicted in temples or on royal monuments, unless they were the most important queens. Likewise, few of the royal offspring of Eighteenth Dynasty kings are known; however, this was not the case for later kings, such as Ramses II in Dynasty 19, who depicted his many children in his Temples of Millions of Years. The depiction of Nefrure in Egypt's temples alongside Hatshepsut after her ascension as king is thus telling of her increasing status. See Robins, *Women in Ancient Egypt*, 36.

29.   There is a great deal of debate about whether Thutmose III and Nefrure were ever married at all. As we are unlikely to find evidence of their sexual relationship—such as texts documenting their offspring—we are left to look for instances of her name as a high-ranking queen. However, nearly every instance of Nefrure's name was removed from the historical record after her death and replaced with the name of another queen of Thutmose III. Therefore, it is difficult to reconstruct their relationship. There is evidence that Nefrure appeared as God's Wife of Amen with Thutmose III in year 22 or 23, only to be erased in favor of a woman named Satiah when Thutmose III began his sole reign. In other words, if Nefrure was the king's Great Royal Wife, then she was removed from that office either because she died or because Thutmose III wanted her gone. See Dorman, *Monuments of Senenmut*.

30.   Although Nefrure was often named as God's Wife, on Hatshepsut's later Red Chapel, depictions of the God's Wife were left unnamed. Three scenes from the Red Chapel show a woman performing as God's Wife, and we might assume that this girl was Nefrure during the reign of Hatshepsut. See Burgos and Larché, eds., *La chapelle Rouge*, vol. 1, blocks 140, 292.

31.   The stela is currently in the Cairo Museum (JdÉ 38546). See Peter F. Dorman, "The Career of Senenmut," in Roehrig, *Hatshepsut: From Queen to Pharaoh*, 108.

32.   Arielle P. Kozloff, "The Artistic Production of the Reign of Thutmose III," in Cline and O'Connor, *Thutmose III: A New Biography*, 297.

33.   Given that most of Nefrure's monumental inscriptions were recarved,

Egyptologists have had to look for traces of her name to reconstruct her titles and thus her place in society as God's Wife of Amen and Great Royal Wife. Some argue that Nefrure was never named King's Wife at all. For instance, there is one stela that may depict Thutmose III and Nefrure together, and here she was marked as God's Wife of Amen, not as Thutmose's wife. This stela was usurped by a later wife, Satiah. It comes from the Ptah temple at Karnak, is now in the Cairo Museum (CG 34013), and dates from the early years of Thutmose III's sole reign. Another stela that may have originally shown Nefrure was found in the funerary temple of Thutmose III at Sheikh abd el-Gurna (CG 34015); her name may have been erased for his mother, Isis (although this is contested by Piccione). For discussion of all these historical documents, see Troy, *Patterns of Queenship*, 164. For an image of the Cairo stela CG 34013, see Peter J. Brand, *The Monuments of Seti I: Epigraphic, Historical, and Art Historical Analysis,* Probleme Der Ägyptologie, 16 (Leiden: Brill, 2000), fig. 51. For discussion of the recutting of the Ptah temple stela, see P. A. Piccione, "The Women of Thutmose III in the Stelae of the Egyptian Museum," *Journal of the Society of the Study of Egyptian Antiquities* 30 (2003): 91–100. This Ptah temple stela shows a woman labeled as the King's Great Wife and the God's Wife of Amen, and this figure could indeed have once been Nefrure. Robins, however, argues that while a sun disk is clearly visible, it is off center, even though this Re element of Nefrure's name was always centered. Because of this, Robins claims that this was originally the name Merytre-Hatshepsut; she was also a wife of Thutmose III, and the sun disk in her name often appears off center. See Robins, "Review of *Patterns of Queenship*."

Chapter Eight: The Setting Sun

1.   For the timing of his change of throne name and its connection to the jubilee, see Uphill, "Joint Sed-Festival," 250.

2.   Made of alabaster, this shrine was built by Amenhotep I; its translucent qualities caught the lamplight. For a discussion of Hatshepsut's new placement of this monument and Thutmose III's later dismantlement, see Blyth, *Karnak*, 52–53. For a reconstruction, see the UCLA Digital Karnak website at http://dlib.etc.ucla .edu/projects/Karnak/feature/AmenhotepICalciteChapel. Hatshepsut seems to have had a penchant for picking the most sacred places in Thebes, dismantling the structures on-site, and erecting her own innovative edifices in their place. She was very confident about her architectural agenda.

3.   The Red Chapel was found dismantled inside of Amenhotep III's third pylon. That is why the original location of Hatshepsut's masterpiece has been much debated. Some Egyptologists think that it was placed in the middle of the Palace of Truth, where the shrine of Philip Arrhidaeus is today; however, her structure seems too big to have actually fit in this space. If it was somehow jammed into her Palace of Truth, such placement would have severely limited the Red Chapel's visibility. Newer Egyptological thinking places the Red Chapel in the Great Festival

Court of Thutmose II, in front of the Palace of Truth, where Hatshepsut could better display her divine predestination and ritual activity to her people and where the structure could better function as a barque shrine with an entrance and an exit. See Franck Burgos and François Larché, eds., *La chapelle Rouge: Le sanctuaire de barque d'Hatshepsout*, vol. 2 (Paris: Éditions Recherche sur les Civilisations, 2008); Warburton, *Architecture, Power, and Religion*, 236; and Blyth, *Karnak*, 57. For a reconstruction of the Red Chapel in different possible locations, see the UCLA Digital Karnak website at http://dlib.etc.ucla.edu/projects/Karnak/feature /RedChapel.

4.   For the Palace of Ma'at, see the UCLA Digital Karnak website at http:// dlib.etc.ucla.edu/projects/Karnak/feature/PalaceOfMaat.

5.   It was during Hatshepsut's reign that we see a new emphasis on solarism and the cults of solar gods. She built solar altars for the first time in sandstone, a material evoking the sun. Bryan writes, "The piety and divine engenderment so consistently expressed by Hatshepsut was a source of inspiration to Amenhotep III. For it is this queen whom the later king imitated, even including a form of her divine birth reliefs and inscriptions in his new Luxor Temple. It was almost certainly her original plan to bring the southern temples of Thebes into a cultic cycle with Karnak that Amenhotep III explored and very nearly accomplished" (Kozloff and Bryan, *Egypt's Dazzling Sun*, 96–97).

6.   A speech of the god Amen recorded on Hatshepsut's Red Chapel includes many ritual duties for the king, including: "Fill the estate, supply the altar. Instruct the *wab* priest regarding their tasks. Advance the laws. Perpetuate the regulations. Enrich the property. Increase that which existed previously. Expand the space of my treasuries. Build without neglecting sandstone or granite. Renew for my temple the statues in good quality limestone. Advance this work for me in the future. Control the monuments of the temples. Install every god according to his (own) regulations. Each one there exactly according to his means. Advance his primeval time for him. Advancing his laws is the joy of a god." For the translation, see Troy, "Religion and Cult," 134.

7.   Old Kingdom and Middle Kingdom kings likely instituted cult activity for royal statues, but we have little direct representation of the practice in their temples.

8.   Another block from the Red Chapel shows just such a priestess. It was carved with a woman's figure labeled as the God's Wife of Amen performing cult activity for the gods in the courtyard of the temple with attendants burning effigies of Egypt's enemies upon a brazier of coals. She was meant to ritually roast these vile combatants alive. This female figure was not labeled as Nefrure, but if Hatshepsut's Red Chapel was carved during the last five years of her reign and if Nefrure was still alive at this point, then the image was likely meant to have represented her. Why she is not named as such remains a vexing problem for Egyptologists. See Burgos and Larché, *La chapelle Rouge*, vol. 1: blocks 140, 292.

9.   See Dorman, *Monuments of Senenmut*, 79, and Schnittger, *Hatschepsut*, 24. There is actually no direct evidence that Nefrure was Amenemhat's mother; see Bryan, "Eighteenth Dynasty Before the Amarna Period," 238. For the suggestion that Satiah was the prince's mother, see Dodson and Hilton, *Complete Royal Families of Ancient Egypt*, 132.

10.   For the argument that Nefrure was being groomed by her mother for the kingship, see Z. Szafrański, "Imiut in the 'Chapel of Parents' in the Temple of Hatshepsut at Deir el-Bahari," in *8. Ägyptologische Tempeltagung: Inter-connections Between Temples*, ed. Monika Dolinska and Horst Beinlich, Königtum, Staat und Gesellschaft früher Hochkulturen 3 (Wiesbaden: Harrassowitz, 2010). Szafrański uses art historical evidence to make his case. The female figure in question is on the south side of the upper terrace at Hatshepsut's temple of Djeser Djeseru. She was recarved and relabeled as Hatshepsut's mother, Ahmes, and Szafrański thinks the image originally represented Nefrure.

11.   Troy, *Patterns of Queenship*, 141.

12.   This stela from Serabit el-Khadim in the Sinai is now in Cairo's Egyptian Museum (JdÉ 38546). See Dorman, "Royal Steward Senenmut," 108.

13.   Troy, *Patterns of Queenship*, 133–38.

14.   Szafrański, "Imiut in the 'Chapel of Parents.'"

15.   When I say that Egyptologists only whisper about Hatshepsut's possible murder, I mean that most do not want such unsubstantiated claims in print. Egyptologists today are loath to make the claim that either Hatshepsut or Nefrure may have been assassinated, probably because they are reacting to the unfounded and heavy-handed patriarchal arguments of early Egyptology (that Senenmut was Hatshepsut's lover, for example, or that she was incapable of directing military campaigns—two claims for which there was never any real evidence), in addition to a healthy fear of appearing sensationalist in the manner of Bob Brier's *The Murder of Tutankhamen: A True Story* (New York: Putnam, 1998). What Egyptologists put in print is often different from what they might say at the bar among friends. In keeping with such hypothetical claims, Warburton places his intimations about Nefrure's murder (and even Hatshepsut's) in a footnote (*Architecture, Power, and Religion*, 55–56n213).

16.   Bryan, "Eighteenth Dynasty Before the Amarna Period," 242.

17.   About forty-two Theban tombs were commissioned by officials of Hatshepsut and Thutmose III, a virtual explosion of private tomb building. In all the previous reigns of the Eighteenth Dynasty combined, only ten tombs were completed in Thebes. See Kozloff, "Artistic Production of the Reign of Thutmose III," 302.

18.   For remarks on innovation during the reign of Hatshepsut, see Dorman, *Monuments of Senenmut*, 109.

19.   For more discussion of the co-option of elites during the reign of Hatshepsut, see Bryan, "Administration in the Reign of Thutmose III," 262, and Warburton, *Architecture, Power, and Religion*, 261–65.

20.   Bryan, "Eighteenth Dynasty Before the Amarna Period," 242.

21.   Kozloff, "Artistic Production of the Reign of Thutmose III," 310.

22.   Hapuseneb probably predeceased Hatshepsut, because she was the only king mentioned in his tomb. Even late in his life, he decided not to include any text or image of Thutmose III. The next First High Priest of Amen was Menkheperreseneb, obviously from a family of Thutmose III supporters, given his name means "Menkheperre (Thutmose III) is healthy!" Bryan, "Administration in the Reign of Thutmose III," 107–8.

23.   Senenmut was given the honor of having his name and image displayed at Deir el-Bahri dozens of times, including in the Punt reliefs and in the images hidden behind the door leaves on the upper terrace and in the Hathor chapel. Besides his many statues commissioned to stand along the processional routes at Karnak, Senenmut also had himself represented at the Mut temple gateway, which was later removed in the same manner as his hidden images at Deir el-Bahri. He also had images and statues set up at Luxor Temple. See Dorman, *Monuments of Senenmut*.

24.   Useramen's tomb only mentions Thutmose III, and he served well into Thutmose III's reign, suggesting that this honor may have been granted by Thutmose III, albeit following Hatshepsut's lead with other officials. See Ziobek, E., "Denkmäler des Verziers User-Amen."

25.   However, some early New Kingdom monarchs did place their burial chambers a short distance away from their actual pyramids. The burial chamber of Ahmose I (first king of the Eighteenth Dynasty) in his pyramid at Abydos was over a kilometer away from his temple. Amenhotep I, the second king of the Eighteenth Dynasty, may have been the first one to place his burial chamber in a remote valley on the other side of a cliff, away from his funerary temple, but until his tomb is firmly identified, we cannot say for sure.

26.   There is a great deal of disagreement about where Thutmose I was buried first and if KV 38 is his original tomb or not. Roehrig thinks KV 38 was indeed commissioned by the early Eighteenth Dynasty king. She also argues that KV 20 was originally made for Thutmose II but taken over by Hatshepsut, that KV 34 was constructed for Thutmose III, and that Hatshepsut added two side chambers to KV 20, with the intention to have herself buried with both her husband, Thutmose II, and her father, Thutmose I. Roehrig contends that the Amduat in her tomb was never completed. See Roehrig, "Two Tombs of Hatshepsut," and John Romer, "The Tomb of Tuthmosis III," *Mitteilungen des Deutschen Archäologischen Instituts Abteilung Kairo* 31 (1975). For a counterargument, see Schnittger, *Hatschepsut*, 59–60.

27.   Hatshepsut's Amduat text was not carved into the live rock but instead onto movable blocks. It has recently been demonstrated by Mauric-Barberio that the Amduat blocks in the tomb of Thutmose I (KV 38) and those in the tomb of Hatshepsut (KV 20) match and that all probably belong to Hatshepsut's reign. Thus perhaps we should assign the innovation of including the Amduat in the royal tomb to Hatshepsut instead of her father; he is the one who can be credited with the radi-

cal decision to move the royal burial to the Valley of the Kings. F. Mauric-Barberio, "Le premier exemplaire du Livre de l'Amdouat," *Bulletin de l'Institut Français d'Archéologie Orientale au Caire* 101 (2001): 315–50. Warburton suggests that agents of Thutmose III moved some but not all of Hatshepsut's Amduat blocks to the tomb of Thutmose I (KV 38) (*Architecture, Power, and Religion*, 205). Tyldesley suggests that the tomb was unfinished and that the blocks were lying on the floor abandoned by the builders (*Hatchepsut: The Female Pharaoh*, 123).

28.   Peter Der Manuelian and Christian E. Loeben, "New Light on the Re-carved Sarcophagus of Hatshepsut and Thutmose I in the Museum of Fine Arts, Boston," *Journal of Egyptian Archaeology* 79 (1993): 121–55.

29.   For a description of the valley temple excavations, see Earl of Carnarvon and H. Carter, *Five Years' Explorations at Thebes: A Record of the Work Done 1907–1911* (Oxford: Oxford University Press, 1912).

30.   From the Second Hour of the Amduat, characterized by mourning and great preparation after the sun god has settled into the underworld. The translation is based on David Warburton and Erik Hornung, *The Egyptian Amduat: The Book of the Hidden Chamber* (Zurich: Living Human Heritage, 2007), 52–57.

31.   For information about ancient Egyptian funerary rituals, see Jan Assmann, *Death and Salvation in Ancient Egypt*, trans. David Lorton (Ithaca and London: Cornell University Press, 2005).

32.   The later tomb of Tutankhamun provides the only comparison for Hatshepsut's possible funerary goods. See Nicholas Reeves, *The Complete Tutankhamun: The King, the Tomb, the Royal Treasure* (London: Thames and Hudson, 1990). For a complete record of the excavation notes and photographs, see the Griffith Institute's website on Tutankhamun's tomb at http://www.griffith.ox.ac.uk/discoveringTut/.

33.   The Book of Hours was often preserved on papyrus, and it was meant to give the dead power over circumstances in the netherworld. The text is broken up into hours, as in the Amduat. For more on this text, see Raymond O. Faulkner, "An Ancient Egyptian 'Book of Hours,'" *Journal of Egyptian Archaeology* 40 (1954): 34–39.

34.   Chapter 148 of the Book of the Dead is the "book for making the transfigured spirit excellent in the heart of Re, causing him to have power before Atum, magnifying him before the foremost of the West, enabling him to go out before the Ennead" and includes the Seven Celestial Cows (the Pleiades or Seven Sisters constellation that moved in the night sky and provided a means of counting the night hours). Also in Hatshepsut's chapel are scenes of the Iunmutef priest—a figure who wears a leopard skin and the sidelock of youth, representative of the eldest son and heir—performing cult offerings and funerary ritual. The chapel walls preserve excerpts from the Pyramid Texts, the oldest known funerary texts from ancient Egypt, which provided protection and necessities to the dead in the next life. For all of these texts, see Marcelle Werbrouck, *Le temple d'Hatshepsout à Deir el Bahari* (Bruxelles: Fondation Égyptologique Reine Élisabeth, 1949).

35.   There is no evidence for it, but Warburton suggests an abdication of power before her actual death: "She certainly did not relinquish power voluntarily at this point, but it is not clear that she died either. However, it should not be forgotten that with the death of her daughter, the possibility of a female dynasty was gone—and there is no reason to believe that her daughter died naturally. It is thus also possible that Hatshepsut did in fact die at this point—but not necessarily accidentally or of natural causes" (*Architecture, Power, and Religion*, 55–56n213).

36.   Hawass, "Quest for Hatshepsut." This mummy belonged to an old, very fat, diabetic woman whose teeth were so worn down that her age was estimated at between forty-six and sixty years. Many other circumstantial signs do not support the identification of KV 60A as Hatshepsut's mummy; for example, not even the brain was removed during embalming. There is no reason to suggest that Hatshepsut received shoddy embalming just because her gender did not fit the office of kingship. If the Egyptians had wanted to harm her after death, they would have done a much more thorough job than poor embalming. Remnants of her burial suggest a traditional and high-cost affair. Furthermore, the estimated age at death of the KV 60A mummy is much older than historical documents allow for Hatshepsut.

37.   Edouard Naville and Howard Carter, *The Tomb of Hâtshopsîtû* (London: A. Constable, 1906). Her anthropoid wooden coffin was also found in KV 4, the tomb of Ramses XI, which was used as a workshop when the royal mummies were being stripped of valuables and moved, indicating that her body remained untouched until the end of the New Kingdom. Other funerary objects of hers were found in the royal cache at Deir el-Bahri (Theban Tomb 320), including a canopic chest, a senet board, and the remains of a chair. For the movement of the royal mummies in the later New Kingdom, see Nicholas Reeves, *Valley of the Kings: The Decline of a Royal Necropolis* (London: Kegan Paul International, 1990).

38.   For more on the shroud of Thutmose III, see Troy, "Religion and Cult," 154.

39.   S. W. Cross, "The Hydrology of the Valley of the Kings," *Journal of Egyptian Archaeology* 94 (2008): 303–12.

40.   But see Nicholas Reeves and Richard H. Wilkinson, *The Complete Valley of the Kings: Tombs and Treasures of Egypt's Greatest Pharaoh's*. (London: Thames and Hudson, 1996), 94–95. Many of Hatshepsut's funerary objects were preserved, which suggests that her mummy is also preserved to us—we just haven't definitively identified it.

41.   Akhenaten's mummy may have been destroyed after the failure of his radical religious changes. Or maybe it was moved back to Thebes as a corrective. For more on the aftermath of Akhenaten's reign, see Dodson, *Amarna Sunset*.

42.   Thutmose I's tomb was likely also looted in antiquity; his coffin was reused by the priest-king Panedjem I in the Theban royal cache. But since the identification of the mummy of Thutmose I has recently been disproved, Hatshepsut's father is still out there somewhere, waiting for discovery. The mummy of her mother, Ahmes, is still missing, too, and maybe Hatshepsut's mummy is with them.

Chapter Nine: The King Is Dead; Long Live the King

1.   The story of this campaign comes from Thutmose III's annals, inscribed in the heart of Karnak Temple. I have adapted it from Lichtheim, *Ancient Egyptian Literature*, 2:29–35.

2.   The Great Green Sea is how the Egyptians referred to the Mediterranean Sea.

3.   Redford, "Northern Wars of Thutmose III," 330–31.

4.   A stela from Armant indicates that Thutmose III led at least two campaigns in Syria-Palestine during the coregency with Hatshepsut. According to O'Connor, his victories imply extensive military campaign experience ("Thutmose III: An Enigmatic Pharaoh," 28).

5.   Because ancient armies were self-sufficient, living off the land with spoils taken from the conquered, campaigns usually took place in late spring and summer. See Redford, "Northern Wars of Thutmose III," 328–29.

6.   P. T. Nicholson and J. A. Henderson, "Glass," in *Ancient Egyptian Materials and Technology*, ed. P. T. Nicholson and I. Shaw (Cambridge: Cambridge University Press, 2000).

7.   Laboury, "Royal Portrait and Ideology," 271.

8.   Laboury argues that "this policy—personal assertion, deep respect for the predecessors and great devotion toward Amun, the god who gives rightful kingship—suggest(s) that the ruler was in need of legitimation after a long partition of his power with Hatshepsut, since they precisely constitute ways to justify claims to the throne" (ibid., 271).

9.   See Christian E. Loeben, *Beobachtungen zu Kontext und Funktion königlicher Statuen im Amun-Tempel von Karnak* (Leipzig: Wodtke und Stegbauer, 2001). Also see the page on the colossal statues at the eighth pylon on Leser, "Maat-ka-Ra Hatshepsut," website at http://maat-ka-ra.de/.

10.   Blyth, *Karnak*, 68–77.

11.   The Akhmenu temple was begun soon after Thutmose's sole reign started. In "Royal Portrait and Ideology," 268–70, Laboury argues that the statues there are very similar to late portraits of Hatshepsut, but with slight differences, including a more masculine body, a deeper depression under the eye, lower cheekbones, a nose with a rounded point, and a chin with a different shape from the side. Laboury sees the Akhmenu statues of Thutmose III, especially CG 42053, as the real face of Thutmose III and most similar to how the young monarch appeared.

12.   Two-dimensional images of sixty-two seated statues are shown, and it is possible that a real, three-dimensional statue group was present in Thutmose I's hypostyle hall between the fourth and fifth pylons, where Thutmose III would have made offerings to his ancestor kings as a respectful heir should. The temple would also have kept portable versions of these statues to bring into the Akhmenu on feast days. See O'Connor, "Thutmose III: An Enigmatic Pharaoh," 19–20, and Redford, "Northern Wars of Thutmose III," 341.

13.   For the names preserved, see the website of Peter Lundström, "Karnak King List," http://xorpid.com/karnak-king-list. For a formal publication of the list, see A. C. Prisse d'Avennes, *Monuments égyptiens* (Paris, 1847), plate 1.

14.   For the timing of the Red Chapel dismantling and subsequent defacing, see Dorman, *Monuments of Senenmut.*

15.   The granite sanctuary of Thutmose III exists only in fragments, but Philip Arrhidaeus's sanctuary is a copy in dimension and subject matter. See Blyth, *Karnak*, 78–83.

16.   Sethe, *Urkunden der 18. Dynastie*, Band 1, 155–76. For more on this important text, see Anthony Spalinger, "Drama in History: Exemplars from Mid Dynasty XVIII," *Studien zur Altägyptischen Kultur* 24 (1997): 269–300. Spalinger argues that the stress on divine nomination indicates some weakness to the claim to the throne by Thutmose III. Those behind the decision to crown Thutmose III thus used an older Middle Kingdom text legitimizing the young Senwosret I (preserved on the Berlin Leather Roll, Berlin 3029, a leather sheet with a copy of Senwosret I's building program, probably copied from one of his own temples, either in the Middle Kingdom or during the early Eighteenth Dynasty) as a source for Thutmose's innovative oracle text. Senwosret I was also said to be chosen by the gods as king and was likewise called a puppy, in reference to his youth. Spalinger maintains that in the reign of Thutmose III we see a new and real self-consciousness of kingship and succession that was not there before: only the king-to-be can understand the gods' revelation and what it means, and the king had to be chosen by the gods, rather than being god incarnate, himself. For further discussion, see also Laskowski, "Monumental Architecture and the Royal Building Program of Thutmose III," 183–237, 219–20.

17.   For example, Laboury argues that the building program of Thutmose III "reveals a certain animosity between the former coregents" ("Royal Portrait and Ideology," 271).

18.   The dating of the death of Nefrure to a time before year 16 is based entirely, if indirectly, on an ostracon from Senenmut's tomb at Deir el-Bahri, but scholars now recognize evidence that Nefrure lived beyond her mother. See Dorman, *Monuments of Senenmut*, 77–78. Some evidence indicates that Nefrure lived many years past regnal year 16 and perhaps even past her mother's death in year 22: (1) a previously mentioned stela from the Ptah temple at Karnak (CG 34013) showing Thutmose III with the God's Wife of Amen Nefrure recut as Satiah; (2) a stela from the funerary temple of Thutmose III (CG 34105) showing the king offering to Amen with his queen, likely originally Nefrure but recut as Thutmose III's mother, Isis, who is called Great King's Wife and Mistress of Upper and Lower Egypt. The tomb of Nefrure was probably located at Wadi Sikkat Taka ez-Zeida, where Hatshepsut's tomb had been prepared when she was queen, because Nefrure's name is carved into one of the boulders at the site. Howard Carter, "A Tomb Prepared for Queen Hatshepsuit and Other Recent Discoveries at Thebes," *Journal of Egyptian Archaeology* 4, no. 2/3 (1917): 107–18.

19.   Given the reoccurring problems of succession, kings increased their harem throughout the New Kingdom. See Bryan, "In Women Good and Bad Fortune Are on Earth," 38–39.

20.   Robins wonders what the king did with all these women, particularly the dozens of women who accompanied the foreign princesses as part of their entourage. She suspects that many of the wives living at the palace never saw the king; they were kept busy producing high-quality goods like fine linen cloth. In many ways, the harem was actually a workshop for high-status goods. See Robins, *Women in Ancient Egypt*, 39–41, and Roth, "Harem," *UCLA Encyclopedia of Egyptology*.

21.   O'Connor, "Thutmose III: An Enigmatic Pharaoh," 27.

22.   Bryan, "Eighteenth Dynasty Before the Amarna Period," 248.

23.   An outer wall of Thutmose III's Akhmenu at Karnak bears an inscription dating to year 23 that records the installation of the eldest King's Son, Amenemhat, as Overseer of Cattle. There is no other evidence of this prince's existence. Dorman suggests Nefrure was alive in year 23 as God's Wife of Amen and King's Great Wife, and was likely the mother of this eldest King's Son. See Dorman, *Monuments of Senenmut*, 78–79.

24.   See Dodson and Hilton, *Complete Royal Families of Ancient Egypt*, 131–32.

25.   Most royal children left no record of their existence, but for evidence of Eighteenth Dynasty princesses recorded on Twenty-First Dynasty mummy labels after their removal from their original tombs and subsequent reburial, see A. Dodson and J. J. Janssen, "A Theban Tomb and Its Tenants," *Journal of Egyptian Archaeology* 75 (1989): 125–38.

26.   Laboury, "Royal Portrait and Ideology," 261.

27.   Dorman, *Monuments of Senenmut*, 173–74.

28.   Ibid., 137, 177–78. The evidence that Senenmut lived into the sole reign of Thutmose III is based on a number of his monuments that can be dated after the death of Hatshepsut. One statue found by a Polish expedition in situ at Djeser Akhet (Cairo Museum statue CG 42117) names only Nefrure and Thutmose III. We also have evidence of another Chief Steward of Amen, a man named Roau, who was a contemporary of Senenmut, and it seems likely that Senenmut lost this influential position to this man. On one of his Djeser Akhet statues, the inscription states that the original location was a temple called Kha Akhet rather than Djeser Akhet, indicating that the statue was not originally placed in Thutmose III's temple but somewhere else. No matter what, Senenmut did not die in year 18 or 19, as previously assumed. Also see Keller's discussion of Senenmut's statue with a Hathor emblem in Roehrig's *Hatshepsut: From Queen to Pharaoh*, 126–27.

29.   Dorman, *Monuments of Senenmut*, 178–81.

30.   Ibid., 158–64. Dorman convincingly argues that it was petty rivalries and personal attacks that sealed the fate of Senenmut's monuments.

31.   Translation from Karl Leser's page on Senenmut: http://maat-ka-ra.de/.

32.   E. Dziobek, "Denkmäler des Vezirs User-Amun," *Studien zur Archäologie und Geschichte Altägyptens* 18 (Heidelberg: Heidelberger Orientverlag, 1998), 144–48.

33.   Bryan, "Administration in the Reign of Thutmose III," 70.

34.   In the later reign of Thutmose III and later in the Eighteenth Dynasty, other officials suffered the same fate as Senenmut, including the vizier Rekhmire, the scribe and royal physician Nebamen, the royal steward Surer, and the queen's steward Kheruef.

35.   It is difficult to connect the destruction of Senenmut's monuments directly to Hatshepsut and her aberrant rule. For example, Senenmut's monuments weren't defaced in the same way or for the same reason as Hatshepsut's and vice versa. On only three of his statues were both Senenmut's and Hatshepsut's names chiseled away, and the removal is inconsistent in any case. On some of his statues, all of Senenmut's names have been removed, while Hatshepsut's remain. See Keller in Roehrig, *Hatshepsut: From Queen to Pharaoh*, 126.

Here is how Peter Dorman reconstructs the destruction of Senenmut's names and images: When Senenmut died, his tomb chamber was sealed and the sarcophagus was left or deposited in the axial corridor of TT 71. A short time after, TT 353 was broken into and defaced. Before Hatshepsut's proscription, Senenmut's name was hacked out in TT 71. Around the same time, at least four of his statues, most of which were dedicated at Armant, were also attacked. Around this time, his sarcophagus was destroyed. When Thutmose III attacked the memory of Hatshepsut, Senenmut's names and images were removed from Hatshepsut's temple of Deir el-Bahri. However, many of Senenmut's statues remained unharmed and on display, as later Ramesside restoration proves. Other Karnak statues show damage but were kept on display as late as Ptolemaic times, as their inclusion in the Karnak cachette suggests (*Monuments of Senenmut*, 178–81).

Chapter Ten: Lost Legacy

1.   Again, this is not to support the so-called heiress theory (see Robins, "Critical Examination," 67–77), but just to stress that maternal bloodline was an important factor in the selection of the next king during the early Eighteenth Dynasty.

2.   This later date for the destruction of Hatshepsut's monuments was first established by C. F. Nims, "The Date of the Dishonoring of Hatshepsut," *Zeitschrift für ägyptische Sprache und Altertumskunde* 93 (1966): 97–100. Also see Blyth, *Karnak*, 51–52, and Dorman, *Monuments of Senenmut*.

3.   See Dorman, *Monuments of Senenmut*, plates 2–4.

4.   This part of Karnak is called the Palace of Ma'at. Much of the proscription in the heart of Karnak happened when Thutmose III erected his granite barque shrine in year 45. See the UCLA Digital Karnak website on the Ma'at suite at http://dlib.etc.ucla.edu/projects/Karnak/feature/PalaceOfMaat.

5.   The defacement usually included hacking with a broad chisel first, then chiseling with a finer tool, and finally polishing the stone surface for later re-carving. In Hatshepsut's Palace of Truth, the finer chiseling is unfinished and nowhere has the surface been polished, as if the workmen stopped in the middle of the proscription process. See Dorman, *Monuments of Senenmut*, 63, and Ann Macy Roth, "Erasing a Reign," in Roehrig, *Hatshepsut: From Queen to Pharaoh*, 277–81.

6.   O'Connor, "Thutmose III: An Enigmatic Pharaoh," 28.

7.   Blyth, *Karnak*, 81–84. It is not clear who walled in the lower part of Hatshepsut's obelisks here, saving them from damage.

8.   See the removed figure of Hatshepsut from the northern obelisk of her first pair placed at eastern Karnak, which is now in the garden at the Egyptian Museum in Cairo. For images, see the obelisk page on Karl Leser's website at http://maat-ka-ra.de/.

9.   See Blyth, *Karnak*, 84–86, and Dorman, *Monuments of Senenmut*, 65.

10.   Dorman, *Monuments of Senenmut*, 65.

11.   For the painstaking work done by the Metropolitan Museum of Art to re-construct these statues, see Hayes, *Scepter of Egypt*, 90–102.

12.   Roehrig, *Hatshepsut: From Queen to Pharaoh*, 103.

13.   Dorman, *Monuments of Senenmut*, 64.

14.   Nims, "Date of the Dishonoring of Hatshepsut," 97–100.

15.   Roth, "Erasing a Reign," 281.

16.   Bryan writes, "Thus the same motivation that would have encouraged support for Hatshepsut's sovereignty—protection of the dynastic line—also sup-ported her dishonoring. The royal ancestry was protected carefully by replacing Hatshepsut's name with those of Thutmose III, Thutmose I, and even Thutmose II" ("In Women Good and Bad Fortune Are on Earth," 34).

17.   Maybe there were other sons of Thutmose III with better connections to Hatshepsut's family who were being passed over. We have no idea if Nefrure was alive during the campaign of destruction against her mother, but members of Hatshepsut's family, descended from Thutmose I and his queen, Ahmes, almost certainly were. Laboury creates an interesting argument for two rival dynastic lines. He says that Thutmose I had children from at least two different beds: Thut-mose II was a son of Mutnofret while Hatshepsut was a daughter of Ahmes. When Thutmose I died, the kingship went to the branch of the family in which a son was still alive—namely, Mutnofret's side. But with the premature death of the latter and the youth of Thutmose III, the other branch of the family created access to the throne through Hatshepsut. To Laboury, the fact that both Thutmose III and Hatshepsut referred only to their own family branches on their monuments sup-ports the idea of a royal family divided: a danger to a very young crown prince, the future Amenhotep II ("Royal Portrait and Ideology," 266–67).

18.   Prince Siamen is known from a statue of the treasurer Sennefer, who

lived under Hatshepsut. See Dodson and Hilton, *Complete Royal Families of Ancient Egypt*, 132–33.

19.   Roehrig, "Eighteenth Dynasty Titles," 111–98, 336–37, 342, and Laboury, "Royal Portrait and Ideology," 265.

20.   Roth, "Erasing a Reign," 281. Hatshepsut needed to be removed only to pave the way for the coregency and sole kingship of Thutmose III's son. After that happened smoothly, all interest in erasing her stopped. Indeed, the names and images of Hatshepsut were not damaged by Thutmose IV (son of Amenhotep II), Amenhotep III, or Akhenaten, the latter so well known for his zealous interest in destroying the names and images of the god Amen. However, Hatshepsut may have been judged harshly by the Ramesside kings because she is missing from the Abydos king list of Seti I.

21.   As the Egyptologist Peter Dorman argues, "The need for the proscription seems to have arisen toward the end of his reign and to have vanished shortly after Amenhotep II became co-ruler, two years before Thutmose III's death" (*Monuments of Senenmut*, 269).

22.   Hatshepsut had done much the same when she had the names and images of her husband, Thutmose II, removed from Egypt's sacred temples. She had obliterated the images of her own brother to position herself as her father's heir and eldest child. The existence of Thutmose II on Egypt's monuments put the success of her own claims to the throne in jeopardy. Thutmose III was just using the same tactic: removing Hatshepsut from Egypt's temples to create a smooth and straight dynastic path for his son Amenhotep.

23.   Laboury, "Royal Portrait and Ideology," 264–65.

24.   The next officeholder was Tiaa, the mother of Thutmose IV.

25.   Robins, *Women in Ancient Egypt*, 150. Merytre-Hatshepsut had no royal blood herself and her receipt of the position was unprecedented. The machinations surrounding appointments to this priestess post are interesting because the accession of Amenhotep II resembles a change in dynasty rather than a linear succession: a king from a new dynasty must quickly assign a new God's Wife of Amen in direct relation to the king. Amenhotep II chose his own mother for the post.

26.   Bryan, "In Women Good and Bad Fortune Are on Earth," 40.

27.   For Hatshepsut's place in Manetho's histories, see W. Waddell, *Manetho* (Cambridge, MA: Harvard University Press; London: W. Heinemann, 1948), 101–19.

28.   Betsy M. Bryan, "Antecedents to Amenhotep III," in *Amenhotep III: Perspectives on His Reign*, ed. David O'Connor and Eric H. Cline (Ann Arbor: University of Michigan Press, 1997), 32.

29.   Bret Hinsch, *Women in Early Imperial China*, Asian Voices (Lanham, MD: Rowman and Littlefield, 2002).

30.   Bryan, "In Women Good and Bad Fortune Are on Earth," 28.

31.   Ibid., 29–30.

FURTHER READING

Allen, James P. *Genesis in Egypt: The Philosophy of Ancient Egyptian Creation Accounts*. Yale Egyptological Studies. San Antonio, TX: Van Siclen Books for Yale Egyptological Seminar,Yale University, 1988.

———. "The Role of Amun." In *Hatshepsut: From Queen to Pharaoh*, edited by Catharine H. Roehrig, 83–85. New Haven, CT: Yale University Press, 2006.

———. "The Speos Artemidos Inscription of Hatshepsut." *Bulletin of the Egyptological Seminar* 16 (2002): 1–17.

Assmann, Jan. *Der König als Sonnenpriester: Ein kosmographischer Begleittext zur kultischen Sonnenhymnik in thebanischen Tempeln und Gräbern*. Ägyptologische Reihe Bd. 7. Kairo: Abhandlungen des Deutschen Archäologischen Instituts Kairo, 1970.

———. *Egyptian Solar Religion in the New Kingdom: Re, Amun and the Crisis of Polytheism*. Studies in Egyptology. London: Kegan Paul International, 1995.

Ayad, Mariam F. *God's Wife, God's Servant: The God's Wife of Amun (c. 740–525 BC)*. London: Routledge, 2009.

Beckerath, Jürgen von. *Chronologie des pharaonischen Ägypten: die Zeitbestimmung der ägyptischen Geschichte von der Vorzeit bis 332 v. Chr.* Münchener Universitätsschriften; Philosophische Fakultät.; Münchner ägyptologische Studien, 46. Mainz am Rhein: Verlag Philipp von Zabern, 1997.

Bietak, Manfred. "Egypt and the Aegean: Cultural Convergence in a Thutmoside Palace at Avaris." In *Hatshepsut: From Queen to Pharaoh*, edited by Catharine H. Roehrig, 75–81. New Haven, CT: Yale University Press, 2006.

———, ed. *House and Palace in Ancient Egypt*, Denkschriften der Gesamtakademie 14. Vienna: Austrian Academy of Sciences, 1996.

Blyth, Elizabeth. *Karnak: Evolution of a Temple*. London: Routledge, 2006.

Bourriau, Janine. "The Second Intermediate Period." In *The Oxford History of Ancient Egypt*, edited by Ian Shaw, 185–217. Oxford: Oxford University Press, 2000.

Brand, Peter J. *The Monuments of Seti I: Epigraphic, Historical, and Art Historical Analysis*. Probleme der Ägyptologie, 16. Leiden: Brill, 2000.

Brier, Bob. *The Murder of Tutankhamen: A True Story*. New York: Putnam, 1998.

Bryan, Betsy M. "Administration in the Reign of Thutmose III." In *Thutmose III: A New Biography*, edited by Eric H. Cline and David O'Connor, 69–122. Ann Arbor: University of Michigan Press, 2006.

———. "Antecedents to Amenhotep III." In *Amenhotep III: Perspectives on His Reign*, edited by David O'Connor and Eric H. Cline, 27–62. Ann Arbor: University of Michigan Press, 1997.

———. "The Eighteenth Dynasty Before the Amarna Period." In *The Oxford History of Ancient Egypt*, edited by Ian Shaw, 218–71. Oxford: Oxford University Press, 2000.

———. "Hatshepsut and Cultic Revelries in the New Kingdom." In *Theban Symposium: Creativity and Innovation in the Reign of Hatshepsut*, edited by José M. Galán, Betsy M. Bryan, and Peter F. Dorman. Occasional Proceedings of the Theban Workshop. Chicago: Oriental Institute, University of Chicago, forthcoming.

———. "In Women Good and Bad Fortune Are on Earth: Status and Roles of Women in Egyptian Culture." In *Mistress of the House, Mistress of Heaven: Women in Ancient Egypt*, edited by Anne K. Capel and Glenn E. Markoe, 25–46. New York: Hudson Hills Press, 1996.

———. *The Reign of Thutmose IV*. Baltimore: Johns Hopkins University Press, 1991.

———. "The Temple of Mut: New Evidence on Hatshepsut's Building Activity." In *Hatshepsut: From Queen to Pharaoh*, edited by Catharine H. Roehrig, 181–83. New Haven, CT: Yale University Press, 2006.

Burgos, Franck, and François Larché, eds. *La chapelle rouge: Le sanctuaire de barque d'Hatshepsout*. 2 vols. Paris: Éditions Recherche sur les Civilisations, 2006–8.

Carnarvon, Earl of, and H. Carter. *Five Years' Explorations at Thebes: A Record of the Work Done 1907–1911*. Oxford: Oxford University Press, 1912.

Carter, Howard. "A Tomb Prepared for Queen Hatshepsuit discovered by the Earl of Carnarvon (October 1916)," *Annales du Service des Antiquitiés de l'Egypte* 16 (1917): 179–82.

Chevrier, H. "Rapport sur les Travaux de Karnak (1933–1934)." *Annales du Service des Antiquités de l'Égypte* 34 (1934): 159–76.

Cline, Eric H., and David O'Connor, eds. *Thutmose III: A New Biography*. Ann Arbor: University of Michigan Press, 2006.

Darnell, John C. "Opet Festival." *UCLA Encyclopedia of Egyptology*, 2010. http://escholarship.org/uc/item/4739r3fr.

Davies, Vivian W. "Egypt and Nubia: Conflict with the Kingdom of Kush." In *Hatshepsut: From Queen to Pharaoh*, edited by Catharine H. Roehrig, 49–56. New Haven, CT: Yale University Press, 2006.

———. "Kurgus 2002: The Inscriptions and Rock-Drawings." *Sudan and Nubia* 7 (2003): 55–57.

———. "A View from Elkab: The Tomb and Statues of Ahmose-Pennekhbet." In *Theban Symposium: Creativity and Innovation in the Reign of Hatshepsut*, edited by José M. Galán, Betsy M. Bryan, and Peter F. Dorman. Occasional Proceedings of the Theban Workshop. Chicago: Oriental Institute of the University of Chicago, forthcoming.

Delange, Elisabeth. *Catalogue des statues égyptiennes du Moyen Empire, 2060–1560 avant J.-C.* Paris: Musée du Louvre, 1987.

Der Manuelian, Peter, and Christian E. Loeben. "New Light on the Recarved Sarcophagus of Hatshepsut and Thutmose I in the Museum of Fine Arts, Boston." *Journal of Egyptian Archaeology* 79 (1993): 121–55.

Dodson, Aidan. *Amarna Sunset: Nefertiti, Tutankhamun, Ay, Horemheb, and the Egyptian Counter-Reformation*. Cairo: American University in Cairo Press, 2009.

Dodson, Aidan, and Dyan Hilton. *The Complete Royal Families of Ancient Egypt*. London: Thames and Hudson, 2004.

Dodson, Aidan, and J. J. Janssen. "A Theban Tomb and Its Tenants." *Journal of Egyptian Archaeology* 75 (1989): 125–38.

Dorman, Peter F. "The Early Reign of Thutmose III: An Unorthodox Mantle of Coregency." In *Thutmose III: A New Biography*, edited by Eric H. Cline and David O'Connor, 39–68. Ann Arbor: University of Michigan Press, 2006.

———. "Hatshepsut: Princess to Queen to Co-Ruler." In *Hatshepsut: From Queen to Pharaoh*, edited by Catharine H. Roehrig, 87–89. New Haven, CT: Yale University Press, 2006.

———. "The Career of Senenmut." In *Hatshepsut: From Queen to Pharaoh*, edited by Catharine H. Roehrig, 107–19. New Haven, CT: Yale University Press, 2006.

————. *The Monuments of Senenmut: Problems in Historical Methodology.* New York: Kegan Paul International, 1988.

————. *The Tombs of Senenmut: The Architecture and Decoration of Tombs 71 and 353.* New York: Metropolitan Museum of Art, 1991.

Dziobek, E. *Denkmäler des Vezirs User-Amun.* Studien zur Archäologie und Geschichte Altägyptens 18. Heidelberg: Heidelberger Orientverlag, 1998.

Favro, Diane, Willeke Wendrich, and Elaine Sullivan. "Digital Karnak." University of California, Los Angeles, http://dlib.etc.ucla.edu/projects/Karnak/.

Feucht, Erika. "Women." In *The Egyptians*, edited by Sergio Donadoni, 315–46. Chicago: University of Chicago Press, 1997.

Flides, V. *Breasts, Bottle and Babies: A History of Infant Feeding.* Edinburgh: Edinburgh University Press, 1986.

Gabolde, Luc. *Monuments décorés en bas relief aux noms de Thoutmosis II et Hatchepsout à Karnak.* Mémoires de l'Institut Français d'Archéologie Orientale 123. 2 vols. Cairo: Institut Français d'Archéologie Orientale, 2005.

Galán, José M. "The Tombs of Djehuty and Hery (TT 11–12) at Dra Abu el-Naga." In *Proceedings of the Ninth International Congress of Egyptologists*, edited by J.-C. Goyon and C. Cardin. Orientalia Lovaniensia Analecta, 777–87. Leuven: Peeters, 2007.

Galán, José M., Betsy M. Bryan, and Peter F. Dorman, eds. *Theban Symposium: Creativity and Innovation in the Reign of Hatshepsut.* Occasional Proceedings of the Theban Workshop. Chicago: Oriental Institute, University of Chicago, forthcoming.

Gardiner, A. H. *Egypt of the Pharaohs: An Introduction.* Oxford: Clarendon Press, 1961.

Graefe, Erhart. "Der angebliche Zahn der angeblich krebskranken Diabetikerin Königin Hatschepsut, oder: Die Mumie der Hatschepsut bleibt unbekannt." *Göttinger Miszellen* 231 (2011): 41–43.

————. *Untersuchungen zur Verwaltung und Geschichte der Institution der Gottesgemahlin des Amun vom Beginn des neuen Reiches bis zur Spätzeit.* Wiesbaden: O. Harrassowitz, 1981.

Griffith, F. L., and W. M. Flinders Petrie. *The Petrie Papyri: Hieratic Papyri from Kahun and Gurob (Principally of the Middle Kingdom).* London: B. Quaritch, 1898.

Habachi, Labib. "Two Graffiti at Sehēl from the Reign of Queen Hatshepsut." *Journal of Near Eastern Studies* 16, no. 2 (1957): 88–104.

Hawass, Zahi. "The Quest for Hatshepsut—Discovering the Mummy of Egypt's Greatest Female Pharaoh." http://www.drhawass.com/events/quest-hatshepsut-discovering-mummy-egypts-greatest-female-pharaoh.

Hawass, Zahi, Yehia Z. Gad, and Somaia Ismail. "Ancestry and Pathology in King Tutankhamun's Family." *Journal of the American Medical Association* 303, no. 7 (2010): 638–47.

Part II: The Hyksos Period and the New Kingdom (1675–1080 B.C.). New York: The Metropolitan Museum of Art, distributed by Harry N. Abrams, 1959.

Hayes, W. C. *The Scepter of Egypt*. Vol. 2. New York: The Metropolitan Museum of Art, 1959.

Hermann, Alfred. *Die ägyptische Königsnovelle*. Leipziger ägyptologische studien, Heft 10. Glückstadt: J. J. Augustin, 1938.

Hinsch, Bret. *Women in Early Imperial China*. Asian Voices. Lanham, MD: Rowman and Littlefield, 2002.

Hohneck, H. "Hatte Thutmosis I. wirklich einen Sohn namens Amenmose?" *Göttinger Miszellen* 210 (2006), 59–68.

Hornung, Erik. *The Ancient Egyptian Books of the Afterlife*. Translated by David Lorton. Ithaca, NY: Cornell University Press, 1999.

Hornung, Erik, Rolf Krauss, and David A. Warburton, eds. *Ancient Egyptian Chronology*. Handbook of Oriental Studies. Sec. 1, The Near and Middle East. Leiden and Boston: Brill, 2006.

Ikram, Salima, and Aidan Dodson. *The Mummy in Ancient Egypt: Equipping the Dead for Eternity*. London: Thames and Hudson, 1998.

Janssen, J. J., and Rosalind Janssen. *Growing Up in Ancient Egypt*. London: Rubicon Press, 1990.

Karkowski, J. "The Decoration of the Temple of Hatshepsut at Deir el-Bahari." In *Queen Hatshepsut and Her Temple 3500 Years Later*, edited by Z. Szafrański, 99–157. Cairo: Warsaw University Polish Centre of Mediterranean Archaeology in Cairo, 2001.

Keller, Cathleen A. "The Joint Reign of Hatshepsut and Thutmose III." In *Hatshepsut: From Queen to Pharaoh*, edited by Catharine H. Roehrig. New Haven, CT: Yale University Press, 2006, 96–98.

———. "The Statuary of Hatshepsut." In *Hatshepsut: From Queen to Pharaoh*, edited by Catharine H. Roehrig. New Haven, CT: Yale University Press, 2006, 158–64.

Kemp, Barry. *Ancient Egypt: Anatomy of a Civilization*. London: Routledge, 1991.

Konner, M., and C. Worthman. "Nursing Frequency, Gonadal Function, and Birth Spacing Among !Kung Hunter-Gatherers." *Science* 207 (1980): 788–91.

Kozloff, Arielle P. "The Artistic Production of the Reign of Thutmose III." In *Thutmose III: A New Biography*, edited by Eric H. Cline and David O'Connor, 292–324. Ann Arbor: University of Michigan Press, 2006.

Kozloff, Arielle P., and Betsy M. Bryan. *Egypt's Dazzling Sun: Amenhotep III and His World*. Cleveland: Cleveland Museum of Art; Bloomington: Indiana University Press, 1992.

Laboury, Dimitri. "How and Why Did Hatshepsut Invent the Image of Her Royal Power?" In *Theban Symposium: Creativity and Innovation in the Reign of Hatshepsut*. Occasional Proceedings of the Theban Workshop, edited by José M. Galán, Betsy M. Bryan, and Peter F. Dorman. Chicago: Oriental Institute, University of Chicago, forthcoming.

———. "Royal Portrait and Ideology: Evolution and Signification of the Statuary of Thutmose III." In *Thutmose III: A New Biography*, edited by Eric H. Cline and David O'Connor, 260–91. Ann Arbor: University of Michigan Press, 2006.

Laskowski, Piotr. "Monumental Architecture and the Royal Building Program of Thutmose III." In *Thutmose III: A New Biography*, edited by Eric H. Cline and David O'Connor. Ann Arbor: University of Michigan Press, 2006, 183-237.

Leser, Karl H. "Maat-ka-Ra Hatshepsut." http://www.maat-ka-ra.de/english/start_e.htm.

Lichtheim, Miriam. *Ancient Egyptian Literature*. Vol. 1, *The Old and Middle Kingdoms*. Berkeley: University of California Press, 1975.

———. *Ancient Egyptian Literature*. Vol. 2, *The New Kingdom*. Berkeley: University of California Press, 1976.

Loeben, Christian E. *Beobachtungen zu Kontext und Funktion königlicher Statuen im Amun-Tempel von Karnak*. Leipzig: Wodtke und Stegbauer, 2001.

Lundström, Peter. "Karnak King List." http://xorpid.com/karnak-king-list.

Mann, Michael. *The Sources of Social Power*. Vol. 1, *A History of Power from the Beginning to A.D. 1760*. Cambridge: Cambridge University Press, 1986.

Maruéjol, F. *Thoutmosis III et la corégence avec Hatchepsout*. Paris: Pygmalion, 2008.

Mauric-Barberio, F. "Le premier exemplaire du Livre de l'Amdouat." *Bulletin de l'Institut Français d'Archéologie Orientale au Caire* 101 (2001): 315–50.

Murnane, William J. *Ancient Egyptian Coregencies*. Chicago: Oriental Institute of the University of Chicago, 1977.

———. "Opetfest." In *Lexikon der Ägyptologie*, vol. 4, edited by W. Helck and E. Otto, 574–79. Wiesbaden: Harrassowitz, 1982.

Naville, Édouard. *The Temple of Deir el Bahari*. Vol. 5, *Plates CXIX–CL: The Upper Court and Sanctuary*. London: Egypt Exploration Fund, 1895.

Naville, Edouard, and Howard Carter. *The Tomb of Hâtshopsîtû*. London: A. Constable, 1906.

Nicholson, P. T., and J. A. Henderson. "Glass." In *Ancient Egyptian Materials and Technology*, edited by P. T. Nicholson and I. Shaw, 195–226. Cambridge: Cambridge University Press, 2000.

Nims, C. F. "The Date of the Dishonoring of Hatshepsut." *Zeitschrift für ägyptische Sprache und Altertumskunde* 93 (1966): 97–100.

Ockinga, Boyo. "Hatshepsut's Appointment as Crown Prince and the Egyptian Background to Isaiah 9:5." In *Egypt, Canaan and Israel: History, Imperialism, Ideology and Literature; Proceedings of a Conference at the University of Haifa, 3–7 May 2009*, edited by S. Bar, D. Kahn, and JJ Shirley, 252–67. Leiden: Brill, 2011.

O'Connor, David. "Thutmose III: An Enigmatic Pharaoh." In *Thutmose III: A New Biography*, edited by Eric H. Cline and David O'Connor, 1–38. Ann Arbor: University of Michigan Press, 2006.

Oppenheim, Adela. "The Early Life of Pharaoh: Divine Birth and Adolescence Scenes in the Causeway of Senwosret III at Dahshur." In *Abusir and Saqqara in the Year 2010*, edited by Miroslav Bárta, Filip Coppens, and Jaromír Krejčí, 171–88. Prague: Czech Institute of Egyptology, Faculty of Arts, Charles University, 2011.

Oriental Institute Epigraphic Survey, ed. *Medinet* Habu. Vol. 7, *The Eastern High Gate*. Chicago: University of Chicago Press, 1970.

Paneque, Christina Gil. "The Official Image of Hatshepsut During the Regency: A Political Approximation to the Office of God's Wife." *Trabajos de Egiptologa* 2 (2003): 83–98.

Piccione, P. A. "The Women of Thutmose III in the Stelae of the Egyptian Museum." *Journal of the Society of the Study of Egyptian Antiquities* 30 (2003): 91–100.

Podzorski, P. V. *Their Bones Shall Not Perish: An Examination of Predynastic Human Skeletal Remains from Naga-ed-Der in Egypt*. New Malden, UK: SIA Publishing, 1990.

Prisse d'Avennes, A. C. *Monuments égyptiens*. Paris, 1847.

Redford, Donald B. *History and Chronology of the Eighteenth Dynasty of Egypt: Seven Studies*. Toronto: University of Toronto Press, 1967.

————. "The Northern Wars of Thutmose III." In *Thutmose III: A New Biography*, edited by Eric H. Cline and David O'Connor, 325–43. Ann Arbor: University of Michigan Press, 2006.

Redford, Susan. *The Harem Conspiracy: The Murder of Ramesses III*. Chicago: Northern Illinois University Press, 2002.

Reeves, Nicholas. *Valley of the Kings: The Decline of a Royal Necropolis*. London: Kegan Paul International, 1990.

Robins, Gay. "A Critical Examination of the Theory That the Right to the Throne of Ancient Egypt Passed Through the Female Line in the 18th Dynasty." *Göttinger Miszellen* 62 (1983): 67–77.

————. "Review of *Patterns of Queenship in Ancient Egyptian Myth and History*, by Lana Troy." *Journal of Egyptian Archaeology* 76 (1990): 214–20.

————. *Women in Ancient Egypt*. Cambridge, MA: Harvard University Press, 1993.

Roehrig, Catharine H. "The Building Activities of Thutmose III in the Valley of the Kings." In *Thutmose III: A New Biography*, edited by Eric H. Cline and David O'Connor, 238–59. Ann Arbor: University of Michigan Press, 2006.

————. "The Eighteenth Dynasty Titles Royal Nurse (mn't nswt), Royal Tutor (mn' nswt), and Foster Brother/Sister of the Lord of the Two Lands (sn/snt mn' n nb t3wy)." PhD diss., University of California, Berkeley, 1990.

————, ed. *Hatshepsut: From Queen to Pharaoh*. New Haven, CT: Yale University Press, 2006.

————. "The Two Tombs of Hatshepsut." In *Hatshepsut: From Queen to Pharaoh*, edited by Catharine H. Roehrig. New Haven, CT: Yale University Press, 2006, 184–187.

Romer, John. *People of the Nile: Everyday Life in Ancient Egypt*. New York: Crown, 1985.

————. "The Tomb of Tuthmosis III." *Mitteilungen des Deutschen Archäologischen Instituts Abteilung Kairo* 31 (1975): 316–51.

————. "Tuthmosis I and the Bibân el-Molûk: Some Problems of Attribution." *Journal of Egyptian Archaeology* 60 (1974): 119–33.

Roth, Ann Macy. "The Absent Spouse: Patterns and Taboos in Egyptian Tomb Decoration." *Journal of the American Research Center in Egypt* 36 (1999): 37–53.

———. "Erasing a Reign." In *Hatshepsut: From Queen to Pharaoh*, edited by Catharine H. Roehrig, 277–81. New Haven, CT: Yale University Press, 2006.

———. "Father Earth, Mother Sky: Ancient Egyptian Beliefs About Conception and Fertility." In *Reading the Body: Representations and Remains in the Archaeological Record*, edited by Alison E. Rautman. Regendering the Past, 187–201. Philadelphia: University of Pennsylvania Press, 2000.

———. "Models of Authority: Hatshepsut's Predecessors in Power." In *Hatshepsut: From Queen to Pharaoh*, edited by Catharine H. Roehrig. New Haven, CT: Yale University Press, 2006, 9–14.

Roth, Silke. "Harem." *UCLA Encyclopedia of Egyptology*, 2012. http://escholarship.org/uc/item/1k3663r3?query=harem.

Schnittger, Marianne. *Hatschepsut: Eine Frau als König von Ägypten*. Darmstadt: Verlag Philipp von Zabern, 2008.

Sethe, Kurt Heinrich. *Amun und die acht Urgötter von Hermopolis, eine Untersuchung über Ursprung und Wesen des aegyptischen Götterkönigs*. Berlin: Verlag der Akademie der Wissenschaften, 1929.

———. *Urkunden der 18. Dynastie, Band 1*. Edited by Georg Steindorff. Urkunden des ägyptischen Altertums 4. Leipzig: J. C. Hinrichs'sche Buchhandlung, 1906.

———. *Urkunden der 18. Dynastie, Band 2*. Edited by Georg Steindorff. Urkunden des ägyptischen Altertums 4. Leipzig: J. C. Hinrichs'sche Buchhandlung, 1906.

Shafer, B. E. "Temples, Priests, and Rituals: An Overview." In *Temples of Ancient Egypt*, edited by B. E. Shafer, 1–30. Ithaca, NY: Cornell University Press, 1997.

Shaw, Ian, ed. *The Oxford History of Ancient Egypt*. Oxford: Oxford University Press, 2000.

Smith, G. Elliot. *The Royal Mummies*. Catalogue général des antiquités égyptiennes du Musée du Caire, nos. 61051–61100. Cairo: Institut Français d'Archéologie Orientale, 1912.

Spalinger, Anthony J. "Covetous Eyes South: The Background to Egypt's Domination of Nubia by the Reign of Thutmose III." In *Thutmose III: A New Biography*, edited by Eric H. Cline and David O'Connor, 344–69. Ann Arbor: University of Michigan Press, 2006.

———. "Drama in History: Exemplars from Mid Dynasty XVIII." *Studien zur Altägyptischen Kultur* 24 (1997): 269–300.

Szafrański, Z. "Imiut in the 'Chapel of Parents' in the Temple of Hatshepsut at Deir el-Bahari." In *8. Ägyptologische Tempeltagung: Inter-connections Between Temples*, edited by Monika Dolinska and Horst Beinlich. Königtum, Staat und Gesellschaft früher Hochkulturen 3, 187–96. Wiesbaden: Harrassowitz, 2010.

Toivari-Viitala, J. *Women at Deir el-Medina: A Study of the Status and Roles of the Female Inhabitants in the Workmen's Community During the Ramesside Period.* Leiden: Nederlands Instituut voor het Nabije Oosten, 2001.

Tougher, Shaun. *The Eunuch in Byzantine History and Society.* London: Routledge, 2008.

Troy, Lana. *Patterns of Queenship.* Acta Universitatis Upsaliensus Boreas 14. Uppsala: University of Uppsala, 1986.

———. "Religion and Cult During the Time of Thutmose III." In *Thutmose III: A New Biography*, edited by Eric H. Cline and David O'Connor, 123–82. Ann Arbor: University of Michigan Press, 2006.

Tyldesley, Joyce. *Hatchepsut: The Female Pharaoh.* London: Viking, 1996.

Tylor, J. J., and F. L. Griffith. *The Tomb of Paheri at El Kab.* London: Egypt Exploration Fund, 1894.

Ullmann, M. "König für die Ewigkeit: die Häuser der Millionen von Jahren." *Ägypten und Altes Testament* 51. Wiesbaden: Harrassowitz Verlag, 2002.

Uphill, E. P. "A Joint Sed-Festival of Thutmose III and Queen Hatshepsut." *Journal of Near Eastern Studies* 20, no. 4 (1961): 248–51.

Vandersleyen, Claude. *L'Égypte et la vallée du Nil.* Vol. 2, *De la fin de l'ancient empire à la fin du nouvel empire.* Paris: PUF, 1995.

Warburton, David A. *Architecture, Power, and Religion: Hatshepsut, Amun & Karnak in Context.* Beiträge zur Archäologie 7. Zurich: LIT Verlag, 2012.

Warburton, David, and Erik Hornung. *The Egyptian Amduat: The Book of the Hidden Chamber.* Zurich: Living Human Heritage, 2007.

Weingarten, Judith. "Hatshepsut and the Tomb Beneath the Tomb." http://judithweingarten.blogspot.com/2009/03/hatshepsut-and-tomb-beneath-tomb.html.

Wente, Edward F. *Letters from Ancient Egypt.* Atlanta: Scholars Press, 1990.

———. "Some Graffiti from the Reign of Hatshepsut." *Journal of Near Eastern Studies* 43, no. 1 (1984): 47–54.

Werbrouck, Marcelle. *Le temple d'Hatshepsout à Deir el Bahari.* Bruxelles: Fondation Égyptologique Reine Élisabeth, 1949.

Winlock, Herbert E. "The Egyptian Expedition 1925–1927: The Museum's Excavations at Thebes." *Metropolitan Museum of Art Bulletin* 23, no. 2 (1928): 3–58.

———. "The Museum's Excavation at Thebes: Excavations at the Temple of Hatshepsūt." *Metropolitan Museum of Art Bulletin* 27, no. 3 (1932): 4–37.

Wysocki, Zygmunt. "The Temple of Queen Hatshepsut at Deir el Bahari: The Raising of the Structure in View of Architectural Studies." *Mitteilungen des Deutschen Archäologischen Instituts Abteilung Kairo* 48 (1992): 234–54.

Zivie-Coche, Christiane. *Giza au deuxième millénaire: Bibliothèque d'étude.* Cairo: Institut Français d'Archéologie Orientale, 1976.

INDEX

ABOUT THE AUTHOR

KARA COONEY is an associate professor of Egyptian art and architecture at UCLA in the Department of Near Eastern Languages and Cultures. She received her PhD in Egyptology from Johns Hopkins University, and her academic work focuses on craft production, coffin studies, and ancient economies. In 2005, she was co-curator of *Tutankhamun and the Golden Age of the Pharaohs* at the Los Angeles County Museum of Art. Cooney produced a comparative archaeology television series with her husband, Neil Crawford, entitled *Out of Egypt*, which aired on the Discovery Channel and is available online from Netflix, Amazon, and iTunes.